LETTERS OF MEDIEVAL JEWISH TRADERS

Letters of Medieval Jewish Traders

TRANSLATED FROM THE
ARABIC WITH
INTRODUCTIONS
AND NOTES BY

S. D. Goitein

PRINCETON UNIVERSITY
PRESS

Library of Congress Cataloging in Publication data will be found on the last printed page of this book.

L.C. CARD: 72-14025

ISBN: 0-691-05212-3

Publication of this book has been aided by The Louis A. Robb Fund of Princeton University Press

This book has been composed in Linotype Granjon

Printed in the United States of America by Princeton University Press Princeton, New Jersey

In loving memory of my eldest brother

MAX MEIR GOITEIN

Executive, gentleman, and humanist

(1895-1940)

PREFACE

Serious books are not always the result of systematic endeavors and orderly procedures. The present volume is a case in point. Its writer is engaged in a comprehensive undertaking: a three-volume book entitled *A Mediterranean Society: The Jewish Communities of the Arab World as Portrayed in the Documents of the Cairo Geniza.* The second volume, with the subtitle *The Community,* comprising some 650 pages, has just been published by the University of California Press. The third and last volume is in an advanced state of preparation. A companion volume to this book, to be called *Mediterranean People: Letters and Documents from the Cairo Geniza, Translated with Notes and Introductions,* also is well under way. Simultaneously with this work on the Mediterranean world hundreds of documents on the medieval India trade have been prepared for editing and translation and are now being checked and rechecked, and new items are added.

One day in November 1971, while working at the Institute for Advanced Study, Princeton, my eyes rested on the vast lawn stretching in front of Fuld Hall, and it occurred to me that it was a felicitous idea of the landscape architect to break the monotony of the lawn by planting a small circle of low crab apple trees in its center. Suddenly it came to my mind that it would be appropriate to make a break in producing large books and turn to writing something short and handy which might be welcome to students, laymen, and scholars alike. A topic for such a book easily presented itself. Most of my scholarly research in the past had to do with rulers, warriors, scholars, poets, and saints. But of late, through the study of the Cairo Geniza, I had become aware of the worthiness of those daring, pious, and often learned representatives of Middle Eastern civilization during the High Middle Ages: the overseas traders. Their letters were available in abundance, and, since these are expressive without being prolix, they provide interesting insights into the personalities of their writers. Before my eyes turned away from the lawn with the crab apple trees, my choice was made.

The originals of only eight out of the eighty items translated in this volume have been edited thus far, six of them by myself. But all of them have been copied and typed, so that they may be regarded as "edited," albeit they have not been published.

The Introduction describes the provenance and present whereabouts of the letters translated, the social milieu of their writers, the organization of the overseas trade, and the goods traded. An Author's Note explains certain details apt to facilitate the use of the book, a List of Abbreviations notes the books, journals, and manuscript collections most frequently used.

There remains for me to express my personal thanks and the gratitude of scholarship to the librarians and officials of the libraries whose manuscripts have been used in this book (see the List of Abbreviations). Most of the manuscripts translated had been copied during the early 1950s, but I possess photostats of all of them and no translation was made without continuous examination of the originals.

This book is part and parcel of my work on the Cairo Geniza, which was made possible during the current year by the National Endowment for the Humanities; the John Simon Guggenheim Foundation; the Lucius N. Littauer Foundation; and the Max Richter Foundation. I wish to extend my heartfelt thanks to the men guiding these institutions for their understanding and encouragement. My membership in the Institute for Advanced Study under the imaginative direction of Carl Kaysen was another fortunate factor furthering my work.

Finally, it is my pleasant duty to thank my young colleague, Professor Abraham L. Udovitch, for his unfailing friendship and, in particular, for reading the manuscript of this book and contributing invaluable suggestions for its improvement. I am grateful to Mrs. Sandra S. Lafferty of the Institute for Advanced Study for her dedicated and painstaking work in typing the manuscript. I would also like to thank the Director and staff of Princeton University Press—in particular Mrs. Polly Hanford, indefatigable editor —for their understanding and helpfulness.

S. D. Goitein

Institute for Advanced Study
Princeton, New Jersey
December 1972

CONTENTS

VI. TWELTH CENTURY AND LATER

VII. ACCOUNTS

AUTHOR'S NOTE

1. With the exception of no. 3, all items in this volume are in Arabic. The translations of Hebrew words or phrases inserted in the Arabic text are italicized.

2. Abbreviations are rendered by full translations, but the English words or parts of words the equivalents of which do not appear in the originals are put in parentheses. For example, the blessing over a dead person, appearing in the original in the form *r"e,* is translated as: *(may he) r(est in) E(den).*

3. Common phrases omitted in the translation are indicated by . . . .

4. References to God are capitalized solely where the word "God" does not precede, as in the opening of letters, often superscribed: "In Your Name," meaning God.

5. Arabic names and words are transcribed as in the second edition of the *Encyclopaedia of Islam*, with the exception that *dj* is replaced by *j*, and *ḳ* by *q*.

6. We spell Fatimids, Fustat, Qayrawān, for Fāṭimids, al-Fusṭāṭ, al-Qayrawān, respectively, and make similar allowances for frequently occurring Arabic names.

7. Biblical names, if appearing in the original in Hebrew, are spelled in the usual English way. When the original has an Arabic form, it is transcribed phonetically, such as Ya'qūb for Jacob.

8. Fractions are rendered in the form they have in the original, where they are written 1/2, 1/4, not 3/4 (see, e.g., no. 64). Fractions calculated by the author are rendered in the usual way (e.g., in no. 27, B).

9. Rhymed prose is indicated by slashes (e.g., in no. 38, A).

10. Words written above the line in the original MSS are put between double slashes (e.g., in no. 15).

11. Parts of a text which are either lost or illegible and replaced by conjecture are enclosed in brackets.

12. Words deleted by the original writers are enclosed in double brackets.

13. Long *ū* in *Abū* ("father of") becomes short in combinations such as *Abu 'l* or *Abu Sḥāq* and is then written without a bar, the sign of length.

ABBREVIATIONS

Amari, *Musulmani di Sicilia*	Michele Amari, *Storia dei Musulmani di Sicilia.* Catania, 1933-1939. 3 vols.
Ashtor, *Prix*	*Histoire des prix et des salaires dans l'orient médiéval.* Paris, 1969.
Assaf, *Texts*	Simha Assaf, *Texts and Studies in Jewish History.* Jerusalem, 1946. Arabic and Hebrew.
b.	Son or daughter of (Hebrew and Arabic).
Baron, *History of the Jews*	S. W. Baron, *A Social and Religious History of the Jews.* New York, 1952-1965. 10 vols. and index.
BM	British Museum, London.
Bodl.	Bodleian Library, Oxford, England. The shelf mark of the manuscript is followed by its number in A. Neubauer and A. E. Cowley, *Catalogue of the Hebrew Manuscripts in the Bodleian Library* (Oxford, 1906), and by the folio of the document under discussion, e.g., Bodl. MS Heb. c 28 (Cat. 2876), f. 38.
DK	David Kaufmann Collection, Hungarian Academy of Sciences, Budapest. One series bears Arabic numerals, and another Roman numerals.
Dozy, *Supplément*	R. Dozy, *Supplément aux dictionnaires arabes.* Paris, 1927. 2 vols.
Dropsie	Geniza manuscripts preserved in the library of Dropsie University, Philadelphia.
EI	*Encyclopaedia of Islam.* 1st ed.
*EI*²	*Encyclopaedia of Islam.* 2d ed.

ENA	Elkan N. Adler Collection, Jewish Theological Seminary of America, New York
Eretz-Israel	*Eretz-Israel: Archaeological, Historical and Geographical Studies.* Jerusalem, 1951———. Hebrew, with English summaries; some volumes have sections in European languages.
f., fs.	folio(s); fragments(s).
Fischel, *Jews*	Walter J. Fischel, *Jews in the Economic and Political Life of Mediaeval Islam.* London. 1937. Reprint, New York, 1969.
Goitein, *Jemenica*	S. D. Goitein, *Jemenica: Sprichwörter und Redensarten aus Zentral-Jemen.* Leipzig, 1934. Reprint, Leiden, 1970.
Goitein, *Jews and Arabs*	S. D. Goitein, *Jews and Arabs: Their Contacts through the Ages.* New York, 1964.
Goitein, *Studies*	S. D. Goitein, *Studies in Islamic History and Institutions.* Leiden, 1966. See also *India Book* and *Med. Soc.*, below.
Gottheil-Worrell	*Fragments from the Cairo Genizah in the Freer Collection*, ed. R. Gottheil and W. H. Worrell. New York, 1927.
Grohmann, *World of Arabic Papyri*	Adolf Grohmann, *From the World of Arabic Papyri.* Cairo, 1952.
Heyd, *Commerce du Levant*	W. Heyd, *Histoire du commerce du Levant au moyen-âge.* Amsterdam, 1959. 2 vols.
Hinz, *Masse*	W. Hinz, *Islamische Masse und Gewichte.* Leiden, 1955.
Idris, *Zirides*	H. R. Idris, *La Berberie orientale sous les Zīrīdes, Xe-XIIe siècles.* Paris, 1962.
India Book	A collection of 354 Geniza documents on the India trade being prepared for publication by S. D. Goitein.

JAOS	*Journal of the American Oriental Society.*
JESHO	*Journal of the Economic and Social History of the Orient.*
JNUL	Jewish National and University Library, Jerusalem, Israel, MS 4° 577, 3. This file contains all the Geniza documents used in this book.
JQR	*Jewish Quarterly Review.*
Lane-Poole, *History of Egypt*	Stanley Lane-Poole, *A History of Egypt in the Middle Ages.* London, 1914.
M.	Heb. *Mār* or Ar. *Sayyidī,* both = Mr.
Maimonides-Meyerhof	*Un glossaire de matière médicale composé par Maïmonide,* ed. Max Meyerhof. Cairo, 1940.
Maimonides, *Responsa*	Maimonides, *Responsa,* ed. Jehoshua Blau. Vols. I-III. Jerusalem, 1957-1961.
Mann, *The Jews in Egypt*	Jacob Mann, *The Jews in Egypt and in Palestine under the Fāṭimid Caliphs.* Vols. I, II. Oxford, 1920-1922. Reprint with Preface and Reader's Guide by S. D. Goitein. New York, 1970.
Mann, *Texts*	Jacob Mann, *Texts and Studies in Jewish History and Literature.* Vol. I, Cincinnati, 1931. Vol. II, Philadelphia, 1935. Reprint with Introduction by Gerson D. Cohen, New York, 1972.
Med. Soc.	S. D. Goitein, *A Mediterranean Society. The Jewish Communities of the Arab World as Portrayed in the Documents of the Cairo Geniza.* Berkeley and Los Angeles, Vol. I, 1967. Vol. II, 1971.
Mez, *Renaissance*	A. Mez, *Die Renaissance des Islams.* Heidelberg, 1922. In order to enable students using the English, French, Spanish, or Arabic translations to find the passage quoted, the number of the chapter is included.

Mosseri — A private collection of Geniza material in the name of Jack Mosseri.

Nahray — A collection of 261 Geniza documents connected with Nahray b. Nissīm (see ch. IV), treated in a Ph.D. thesis by Murad Michael. The numbers following *Nahray* refer to Dr. Michael's thesis.

REJ — *Revue des Études Juives.*

Serjeant, *Islamic Textiles* — R. B. Serjeant, "Material for a History of Islamic Textiles up to the Mongol Conquest," *Ars Islamica,* 9-16 (1942-1951).

Shaked, *Bibliography* — Shaul Shaked, *A Tentative Bibliography of Geniza Documents.* Paris and The Hague, 1964.

Steingass, *Persian-English Dictionary* — F. Steingass, *A Comprehensive Persian-English Dictionary.* London, 1947.

Tarbiz — *Tarbiz. A Quarterly for Jewish Studies.* Hebrew, with summaries in English.

TS — Taylor-Schechter Collection, University Library, Cambridge, England. The collection is kept in glasses, in bound volumes, and in boxes. For example:

1. No. 251 of the series of glasses, 12 inches long is marked thus:
   TS 12.251

2. Folio 7 in volume 12 of the series of volumes 10 inches long:
   TS 10 J 12, f. 7

3. Boxes are marked either with Arabic numbers or with letters (G, J, K, and so on), or with the word "Arabic."

4. NS designates new series. It is followed by the number of the box and the folio.

5. NS J designates boxes of the new series which contain documents exclu-

TS (cont'd.)	sively and which bear no numbers. Only the folio is cited.
ULC	University Library, Cambridge, England. Collections of Geniza material in the library other than the Taylor-Schechter Collection.
Wahrmund, *Handwörterbuch*	A. Wahrmund, *Handwörterbuch der neuarabischen und deutschen Sprache.* Giessen, 1898. 2 vols.
Yāqūt	*Jacut's Geographisches Wörterbuch*, ed. F. Wüstenfeld. Vols. I-IV. Leipzig, 1866-1870.
Zion	A Quarterly for Research in Jewish History. Hebrew, with summaries in English.

LETTERS OF MEDIEVAL JEWISH TRADERS

CHAPTER I

Introduction

1. Provenance and present whereabouts of the letters translated

Anyone looking at the title of this book will be tempted to ask: Why Jewish? Why should we single out one of several communities active in the trade of the Islamic countries during the High Middle Ages? The answer is simple: From that world and that period, only the letters and other papers of Jewish overseas traders have thus far been found. Their preservation was due to very special circumstances.

All the letters translated in this volume were originally found in the so-called Cairo Geniza. Geniza (pronounced gueneeza) is a place where discarded writings on which the name of God was or might have been written were deposited in order to preserve them from desecration. This pious precaution was a general Middle Eastern custom, shared by Christians, Muslims, and Jews. But only the Jews seem to have developed the practice of burying their sacred writings no longer in use, a custom still widely observed.

Most of the papers of the Cairo Geniza were preserved in a room specifically set aside for that purpose and attached to a synagogue. Hundreds of thousands of leaves have been saved, mostly of religious, or otherwise literary, character. Unlike other genizas, however, the Cairo Geniza also comprises a huge quantity of writings of a purely secular character, such as official, business, learned, and private correspondence, court records, contracts and other legal documents, accounts, bills of lading, prescriptions, etc. Since only discarded writings were thrown into the Geniza room, it is natural that most of the material is fragmentary. Still, the number of writings extant in their entirety, or at least forming meaningful units, is considerable. I estimate that about 1,200 more or less complete business letters have been preserved and identified as such by me. Thus, the eighty letters presented in this volume contain about seven percent of the total. I do not claim at all that the pieces chosen here are uniquely representative. Alongside items of special interest, others of a more humdrum character have been translated. Another author might have selected another eighty pieces equally apt to illustrate the mercantile world of the medieval society of the Arabic speaking Mediterranean area.

The appellation Cairo Geniza needs some qualification. The city of Cairo was founded by a Fatimid caliph in the year 969 when Egypt was conquered by his troops. The ancient capital of Islamic Egypt (al-)Fustat, sometimes inaccurately referred to as Old Cairo, was situated about two-and-a-half miles south of the new foundation and remained the economic center of the country throughout the eleventh and the first half of the twelfth century. This is precisely the period in which most of our letters were written, as is evident from this breakdown:

	Total
Letters from the eleventh century (may include last decade of the tenth) nos. 1-5, 11-36, 63-67, 69-73, 74, 77	43
Twelfth century (may include last decade of the eleventh century) nos. 6, 7, 9, 37-42, 48-60, 68, 75, 79	25
Thirteenth century (includes one item from the end of the twelfth) nos. 8, 10, 43-47, 61, 62, 76, 78, 80	12

The synagogue with the Geniza chamber was that of the "Jerusalemites" or "Palestinians," that is, the ancient, pre-Islamic congregation of Fustat, which adhered to the rites and customs of the Jews of Palestine. The immigrants from Iran and Iraq, referred to as "Iraqians" or "Babylonians," possessed another place of worship, originally a church, which they had purchased from the Coptic Patriarch in 882.[1] A third Jewish community of Fustat was that of

[1] Until recently it was generally assumed that the Geniza chamber had been attached to the building which originally was a church (see, e.g.,

the Karaites, a dissident sect recognizing the sole authority of the Bible and repudiating that of the "Rabbis" of the Talmud, the post-biblical writings sacred to the main body of Jews who were referred to as "Rabbanites." In the eleventh century the Karaites were very prominent in commerce and banking, as well as in the government bureaucracy and medicine, but, naturally, they had no reason to deposit their discarded writings in a Rabbanite place of worship. Still, some interesting items addressed to Karaites found their way into the Geniza, as for example, nos. 11 and 69, and there are many references to them throughout. (See index, s.v. Karaites and Tustarīs.)

At least twenty out of the eighty items included in this volume were addressed to places other than the capital of Egypt. As the title of this publication and selections 1-10 indicate, the letters originated in practically all Islamic countries extending from Spain and Morocco in the West to India in the East. Letters with a destination other than Cairo-Fustat reached the Geniza for a great variety of reasons, but mostly because the recipients had traveled there.

As a rule, business letters from the area and the period covered by this book were written in Arabic. This was not classical Arabic, nor simply a vernacular, but a semiliterary language of rather regular usage and considerable expressiveness. Jews wrote this language with Hebrew characters. Since everyone had learned Hebrew as a little boy while attending school, where Bible-reading was the main subject of study, all were familiar with Hebrew letters, while the far more difficult Arabic script had to be practiced with a private tutor. Moreover, the writers often interspersed their Arabic text with Hebrew words and phrases.[2] Needless to say, the better merchants were fluent in the Arabic script as well, as we see from the addresses which are often in Arabic characters, or from express references, as in no. 9. Selection no. 62, a letter to a qadi, or Muslim judge, is, of course, in Arabic characters, while no. 3 is in the

---

Paul E. Kahle, *The Cairo Geniza*, New York, 1960, p. 3). But, as I have shown in *Med. Soc.*, II, 148-149, it was the Iraqians who acquired the church when they were in need of a place of worship for themselves, while the "Jerusalemites," the original Jewish inhabitants of Fustat, already possessed a synagogue there in Byzantine times.

2 The translations of Hebrew words and phrases are printed in italics.

Hebrew language, because its writer was an Italian, and not an Arabic-speaking, Jew.

The treasures of the Cairo Geniza became known to the scholarly world (and to antiquity dealers) shortly before 1890, when the time-honored synagogue of the Palestinians was pulled down and replaced by another building. Libraries and private collectors in Europe and America acquired considerable quantities of the documents found there. Finally, in 1897, Solomon Schechter, then Lecturer of Rabbinics at the University of Cambridge, England, with the assistance of Dr. Charles Taylor of St. John's College, succeeded in removing the total remaining content of the Geniza chamber to the University Library, Cambridge. The Taylor-Schechter Collection now contains perhaps three times as much as all the other Geniza collections taken together. Other important collections represented in this volume are those of the Bodleian Library, Oxford, the British Museum, the Jewish Theological Seminary of America, New York, Dropsie University, Philadelphia, the David Kaufmann Collection, Budapest, Hungary, and the private Mosseri Collection. There are a dozen other collections, almost all of which contain material suitable for this volume.[3]

2. The traders' world

With a few exceptions, this book is confined to letters, including accounts which used to form parts of letters. Naturally, a great variety of papers others than letters dealt with commerce, such as legal documents issued at the conclusion or the dissolution of a partnership, the granting or payment of a loan, the sale of a house, a slave, or a book, or any other transaction for which written statements used to be made. Court records connected with commerce are another extremely frequent type of document found in the Geniza. In this volume, I wished to present the subjective aspect of trade, trade as seen by the people who were engaged in it, and this is most directly expressed in their letters.

Because of the general insecurity and the slowness of communications, international trade was largely dependent on personal rela-

[3] The story of the documentary Geniza is told in detail in *Med. Soc.*, I, 1-28, in Goitein, *Studies in Islamic History*, pp. 279-295, and briefly in *EI*^{2}, III, 987-989.

tionships and mutual confidence. A man shipping goods overseas normally had to wait months before he could know what happened to them. He had to rely on his friends in the country of destination for the proper handling of his affairs. Mostly, although by no means exclusively, friends were chosen from one's own religious community. This was natural under medieval conditions. The clubhouse of the Middle Ages where one met one's peers daily, or, at least, regularly, was the mosque, the church, or the synagogue. A Spanish Jew traveling to India would pray in the synagogues of each of the larger cities of Sicily, Tunisia, Egypt, and Yemen, and thus become personally acquainted with everyone who counted. Thus, coreligionists became natural business friends. The religious community functioned like an extended family. The few longer Arabic business letters on papyrus from the ninth and tenth centuries (which have been edited by A. Grohmann, D. S. Margoliouth, and A. Dietrich) were also exchanged between members of the same religious community, either Christians or Muslims.[4]

Religion was conducive not only to the formation of business relationships, but also to their proper conduct. Again and again a man's piety and fear of God are invoked when he is reminded to adhere to good business practices or when he is praised for his excellent handling of his friends' affairs.[5]

The modern reader is inclined to regard the continuous references to God in these letters as a mere *façon de parler*. This is not the case. God was conceived as the creator of all that happened in nature and in human life, including man's thoughts, decisions, and actions. He was, so to say, the most active substance in the physical world. Therefore, keeping him constantly in mind and mouth was the most practical thing a good businessman could do.

Moreover, man's very limited ability to defend himself against the whims of nature, such as storms at sea, famines, epidemics, and other cases of illness, as well as his helplessness in the face of a ruthless government or the constant menaces of piracy and war

[4] Adolf Grohmann, *From the World of Arabic Papyri*, Cairo, 1952 (where further literature on Arabic papyri); Albert Dietrich, *Arabische Briefe aus der Papyrussammlung der Hamburger Staats- und Universitäts-Bibliothek*, Hamburg, 1955; D. S. Margoliouth, *Catalogue of Arabic Papyri in the John Rylands Library, Manchester*, Manchester, 1933.

[5] E.g., no. 1, sec. C; nos. 11, 17, 23, secs. B, D, F.

developed in him a feeling that he was not the master of his own destiny, that he was delivered into the hands of a higher power. "Fate," albeit not absent from our letters, occurs in them rarely. God, the personal God, served the purpose better; he was a friend and father, with whom one conversed in prayer at least seven times a day; he knew one's innermost thoughts and most secret deeds, and one could always find a little, or not so little, sin, for which one was punished when something went wrong. All the good came from God and "he who hopes for the good will obtain it; God does not break his promise" (no. 32). Hence the astounding equanimity apparent in many Geniza letters and the generally optimistic approach to life displayed in them despite frequently dire living conditions. Religion was undoubtedly the strongest element in a merchant's mental makeup, and religion meant membership in a specific religious community.

Trading, naturally, was interdenominational and international. Several letters of this volume make mention of non-Jewish business friends and even partners. The trade with Christian Europe was largely responsible for the flourishing state of the mercantile communities on the southern shores of the Mediterranean during the eleventh century, as shown in *Med. Soc.* I, 44-47, where it is emphasized, however, that this trade was in the hands of Christian, not Jewish, merchants. Consequently, this exchange with Christian Europe is reflected in this collection mainly by indirect reference. Number 4, a letter from Amalfi, Italy, is the only example from the eleventh century of Arabic-speaking Jewish merchants doing business in a Christian port of Europe; there is none from the twelfth; and again only one, no. 8, this time concerning Genoa and Marseilles, from the thirteenth century. An important element of mutual understanding was the fact that the business ethics of the three monotheistic religions were essentially identical, although individual writers formulated them differently in their own original fashion.[6]

Besides the barriers of religion there existed the dividing lines of economic position and social class and sometimes it appears that the latter were stronger than the former. The reader of this volume

[6] A good introduction to the business ethics of Islam is provided in the article "Tidjārah" in *EI*[1], IV. About Hindus see the introduction to ch. V, below.

will quickly acquire a feeling for the social position of a writer, namely, whether he addresses an equal or a person of a higher or lower state than his own. In practically every letter the recipient is wished that God may preserve his "honored position" (Arabic *'izz*). For "man's fate depends on his place in society."[7]

Yet a spirit of equality pervaded that highly differentiated world. The way in which a former slave addresses a merchant prince and great communal leader (no. 13) is characteristic in this respect. The root of such brotherly attitude was again religion: one feared the same God, who was very near to all his children, high and low, and frequented the same place of worship, which was usually of limited size. Moreover, in both Judaism and Islam, scholarship conferred social prestige. A learned middle-class merchant—a rather common phenomenon—ranked as high in society as a rich and powerful supplier of the court. It seems also that the long months spent together in foreign parts on perilous voyages brought people close together, for "strangers are kinsmen to one another" (n. 78).

As is evident from the content of several of the letters translated below, some of their authors were learned persons, and some, such as Nahray (ch. IV), Abraham Yijū (nos. 38, 39, 40), and Ḥalfōn b. Nethanel (no. 59) were scholars. Besides biblical studies and, of course, the command of Hebrew (including Aramaic, the language in which a large section of the post-biblical Jewish literature is written), they were versed in Jewish law and lore, as is evident from the legal opinions which they wrote on the reverse sides of business letters received by them. This vast body of writings was studied first "for Heaven's sake," that is, because study was worship, but also for practical reasons: one studied the law because it was applied in life, and attorneys, who take care of these matters in our own time, were practically unknown in those days. In addition, Abraham Yijū was a poet, or rather, a maker of verses, and Ḥalfōn a connoisseur in several fields, such as poetry, philosophy, and some of the sciences.

Islam, as already alluded to in passing, took a similar attitude

[7] TS 13 J 8, f. 27, l. 27. The letter concerned is personal, not commercial. (A young man asks his prospective father-in-law not to divulge that he had asked him for the hand of his daughter, for he would lose face if he were repudiated.)

toward learning and the learned; the learned merchant has indeed been described as the bearer of medieval Islamic civilization. I wonder, however, whether this was not a more general medieval phenomenon. In the thirteenth century Norwegian *King's Mirror*, a young man who wished to become an overseas trader instead of joining the service of the king, received this advice from his father —among many other instructions: "Finally, remember this, that whenever you have an hour to spare you should give thought to your studies, especially to the law books; for it is clear that those who gain knowledge from books have keener wits than others, since those who are the most learned have the best proofs for their knowledge."[8]

There was very little contact between the world of the traders and that of the government and the army. The top merchants who acted as suppliers to the court naturally were close to the ruling circles, such as the recipients of nos. 1 and 11 or the writer of no. 12. The government provided naval escorts as a protection against pirates and enemy attack, as in nos. 69-70, which were, however, often ineffective, as proved by nos. 9 and 73. Syria was notorious for its lawlessness, and the caravans had to be protected by special guards paid by the merchants (no. 16, sec. A). Customs dues were not particularly oppressive. Complaints appear only in the times of political decline, as at the end of Almoravid rule in Morocco (no. 7), in disorderly Yemen (no. 43), or in later Ayyubid times in Egypt (no. 8, sec. B).

The government reserved for itself the right of buying first. When a boat carrying oil, wax, silk, or any other goods regarded as essential for the court or the army, arrived in a port, the government would prohibit the unloading until it had made its own purchases (see, for instance, no. 14). Powerful officials would assert the same right for themselves (no. 11, sec. C). A foreign Muslim ship would be seized and emptied of its entire cargo when it was needed for a war—a procedure that of course upset the dispositions of the merchants affected (no. 50). A boat from a Muslim country, albeit

[8] James Bruce Ross and Mary Martin McLaughlin, *The Portable Medieval Reader*, New York, 1956, p. 146. From *The King's Mirror*, trans. L. M. Larson, New York, 1917.

owned by a Jew, was liable to seizure when driven by a storm to Christian territory, as no. 76 shows, but local contacts were apt to save the proprietor from such a mishap. Government supervision of the mores of the travelers, as attested in no. 80, was exceptional, and not general practice.

Christian and Jewish merchants used to settle their disputes and other legal affairs before their communal courts (see *Med. Soc.*, II, ch. VII, and in this book, nos. 17, 18, 33, 34D, 36, 37A, 39B, 45B, 46, 47, 48, 51, 54, 56, etc.). Since, in those days, law was personal rather than territorial, that is, a man normally was judged in accordance with the law of the denomination to which he belonged, the Jewish merchants traveling between Spain and India were subject to the same law everywhere and often knew the prominent judges and jurisconsults from their writings or personally or both. If a merchant was learned, he himself often served as an assistant judge, or, where no local authority was available, formed a court with others. Any non-Muslim could apply to a Muslim, that is, government, court, as alluded to in no. 17, but this was strongly resented, as is evident, for instance, from the content of no. 56 and the tenor of the report contained in no. 79. All in all, the organization of law in medieval Islam markedly enhanced the cohesiveness of the non-Muslim communities and the communal attachment of the merchants.

3. The organization of the overseas trade

This volume is concerned with the traders rather than the trade, that is, with the sociological rather than the economic aspects of the overseas commerce. But, naturally, the former cannot be properly appreciated without some knowledge of the latter.

The organization of the overseas trade was effected largely through partnerships, countless varieties of which appear in the Geniza papers, as is evident from the discussion of the subject in *Med. Soc.*, I, 169-186.[9] The rich Islamic material on this vital instru-

[9] Three partnership agreements from the Cairo Geniza were published by A. L. Udovitch in *Studia Islamica* 32 (*Joseph Schacht Memorial Volume*), 289-303. Thirty more partnership documents, all differing with regard to the socioeconomic circumstances and mostly also the legal stipulations, are translated in my forthcoming book *Mediterranean People: Letters and Documents from the Cairo Geniza, Translated with Introductions and Notes.*

ment of economic life has been brought to the attention of the scholarly world in an important recent publication.[10] To be sure, the very great merchants possessed sufficient capital for financing comprehensive overseas undertakings with their own resources (see, for example, nos. 69 and 70). They employed agents in the home ports to ship their goods and permanent representatives in the main centers of trade abroad. But even they would not disdain the conclusion of many partnerships of limited size, as manifested in nos. 1, sec. B, and 14, both referring to the merchant prince Joseph Ibn ʿAwkal who lived around 1000. The economically strongest, like our own great companies, endeavored to become still stronger through partnership, as when the Muslim Bilāl, who later became the ruler of southern Yemen, and Maḍmūn, the leader of the Jewish community of Aden and superintendent of its port, united in constructing a boat for the Aden-Ceylon route or in shipping huge quantities of goods to the capital of Egypt, as we learn from no. 37, secs. B and C. Middle-class merchants who produced the bulk of writings preserved in the Geniza, usually conducted their business ventures in cooperation.

For an easier understanding of the letters translated in this volume, one characteristic of the Mediterranean partnership should be kept in mind: the relationship of partners could be maintained during a lifetime or even through generations, as in nos. 22 and 25, but it was customary to make a contract for each business venture, which could be defined by a certain time limit, such as a year, or a specific undertaking, such as "a travel to Yemen and beyond."

"Informal cooperation," based on "formal friendship," was another and widely applied method of overseas trade. I purposely placed the angry letter from Qayrawān, Tunisia, at the beginning of the book because it emphasizes again and again the true character of business "friendship," as it was called. The writer does not wish to become the official representative of the addressee; all he wants is "that you exert yourself for my goods there as I do for yours here" (no. 1, secs. A, C, F, H). The services rendered for a "friend" and expected from him were manifold and exacting, as the long list in *Med. Soc.*, I, 164-169 shows, and there is little doubt

[10] Abraham L. Udovitch, *Partnership and Profit in Medieval Islam*, Princeton, 1970.

that the relationship varied from one pair of friends to another.[11]

The bonds of friendship were strengthened by marriages concluded between families all over the Mediterranean area, including the India route (see no. 9). Blood relationship was felt to be even stronger than the ties of marriage. A family business, comprising a father and his sons, brothers, or a merchant and his nephew, was the natural form of mercantile cooperation, conspicuous especially during the eleventh century, as is proved by many examples in this volume. But cooperation never meant common property. Accounts were kept strictly separate. Fathers groomed their boys to do business on their own account, as in no. 22, sec. F, and granted them only a modest share in the family income as long as they were dependent (see no. 40, sec. E).

Bond-servants who acted as commercial agents of their masters also must be regarded as belonging to the family business. For a slave was no stranger; he was a member of the household. Bama, the Indian slave so often mentioned in the correspondence of his master, is referred to as brother, he is addressed with the title "sheikh," like any other respectable merchant, and greetings are regularly extended to him in the letters still read by us (see no. 38, n. 18). The status of a bond-servant depended, of course, on that of the master whom he served, as the story included in no. 79 so palpably demonstrates. Male slaves able to serve as confidants and to do overseas business were costly and only the greater merchants could permit themselves such a luxury, as is evident from the examples occurring in this book. It must have been customary to free such bond-servant agents at a comparatively early stage of their lives, that is, when they still were able to do business for themselves, for the cases of freedmen carrying on a business of their own, like the one in no. 13, are at least as frequent in the Geniza as those still in bondage and working for a master. I imagine that a merchant with small children took a slave as his confidant, but as soon as his sons were old enough to assist him, he freed the slave, lest he should become too powerful in the house, as happened so often in Islamic governments. The Geniza is apt to contribute

[11] The subject is treated in a wider context in S. D. Goitein, "Formal Friendship in the Medieval Near East," *Proceedings of the American Philosophical Society* 115 (1971), 484-489.

material to the study of this interesting social phenomenon, which has parallels in various other human societies.

A ubiquitous element of medieval trade was the *dallāl*, usually translated as broker, auctioneer, or middleman, the person who fulfilled the economic function of advertisements and other modern means of publicity. He cried out the goods offered for sale in the bazaar and brought them to the knowledge of customers in other ways. The writers of our letters rarely have opportunity to mention him, but the accounts often list the commission paid to a dallāl, as in no. 64, secs. A and D.

In addition to partnerships, "friendships," family connections, and agents and brokers of various types, overseas trade relied on an institution which, more than any other, has been brought into the broad light of history through the Cairo Geniza documents: the office of the representative of the merchants. The *wakīl al-tujjār* originally was the legal representative of absent foreign merchants, and often himself a foreigner or a descendant of one: a Spanish Jew in the port city al-Mahdiyya, Tunisia (no. 70, n. 6); a Maghrebi in Alexandria, Egypt (no. 28, n. 24); a man from Aleppo in Ramle, Palestine (no. 5, n. 20). The prominent wakīl of Fustat, Abū Zikrī Judah b. Joseph Kohen, to whom letters 9 and 37 are addressed, was called Sijilmāsī, and probably had traveled to that remote city in southern Morocco, if he was not born in that place, while his father sojourned there on business.[12] The representatives of the merchants in Aden, South Arabia, Ḥasan b. Bundār and his son Maḍmūn (nos. 36, 37, 38 sec. C, etc.), probably hailed from Iran. I have come to this conclusion not only because of the Persian name of the founder of the family, Bundār, but for various other reasons, the explanation of which would take me too far afield.

Thus, the function of the representative of the merchants was

[12] See no. 41, n. 6. Judah's father might have married in Sijilmāsa and remained there until a son was born to him. Judah's grandfather and namesake was the leading Jewish scholar and religious authority in Egypt (see the introduction to no. 9). "Dynastic" marriages were as common among the families of divines as among those of the leading merchants. In 1037, the head of the Iraqian Jewish community of Fustat married the daughter of the Jewish judge of Sijilmāsa, which would have formed an exact precedent for Judah's father. About such marriage connections between families living in countries remote from one another see *Med. Soc.*, I, 48-49.

essentially the protection of the interests of persons who were absent from a town or were foreigners there. He kept a warehouse, which served for the storage of goods, as a bourse where business was transacted, and as a mail office. He received merchandise sent to him from abroad, sold it, and distributed the proceeds to the partners who had invested in the relevant business venture (no. 40, n. 11). He took care of the goods, money, and claims of merchants who had perished at sea or otherwise died abroad, and tried to alleviate the lot of the families who had suffered this privation (no. 37). On top of all this, he of course did business for himself. Muslim representatives of merchants are usually referred to with the title qadi, or judge, which means that they also issued the legal documents needed for business transactions. Letter 62 is addressed to such a qadi, but one who was not the proprietor of a warehouse, but sat in one acting as a notary. Most of the Jewish wakīls referred to in this book were learned enough for drawing up legal documents, but it seems they were occupied with work more lucrative than the time-consuming labor of a legal clerk.

The office of the representative of the merchants has been discussed by me in *Med. Soc.*, I, 186-192. A renewed scrutiny of the Geniza papers in comparison with the widely diffused Arabic literature on the subject may provide additional insights. There is little doubt that the Islamic wakīl al-tujjār, or shāh-bender ("the king of the port"), or whatever he was called, was the prototype for the consuls of the Italian and other merchants' colonies in the Levant, and a comparative study might be conducive to a better understanding of both institutions.

4. The goods

The character of a trade, and even of a trader is considerably influenced by the nature of the merchandise with which he trades. Everyone understands that the matters to be attended to by a druggist are very different from those to be tackled by a horse-dealer. Therefore a note about the commodities handled by the writers of our letters might not be out of place.

With one or two exceptions, the 150 or so commodities mentioned in this book, as unfamiliar as some of them may appear to the modern reader, were common items in the medieval trade and also recur in other Geniza letters. Their provenance, movements, prices, use, and economic significance can thus be conveniently studied on the basis of rich and reliable source material. It is not intended to pursue this study here. I wish, however, to give a short survey of the goods traded by the writers of our letters so that the reader may become familiar with the world in which they moved. The notes provide additional information wherever needed.

In view of the bewildering variety of goods appearing in this book one might be tempted to assume that these people traded with practically everything. Nothing is further from the truth.

The main food items, such as wheat, beans, and barley, are not included here; neither are sheep and other meat cattle, nor beasts of transport, such as donkeys, mules, and camels. No one traded in building materials, whether timber, bricks, or stones. Weapons and slaves, great items of both international and local trade, are entirely absent from the Geniza correspondence. To be sure, all these were items in general use. Therefore we read that people acquired them for themselves, their relatives and friends, or the community. There were also exceptions confirming the rule: for example, we would find a document proving that a Jew traded in commercial quantities of wheat. But such exceptions are rare.

The choice of the goods traded depended in a large measure on the community to which a trader belonged. The international commerce of the Jews was closely intertwined with the local Jewish industries and retail business. Then, as in modern times, Jews were prominent in textiles. Therefore, threads, fabrics, and clothing take a place of pride in the letters translated here. I hurry to add: had we a similar collection from the hands of Muslim or Christian traders, the picture would have been exactly the same. In the Middle Ages, textiles were the number one item of commerce in both general and luxury goods. According to a Muslim legend, Abraham was a clothier; to the best of my knowledge, no Jewish source exists for this legend.[13] The pious and learned Muslims who mostly found their livelihood in the bazaars of the clothiers, simply could not

[13] A Jewish legend to this effect could hardly have originated in view of the express testimony of the Book of Genesis which depicts the patriarch Abraham as a cattle breeder.

imagine that Abraham, the father of faith, could have done anything other than trade in textiles.

Dyeing, a difficult craft in view of the primitive materials then available and the high demands made of the artisan,[14] was closely connected with the textile industry and also largely Jewish. Jews even had the reputation of possessing professional secrets which they refused to communicate to anyone not within the fold. But again, it would be entirely wrong to assert that the Jews enjoyed a monopoly in this field or, vice versa, that they were forced into it because it was regarded by some as a despised profession. Anyhow, the Jewish overseas trade handled great quantities of dyeing materials coming from practically all parts of the world frequented by it: the Far East, India and Yemen, Egypt, Palestine and Syria, Tunisia and Morocco. By chance, only the most common dyeing stuffs occur in our letters.

In the professions of druggist, pharmacist, and perfumer the Jews were represented out of all proportion to their number. These were the most popular occupations among them. Consequently, medical plants and preparations, spices and aromatics, as well as perfumes and incenses constituted the main items of the Jewish overseas trade. About one-third of the commodities listed in the index of this book belong to this category.[15]

Copper, together with its alloys, is the metal most frequently mentioned in our letters. The reason for this is, of course, that most utensils and containers, for instance in the kitchen, which are manufactured today from a great variety of materials, were then made of copper. The Arabic terms for copper, bronze, and brass often are used indiscriminately (see no. 39, n. 8). In addition, the reader should be alerted to the fact that "copper," when not expressly described as raw material, could also mean old or broken copper vessels sent to a place where they would be melted down and used for the fabrication of new ones.[16] Tin, the usual alloy of copper,

[14] See no. 11. About the color-intoxication of medieval people see *Med. Soc.*, I, 106-107.

[15] The Geniza material about these professions is presented in *Med. Soc.*, II, 261-272, where an attempt is also made to explain why they were so popular among Jews.

[16] The same use is seen in the lists of trousseaux, which are mostly divided

and lead, used in many chemical processes, also were great items of commerce.

Iron, a most prominent commodity of export from India to the Arab world and handled by Jewish merchants, was next to absent from the Geniza papers related to the Mediterranean trade. Once it is mentioned there, the Hebrew word is used, probably because the writer assumed that the iron, if discovered, would be seized by the government. (The secret police was believed to know the Hebrew characters, but not the language.) Jews were black- and coppersmiths and manufacturers of various implements made of metals and preparations from chemicals, but were not particularly conspicuous in these industries. Thus the Jewish prominence in the metal trade probably went back to some ancient tradition. When the Arabs invaded the island of Rhodes in the eastern Mediterranean in 672 or 673, they destroyed the famous colossus, one of the seven wonders of the ancient world. Its copper, weighing 880 camel loads, was bought by a Jewish merchant in Emesa, Syria, who certainly was no novice in the copper trade. An Iranian source of the twelfth century speaks of a Jew who had leased copper mines in that country from the government. When we find a Tunisian Jew operating a bronze factory in India (no. 39), we can safely assume that this newcomer to the subcontinent only followed the examples of other Jews who preceded him. The trade in metals and chemicals is well represented in our collection.

Throughout the Muslim world Jews were active as gold- and silversmiths. But the products of this industry were sold individually and were not traded wholesale. Pearls and precious stones were a great commodity of international trade, and so were the cheap mass articles serving as ornaments, such as beads, corals, cowrie shells, and lapis lazuli. Jews were very prominent as glassmakers. But this industry is referred to in documents in greater detail than it is in letters.

Olive oil, wax, and soap were imported to Egypt in large quantities, mainly from Tunisia, and so were dried fruits, mostly from southwest Asia. Sugar, on the other hand, was produced in Fustat

---

into these sections: jewelry (including gold and silver vessels), clothing, bedding, copper (meaning household goods).

and exported from there all over the Mediterranean. Jews were prominent in the food industry as makers of sweets, cooked foods, and lemonades, but these people seem to have been small vendors and hardly of significance for a flourishing international trade. Naturally, oil and wax were needed for lighting, for which the local linseed oil also was used. Because of the heat, the nights were reserved for entertainment and study and the consumption of lighting fuel was high. The Jewish community of Fustat was praised for its zeal "for study throughout the night until daybreak." (Their letters do not give this impression.)

By chance, two other commodities of wide use in daily life, and consequently often referred to in Geniza writings, are almost absent from our selection. Cheese was the main protein food of the poorer population, and despite Egypt's extended sheep breeding, cheese had to be imported from Sicily, Crete, and other places. Here (no. 39, n. 21), cheese, especially prepared for use in a Jewish kitchen, is sent as a present from Aden to India. Wine, in good Mediterranean fashion, was taken by Christians and Jews with their daily dinner. Every respectable household had a good supply, and wine merchants have left us their accounts. Despite Koranic prohibition wine was openly sold in the bazaars of Cairo in those days, and the shipowner with the family name "Son of the Wine-seller" in no. 73 certainly was a Muslim.[17] In classical antiquity salted tuna fish was an important Mediterranean article of trade. In the Geniza, it appears solely as a present, sent from Tunisia to Egypt (as in no. 22, sec. J), probably because the Jews had no part in that wholesale trade. But Jewish fishmongers are repeatedly referred to in the Geniza, even a tuna fish-seller (or perhaps fisher, for in the document concerned his future wife promises never to leave the house except with his permission and gives him the right to lock her in, a right enjoyed by Muslim, but not by Jewish, husbands; in exchange she receives some special privileges).

One of the most exacting aspects of medieval sea transport was the proper packing and wrapping of the goods. The storms tossed those sailing ships around, the bales were torn apart and the goods contained in them damaged by seawater. "Eight bales of flax, seven

[17] It could have been a nickname.

of which had been torn open," we read in no. 23, sec. C, and similar statements are contained in no. 22, sec. D; no. 25, sec. C; and elsewhere. The bales of flax damaged by seawater were a constant rubric in the account books, as in no. 63. The goods were wrapped in canvas and protected by oxhides, an item of import from Sicily. Because of the availability of hides in the West parchment remained in use there for letters far longer than in Egypt, where we find it used only in sacred or otherwise precious books and in important legal documents.

Paper was produced everywhere, but varied so much in quality that we find it shipped from one country to another in huge quantities, e.g., in nos. 15 and 16. In the India trade, small amounts of paper, Egyptian, Spanish, etc., were sent as presents from Aden to India. Many of the letters sent to India and which we now hold in our hands must have remained with their recipient for ten or fifteen years, and one wonders how they were protected against termites; those expert dealers in spices and medical plants probably knew how to overcome those voracious insects. The local Indians did not use paper in the twelfth century. Our letters permit us also a few glimpses into the book trade.

Finally, gold and silver coins and other means of payment also should be classified as "goods"; at least they were regarded as such by the writers of our letters. A variety of coins were on the market, but the general movement of specie was from the West to the East, from Spain and North Africa to Egypt and from there to India and the Orient. Promissory notes were the most common means of payment inside a country, while the *suftaja*, usually translated as "bill of exchange," but more correctly described as cashier's check (see no. 70, n. 18) was used for larger transactions, often those conducted between two countries.

In order to counteract the perils of transport and the whims of the overseas markets, merchants usually spread the risk by shipping a variety of goods and by limiting the size of the shipments. Occasionally, however, we find extravagant quantities of one commodity only and that at a time of war, as in nos. 17, 69, and 70, where unusual numbers of bales and bags with Egyptian flax went westward. Shall we assume that in wartime there was a boom for Egyptian flax during the first half of the eleventh century as there was one for Egyptian cotton during the American Civil War over 800 years later? Or were there sudden developments in Europe or the Maghreb which justified such risks? The Geniza letters are apt to alert us on many aspects of medieval socioeconomic history. They offer a most promising field of study, provided that study is based on sound philological work—I mean the exact reading of the texts and correct translations. The collection offered here should be regarded as experimental, for we are still in the very midst of the research.

CHAPTER II

Geographical Setting

Two LARGE areas of medieval commerce, the Mediterranean and the India trade, are covered in this book. The hub of the Mediterranean was the Islamic principality which comprised Tunisia and Sicily; it is represented here mainly, but not exclusively, by (al-) Qayrawān, the inland capital of Tunisia, and its seaport al-Mahdiyya, and by Palermo, the capital and northern seaport of Sicily, and other ports of that island. The backbone of the India trade was formed by three centers: Qūṣ (no. 10) and other towns in Upper Egypt, to which one traveled from Cairo on the Nile; 'Aydhāb and other ports on the Sudanese coast, which were reached from Qūṣ by crossing the desert; and, above all, Aden in South Arabia. The twin city Cairo-Fustat, the capital of Egypt, formed the terminal for both the Mediterranean and the India trade and served as distribution center for the goods of both. Alexandria, although the main port of Egypt, was commercially of secondary importance. All great transactions were made in Cairo-Fustat.

In Roman and Byzantine times, the opposite situation prevailed. Alexandria was then the economic, administrative, and cultural capital of Egypt. For in those days the Mediterranean was an inland sea dominated by Rome, and Egypt looked westward. In Islamic times, that sea was plagued by almost continuous warfare. The capitals of the Islamic states, such as Qayrawān, Cairo, and Damascus, were therefore situated far away from the sea. Caesarea on the seashore of Palestine, the administrative center of the country under the Romans, was replaced by inland Ramle (see no. 5).

Several of the countries and regions most vital to the medieval trade are represented here mostly by reference only, or even solely by implication. Sudanese gold fed the entire economy of the age, yet we do not have a single letter from the Sudan nor even a report

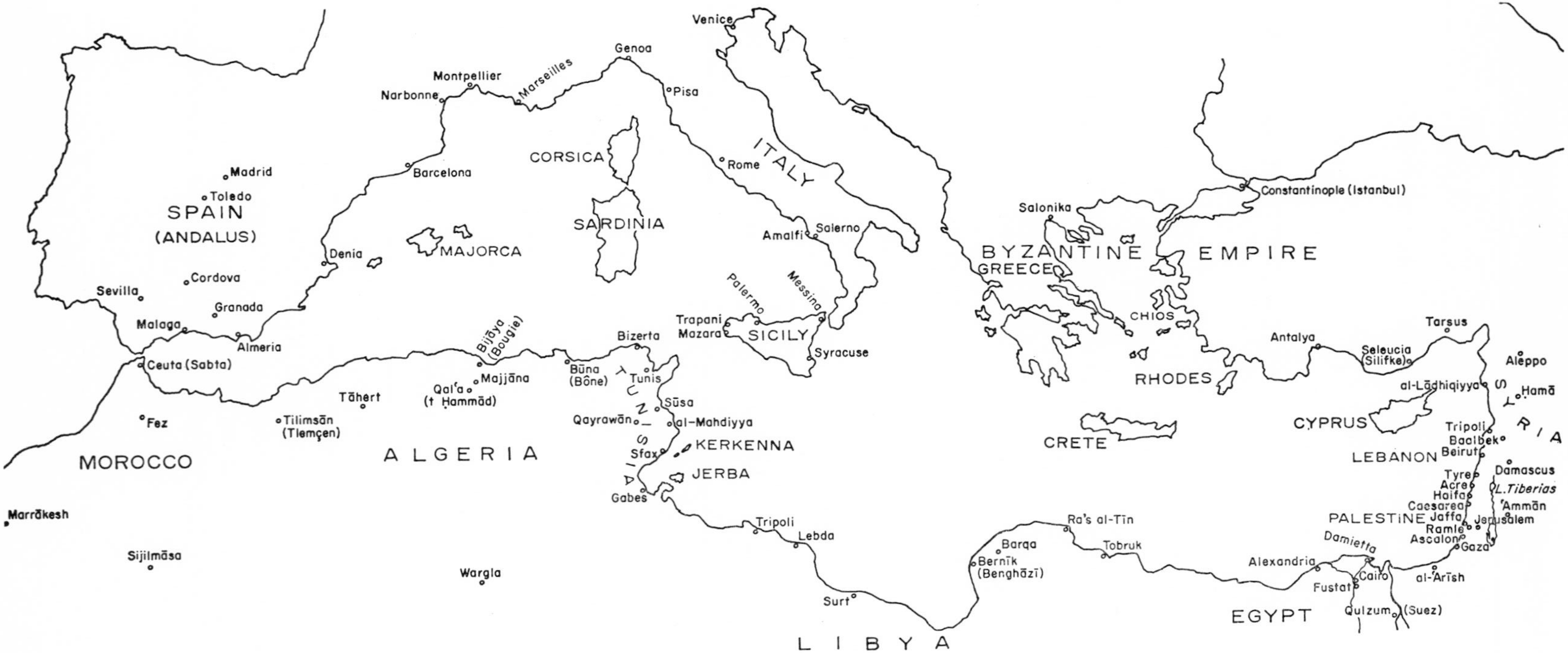

Map I. The Mediterranean Route

of a voyage made there. But Sijilmāsa, the Moroccan "desert port" and terminal for the caravans going south to the Sudan and east via Qayrawān to Cairo, is repeatedly mentioned in our letters. Spain and Morocco, which both produced some of the main commodities of the international trade, such as silk and copper, or potash alum and antimony (kohl), are represented by only a few items. The examples from Iran and Europe (nos. 2, 4, 8) are exceptions confirming the general absence of such letters. The west coast of India is represented in my collection of India papers by sixteen of its ports, whereas the east coast, Malaya, and Sumatra appear only by reference, as here in nos. 45-47.

Thus, the bulk of this book is made up of letters exchanged within the inner circles of the two great trade areas: between Egypt and Tunisia-Sicily in the West and Palestine and the Lebanese coast in the Northeast; and between Aden and Egypt on the one hand and the west coast of India on the other. A considerable part of the goods mentioned were grown, processed, and used within these inner circles, such as the Egyptian flax exported to Tunisia-Sicily and coming back to Egypt in the form of finished fabrics and textiles. But the major portion consisted of reexports, such as the countless Oriental products which moved through or from India, then through Aden, Egypt, and Tunisia-Sicily to Spain and Christian Europe, or Spanish silk and copper, which traveled in the opposite direction. Thus the correspondence translated in this book comprises a far wider geographical area than that indicated by the places of dispatch and destination of the letters.

This chapter intends to give the reader a general idea of the geographical setting, but does not present all the localities occurring in this book. Jerusalem, for instance, is the scene of nos. 19-21 and 32, but does not appear here at all.

1 AN ANGRY LETTER FROM QAYRAWĀN

the Capital of Ifrīqiya (Tunisia), to Fustat, the Main City of Egypt, about Business in Spain and in the Writer's Place

Ca. 1000

Joseph b. Jacob Ibn 'Awkal, the recipient of this letter, was a merchant prince active in the capital of Egypt from the end of the tenth century through the first third of the eleventh. One of his offices was in the *Dār al-Jawhar*, the gem bourse, of Fustat, and he specialized in luxury articles such as pearls, gems, and crystals. But his business encompassed practically all the goods usually traded between the western and eastern Mediterranean during the eleventh century and which on a smaller scale were simultaneously handled by merchants of far lesser stature. These included many varieties of flax, then the staple export of Egypt, also sugar, its main industrial product, and, of course, textiles, manufactured in or brought to that country; pepper and other spices, medical herbs, and odoriferous woods, also dyeing materials, such as brazilwood, indigo, and lac, coming from the Far East and reexported to the Muslim West and Europe; the products of Spain and Sicily, above all silk of various types and qualities, and metals such as copper and lead; textiles, olive oil and soap, wax and honey, imported from Tunisia; and last, but not least, specie, which, drawing on the rich sources of Sudanese gold and Spanish silver, was abundant in the West but scarce in Egypt. The difference between a great merchant like Ibn 'Awkal and less prominent members of the profession consisted in the quantity and quality, but not in the variety, of the goods traded.[1]

In addition to his manifold commercial activities, Ibn 'Awkal played an important communal role as the representative of the *yeshivas*, the two Jewish high councils and academies of Baghdad, which were the spiritual centers of the Diaspora. The questions on points of religious law of the Jewish communities of North Africa and Egypt as well as their donations were forwarded by him to Baghdad, and the answers and accompanying letters were sent by him to the addressees, after first having been copied in his offices as

[1] A more detailed list of items handled by a less prominent merchant is presented in *Med. Soc.*, I, 154.

a matter of precaution. Hundreds of such copies have survived in the Geniza, but not a single letter showing Ibn 'Awkal in *commercial* relations with Iraq or Iran has been found. For one letter from southern Iran addressed both to his father and to him, and written partly in Arabic and partly in Judeo-Persian, includes a request that they transmit 90 gold pieces worth 100 mithqāls, or dinars, to an acquaintance in Fustat, but contain no indication of commercial activity.[2]

How, then, are we to explain the strange geographical dichotomy between Joseph Ibn 'Awkal's commercial and communal activities? His family, like many other Jewish families in the West, originated in Iran, as is proved by the fact that father and son are addressed in the Persian language. Further family ties connected them with Tunisia and Sicily. Thus it stands to reason that Joseph's grandfather had emigrated to the Muslim West, where his father and he himself acquired that high standing in the North African communities which enabled them to become the representatives of the North African diocese when the family moved to Egypt, following the Fatimids who conquered that country in 969. Joseph himself had personal experience solely in Spain, Sicily, and North Africa. Therefore, when taking up residence in Egypt, he restricted his business activities exclusively to the Muslim West. Among the fifty or so items addressed to him which are preserved in the Geniza there is none from Asia, not even one from the ports of the eastern Mediterranean. The Judeo-Persian letter mentioned before is an exception which confirms the rule.

Forty-six letters and accounts destined for Joseph Ibn 'Awkal, partly also for his father and sons,[3] have been edited by me with Hebrew translations and comments, or, if they were too much damaged, described and discussed in the periodicals *Zion* and *Tarbiz*.[4] An excellent and most useful analysis of the entire material, including the few texts edited by others, and an English trans-

[2] TS Arabic Box 42, f. 176, not yet edited at the time of the writing of these lines. See also no. 2, n. 1, below.

[3] Four sons and two daughters are referred to in the Geniza papers. He might have had more.

[4] *Zion* 27 (1962), 156-165. See also *Tarbiz* 34 (1965), 162-182; 36 (1967), 366-395; 37 (1967-1968), 48-77, 158-190; 38 (1968), 18-42. See also letters nos. 3 and 4, below.

lation of seventeen major items have been provided by Norman A. Stillman.[5]

The letter presented here well illustrates Mediterranean trade at the opening of the eleventh century. Tunisia naturally had lost much by the transfer of the Fatimid court and army to the newly built imperial city of Cairo, Egypt. But it still served, together with Sicily, as a commercial intermediary between Muslim Spain, western North Africa, also Christian western Europe, and the Muslim East. The caravans of Sijilmāsa, the desert entrepôt in southern Morocco, which imported the riches of sub-Saharan Africa, still passed through Qayrawān, then the capital of the country now known as Tunisia. Our letter exhibits both the first intimations of decline and the pride of a city which once was the hub of the Mediterranean.

The main types of business cooperation: informal "friendship" based on reciprocal services, formal partnership, and outright commission, are represented here with the first being the most prominent. Another recurring problem of overseas trade, namely, whether the correspondent should follow the instructions of the sender of a shipment or act according to his own lights in view of changing market conditions, is much ventilated.

The family name of the writer of our letter, Ibn al-Siqillī, shows that one of his ancestors had emigrated from Sicily to Qayrawān. Two of his sons were engaged in the trade between Spain and Egypt, one of them acting as business correspondent of Ibn 'Awkal, like his father.

The letter is one of the earliest addressed to Ibn 'Awkal. For in another letter, sent from Qayrawān in July 1008, his two sons Hillel and Benjamin, to whom greetings are extended here, appear already as partners in the family business (see n. 23, below). Moreover, the tone of our letter, despite its repeated emphasis on Ibn 'Awkal's high rank, is rather disrespectful, which also suggests an early stage of his career.

David Kaufmann Collection, Budapest, DK 13.[6]

[5] *East-West Relations in the Islamic Mediterranean in the Early Eleventh Century: A Study in the Geniza Correspondence of the House of Ibn 'Awkal.* Ph.D. dissertation, University of Pennsylvania, 1970, pp. 69, 416. Cited hereafter as Stillman, *East-West Relations.*

[6] Ed. S. D. Goitein, *Tarbiz* 37 (1968), 64-70, trans. Stillman in *East-West Relations*, pp. 267-279.

I am writing to you, my esteemed elder, master, and chief, may God prolong your life and make lasting [your honored position],[7] well-being, and security, on Elul 23.[8] I am safe and in good health, many [thanks be to God]. [I am yearning for] the sight of your blessed countenance; may God unite us in the best of circumstances and in perfect happiness.

A. Brazilwood[9] sent to Spain contrary to the instructions of Ibn 'Awkal

Your enjoyable letters have arrived and I have gathered from them that you are fine; may God ordain that it should always be so; may he ever increase his boons to you and shower upon you his favors.

My elder and master, you say that I *took* the brazilwood and sent it to Spain. I did not take it for myself, nor have I made any profit from it. Rather, it caused me losses. I acted thus because I rely upon you and because you are helpful to me with your high rank in matters of the goods sent by me to you on my account. I was sure that you would write me exactly the opposite of what you have written, which offended me so much and for which I do not know any reason. Your shipment was sent in Iyyar (April/May) and mine was sent to you in Av (July/August); could your consignment possibly have come from Spain and made all this in two months? And even if this was possible, would you not have acted similarly?[10]

[7] Here and throughout, the manuscript is damaged by little holes. Standard phrases are restored without comment.

[8] Late in August or early in September, in time to be sent with the very last boat sailing.

[9] This Indian red dye, also called sappan wood, was an important item of medieval international trade and is mentioned in countless Geniza papers. See also *EI*[2] s.v. *Bakkam*.

[10] Ibn 'Awkal obviously had insinuated that the writer had profited from sending his brazilwood to Spain. Between the Jewish months of Iyyar (April/May) and Av there are two other months. What he seems to say is this: You sent your brazilwood from Egypt in May; now, you assume, it has arrived here, was forwarded by me to Spain, sold with great profit, and other goods bought there had been brought here, which helped me to finance my shipments to you, which were sent early in August. Is this technically possible?

B. Silk sold in Qayrawān instead of being sent to Fustat

You w[rite in your letters that] I should send you the 420 pounds of silk. But one-third of this is my brother's investment, besides which he is entitled to a third of the profit along with you. Moreover, the merchants are unanimously of the opinion that silk sells in Qayrawān better than in Fustat. Here (a pound) sells for 1 1/2 dinars of Qayrawān standard weight.[11] I wished I had immediately forwarded to you your share, as you instructed me, for most of the proceeds are still outstanding and I have debited myself with all that is due my brother and due you. I have received payment for 100 pounds from Salāma of al-Mahdiyya only eight days before the writing of this letter. With Ibn al-Ṣabbāgh ("Mr. Dyer") there is also a debt outstanding, for I sold to him on credit. I also lost much money which was due us from the colorists,[12] but did not charge anything to the two of you, for my brother settled his accounts with me before his departure and took what was due him. And this is my reward from you after all this.

C. Cash sent in the Sijilmāsa caravan

I sent you 100 less one-quarter 'Azīzī dinars[13] in the caravan of the Sijilmāsis[14] with Abu 'l-Surūr b. Barhūn.[15] This was taken from my own money, for at that time I had not received a penny from the price of the silk. I acted thus because of my esteem for

[11] There was only a negligible difference between a gold dinar struck in Qayrawān and one in Egypt. The standard price for a pound of silk around the middle of the century was 2 dinars. See *Med. Soc.*, I, 222.

[12] Ar. *lawwānīn*, repeated at the end of the letter, but not found by me anywhere else. The word is derived from *lawn*, "color," and it stands to reason that these "colorists" had to do something with the dyeing of silk, but exactly what, I do not yet know.

[13] Coined under the Fatimid caliph al-'Azīz (975-996).

[14] See the introduction. The ship which was to carry this letter was expected to travel faster than a caravan which moved slowly and made prolonged halts during which the merchants would do business. It seems, however, that at that early time travel by land was regarded as safer.

[15] This is Isaac b. Abraham of the famous Tāhertī family. The biblical Isaac, which means "the one who laughs" (Genesis 21:1-6), had as its Ar. equivalent Abu 'l-Surūr ("Joyful"), while Barhūn was the Maghrebi form of endearment for the name Abraham.

you and because of your illustrious position, your noble character, and piety.[16] All I ask from you is that you act with respect to my goods sent to you in the same manner as I acted with your goods sent to me.

D. No share in a most profitable sale of pearls

Then you sent those pearls and I worked hard collecting their price. For how long shall this go on?! Should I not have taken one quarter of the profit? Through me you have made a profit of close to 1 dinar per dinar, and all this was of no advantage to me. I expected only that you would exert yourself for me, at least that you would send me what you owe me. Had I owed you 2,000 dinars, would I withhold them from you? Would they not reach you (even) by sea to your satisfaction?[17] If you had sent my money, I would have made good use of it—as you have made of yours. And what had happened if, God forbid, your goods had traveled a second time and entered my account?[18] How would I then stand before you? But God, may he be praised and exalted, knows my good intentions, and he rewards every man according to his intention.

E. Ibn 'Awkal failed to satisfy the writer's creditors

What disturbed me most was your failure to pay to Ibn Yazdād[19] and Salāma, the son-in-law of Furayj,[20] the sum that I asked you to pay them or to give them the equivalent in goods, although I had advised you expressly to do so. You have withheld payment from them, while this is a debt upon me. And this, at a time when your merchandise was in Spain![21] Their letters vituperating me have

[16] "Piety" (*diyāna*) in a business letter means meticulous behavior toward one's fellow merchants.

[17] Ibn 'Awkal had withheld some sums owed the writer in view of the unsatisfactory brazilwood transaction (sec. A, above). Ibn Siquillī retorts that he would honor any obligation and send even a very large sum by sea, meaning quickly and on his own responsibility.

[18] This refers to a second shipment of brazilwood (sec. G, below).

[19] A Persian name, meaning "God has given." This man is probably identical with Joseph Ibn Yazdād, mentioned in a Karaite document dated 1004 (ed. Mann, *Texts*, II, 196-198).

[20] Probably a diminutive of the common name Faraj, "delivery, salvation."

[21] That is, not in my hand.

now come here to everyone and my honor has been disgraced. Had you only made promises to them and said: "He has given instructions for you," they would have been patient and I would have been spared those vituperations.

F. False rumor that the writer had asked Ibn 'Awkal to become his representative in Qayrawān

Our Maghrebi friends[22] told me what they had heard in your name from Abu 'l-Khayr b. Barhūn,[23] that I had written to you asking you to replace Ibn Majjānī[24] by myself. I have not wanted this. I am not prepared to undertake it, nor have I any need for this. What I do need is to benefit from your high position and that you exert yourself for my goods as I do for yours. What I did say is that you should entrust me with your affairs just as I entrust you with mine. But after having taken care of someone else's affairs or having formed a partnership with him, God forbid that I and my honor should then be treated in this improper way. I never withhold a penny from anyone else, nor is any claim made against me at any time.[25]

G. Special arrangements for a second shipment of brazilwood to Spain which did not materialize

I had made an agreement with Faraḥ ("Joy") of Fez with regard to the remainder of the brazilwood, to the effect that I take it and send it to Spain [at a c]ommission, but on the condition that I will bear *responsibility* (for its loss). Each qinṭār (100 pounds) was appraised at 12 dinars in the presence of a number of our friends.

[22] Ar. *aṣḥābnā*, which usually means "coreligionists," that is, Jews. But since so many Maghrebi Jews participated in the Mediterranean trade, the literal translation "friends" is perhaps more appropriate here.

[23] This is Moses, called Abu 'l-Khayr ("The Good One"; see Exodus 2:2), son of Abraham Tāhertī, who, like his brother Isaac (see n. 15, above), often traveled to Egypt. The letter dated 1008, mentioned in the introduction, was written by a third brother, Ṣāliḥ. See *Tarbiz* 37 (1968), 158.

[24] This is the father of the writer of letter no. 18, below.

[25] My Heb. translation of lines 33-34 (*Tarbiz* 37 [1968], 68), must be revised according to the version provided here.

You, not I, had to have the choice since all this was to be on your behalf.[26] Finally, Faraḥ did not do it.

Thank God that this did not materialize, for you would have treated me in this matter as you have done before. But, by God, my master, the profit with this would have been even greater than with the first shipment. For this year brazilwood which I had bought in Qayrawān for 265 dirhems was sold on my behalf for 125 dinars.[27] God knew my good intentions and spared me many troubles in a matter from which I would not have had any advantages.

H. Conclusion and P.S.

(Another twenty-four lines reiterate the arguments made before. Three times the writer again emphasizes the urgency of satisfying his creditors; see sec. E, above.)

I do not dare to say to you: "Send me your things and I shall handle them,"[28] fearing that you may tell stories about me that I have asked you to put me in Ibn al-Majjānī's place.[29] I do not need this. The little we have here in the Maghreb is worth the abundance you have over there. But after all, I am your servant and prepared to deal, for your profit and without advantage for me, with anything you might send me. By God, my lord, this will give me only pleasure. God knows.[30]

Kindest personal regards to my master, the elder, and to his two sons Hillel and Benjamin, may God protect and keep them.

(In the margin:)

I copied for you from my account book[31] the account for the sale of the silk, and the expenses involved from beginning to end,

[26] It was agreed that Ibn 'Awkal should be free to decide which form of business cooperation he preferred.

[27] Even if we assume that the dirhems referred to were of highest silver content and worth about 1/12 of a dinar (see *Med. Soc.*, I, 370, sec. 4; 377, sec. 30), a profit of over 500 percent would have been made here. Even a profit of "almost 100 percent" (sec. D) was exceptional. As a rule, their profits were surprisingly low (see *Med. Soc.*, I, 202ff.).

[28] The usual conclusion of a business letter.

[29] See sec. F, above.

[30] Here is a short note about a payment of 1 dinar to one Ibn 'Allān. About this family see no. 17, below.

[31] The account book, *daftar*, was accepted by the courts as a legal proof.

including a description of each item and showing how it was sold without any loss for you. May God replace that which has gone . . . for what has remained with the "colorists" can never be recovered. Please examine the account and take notice of all its details. If you have any doubts, let me know and I shall give you the necessary explanations, if God wills.

(Address:)

To my master and chief, the [illustrious] elder, Abu 'l-Faraj,[32] may God prolong his life and make permanent his honored position and prosperity, Yūsuf (Joseph) b. Ya'qūb (Jacob) Ibn 'Awkal—(may his) s(oul) r(est in peace). May God be his friend, protector, helper, and shepherd.

From Samḥūn b. Dā'ūd Ibn al-Siqillī ("Generous," son of David, the son of the Sicilian). Miṣr (Fustat) i[f God wills].

(In Arabic characters:) In Miṣr, if God wills.

2 FROM IRAN TO EGYPT

March 5, 1026

Geniza letters sent from Iran to Egypt are conspicuous by their absence. A note written partly in Arabic and mostly in Hebrew characters and Persian language was sent around the year 1000 from southern Iran to Jacob Ibn 'Awkal and his son Joseph in Fustat.[1] A few letters entirely in Persian have also been found, but these were mostly written in places west of Iran.

The reason for this deficiency was the same as that accounting for the scarcity of regular business letters from Spain to Egypt despite the manifold commercial ties between these two countries. Given medieval travel and market conditions, the distances between Egypt and Iran or Spain were too great for the smooth conduct

[32] This byname, "Delivery" was given to Ibn 'Awkal later in life, probably after he recovered from a serious illness. Originally he, like any other Joseph, was called Abū Ya'qūb, "Father of Jacob."

[1] TS Arabic Box 42, f. 176. About Ibn 'Awkal see no. 1, above. The note gives also Baghdad as Ibn 'Awkal's address, probably a branch of his firm to which the consignment from Iran was sent.

of day-to-day commerce, for which constant adaptation to an ever fluctuating market was required. An analysis of this letter implicitly illustrates this situation.

The letter was sent from al-Ahwāz, the capital of a province of the same name in southwestern Iran. It was addressed to the three senior Tustarī brothers in Fustat, who conducted one of the most prominent firms in that city.[2] Tustar, the city from which their name is derived, is also situated in that Iranian province. But it seems that before moving from Iran to Egypt the Tustarī family lived in Ahwāz, as is evidenced by a Judea-Persian law record from that city, dated January 18, 1021, reporting that their sister Hannah made a certain claim there in her own name and that of her brothers. Our letter also indicates that they possessed property there.[3] Thus the business conducted between Iran and Egypt actually was an inner-Persian affair: that is, it was emigrants from Iran who maintained relations with their native country and who still had relatives and possessions there.

Furthermore, the goods traded, both those sent from Iran and those ordered from Egypt were so-called *a'lāq*, choice textiles of high value which could be easily transported. It was a trade of limited volume. It is interesting to note that all firms concerned, the senders, addressees, and the carriers of the consignments, were family businesses, consisting either of brothers or of father and son, for which see *Med. Soc.*, I, 165, 180-183.

All names in this letter and the contemporary law record from Ahwāz are either Arabic or Hebrew, but the writer of the letter was Persian, as is betrayed by his faulty Arabic grammar. For instance, Persian, like English, has no masculine and feminine endings; Arabic has them in abundance. Therefore our writer makes the same mistakes as American students trying to learn Arabic in

[2] See *Med. Soc.*, I and II, indexes, s.v. The Tustarī brothers mentioned by the Muslim historians (see Fischel, *Jews*, p. 72), were the sons of Sahl, the eldest of the three addressed here.

[3] Bodl. MS Heb. b 12 (Cat. 2875), f. 24, ed. D. S. Margoliouth, "A Jewish-Persian Law Report," *JQR* 11 (1899), 671-675. For further study of this document see Jes. P. Asmussen, "Judaeo-Persica II," *Acta Orientalia* 29 (1965) 49-60, trans. D. N. MacKenzie in *Journal of the Royal Asiatic Society* (April 1966), p. 69. Additional comments in Shaul Shaked, "Judaeo-Persian Notes," *Israel Oriental Studies* 1 (1971), 180-182.

that he confuses the genders. Quite a number of Persian names have been preserved in the Geniza (see *Med. Soc.*, I, 400, n. 2), but the majority of the Persian Jews living around 1000, as far as they had no Hebrew names, must have borne Arabic names, just as did their compatriots, the Persian Muslims.

University Library, Cambridge, Taylor-Schechter Collection, TS 13 J 25 f. 18.

A. Acknowledgment of Letter

May God prolong the life of my lords, the noble elders, and always help and support them and make their prominent position permanent.

I am writing to you from al-Ahwāz on Friday the 12th of Muḥarram of the year 417.[4] I am well, praise and thanks to God.

God knows the strength of my longing for you—may he always support you—and I ask him to ordain our coming together when his sanctuary will be built.[5]

Your letter has arrived—may God always support you. I took notice of its content and was happy to learn that you are well. I praised God, the exalted, for this. I understand that you have most kindly dispatched that consignment and hope it will arrive with God's support and gracious help. May he reward you well.[6]

B. Specifications of Goods Sent

My impositions on you are manifold, but I am no stranger to you. I have sent you through my lords the elders, the sons of Zakariyyā—may God make their honored position permanent—four chests, two of them sewed up, each containing ten robes, a third chest with a complete set of . . . ,[7] a fourth one with four gilded

[4] March 5, 1026, the Muslim date. Only letters which were supposed to be on their way for many months were dated with such exactness. The text has "seven and ten," *sb' w-'shr*, instead of "seventeen."

[5] This pious wish does not mean that the writer defers the hope for a meeting to the time of the Messiah, but implies his confidence in seeing the Temple of Jerusalem rebuilt during his own lifetime.

[6] The meaning of this phrase: your service is of such great value that only God is able to reward it adequately.

[7] Two holes in the manuscript. Visible: *zṛ 'wy*, probably a Persian word beginning with *zar*, gold.

mantles[8] of first quality. My lords know better than I how to handle this.

I also sent with them, I mean, the sons of Zakariyyā, may God keep them, a box covered with leather containing a Ṣāḥibī[9] robe of *khazz* silk and a gilded Ṣāḥibī garment of khazz, first class, with *ibrīsim* silk.[10] I hope that, with God's support and gracious help, everything will reach you in good condition and that after arrival you will handle its sale at your discretion and then purchase with its proceeds whatever you deem fit.

I am upset about the sinking of the consignment. Please handle this matter as you deem fit, for your money and mine are one and all profit I make comes from your pocket.[11]

C. An Apology

You wrote me [about] the two stores. I have nothing further to add in this matter. I know well that this and other property are exclusively yours, while the elder Abū Ṭayyib has no share in this or other possessions.[12] I noticed that the price offered for the property was insufficient, but people were eager to get it for that value. For this reason I told the messenger that it belonged to Abū Ṭayyib,

[8] Text: *r'd't*, which I take as an attempt to form an Arabic plural of *ridā*, mantle.

[9] The term is not noted in Serjeant, *Islamic Textiles*, but I have little doubt that it refers to the famous Būyid vizier Ibn 'Abbād al-Ṣāḥib, who died on March 30, 995, and who used to distribute robes of honor made of light silk (*khazz*; the same word as used here). See Mez, *Renaissance*, ch. 7, p. 96. Steingass in *Persian-English Dictionary*, p. 779*a*, says "kind of striped silk."

[10] Khazz was a light and *ibrīsim* a heavy type of silk; see Mez, *Renaissance*, p. 96, and Serjeant, *Islamic Textiles*, pp. xv-xvi, 65.

[11] Goods were sent from Egypt by sea to Tyre or another port on the Lebanese coast and from there overland to Iran. Losses by shipwreck were variously the responsibility of the sender, recipient, or carrier, depending on the condition on which the consignment was sent.

[12] The Tustarī brothers had sent a messenger to handle their possessions in their native city, among them the sale of two stores. The writer wished to preserve them for one Abū Ṭayyib ("Mr. Good"), no doubt identical with Ṭōv (Heb. "Good") b. David, a nephew (sister's son) of the Tustarīs (see Ms. Meunier, ed. I. Ben Zvi, *Zion* 3 [1938], 182, ll. 15-16). When the Tustarīs heard that the writer had informed their representative that the stores belonged to Abū Ṭayyib, they were furious. Obviously these stores were inherited, and according to Jewish law, a sister does not inherit together with her brothers.

may God keep him. Had I known that you did not like this, I would not have said so. I did it out of compassion for him so that it should not slip out of his hand. But I hope that God will grant the return of the messenger; then I shall personally assist him in the sale so that it will bring whatever God will grant.[13]

D. Recapitulation of a Previous Order

In a previous letter I had asked you,[14] may God always be your support, to kindly buy certain textiles for me, namely: a Dabīqī[15] robe with a border, first class; a Dabīqī turban,[16] forty cubits long[17] with sparkling fine . . . and beautiful . . . and a Dabīqī cloak (*īzār*), first class, . . . (7-8 words) eleven by eleven. It was sent to me by you and in its basket there was a robe.

Also, three sets of *qaṣab*,[18] one pistachio-colored, one "ample,"[19] and one khalūqī.[20] The veils should be large.

Also a sumac-red veil, a lilac turban, a Dabīqī kerchief, and a towel.[21]

[13] The source referred to in n. 12 states that Ṭōv received a loan of 4 1/2 dinars. The writer assures the Tustarīs that he would try to get a good price and would pay no attention to Ṭōv's claims. People mostly preferred to keep business and charity separate, albeit religion taught otherwise. See *Med. Soc.*, II, 142.

[14] Here the writer goes over to the dual. Whether the original letter had been addressed to only two of the three brothers, or whether this change is due to the faltering Arabic grammar of the writer, cannot be decided.

[15] Fine Egyptian linen.

[16] Persian *sarpīč*, lit., what is wound around the head. The Hebrew alphabet possesses no sign for *č*(tsh); it is expressed here by *g*, representing Ar. *j*, which substitutes for Persian *č*.

[17] During the time of the Fatimid caliph al-'Azīz (thirty years prior to the writing of our letter), Dabīqī turbans 100 cubits long were the great fashion in Egypt (see Mez, *Renaissance*, ch. 25, p. 433). Our business letter shows that the Muslim antiquarian Maqrīzī reporting this knew what he was talking about. The incredible fineness of the Dabīqī together with the predilection for huge, bulging turbans explains these strange measures. It is impossible to define the length of the cubits intended here exactly since they varied from town to town. Two feet might be a reasonable average. See Hinz, *Masse*.

[18] A wide-meshed linen interwoven with gold or silver threads, often mentioned in the Geniza. "Set," i.e., complete attire of a woman, containing at least one robe, hood, and veil.

[19] A *mawfūrī*, not yet found elsewhere.

[20] Khalūq is an aromatic plant (*galia muscata*, Wahrmund, *Handwörterbuch*, s.v.); probably its color is intended.

[21] Text: *mshfh*, which is either *mishshafa* with *n* assimilated, or *minshafa*

Please do not stop writing me about your welfare and your concerns so that I may, God willing, deal with them as is incumbent on me.

(Address in Arabic characters:)

(To) my lords, the noble elders, Abu 'l-Fadl, Abū Ya'qūb, and Abū Sahl, (that is,) Sahl, Joseph, and Abū Sahl,[22] the sons of Israel b. *Hdr.*[23]

(From) their servants Ephraim b. Sa'īd and Ṣāliḥ b. Ephraim.

3 ITALIANS TRAVEL TO THE EAST

Beginning of Eleventh Century

This unusual letter is written on vellum in large, calligraphic characters, the like of which were used in books and Torah scrolls, not in letters. The writer no doubt was a professional scribe himself, for he sends greetings to his teacher, a copyist (sōfēr), and to another scribe. He was an Italian, whose native city cannot have been situated far away from Amalfi, for he refers to persons living there by their first names only and asks to forward greetings to a person in Naples. Since he was so pathetically shy of water, he was perhaps a landlubber, which would suggest Benevento, known as having a Jewish community as his hometown. His Hebrew betrays the high standard of biblical and talmudic studies among the Jews of Italy at the turn of the first millennium, to which this letter must be attributed.

---

with *n* omitted by the scribe. *One* "towel," often described as imported from Europe (Sicily), regularly appears in lists of trousseaux. It was large enough to serve as a wrapper for clothing sent overseas (TS NS Box 323, f. 1). This ceremonial family towel probably was destined only for guests wiping their hands after washing them before and after meals.

22 Abu 'l-Fadl was the kunya of Sahl; Abū Ya'qūb, that of Joseph; and Abū Sahl, that of Sa'īd. The repetition of the kunya Abū Sahl instead of inserting the name Sa'īd probably was a mistake.

23 The father of Israel was called Jacob. I take *Hdr* as Heb. *Hadar* (*ha-yeshīvā*), "Splendor (of the yeshiva)," an honorary title conferred on him because of his donations.

The writer describes the double punishment he received for leaving his parents against their wish: his complete disenchantment with his Eastern teachers, in the search of whom he had undertaken the perilous journey, and the suffering of shipwreck with its horrors and losses. But he concludes on an optimistic note. He hopes to settle in the Land of Israel and finally to be united there with all his beloved.

The top and bottom of the parchment sheet are eaten away and large holes extend crosswise throughout its midst where it was folded. A translation of the highly interesting first part would require too long a commentary because of the many deft allusions to talmudic texts. In short, he says that the would-be great teachers whose publicity had deafened his ears and caught his eyes proved to be fakes living on the work of preceding generations. Like most travelers our scribe carried merchandise with him.

University Library, Cambridge, Taylor-Schechter
Collection, TS 12.144[1]

I faced death and unbearable dangers from the day I parted from my parents, whom I disobeyed. Likewise, when I visited Amalfi,[2] there were difficulties when I was preparing to leave the city. Disturbances surrounded [it?] and I wondered why all that should happen. M. Hananel and M. Menaḥēm—may they be remembered with a thousand blessings—were very good to me. [They introduced me] to the merchants, and all my dealings were carried out according to their instructions; also all other matters, such as the customs to be paid to the city, [. . .]. They also tried to persuade us[3] not to continue our way. But we did not listen, for thus it was destined by God.

We arrived in Palermo[4] on the [. . .] and paid customs for everything in addition to duties imposed on us for the . . . of the sailors

[1] Ed. Assaf, *Texts*, pp. 134-137. The translation begins in l. 10, where I read *we-hinnē rā'ū 'ēnay shaḥat.*

[2] Spelled *m'lfy* (Malfi), as fitting an Italian writing Hebrew, and not *mlf* (Malf), as in the letters of Jews whose mother tongue was Arabic.

[3] The writer was accompanied by two fellow travelers.

[4] Called by its Arabic name (Ṣiqilliyya "Sicily"), spelled Ṣoqiliyāh. For the Italian ear Arabic *ṣ* colored the following *i* to *o*.

of the ship.[5] We were [there] a week and waited. Finally we found a large ship there which sailed to Alexandria, Egypt. We paid the fare and embarked before the New Year Holiday. But on the fifth of the month of Tishri,[6] on Monday at noon time, a storm broke loose upon us [. . .], storming upon us for three days. On the third day the ship began to leak and water penetrated into it from all sides. [We worked hard] to reduce its load and to bale the water out, for there was a big crowd on the ship, about four hundred persons [. . .]. The sea became ever wilder and the ship was tossed about with its entire load. All the people lay down, for no strength was left to anyone, [and cried to] God. Then they approached the captain and pleaded with him, saying, "Save us! Turn the ship toward the land as long [as there is daylight], before the sun sets, when everything will be lost." And all cried with a loud voice. The ship was steered toward the coast and all embraced one another, trembling.[7] I am unable to describe how we[8] cried. For when I saw that those who knew how to swim had given up hope for life, what should I do who cannot stand water as high up as the ankles?

Finally, the ship touched ground and cracked asunder, as [an egg] would crack when a man presses it with his two hands. Passengers began to drown here and [there and pieces from] the ship floated above them. We three stood on a cabin on the uppermost part of the ship and did not know how to escape. People from below called us saying: "Come down quickly, each of you, catch a piece of wood and ride upon it, perhaps God will grant you rescue." [We] cried to God with a bitter voice, but when [I] saw that everyone was riding on a piece of w[ood I said to . . .] and to Elijah:[9] "Why should we sit here, let us do as they do." I emitted a loud cry [and moved. We went down] together, one helping the

[5] There is a hole at this point caused by the middle fold of the sheet and only the remnants of the letters are visible. It was customary for passengers to pay a small compensation to the sailors, but this had to be done at embarkation.

[6] This day always falls in September. The New Year is celebrated on the first two days of Tishri.

[7] The text clearly has *we-ḥōrēd* (for the more common *ḥārēd*), and not *hūrād*, as in the printed edition. My summary of the account in *Med. Soc.*, I, 321, is to be corrected accordingly.

[8] The writer and his companions; see nn. 3, 9.

[9] One of his companions.

other, [praying] to Him who hears Israel. [. . .] and he got upon a piece of wood.

(Here the first page of the manuscript breaks off. On the reverse side the remainders of six lines are preserved, which despite their entirely fragmentary character are not without interest. Line 2: ". . . much from the sea," alluding probably to the fact that many of the goods were salvaged, as happened often with ships foundering near the seashore. Line 4: "Money is nothing . . . I shall replace," which shows that the traveler had suffered losses, but felt himself able to recover. Finally, he announces that his companions would settle in Tyre, then the greatest port on the Lebanese coast, which he, however, defines as situated in the Holy Land,[10] and expresses the confidence that God would place him[11] there, too, to become "a plantation of pride."

Thus it seems that the letter was written in Egypt. The disappointing teacher was perhaps Elhanan b. Shemarya (first quarter of the eleventh century), who created much publicity for his school, but whose eminent position was mainly inherited from his renowned father.

The persons in Italy to whom greetings were extended bore Hebrew names, with one exception: Benin(et)to, spelled *bynynṭw*.)

4 FROM AMALFI, ITALY, TO AL-MAHDIYYA, TUNISIA

Middle of the Eleventh Century

Both literary sources and the Geniza documents indicate that close relations existed between Tunisia and (then Muslim) Sicily on the one hand and the seaports of southern Italy, such as Amalfi and Salerno, on the other. But no correspondence illustrating these relations has been preserved, since the recipients of letters from either side had no reason to carry them all the way to Fustat, where the Geniza chamber was located. The fragment translated below

[10] This confusion originated through the ambiguity of the Arabic term Shām, which comprised Syria, Lebanon, Israel, and Jordan.

[11] The manuscript clearly has *we-yiṭṭāʿēnī.*

escaped destruction for a simple reason: its reverse side is almost completely blank. The recipient, on his way from Tunisia to Egypt (as anticipated in the letter), took it with him in order to use it as scrap paper; and he had already done so, as we see, for the upper part of the sheet (the reverse side of which also contained the address) is torn away.

The fragment begins in the middle of a sentence. The writer is a merchant from Alexandria who had bought pepper, *lubān* (see n. 9), and other Oriental goods in order to sell all or part of them in Amalfi on his way from Egypt to Tunisia. The ship in which he traveled, pursued by pirates or an enemy, was forced to flee as far north as Constantinople and again had to take refuge in Crete. Thus, instead of the fifteen to twenty-five days normally required for the journey from Alexandria to Amalfi (see *Med. Soc.*, I, 325-326), they were on the high seas for over seventy days. When they arrived in Amalfi they found the economy of the city ruined by a heavy imposition. The writer and his companion, or perhaps companions, waited now until business in Amalfi would revive and meanwhile sent instructions to his business friend in al-Mahdiyya regarding the disposition of his goods that had been sent directly from Egypt to al-Mahdiyya. He was sure that his business friend would leave for Egypt long before he himself would be able to leave Amalfi for al-Mahdiyya.

In a postscript, he reports that he and one of his companions went to see Yuḥannā (John, an exclusively Christian name), presumably a merchant in Amalfi who owed something to the person referred to, and that, as of that time, John had neither given a reply nor delivered anything.

Whether Yuḥannā was an Arabic-speaking Christian, perhaps originating from Tunisia, who had settled in Amalfi, or a native Amalfian, I am unable to decide. During the eleventh century, Christianity was still very much alive in Tunisia, as is evident from the material presented in Idris, *Zirides*, pp. 757-764, and index, p. 872, s.v. christianisme.

An Italian version of this letter was provided by me as an appendix to a paper by Armand O. Citarella, "Scambi commerciali fra l'Egitto e Amalfi in un documento inedito della Geniza di Cairo," *Archivio Storico per le Province Napoletane*, 10 (1970),

3-11. See also Citarella's "Patterns in Medieval Trade: The Commerce of Amalfi before the Crusades," *JESHO*, 18 (1968), 531-555.

University Library, Cambridge, Taylor-Schechter Collection, TS 8 Ja 1, f. 5.

. . . we suffered hardship and did not hear about the escape,[1] for we came near[2] to the ca[pital] Qaṣanṭīnā (Constantinople). After we had cruised on the sea for eighteen days he[3] attacked us again. Then it became evident that they[4] were on their way to one of the coasts of the Muslims. So we returned to Crete.[5] We did not cease to gulp our blood[6] until we arrived in Amalfi after more than seventy days.[7] This was not enough: We came to a town whose property had been confiscated[8] and we did not find anyone who would buy any goods from us, be it pepper or olibanum (lubān)[9] or anything else, not even one dirhem's worth. We put our goods in warehouses and are now waiting for God's help. I do not worry for my own things. I worry for you and your goods that I am unable to sell. I really regret this very much.

(The writer now gives orders to the recipient in al-Mahdiyya to sell one bale of indigo and six bales of flax and smaller items which had been sent by him from Egypt to Tunisia directly. From the proceeds the recipient was permitted to take a loan of 280 dinars[10]

[1] The escape—probably of another ship which had reached al-Mahdiyya a long time ago and about which the recipient had written to the writer.

[2] Text: *jīnā ʿalā.*

[3] Pirates or an enemy previously referred to.

[4] Such a change from singular to plural is not uncommon. The writer now had in mind the ships of the attackers.

[5] This shows that they had already reached a point west of Crete.

[6] Text: *najraʿ dimāʾanā.* I have not seen this phrase before. It probably means: we lived in utmost dread, but could also mean: we tried to inspire ourselves with courage.

[7] Text: *nayyif wa-sabʿīn*, usually defined as meaning: approximately 72-73.

[8] Text: *balad muṣādar,* mostly used in connection with the confiscation of the property of a high government official.

[9] Whether *lubān* really means here and in many other Geniza letters the frankincense plant cultivated in South Arabia and Somaliland, or something quite different (high-valued benzoin, as I learned from O. W. Wolters) needs further inquiry. As far as my memory goes, the term occurs only in letters going from Aden westward.

[10] The letter indicating 80 is not clear.

for himself and to leave the balance with a friend until the writer would arrive in the Tunisian port. The recipient was also to take with him to Alexandria a qinṭār, or hundredweight, of sarcocol, *anzarūt*,[11] belonging to the writer, as well as a pitcher with oil and a jug with soap for his family. After greetings to three other friends, overflowing to the margin, he adds:)

Please inform the elder Abu 'l-Faḍl b. Salmān that I went to see *Yuḥannā* (spelled *yḥn'*), I and the elder Abū Sahl, and gave him the letter,[12] but he did not answer it. Until now I have been reminding him, to find out what he would say. If I get something from Yuḥannā, I shall send it to him.

5 REPORT FROM RAMLE, PALESTINE

About Merchandise and Provisions Bought in Tripoli and Tyre, Lebanon, and a Disastrous Sea Voyage Back
Shortly after 1065

Ramle, situated between the Mediterranean and the hills of Judea, served as the administrative and commercial center of Palestine until the advent of the Crusaders. Coastal Caesarea, the other Palestinian town mentioned in this letter, had occupied the same position in Roman and Byzantine times, but had decayed into insignificance by the eleventh century.

The writer of the letter was a Maghrebi merchant, who commuted between Egypt and the eastern shores of the Mediterranean, trading, since at least 1050,[1] Egyptian flax in exchange for the silk of Lebanon and Cyprus and the cotton of Syria. Our letter must have been written in 1066 or so, when Egypt was ravaged by a terrible famine, and the merchants were eager to secure whatever

[11] A plant used as a drastic purgative and as a medicament for the eyes. A common article in the Mediterranean trade.

[12] Sent by the recipient to the writer. The names Abu 'l-Faḍl and Salmān were common in the eleventh century and are not helpful in identifying the man.

---

[1] JNUL 1, *Nahray* 23, dated spring 1052, and referring to previous trips to the coasts of Lebanon and Syria.

victuals they could lay hands on for their families and friends.[2] To be sure, figs, raisins, and other fruits were staple exports of southwest Asia to Egypt.

The recipient was Nahray b. Nissīm, a Tunisian merchant-banker, scholar, and communal leader, who spent most of the last fifty-one years of his life (1045-1096) in Egypt. Chapter IV is dedicated to him.

University Library, Cambridge, Taylor-Schechter Collection, TS 8 J 19, f. 27, *Nahray* 84.

I trust in God.[3]
Praised be the Lord who resurrects the dead.[4]
My master and lord, may God prolong your life, make your well-being and happiness permanent, and keep away from you all evil in his mercy. I am writing from Ramle on the 8th of Teveth (approximately: January), feeling well in body, but being worried in my mind.

A. The Sea Voyage

I set sail[5] for Jaffa, the port of Ramle. But a wind arose against us from the land. It became a storm, chasing and driving us out to the high sea,[6] where we remained for four days, giving up all hope for life. We were without sails and oars, the steering rudder and the sailyards were broken, and the waves burst into the barge (*qārib*). We cried: "Allāh, Allāh," for our ship was a mere riverboat (*'ushārī*), small as a ferry (*ma'diya*). We threw part of the cargo overboard, and I gave up all hope for my life and my goods. I vowed 1 dinar from the proceeds of the *silk*.[7] Finally, God in his glory and

[2] The writer emphasizes this in a letter, sent seven weeks earlier from Tripoli, Lebanon (TS Or 1080 J 17, *Nahray* 85).

[3] The use of this verse from the Qur'ān (11:56) as superscription of a letter written in Hebrew characters was rare and confined, if I am not mistaken, to Maghrebis.

[4] A benediction pronounced when someone had been rescued from a great danger.

[5] From Tyre, Lebanon, whereto he had traveled from Tripoli, as announced in the letter referred to in n. 2, above.

[6] Text: *kharaj lanā rīḥ min al-barr bi-naw sayyabnā* (see Dozy, *Supplément*, I, 710*b*) *dakhal bina waṣṭ al-baḥr*. East winds blowing from the desert in November are occasionally very pernicious.

[7] The strange use of the biblical word *shēsh* for silk as a kind of secret

majesty granted us to reach Caesarea, but my clothes and goods were completely soaked. I did not find a place to stay and to spread out my things. So I took domicile in the synagogue, where I remained for five days.

B. In Ramle

When I arrived in Ramle, I had to pay customs to a degree I am unable to describe. The price in Ramle of the Cyprus[8] silk, which I carry with me, is 2 dinars per little pound.[9] Please inform me of its price and advise me whether I should sell it here or carry it with me to you in Miṣr (Fustat), in case it is fetching a good price there. By God, answer me quickly, I have no other business here in Ramle except awaiting answers to my letters. About 3 dinars worth of goods of mine were jettisoned from the barge; may God, the exalted, restore the loss. If you want me to carry the silk with me, instruct Makhlūf b. Muḥsina[10] (write him!) to pay me 2-3 dinars, or have Abū Barhūn[11] write to his brother Ya'qūb (Jacob) to give me this sum so that I do not have to sell my clothing or the silk.[12] A man like you does not need to be urged. I know that my money and yours[13] are one. Moreover, you have a share in this. I need not stress the urgency of a reply concerning the price of silk from Shām (Syria-Lebanon) and from Cyprus, and whether I should sell it here or carry it with me.

---

code originated perhaps in the time when the trade in this commodity was not without danger.

8 Spelled here *q'brsy*, which expresses, I assume, a pronunciation of the word as *qĕbris*. Below: *qbrsy*.

9 Meaning the Egyptian pound, which had approximately the weight of the present day USA pound; see *Med. Soc.*, I, 360. The pound of Ramle weighed about five times as much (see Hinz, *Masse*, p. 30). The standard price for an Egyptian pound of silk was 2 dinars (see no. 1, n. 11, above). Understandably, our traveler hoped to obtain more.

10 "Substitute" (given by God for a child that had died), "son of The Beneficent Woman."

11 "Father of Abraham," meaning a man called Isaac.

12 Even important merchants did not carry much cash with them. The price of the jettisoned goods worth 3 dinars had been sufficient for the traveler to cover his expenses, had they not been lost.

13 Text: *al-mālayn*, literally, "the two moneys."

C. Consignments from Tripoli

I wrote you from Tripoli and informed you that I had sent four bundles of cotton and twenty-one pieces[14] of figs to Alexandria. I wrote to M. Mardūk,[15] asking him to receive this shipment. With Yaḥyā b. al-Zaffāt[16] I sent two bags and one basket with wheat, red earth,[17] and two baskets with raisins and figs. I instructed him to deliver these to Mardūk. Your share in the basket (of wheat)[18] and the figs is 8 dinars, and your share in the silk also 8 dinars. I hope you have written to Alexandria instructing Mardūk to take care of the matter, and also to attend to the sacking (*khaysh*). Also write him to send you either the proceeds, or the goods to be bought for them, or broken dinars.[19] And by God, answer. I have no business other than waiting for your letter. By God, do not neglect this. By the bread (we have eaten together), as soon as this letter arrives, send the answer to the warehouse of the representative of the merchants, Abu 'l-Barakāt Ibn al-Ḥulaybī.[20] A man like you needs no urging.[21]

D. News from Fustat

Describe to me the prices in the city (Fustat), and especially with regard to wheat and bread—I need not urge you to write me about this—as well as concerning the state of my father and the family. Special regards to you, and also to those who ask about me. Please honor me with any concern you might have. Regards also to Joseph

[14] The dried figs were pressed into huge cakes.

[15] The Ar. equivalent of Mordechai, a name common in those days only among Persian Jews. This Mardūk (b. Mūsā) was from Tripoli, Libya, and a representative of the Maghrebi merchants in Alexandria.

[16] "Trader in pitch, tar," an important commodity (used, e.g., for calking ships).

[17] Ar. *makra*, mentioned in the Geniza letters regularly as used for writing on bales.

[18] This is clearly evident from the letter written in Tripoli (n. 2, above). The recipient's share might have been very small, as little as one-tenth. That letter made mention also of a consignment of rice.

[19] To be sold to the caliphal mint. In one way or another, the writer wished to have his money in Fustat, and not in Alexandria. It was winter, wherefore he intended to travel overland direct to Fustat.

[20] "The little man from Aleppo," known also from other Geniza documents.

[21] Such importunate repetitions were the rule, not the exception.

and his mother.[22] How are they? Regards also to our friends. And Peace.[23]

(Address:)

To my lord and master Abū Yaḥyā Nahray, son of Nissīm, (*may he*) *r*(*est in*) *E*(*den*), may God prolong his life and make permanent his honored position, strength, and happiness.

From Ya'qūb (Jacob) b. Salmān al-Ḥarīrī[24]

(Repeated in Arabic characters. What follows is also in Arabic characters:)

To Fustat, the House of Exchange, the office of Ibrāhīm b. Isḥāq, the Jewish banker.[25]

(Note of the mail agency; in another pen and script:)

To my lord, the shaykh Abū 'Alī al-Ḥusayn b. Mufrij, from 'Abd b. Muḥammad b. Qaysar.

Fustat, if God will. Deliver and receive reward.[26]

6 NOTE FROM ALEXANDRIA

About an Errand Done in Spain for a Business Friend in Fustat
Ca. 1110

This short note is perhaps more characteristic of Egypt's role in the Mediterranean trade than the many long business letters preserved in the Geniza. It speaks of gold from Morocco, silk from Spain, ambergris, which was found in the Atlantic Ocean, and of musk and civet perfumes, which were imported from far away Tibet

[22] The writer's wife and son. This shows that the recipient was a close friend and, most likely, a relative.

[23] Written in Ar. characters, in abbreviated form.

[24] "The Silkworker," a family name.

[25] This is Abraham b. Isaac the Scholar (see *Med. Soc.*, II, 512, sec. 10), whose intimate friendship with Nahray is evident in Geniza documents through forty-five years (1050-1095).

[26] The receiving mail agency is identical with that mentioned in *Med. Soc.*, I, 292, bottom. The Ramle agency was different from that forwarding the letter (TS 13 J 36, f. 6). Qaysar is derived from Caesar, but is a good old Arabic name. "Deliver and receive reward" obviously means here "Payment after delivery."

or Indochina and the Malay archipelago. It is addressed to a merchant bearing the family name of al-ʿAfṣī, which means a trader in gall, an important commodity brought to Egypt from northern Syria. Even more remarkable than the geographical diversity of the origin of the products mentioned is the extremely casual way in which the writer speaks about his safe arrival in Alexandria from Spain. It is also noteworthy that both the sender of the letter and its recipient, as well as the three merchants mentioned in it, are known from other Geniza documents.

Bodleian Library, Oxford, MS Heb. d 66 (Cat. 2878), f. 52.

In (Your) name, O Merci(ful).

A

I am writing these lines to my lord, the illustrious elder—may God prolong your life and make permanent your exaltedness and high position—to inform you that the Kohen al-Fāsī[1] sent to me a bar of gold for you from Fez with the notification that he sold civet perfume for you for 7 1/2 and 1/8 Andalusian mithqāls. He asked me to sell the gold in Almeria[2] and to buy silk with the proceeds. However, I did not think that this was the right thing to do, and decided to leave the gold as it was sent to me. Now, God in his mercy decreed my safe arrival, whereupon I sent it to you with Binyām al-Rashīdī,[3] the perfumer. Kindly compose my mind by the acknowledgment of its arrival. When I come, I shall, God willing, deliver the letter addressed to you in person.

B

One of the friends of the aforementioned Kohen sent a quantity of ambergris with me and asked me to sell it through you; you are to buy me good "fivers" of musk[4] for the money—may I never be deprived of you and never miss you. The weight of the ambergris

[1] A family name derived from the town Fez in Morocco. Here, we find that merchant actually living in Fez.

[2] A port on the east coast of Spain.

[3] A family name derived from Rosetta, Egypt. Binyām is Benjamin.

[4] Musk was traded in "fivers," *khumāsiyyāt*, perhaps a package weighing 5 dirhems (*India Book*, passim).

is 225 dirhems, together with the piece of cloth and the canvas. It will be brought to you by my brother Abu 'l-Barakāt. As soon as you take delivery, sell it without any slackness or delay for whatever price God grants and apportions.

C

Accept from me the best of greetings, *and may the welfare of my lord continue to increase forever.* As soon as the ambergris is sold, buy "fivers" of good musk with the money. If I can do anything for you, please honor me with the task. Do not be offended by the form of these lines.[5] I wrote them *on the Eve of the Sabbath*, after having taken my bath. Therefore, please—may God honor you—excuse me and remove any blame from me. *And Peace!*

(Despite this polite request, the writer repeats a third time the demand that the ambergris should be sold immediately after its arrival. He also asks to be informed about its weight without the wrapping.)

(Address, written upside down, as usual:)

To Miṣr (Fustat), may God protect it, to my lord, the illustrious elder Abū Sa'īd al-'Afṣī[6]—may God prolong his life and make permanent his honored position and prosperity.

His grateful Abu 'l-Ḥasan, son of Khulayf, the Alexandrian—*m(ay he rest in) p(eace!)*

7 FROM A SPANISH MERCHANT IN FEZ, MOROCCO, TO HIS FATHER IN ALMERIA, SPAIN

1140 or slightly earlier

This rare specimen of a business letter going from Morocco to Spain provides interesting information on several points. Cheating

[5] The letter is written calligraphically, but its style is somewhat brusque and importunate.

[6] "The Merchant of Gall." This was a family name. The person concerned, as we learn from this and other Geniza letters, was a "perfumer," a dealer in perfumes and drugs.

at customhouses seems to have been uncommon in the eleventh and twelfth centuries, probably because the rates, as the Geniza data show, were reasonable. Customs were paid not only at frontiers, but at the gates of any larger city, and no discrimination was made between local people and foreigners. When, however, such discriminations were introduced, as was done in Sicily at the end of the Muslim rule, then we often read in the Geniza papers about attempts of foreigners to pass off their baggage as belonging to local people. Here, we learn the same about Fez.

The letter also gives us a good general idea of the writer's business. He dealt with precious textiles, probably manufactured in Cairo, or even farther east; with copper imported from Spain; with products of the eastern Mediterranean, such as indigo and scammony; and with the staples of the Orient, such as lac. Naturally, he exported Moroccan local products, for instance, antimony, which is expressly mentioned. The letter also casts interesting sidelights on his commercial techniques and his general frame of mind.

The letter is written with a thin pen, then in common use in Spain, on good quality, whitish paper. But the form of the Hebrew script is entirely different from the fleeting cursive cherished by the more literate men of that country and is similar to the types used in the Muslim East. In his Arabic usage, however, the writer, even if originally an Easterner, had adapted himself to his environment; he writes *ḥlw*, "sweet," meaning "good," and *mly*, "full," meaning "rich"—usages not found in the contemporary Geniza letters from the eastern Mediterranean. He might be identical with the writer of letter no. 60, but that one is written with a thick pen, which makes it difficult to compare the two scripts.

The first five lines are badly damaged, but most of the missing words can be safely restored.

How did this letter find its way into the Cairo Geniza? It is reasonable to assume that the recipient, like countless others, fled to escape from the Almohad persecutions (as from 1145, approximately) and found his refuge in Egypt.

University Library, Cambridge, Taylor-Schechter
Collection, TS 12.435.

In (Your) name, O Merci(ful).

To my master and lord, my succor and supp[ort], may God prolong your life and m[ake permanent your high rank] and lofty position. May he crush those who envy you and not withhold from you [success]. May he substitute me [as ransom for all evil that might befall you and may he] never leave me [alone, being without you. May he let you suc]ceed in obeying him and eliciting his favor. May he unite us in happiness, soothe my solitude by your appearance and relieve my grief through your presence. Lo, he listens to our prayers and answers quickly.

I arrived in Fez on Friday, 2nd of Marheshvan.[1] At our arrival we were met by the *informers* and they found out exactly the number of the loads (belonging to us). They went to the superintendent of the customs and told him. On Sunday morning he sent for me and for Ibrāhīm and said to him: "Are you prepared to give an oath that all that arrived with you is entirely your property and that this man has no share in it?" Then he said to me: "Are you prepared to swear that nothing at all was brought by you to this place?" There was much talk, but he clearly knew that five camel loads had arrived with me. After great troubles it was agreed that the governor[2] would take 10 mithqāls; the superintendent of the customs, 3; the informers, 2; and the employees, 1/2. I was sick for three days out of anger and sorrow. Had I possessed here the same courage as I usually have in Almeria, I would have escaped with less than this. But I consoled myself with the solace of one who has no choice. I also said to myself, perhaps God may grant us some compensation for the loss. On the day of my arrival it was 3 and 2; today it is 2 and 4.[3]

By God, if you can avoid it, do not go abroad. If God wills, I shall set out for Marrākesh with the very first company[4] traveling

[1] Late September, early October.

[2] Ar. *qā'id*, corresponding to *amīr* in the East. Large cities, such as Alexandria or Fez, were administered by a military governor.

[3] Obviously an example of profit already made. I understand the numbers thus: on the day of the writer's arrival a certain standard commodity was worth 3 dinars and 2 qīrāṭs; at the time of the writing, it was already (3 dinars and) 2-4 qīrāṭs.

[4] The long way between Fez and Marrākesh led mostly through inhabited country, not through deserts. Therefore, one traveled not in a big caravan,

there, and, if necessary, inform you about the situation, whereupon you may make your decision. I have no other aim, by God, than saving you from trudging along the streets and traveling overland.[5] May God turn everything to a good end!

I should also like to inform you that I spread out the *niṣfiyya*[6] clothes, and the very first garment that fell into my hands was spoiled by water in all its folds. I went out of my mind, but God, the exalted, had willed that only this one was spoiled. This happened because we had much rain on the way, but God, the exalted, granted rescue. As of late today I sold ten pairs of them for a total of 80 dinars, inclusive of the ten bad ones[7] and the one spoiled by water.

I bought first-class, excellent antimony (kohl), about twenty qinṭārs, the qinṭār for 1 dinar. If you think that I should buy more, send me a note and let me know.[8]

For the lac I was offered 24 (dinars). I am holding on to it, perhaps I shall get 25.[9]

The good elastic (?)[10] copper is worth here 9 dinars a qinṭār.

---

but in smaller groups, called *ṣuḥba*, large enough for protection but of limited size, making for mobility. See *Med. Soc.*, I, 277.

[5] Although one had to cross the sea to get to Morocco from Almeria, it was not the sea voyage, but the uncomfortable locomotion by land which was disliked most.

[6] A precious piece of clothing, ordered in Cairo by a merchant from Aden (*India Book* 50), or sent as a present from Fustat to Lucena, Spain (ibid. 102). *Niṣfiyya* was apparently sold in pairs. See Dozy, *Supplément*, II, 680*b*, and Serjeant, *Islamic Textiles*, 15-16 (1951), 66.

[7] Ar. *wakhsh*, a Maghrebi word. The receiver of the letter knew of course that the clothes sent were of differing quality.

[8] Morocco was a country of export for kohl. In Egypt the price of this commodity was five times as high. See MS Westminster College, Cambridge, England, Fragmenta Cair. Misc. 50 (dated 1098) and TS 12.434 (approximately the same time).

[9] Lac was an Oriental commodity very much in demand in the Mediterranean countries and referred to in scores of Geniza letters and accounts. Its price per qinṭār varied from 15 dinars (TS 13 J 29, f. 10, l. 16 from al-Mahdiyya, Tunisia, eleventh century) to 50 (TS 13 J 19, f. 29*v*, l. 6, from the same place, early eleventh century).

[10] Copper was one of the great exports from Spain to the East, and many types are mentioned in the Geniza. But "elastic (lit. palpitating) copper," *rajīf* or *rijjīf*, has been found only here. Prices varied from 5 to 25 dinars, certainly depending on quality, place, time, and circumstances.

Scammony[11] is worth 3 dinars a pound. Inquire, and if it reaches that price in Almeria, sell it. Otherwise send me one half (of what we have) and leave there the other half.

All our lac and niṣfiyyas are in the house[12] of Ibrāhīm, for I did not want to leave anything at all with me in the house. I may be able to sell all the niṣfiyyas in Fez.

Please take notice that indigo is very much in demand here in Fez.

I should also like to inform you that everyone, Muslims and Jews, tell me that Ibn Ṭalw[13] will pay me all he owes us, as soon as I arrive,[14] for he is very rich today.

Hatred (of Jews)[15] is rampant in this country to a degree that, in comparison with it, Almeria is a place of *salvation*.[16] May God the exalted grant rescue and a good end in his mercy.

(Address, right side:)

To my lord, succor, and support, my father,
Japheth ha-Levi b. 'Ullah (may he) r(est in) E(den).[17]

[11] Scammony, called in Arabic and in the Geniza letters by its Greek name *saqamūniya* (from which the English word is derived, too), or more frequently, as here, *maḥmūda*, "the praiseworthy (medicament)," is a plant growing in the countries of the northeastern Mediterranean, whose resin was and still is used as a strong purgative. It was exported as far as Morocco in the West and India in the East. The price given here is paralleled by other data in the Geniza papers.

[12] Ar. *bayt*, which, in the East, then meant "room." But here, I believe, the meaning "house" is more appropriate. Since these Spanish merchants constantly traveled to Morocco they possessed a house there. Many other such instances are alluded to in the Geniza papers. See *Med. Soc.*, I, 61.

[13] Could be pronounced also *Ṭilw*. This old Semitic word has many meanings in Arabic, designating in general a young mammal.

[14] In Marrākesh, it seems. One sees again that collecting one's assets was as time consuming as selling one's merchandise.

[15] The problem of medieval "antisemitism" is treated in *Med. Soc.*, II, 278-284.

[16] This remark is sarcastic, meaning that Almeria itself had a bad reputation in this respect. A letter from that town (*India Book* 129, l. 24 and top, l. 4) says: "The 'hatred' has eased a little."

[17] It is likely that this man was a son of 'Ullā ha-Levi al-Dimashqī, the recipient of nos. 53-56, below. That a Damascene merchant settled in Fustat should send one of his sons to Almeria, Spain, to take care of his business there, was natural in the early twelfth century when the direct route between Spain-Egypt had become much frequented.

Forward, and you will be rewarded![18]
(Left side):
His son [[19]
May he become his ransom.

8 MERCHANTS FROM EGYPT AND THE MAGHREB VISIT GENOA AND MARSEILLES

Early thirteenth century

The fragment translated is the third sheet of a business letter. This is very uncommon, since merchants and clerks used to cut their paper in such a way that one sheet, at most two, provided sufficient space for what they intended to write. Equally uncommon is the content: Mediterranean trade in the thirteenth century. Very little material about this subject has been found in the Geniza. This is mainly to be explained by the fact that by that time most of the well-to-do merchants had moved from Fustat, where the Geniza was located, to Cairo. But since references to the India trade are found from this period in considerable number, a shift from the Mediterranean to the India trade must have occurred in the course of the twelfth century.

Script and style, and, in particular, the reference to the Jewish judge Menaḥēm of Cairo and the mail carrier Khuḍayr assign this sheet approximately to the second or third decade of the thirteenth century.[1] The recipient of the letter is constantly addressed with

[18] Namely, by God, who will grant you a safe journey as reward for your kindness. Ar. *balligh tusdā*, for which in Tunisia and the East they wrote *tu'jar*.

[19] The end of the line is torn away, but I believe nothing was written here. Not mentioning one's own name was an expression of particular affection and intimacy.

---

[1] *Med. Soc.*, II, 514, sec. 26.

the title "our lord." This address could refer either to the Nagid, or head of the Jewish community, or its chief judge. Abraham Maimonides, the Nagid at that time, was a court physician and was not involved in business as was the person addressed here; moreover, he is expressly mentioned in the letter. On the other hand, the chief judge, Hananel b. Samuel,[2] like his father, appears in several Geniza documents as a munificent benefactor.[3] From the profession of Jewish judge alone one could not acquire riches. Our letter shows him as a kind of silent partner with a brother, presumably Solomon (b. Samuel), to whom greetings are extended in the letter of a French rabbi, writing in 1211, after Hananel, but before Abraham Maimonides, who, at that time, was still very young.[4]

After having written four pages of about forty lines each, the writer was obviously tired and made a great many mistakes (see n. 11). But his handwriting is of remarkable clarity and regularity.

Strange as it may seem, this letter is the only instance known to me from the "classical" Geniza period of Jews from Islamic countries doing business in Genoa and Marseilles.

University Library, Cambridge, Taylor-Schechter
Collection, TS Arabic Box 53, f. 67

A. STUDY, NOT BUSINESS

...he should neither sell nor buy, and your servant imposes this on you since you are in a position like that of the tribe of Issachar.[5]

[2] Ibid., 515, sec. 31.

[3] TS 10 J 17, f. 4, *India Book* 37. Mosseri L 291, l. 10, ed. Mann, *Texts*, I, 463, TS NS Box 321, f. 13. He is referred to as "our lord" in ULC Add. 3415, dated 1237.

[4] TS 24.41, l. 29, ed. Mann, *Texts*, I, 410.

[5] Deuteronomy 33:18. This biblical passage was applied to two brothers, one dedicated to study and staying at home like Issachar (cf. I Chronicles 12:32), and the other traveling abroad and earning money for both (see Ginzberg, *Legends of the Jews*, II, 144). The writer of our letter had a son in Fustat who was supposed to study, but obviously was more interested in business. His father admonishes the judge to look after him, since he, the judge, stayed in Fustat and derived profit from his business connection with his widely traveled brother.

B. Prices in Alexandria

Goods are selling well here: Indigo, 22 (dinars).[6] Olibanum,[7] around 7. Cinnamon, 12.[8] Brazilwood,[9] 60. But the quickest sales are those of pepper.[10] The sale price is standardized at 46 per load leaving the city.[11] Here in Alexandria one has to pay 1 dirhem for each dinar's worth brought into the city, and for local sales beyond one-fourth (of the quantity imported), 5 dinars per load plus 1 1/2 dinars for the dragoman and the agent.[12]

C. Visits to Genoa and Marseilles

I have made an agreement with Khuḍayr[13] to carry this basket[14]

[6] Meaning: a qinṭār, or 100 pounds of this commodity were sold for 22 dinars. Many types of indigo—Indian, Yemenite, Egyptian, Palestinian (called 'Amtānī, from 'Amtā, a locality in the Jordan valley), and Persian—were on the market, and used to be weighed with different types of weights. Their prices also differed widely. A price comparable to the one mentioned here is cited in an almost contemporary inquiry submitted to Maimonides, viz., 37 dinars for 1 1/3 qinṭārs = 27 3/4 per qinṭār (Maimonides, *Responsa*, I, 153). In the Geniza we also encounter prices of 20 dinars (TS 12.248, *Nahray* 75) and less per qinṭār.

[7] Ar. *lubān* (see no. 4, n. 9, above). In an almost contemporary letter from Alexandria (TS 16.215, l. 35, *India Book* 187), the price is 6 1/2 dinars per qinṭār. But in a price list from Fustat dated 1133 (TS 13 J 33, f. 1, *India Book* 85), it is 12 dinars.

[8] Almost the same price (12 1/2 dinars per qinṭār) occurs in a letter from Alexandria written about 170 years earlier. Bodl. MS Heb. a 2 (Cat. 2805), f. 18, l. 17, *Nahray* 44.

[9] Ar. *baqqam* (see no. 1, n. 9, above). This dye was often traded in camel loads, *ḥiml*. This must be the case here. In TS 13 J 33, f. 1, dated 1133 (see n. 7), a load cost 90 dinars, but two hundred years prior to our letter (Bodl. MS Heb. c 27, f. 82 [Cat. 2835, no. 44], top) the price for a qinṭār was 10-12 dinars in al-Mahdiyya, which is very close to the price quoted here. One standard load contained five qinṭārs.

[10] For the prices of pepper see *Med. Soc.*, I, 220-222, and E. Ashtor, *Histoire des Prix . . . dans l'orient médiéval*, Paris, 1969, pp. 138ff.

[11] Text *wyqṭ' b'* (for *bay'*) *kl khrj* 46 *'l-ḥml.* For other slips see nn. 17, 21, 22, 24, 25, 31, 34.

[12] This thirteenth century customs tariff is considerably higher than those in force in Fatimid times. See *Med. Soc.*, I, 343-344.

[13] Diminutive of *Khiḍr*, the Muslim name of the prophet Elijah, common in various derivations, also among eastern Jews (cf. the name *Khadduri*). This Khuḍayr operated a commercial mail service between Alexandria and Cairo. For example, see David Kaufmann Collection, DK IXv, l. 4 (a letter to the judge Elijah b. Zechariah).

[14] With saffron. See n. 15.

and to bring it to you for 6 (dirhems)—he says for 8[15]—and I have notified you to keep the sum either with yourself or deposit it with our lord, the head (of the community).[16] In the hand of your servant there are still . . .

If the saffron cannot be sold in its entirety, I suggest you place the rest with Abū 'Alī b. Dā'ūd, if this is all right with you, or anyone else in whom you have confidence. Any sale should be certified by a notary, except if my lord is present during the counting and weighing of the money paid and if it remains in your possession.

This consignment is the property of R. Isaac b. Ibrahīm al-Tu'ātī,[17] but *no one knows this*[18] except myself. I mention this to you, so that in case anything happens,[19] our lord may give witness against me in favor of its real proprietor. By God, my only intention was to fulfill my duty. These are little matters, to reveal which would be embarrassing to me.[20] For[21] the proprietor of this saffron happened to be in Genoa when I was in Marseilles, and when he heard of me, he traveled there and delivered my goods to me. May God grant him a good reward. No heedlessness is permissible with regard to his rights.

[15] The final price would be fixed after arrival.

[16] Unlike his father Moses Maimonides, Abraham presided over a rabbinical court in person. The writer thought that it would perhaps be proper to deposit the saffron or its price in the trust of a court other than that of his brother, the judge, since the latter was a silent partner in the business.

[17] Tu'at, usually spelled *Touat* in the French way, is an oasis in the Western Sahara, formally inhabited also by Jews (see A. Chouraqui, *Les Juifs d'Afrique du Nord*, Paris, 1952, p. 34). Touaty is a family name still found among Jews from North Africa (see M. Eisenbeth, *Les Juifs de l'Afrique du Nord, démographie et onomastique*, Alger, 1936, p. 182). The person mentioned here is certainly the most ancient attested and datable instance of its use. The name does not necessarily mean that either the man involved or his ancestors had lived in that oasis, but might simply indicate that he or they used to travel there for business. Text: *'l-t'wty* for *'l-tw'ty*.

[18] In Hebrew, indicating that this should remain a secret. Why the Maghrebi merchant wished that the shipment should not be identified as his, is not evident. The writer seems not to have ascribed much importance to this wish (see n. 20), but was resolved to act as asked.

[19] If the writer should perish on his forthcoming business trip. See n. 27, below.

[20] This passage seems to mean that revealing the name of the real proprietor would not have made much difference.

[21] Text: *l'*, a slip for *l'n, li'ann*.

D. Maghrebi silver

May our lord not neglect the dirhems sent with Khuḍayr. Send a messenger to the Maghrebis[22] as soon as the letters for them arrive. Charge my account for his payment and I shall charge theirs.[23] If they have already left for Alexandria, open the letters and read them. You will find in them the weights of the (various consignments of) silver indicated. Then may our lord—may God give him success—go up to Cairo to the sons[24] of his h(onor), and h(oliness), (our) m(aster and) t(eacher) Menaḥēm and supervise the change, since the Maghrebis will not be present[25] themselves, take the equivalent (in gold) immediately, send it with Khuḍayr and tell him that this sum is the price of the *qaṣab*.[26]

Any service or request our lord may have, please honor your servant with it. And do not forget to include me in your prayers.[27]

P.S. 1. About two turbans

I also sent you with Khuḍayr a paper bag with two plain white turbans (to be sold at a) minimum price of 150 (dirhems). May our lord kindly place them with ʿImrān al-Marrākushī (Amram of Marrākesh, Morocco), if he is in town, otherwise, with al-ʿAfīf al-Ḥarīrī,[28] who may give them to anyone for sale, but should not

[22] Text: *ḳhlfh*, a slip for *ḳhlfhm*.

[23] Silver dirhems had been sent to Alexandria for Maghrebi merchants returning from an Oriental trip. The writer forwarded the dirhems with Khuḍayr to Fustat-Cairo according to instructions received. Letters for these merchants, also sent to him, were forwarded by him with a different mail carrier —a usual measure of precaution. The writer was informed of the contents of these letters, but he could not know where the merchants were at the time. He therefore asks the judge not to wait for an opportunity to forward the letters, but to send them with a special messenger, which could be expensive. If those merchants were still south of Cairo, the judge would have to await their instructions; if they had already arrived there, they would take care of the silver themselves. The writer gives instructions in case that they had already left for Alexandria on their way home.

[24] Text: *'wl'*, for *'wl'd, awlād*.

[25] Text: *yṣrw*, for *yḥṣrw* (*yaḥḍuru*).

[26] Linen decorated with gold and silver threads. It seems that for reasons of safety the messenger had been told that he carried *qaṣab*.

[27] For the writer was again embarking on a sea voyage as announced no doubt in one of the two sheets lost.

[28] The first word is a title ("the honest"), mostly given to officials or agents

neglect the matter. They should obtain a price higher than here in Alexandria, namely 75 apiece, but in any case not less.[29]

P.S. II. About some other textiles

I wrote to the elder al-ʿAfīf concerning the shawl[30] of Ibrahīm, but he is a poor letter writer. I have also mentioned to our lord that it is worth 3 (dinars). The mantles[31] are with Khuḍayr or with ʿIwaḍ b. Jawhar al-Mubashshirī.[32] He will arrive with the transport on Tuesday,[33] for he will leave Alexandria on the last day of the Holidays.

Your servant congratulates our lord on this feast. May God grant our lord *many pleasant years and may he live to behold the beauty of the lord and to visit every morning in his Temple.*[34]

P.S. III. About pious foundations

(Twelve, largely effaced lines and one long line running on the margin indicate that the writer was an almoner who supervised the collection of the rents of houses donated to the community and the distribution of the available funds to the poor and other deserving persons. He speaks about six collections of rents, his own letters to the Nagid in this matter, and about one Maʿānī, of whom it was said that he was only a cantor.[35] A man with this name is mentioned

---

of low rank, the second a common family name, "Silkworker"; see no. 4, n. 24, above.

29 The turbans were probably imported from Sicily (see S. D. Goitein, "Sicily and Southern Italy in the Cairo Geniza Documents," *Archivio Storico per la Sicilia Orientale* 77 [1971], 14). The price of 75 dirhems (approx. 2 dinars; see *Med. Soc.*, I, 382, secs. 60, 61) is paralleled in the Geniza documents.

30 Ar. *ʿarḍī*, probably called so because its breadth was larger than its length. Used by both men and women and often sent as a gift. The price mentioned here was normal. In TS NS J 344, probably from the same time: "about 60 dirhems." See also Ashtor, *Prix*, p. 168. The examples could be multiplied.

31 Text: *'rdh* for *'rdyh* (*ardiyah*) plural of *ridāʾ*.

32 ʿIwaḍ ("Compensation," so called when born after an elder brother had died) was the son of the freedman "Jewel," whose former master was called Mubashshir.

33 Text: *'l-thl'th*, for *'l-thl'th'*.

34 Psalm 27:4, a common good wish for the holidays in the Geniza letters. He writes "in the temples," *bhyḳlyw*, slips to the very end.

35 Ar. *muṣallī*, a late term.

as an influential communal official in Alexandria in a letter from this period.[36] But the passage is too damaged for safe reconstruction.)

9 AFTER CAPTURE BY INDIAN PIRATES

A Representative of Merchants in the Capital of Egypt, Stuck in Broach, North of Bombay, after Having been Captured by Pirates, is Invited by his Brother-in-law in Mangalore, Southern India, to Join him in his own Ship on the Way back to Aden
Ca. 1145

The writer of this letter, Maḥrūz ("Protected by God") b. Jacob, was a *nākhodā*, or shipowner, who commuted in his own boat between Aden and India. Occasionally we find him in the capital of Egypt, where his sister was married to the recipient of this letter, Judah b. Joseph ha-Kohen, representative of the merchants there. Judah's own sister was married to Maḍmūn, representative of the merchants in Aden (see no. 37, introduction). Thus we see that these India traders bolstered their economic positions by carefully arranged family bonds.

Judah b. Joseph ha-Kohen was the grandson of his namesake, the Rāv, or Master, who was so prominent in the Jewish community of Egypt during the second half of the eleventh century (see no. 35, nn. 1, 2, below). In more elaborate addresses he, like his grandfather, is called "Scion of the Gaons," and, like the latter, he himself signs documents with the title "Scion of Yehōseph (same as Joseph), the righteous priest," referring to the first member of the family, who, after emigrating from Baghdad to Jerusalem, became president of the High Court there at the end of the tenth century.[1] Such transitions from religious and legal to commercial leadership and vice versa were natural to the bourgeois society of

[36] TS 13 J 21, f. 30, l. 12, ed. J. Braslavsky, *Eretz Israel* 3, p. 208.

---

[1] See the genealogical lists and discussion in Mann, *Jews in Egypt*, II, 62-63.

the medieval Middle East and common to the three monotheistic religious communities.[2]

Bodleian Library, Oxford, MS Heb. b 11, f. 22 (Cat. 2874, no. 21).
India Book 133.

IN (YOUR) NAME, O MERCI(FUL)!

"Your hand shall be lifted upon your adversaries, and all your enemies shall be cut off."[3]

I am writing to you, my lord and master, my chief, the illustrious elder—may God prolong your life and make permanent your prominent position, may he be for you and with you and guard you in all your affairs. I am writing to you out of a strong longing; may God make us meet together presently in the best circumstances in his favor and bounty, if God wills, for it is up to him and it is in his power alone.

I wish to inform you, my lord, that I had previously written to you at Tāna.[4] Meanwhile the accompanying boat of the ship[5] arrived, and its soldiers told us that the ship in which your excellency my lord traveled was taken by pirates, and I was very sad about this. But afterwards I praised God and thanked him, when I heard that your life was saved. "*O that men would praise the Lord for his goodness.*"[6] Everything can be replaced except life; I would indeed like to mention to you, my lord, that your servant had a large shipment in the boat of Fōfalī ("Betel-nut merchant"), then God ordained what happened (i.e., everything was lost); in the end, however, God compensated me—praise and thanks to him. Likewise, my lord, do not be sad. God will replace your loss to you soon;

[2] India with its castes might have been different.

[3] Micah 5:8. Intended as a good wish for the pirates.

[4] Spelled Thana today, "21 miles northeast of Bombay city," S. Maqbul Ahmad, *India and the Neighbouring Territories, etc.*, Leiden, 1960, p. 106, and passim (see index). This and the following Indian localities occur also in other Geniza letters.

[5] A large, ocean-going ship carrying freight and passengers was usually accompanied by a smaller vessel serving as lifeboat. The soldiers stationed on it for the protection of the ship on which Judah traveled, made off as soon as the pirates made their appearance.

[6] Psalm 107:8. Usually said on such occasions.

you will live, if God wills and God will compensate you many times.

Your servant thought that your honor my lord was in Tāna, and I had previously sent letters to the nākhodā Tinbū, advising him to pay to my lord 21 mithqāls (Egyptian dinars) or more. Afterwards, however, my lord the Sheikh Abu 'l-Qāsim Ibn Qaṭṭān ("Dealer in cotton") came to Mangalore. I inquired about you and he told me that your excellency was in Broach.[7] In all circumstances please come quickly to Mangalore and do not tarry, for I am waiting here in Mangalore and—if God wills—we shall embark on our way home as soon as possible. It is better for you to travel from Mangalore with me than to travel in the ships of foreign people. Please remember that there is no difference between us, my money is yours, it is just the same. The boats[8] start presently from your place, from Kanbayāt,[9] and from Tāna; please set out immediately so that you reach Mangalore with the vessels which, God willing, will soon be arriving in Malibārāt,[10] Kayākannūr,[11] and Mangalore. If, my lord, you need any gold, please take it on my account from the nākhodā Tinbū, for he is staying in Tāna, and between him and me there are bonds of inseparable friendship and brotherhood.[12]

You would certainly like to know, my lord, that a sum in favor of your excellency remained with me on account of the silk. With it I bought twelve [. . .] and sixteen large [bahārs][13] peppers for

[7] About four days' travel north of Tāna. Maqbūl (see n. 4, above), p. 102.

[8] Ar. maṭāyā, a general word for mounts, riding animals, means of locomotion. The word may mean also carts drawn by oxen. The Middle East, throughout the Islamic period, was practically unfamiliar with any form of carriages and therefore had no word for them, see *EI*², s.v. *'Adjalah.* Carts drawn by oxen were common in India and here possibly reference is made to convoys of them setting out at fixed periods. But see no. 10, n. 4, below.

[9] Present day Cambay on the gulf with the same name, still north of Broach.

[10] Malibār or Manibār is Malabar, but meaning both a region and a place on the southwestern coast of India.

[11] Kayākannūr, explained by Professor A. L. Basham as "Lesser Cannanore," *ḳay* meaning "lesser" in Tamil, the language spoken in those parts. Not found in any other Geniza paper.

[12] Tinbū, apparently a Hindu. Abu 'l-Qāsim, who was mentioned before in deferential terms, was a Muslim.

[13] The terms "large" and "small" were applied to the *bahār*, usually 300 pounds in our papers. See no. 37, n. 35, below.

you, and I dispatch this for you under God's protection from Mangalore with the "Blessed" ship—may God ordain her safety.[14]

Attached to this letter, is another one in Arabic characters of the same content as this letter; please notice this. And again, my lord, do not take to heart what you have lost; you have, my lord, praise be to God, plenty to have recourse to and to be compensated with. When life is saved, nothing else matters. Nor do I need to urge you again to come to Mangalore.

Accept, my lord, copious regards for your noble self and convey copious regards to the elder Abu Sa'd. The writer of these lines,[15] Abraham b. Yijū, conveys to your excellency copious regards, and those who attend the writing of this letter do the same. *May the well-being of my lord grow indefinitely and never become reduced.*

(Address:)

To be delivered to my noble lord, the light of my eyes, his honor, (our) M(aster) and T(eacher) Judah ha-Kohen, the wise and understanding, the son of his honor, greatness, and hol(iness), (our) M(aster) and T(eacher) Joseph ha-Kohen, may his soul be satiated with pleasures in the Gardens of Eden until he will be quickened at the end of the days.

From his servant Maḥrūz, the son of Jacob, (may he) r(est in) E(den).

Given in trust (i.e., no fees for delivery).

10 MEMO FROM THE INDIA ROUTE TO QŪṢ, UPPER EGYPT

This tersely written memo is instructive in many respects. Its time is fixed by the references in secs. 4 and 7 to the Jewish chief judge of Cairo Menaḥēm b. Isaac b. Sāsōn, who was active during the first third of the thirteenth century (see no. 8, n. 1, above). The

[14] The "Blessed" (ship) belonged to Maḍmūn of Aden (see no. 37, below) and operated between Aden and Mangalore. *India Book* 28*v*, ll. 5-6.

[15] The letter is a beautiful example of Abraham Yijū's calligraphy. The letter in Arabic characters probably was written by Maḥrūz himself and was destined to be shown, if necessary, to his non-Jewish business friends, especially Tinbū. The Hindu shipowner certainly knew Arabic.

recipient of the shipment noted in sec. 6 is also known to have lived at that time. The fact that presents are sent to the Jewish chief judge in Cairo, but none to any dignitary in Fustat, suggests that the sender of the memo lived in Cairo rather than Fustat. This explains why the Geniza has preserved only this memo and the fragment of another (*India Book* 299) from the hand of this India trader despite the very considerable size of his business and the great number of his Muslim and Jewish business friends. He lived in Cairo and therefore had no opportunity to deposit his papers in the Geniza, a chamber in the ancient synagogue of the Palestinians in Fustat. Our memo, naturally, arrived there through its recipient.

The addressee lived, or more likely, only sojourned, in Qūṣ, Upper Egypt sec. 5). One traveled on the Nile upstream from Cairo to Qūṣ, and from there through the desert to ʻAydhāb, the Sudanese port on the Red Sea, which once was a great emporium, but has disappeared from the map since (see sec. 14). The memo was most likely written in Aden, South Arabia, since the spices, perfumes, and textiles listed came from different parts of India and other countries of the Far East and were assembled in that South Arabian port before being forwarded to the West. Despite the great variety of goods listed, entire categories of merchandise are absent from this thirteenth century memo, as for example, metals, especially bronze vessels and iron, which so frequently appear in the India papers of the twelfth century.

Ten different carriers transport the goods destined for a single recipient. This practice is indicative of the lack of security on the trade route. In the memo (*India Book* 299) the writer indeed alludes to dangers, i.e., political troubles, that will be reported by the travelers orally.

Two of the shipments were addressed not to the recipient of this memo but to his son, who, as was customary, bore the name of his grandfather. Throughout the centuries it was a common practice among the merchants to let their sons do business on their own account at an early age in order to groom them for the profession of independent, self-reliant traders (see nos. 22, sec. F, and 57, and *Med. Soc.*, II, 191-192).

University Library, Cambridge, Taylor-Schechter Collection,
TS Arabic Box 30, f. 145. *India Book* 156

(To) M. Mufaḍḍal Ibn Abī Sa'd ("Excellent, son of Fortunate").[1]
God is sufficient for me.[2]
These items have been sent by your servant to my lord—may God make permanent his honored position.

I

With the sheikh Yaḥyā b. Abi 'l-Qāsim al-Sakhāwī[3] in the "mount"[4] of Ibn al-Naffākh ("Hornist," "Blower of the Horn"):
3 bales with lac, each weighing 400 pounds
2 bales, "mixed,"[5] one half pepper and the other ginger, each weighing 1 *bahār*[6]
1 bale cleaned clove,[7] weighing 40 gross mann[8]
1 bale clove stalks, weighing 50 mann
Everything is marked: Mufaḍḍal Ibn Abī Sa'd.

[1] Hastily added in vertical lines on the upper left-hand corner of the sheet. He is the recipient of the memo. See secs. 1, 2, 9, 13, 15.

[2] Ar. *Allāhu ḥasbī*; this is an abbreviated and inverted form of a Koranic phrase which is often found at the *end* of letters, e.g., nos. 29 and 33, below.

[3] Of course a Muslim, since Abu 'l-Qāsim was the byname of the prophet Muhammad. Sakhāwī was a common Egyptian family name.

[4] Ar. *maṭiyya* must denote here a type of boat or its name. No. 9, n. 8, above, refers to inland India, but there, too, boats of a local type could be intended.

[5] Ar. *khulṭa*, which means "partnership" in the Mediterranean trade, but denotes in the India papers "a mixture of pepper and ginger." The addition "one half pepper, the other ginger" denotes the *quantities* of the mixture, not the fact, which is already indicated by the Ar. term. See *India Book* 55, l. 2; 73, ll. 27-28; 208, l. 36. This mixture, which appears even in price lists (see *India Book* 85, ll. 20-21), must have been known also to European merchants, but I do not find it in Heyd, *Commerce du Levant*, II, 619-623.

[6] Usually, 300 pounds; see no. 37, n. 25, below.

[7] The dried flower bud of the clove (*clou de girofle*) had to be separated carefully from the stalk and all other parts of the plant. The stalks themselves were also sold, but for a much lower price, of course; see what immediately follows and Heyd, *Commerce du Levant*, II, 607.

[8] The *mann* mentioned in the Geniza papers generally is equivalent to something less than 2 Egyptian pounds (see also Hinz, *Masse*, p. 16). The term translated here as "gross" is a mere guess. Ar. *muṭarraḥa*, the only suitable meaning of which is "extended, increased (said of the height of a building)." Wahrmund, *Handwörterbuch*, II, 129, 829.

2

For the elder Abū Naṣr, the twin brother[9] of my lord, as an equivalent of what was due him, with Futūḥ[10] a bale of pepper weighing 140 pounds. Marked. . . .[11]

3

With the same a bale containing three bags of cleaned clove, marked: Mufaḍḍal Ibn Abī Sa'd.

4

A bag[12] for *our lord* Menaḥēm weighing 2 1/2 mann. His name is written on it.

5

A bag for the Jew from Majorca[13] who is with you in Qūṣ, weighing 1 mann. *Mayurqī* is written on it.

6

A bag for the elder Makārim ("Nobility") b. Mufaḍḍal b. Nänū[14] from the elder Ibn Walīd, weighing 2 and 5 mann. (Written on it in another hand:) "Ṣayrafī."[15]

7

A bag containing a precious turban made of *lālas* (fine red silk), a *bukhnuq* (shawl), and a white *burda* (robe) without a border

[9] Ar. *ṣinw* used thus today, but meaning in classical Ar. "brother, brother from both father and mother, son, cousin." Not common in the Geniza.

[10] "Openings" or "Conquests, Victories," a very common Jewish name at this time.

[11] Squeezed in, written in Ar. letters; but finally the writer forgot to note which was the mark.

[12] Namely, of clove, the standard present, brought or sent home by India traders.

[13] The well-known Spanish island. People and goods originating from there are repeatedly mentioned in the Geniza. This shipment was a charity.

[14] Mufaḍḍal b. Nānū (here with Imāla Nänū), the father of this man, contributed to the public appeals described in *Med. Soc.*, II, App. C, secs. 30, 31, 139. Nānū is a children's word, like British *nanny*. See ibid., 508.

[15] "Banker," "Money Changer," the family name of the recipient.

for *our lord* Menaḥēm. Marked (in Arabic characters:) Mufaḍḍal Ibn Abī Sa'd.

8

A bag with (Chinese) rhubarb, canvassed. Abu 'l-Ḥasan b. 'Aṭiyya ("Handsome, son of Gift") sent this to Ṭāhir[16] b. Ibrahīm ("Pure, son of Abraham").

I instructed him[17] to deliver everything to my lord.

9

With Maḥāsin ("Favors"), son of the man with the parted beard: a flask with musk, weighing 12 1/2 mithqāls. Marked: Mufaḍḍal Ibn Abī Sa'd. Also with him a bag of odoriferous wood, weighing 1 mann; in the middle of this is a piece of cloth containing a unit[18] of ambergris.

10

A bag with three lālas turbans, a lālas *'arḍī* (broad shawl), and a fine cotton robe, all marked: Abu 'l-Qāsim, the son of the Physician.[19] If Abu 'l-Qāsim is in town, he should accept delivery. Otherwise, my lord should receive it.

11

With him also: a bale with lālas textiles packed in leather, marked: Abū Sa'd b. Mufaḍḍal Ibn Abū (!) Sa'd, namely:

3 Volga[20] robes
11 small lālas turbans
2 large turbans
5 broad shawls with black borders
Total 21 pieces

[16] All very common Jewish names.

[17] Futūḥ, mentioned in sec. 2.

[18] Ar. *bay'a,* lit., a sale.

[19] A Muslim business friend. See n. 3, above.

[20] Ar. *arthī,* from *arthā,* the name of the Volga river, from the shores of which the Muslim peoples received the black sable and other furs. See Serjeant, *Islamic Textiles,* 15-16, p. 74. These Indian robes of fine red silks had borders of fur. Cf. sec. 7, above, where it is stated that a robe sent to the judge had no border.

Cleaned lālas: 4 untailored pieces[21]
3 large turbans
3 small turbans
3 broad shawls
Total of cleaned lālas: 13 pieces
(In the margin:) 2 harnesses[22] of wood for the elder Abu 'l-Surūr b. Maṣlī'aḥ.[23]
Grand total: 39 pieces[24]
I instructed him to deliver everything to my lord.[25]

12

With 'Aṭā' Allāh b. 'Abd al-Khāliq[26] a bale with cleaned clove, weighing 52 1/2 mann. Marked: Abū Sa'd b. Mufaḍḍal Ibn Abū Sa'd.

13

With Aḥmad b. Ḥasnūn a bale with cleaned clove, weighing 40 gross mann, and a bale with clove stalks, weighing 50 mann. Marked: Mufaḍḍal Ibn Abī Sa'd.

14

In the "nailformed" (boat)[27] of Ibn Hiba[28] what had been sent via 'Aydhāb, when the ship sank and the cargo was partially saved:
2 remainders from the pepper and ginger, weighing 814 pounds
a remainder of lac, weighing 450 pounds
a bale of lac, weighing 130 pounds. Marked: Abū Sa'd b. Munajjā.[29]

[21] Ar. *maqṣūr ajlām*, which I take as derived from Aram.-Heb. *glm*, "untailored piece." See n. 30, below.

[22] Ar. *m'shrtyn*. The tentative translation is taken from Dozy, *Supplément*, II, 131 *a-b*.

[23] "Successful" (Heb.), a name with messianic undertones. See Isaiah 48:15.

[24] Even with the wooden pieces the total seems to be not more than 36. Such mistakes are extremely rare.

[25] Although the shipment was addressed to his son.

[26] "Gift of God, son of the Servant of the Creator," a Jew, as is evident from *India Book* 299.

[27] Ar. *mismārī*.

[28] "Gift," a name common to Muslims and Jews.

[29] "Saved," Ar. equivalent of Joseph, who was saved from the pit. See no. 55, below.

15

For my lord, out of the total load carried by Afḍal and Abu 'l-Surūr: a remainder of pepper weighing 357 pounds, marked Mufaḍḍal Ibn Abī Sa'd. All this is sent to you with Rashīd, the servant of Ibn Hiba and Qāsim Ibn al-Qathīf.

16

Also with Qāsim Ibn al-Qathīf a bale packed in leather and canvas, marked Abū Sa'd b. Munajjā, containing ten lālas robes, untailored[30] and of utmost fineness.

And peace.

[30] Ar. *thiyāb ajlām.* See n. 21, above.

CHAPTER III

The Eleventh Century

THE ELEVENTH century was the golden age of the overseas trade on the Islamic side of the Mediterranean. Over half of the letters translated in this volume originated in that period (see the Introduction, sec. 1). Most of the details on international commerce provided in *Med. Soc.*, I, refer to that century and the same is true of the general Introduction to this book. Thus, there is no point in providing this chapter with another introduction. Letters 11-14 and 17 illustrate the affairs of the leading merchants, while nos. 22 and 25 are typical examples of full-fledged business letters of the middle class. The reader is advised that these two groups represent the most numerous and most instructive business letters in the Geniza. A short summary of my finds with regard to the Mediterranean trade of the eleventh century is found in my essay "Mediterranean Trade Preceding the Crusades," *Diogenes* 59 (1967), 47-62.

11 FROM THE CORRESPONDENCE OF TWO GREAT MERCHANT FAMILIES

Ca. 1010

Great families, strong through their wealth, far-flung connections, and sheer manpower, loom large in the Geniza correspondence of the eleventh century. But even in letters directed from one family partnership to another, it was customary that an individual, normally the senior member of one family, addressed his opposite number personally. Thus, in our letter, the address is written in the name of the two firms: the three senior Tustarī brothers in Cairo-Fustat are addressed by two Tāhertī brothers in

Qayrawān, Tunisia.[1] Two other Tāhertī brothers were in Egypt at that time. But throughout the letter Mūsā (Moses), the dean of the Tāhertīs, speaks to Sahl, the eldest of the Tustarīs (and father of the famous Abū Sa'd, who later became a most influential person at the Fatimid court).[2]

The goods referred to in this letter mostly were high-priced textiles, each of which was traded individually. Such items were given at weddings and other special occasions and transmitted from parents to children as precious heirlooms. Our writer emphasizes that the most valuable textiles were the old ones.

The warm words of admiration and friendship in this letter are by no means commonplace. They are all the more remarkable as the writer was a prominent representative of rabbinical Judaism—he became indeed a "member" of the Jerusalem yeshiva in, or around, 1022[3]—while the Tustarīs belonged to a dissident sect, the Karaites.[4]

As our letter shows, the two Tāhertī brothers then in Egypt were still novices in the Eastern trade at that time, while in 1024 they were already well established there.[5] The junior Tustarīs, the three sons of Sahl, are referred to here as "your boys" and the writer clearly had known the father of the three senior brothers. Thus our letter was probably written during the first decade of the eleventh century.

University Library, Cambridge, Taylor-Schechter Collection, TS 12.133

A. Words of thanks and appreciation

I am writing to you, eminent elder and leader of the profession—may God prolong your life, make your welfare and happiness per-

[1] For the Tustarīs see no. 2, above, and no. 69, below; for the Tāhertīs see *Med. Soc.*, I, 181, and no. 1, n. 23, above, and nos. 12, 13, 25, 26, 27, 30, 63, 71, below.

[2] Killed in 1047. See *Med. Soc.*, I, 165 and here, no. 20, sec. B, below.

[3] TS NS Box 320, f. 16, ed. S. D. Goitein, *S. W. Baron Jubilee Volume* (forthcoming).

[4] S. M. Stern, "A Petition to the Fatimid Caliph al-Mustanṣir Concerning a Conflict within the Jewish Community," *REJ* 128 (1969), 211.

[5] See no. 63, below.

manent, and increase his b[enefactions] to you and for you—on Marheshvan 9th.[6] I am well and in good health, thank God.

Your letters have arrived, my lord—may God support you—and I was happy to learn that you were well. I praised God for this and asked him to make this permanent in his grace.

Likewise, my lord, [the letters] of my two brothers—may God keep them—have arrived reporting how kind you have been to them and how much care you have given to their affairs. [They] thanked God[7] for this, my lord, in the presence of all those who know you[8] and those who do not know you.

And I ask God to multiply people like you in the nation,[9] for you are its ornament. By my father—(may he) r(est in) p(eace), although I am now back with my family, I am extremely unhappy[10] to be separated from you. For being with you makes the soul strong with God. I ask God to make your present state permanent, and to keep you alive until you see your boys as my lord, the elder,[11] (may he) r(est in) p(eace), has seen you, namely that they will presently become even more successful than you.[12]

B. Shipment for the top merchant in the city

Your shipment for the elder, my lord Abū Zikrī[13]—may God support him—has arrived, my lord. These are unique, exquisite pieces, each having feathering[14] on its . . . ,[15] incomparable. The festive

[6] Early October. The letter was sent overland, not in a boat.

[7] Instead of saying: "He praised him," one said: "He thanked God for having created such a man."

[8] From here to the end of the next paragraph "you" is in the plural.

[9] *Umma,* meaning Jews, whether Rabbanite or Karaite.

[10] Ar. *mutanaghghiḍ shadīd al-tanaghghuḍ,* a strong expression.

[11] The addressees' father.

[12] Saying to a father that his sons were or would be "better" than he made him happy. But the construction of the sentence is awkward: *ḳamā annahum al-sāʿa ḳhayr minḳum ḳull waq*[*t*]. There is a dot on the first *ḳ*, meaning perhaps that *ḳamā* is to be deleted.

[13] About him see the next selection, no. 12, below.

[14] Ar. *murayyash,* a common term in the Geniza trousseaux (also in the form *murāyash*). Perhaps derived from *rīsha,* lit., "feather," a needle with precious stones. See Dozy, *Supplément,* 1, 575*a*.

[15] Text: *fī mʿzʾh*. The reading is clear.

costume[16] is even finer. It has been said that he was [offered] 60 dinars in cash for it. But he refused to sell it, for he wished to wear it himself. The lead-gray robe is better than everything. I have forwarded your letters to him.[17]

The servant, my lord, did not have this much inconvenience.[18] The man[19] seeks your friendship, [. . .] and (marital) connection with you and wishes to derive profit from your honored position and your advice for his undertakings. Had he a son fit to serve you as an apprentice, he would have been honored by this.

His letters will be sent to you in the pilgrims' caravan.[20]

C. The writer's own shipment and orders

The cloaks[21] sent by you have arrived, and I wish to thank you for your kindness and exertion in this matter. You noted also that the rest of the order had been carried out. All you have sent, my lord, is fine, but I wish to ask you to buy everything all over again, for the three robes striped with curved lines,[22] as well as the white robe which I wanted to have for me as a mantle, were taken from me by a man who imposed on me. Present circumstances make such

[16] Ar. *ḥulla,* denoting the complete festive attire of either a man or a woman. For 60 dinars a family could live in those days for about three years. One could have a ḥulla of course for a fraction of this price. The highest price for a ḥulla found thus far in the Geniza outside this letter was 20 dinars for one ordered in Tinnīs by Nahray b. Nissīm. See TS 10 J 20, f. 16, l. 12, *Nahray* 128, where his correspondent writes somewhat incredulously: "If you are serious about the order of the ḥulla for this price write how you want the color and other details."

[17] Refers to letters received after the shipment referred to before. The Tāhertīs served as representatives of the merchants and as such received letters for persons momentarily out of town.

[18] The Tustarī had apologized for causing some inconvenience to Abū Zikrī's *ghulām,* slave or employee, presumably by charging him with some errand for himself. Our writer replies that Abū Zikrī would not mind; had he had a son fit to serve the Tustarīs as an apprentice, he would have sent him to them.

[19] Abū Zikrī.

[20] Abū Zikrī had sent letters to Moses for forwarding to Egypt. Moses did not enclose them with this letter, but waited for the caravan of the pilgrims to Mecca which, although moving slowly, was regarded as safer.

[21] Ar. *ḳisawāt,* could serve also as robes (see below) and bedcovers.

[22] Ar. *mu'arraj,* the translation according to Steingass, *Persian-English Dictionary,* p. 1271*a,* and Wahrmund, *Handwörterbuch,* II, 841*b.*

things necessary; I cannot go into detail about this. May God save us from what we fear. All I could say was that those garments were for sale.[23]

I would like the robe to be deep red, as red as possible, and the white and yellow also to be of excellent color. I did not like the color of the yellow which arrived. Also, the white robe which is to serve as mantle should be of the same quality. The best robes manufactured are the old ones. It should be cut in two pieces.[24] Its price should be 2[5 dinars], or as you deem proper; 1 dinar more on a robe having your approval is preferable to one not so good.

The Sig[laton][25] robe is of extreme beauty, but it is not the color which they ordered. For this is white and blue, but instead I w[ished to have] one of the blue onion color,[26] an open color, according to your taste. I wish to have the very best, as chosen by you.

I wish also to have two lead-gray robes with borders "filling your eyes," each worth about 25 dinars, or a little more, provided they are first class. Act according to your own judgment. I know that you, may God support you, are eager to save a dirhem for me more than I do, and you have also the capacity to do so.

Also (buy me) a white *rāzī* robe.[27]

The festive costume which I have ordered before, should be like the one you sent to [my lord] Abū Zikrī Judah—may God support him.[28] If you cannot obtain one like that, then it should be red, striped with curved lines, like the robe which (my lord) Abī

[23] Tāhertī wanted to have these pieces for persons who had individually ordered them and partly also for his own family. But he was forced to sell to Muslims under the veiled (or open) threat that the old discriminatory laws on clothing for non-Muslims would be invoked. They were indeed renewed, perhaps only temporarily, under the Zirid ruler of Qayrawān, Mu'izz b. Bādis (1016-1062). See Idris, *Zirides*, p. 767.

[24] While the robe, *thawb*, used as upper garment, was cut in one piece, this one, which should serve as a *ḳiswa*, or mantle, was to be cut in two.

[25] This heavy fabric of damask silk was extremely popular in the Middle Ages, and, in later times, almost regularly deep blue (see Heyd, *Commerce du Levant*, II, 700). In our period, it used to be, as here, of *two* colors.

[26] Ar. *baṣalī*. I assume the reference is to the pale purple color of an onion cut open. The term "open color," *maftūḥ*, seems to mean "light."

[27] Made in Rayy, a great industrial center in Iran of those days, or in the style imported from there.

[28] See n. 13 above.

Ibrahīm ʿAyyāsh[29] had had made for himself and I do not care if it costs 1 or 2 dinars more.

The package forwarded by my lord Abi ʾl-Ḥasan (?) ʿAlī, the son of the sister of the elder ʿAllāl,[30] has arrived. But the *ʿattābī*[31] does not have such good going here. All that was obtained for the package of ʿattābī was 20 dinars.

(There follow about twenty partly effaced words).

D. Urgent Appeal for the Writer's Brothers

I have another wish, my lord. Should a caravan set out in which trustworthy Muslims, who have given you sureties, will travel, let the merchandise of my brothers be sent with them as if it were yours. They would profit from this in many respects.[32]

The balance for the garments ordered will be sent to you with the pilgrims' caravan in a purse of gold dinars.[33]

My lord, I do not need to entreat you to take care of my brothers—may God keep them—their soul lives only[34] . . . because they are with you. In a place where you are they are no strangers. May God protect me through you.[35]

(There follows a short, only partly preserved passage dealing with a lawsuit concerning a flask worth 22 dinars, probably containing musk).

[29] Meaning "Long-lived," one of the many Ar. equivalents of Heb. Ḥayyīm. This ʿAyyāsh was a brother-in-law of Abū Zikrī and his commercial representative in Egypt (see no. 12, below). He should not be confounded with his namesake, frequently mentioned in the Geniza, who lived a generation later.

[30] It was common practice for a young man to serve as an apprentice with an uncle. Long after having become an independent merchant he still would be styled "the nephew of Mr. So-and-So."

[31] *ʿAttābī* (from which Eng. *tabby* is derived). A silk taffeta, originally produced in Baghdad, was manufactured at that time in many different parts of the Islamic world. See Serjeant, *Islamic Textiles*, index, s.v., and no. 60, n. 4, below.

[32] It would be safer, cheaper, and also quicker. For otherwise they would have to wait for the next seafaring season opening late in April.

[33] Meaning that the payment would be in cash and immediately and not by calculating the reciprocal debts and assets.

[34] Partly effaced and torn away and followed by four other effaced words.

[35] Meaning: By keeping you alive and prosperous God protects also me.

E. Conclusion

A letter from you, my lord, with a report on your state and welfare and any order you may have will give me pleasure and will be sure of my recognition and thanks. Best regards to your dear selves and to my lords Abū Naṣr, Abū Sa'd, and Abū [Manṣūr][36]—may God let you see all your hopes fulfilled in them—and to all encompassed by your care.

(Address. Right side:)
To my elder and illustrious leader Abu 'l-Faḍl, Abū Jacob, and Abū Sahl, Sahl, Joseph, and Sa'īd, the sons of Israel, may God prolong their lives.[37]
(Left side:)
From Mūsā and Isaac, the sons of Barhūn, (may his) s(oul) r(est in peace).

12 RECIPROCAL SERVICES

Ca. 1020

This short letter, written on vellum, illustrates well what has been described in *Med. Soc.*, I, 164-169, as *informal business cooperation.* Abū Zikrī Judah, the leading Jewish merchant of Qayrawān, referred to in sec. B of the preceding letter, asks one of the Tāhertī brothers sojourning in Egypt to assist his brother-in-law in the management of his, Judah's, affairs in that country. On his side he had taken all the necessary steps to ensure that the Tāhertī's goods would be sent from Tunisia to Egypt safely and quickly.

Judah was able to do so because he was closely connected with the

[36] These were the sons of Sahl, the eldest of the three senior Tustarīs, who alone is spoken to in the letter. See, e.g., Mann, *Texts*, I, 375.

[37] It was customary to address a person first with his honorific byname, the *kunya*, followed by a blessing, and then to give his full name. The names are to be understood therefore as follows: Abū 'l-Faḍl Sahl, Abū Jacob (rather Ya'qūb, but spelled here without *w*) Joseph, Abū Sahl Sa'īd.

It should be noted that in Tunisia, in this period, the kunya was often introduced by Abī, not Abū. Since there was no complete consistency in this matter and in order to avoid confusion I spell it Abū throughout.

"Sultan" of Tunisia[1] and especially with "the Illustrious Lady," the Sultan's aunt, who ruled the country in the early years of his reign until her death in October 1023.[2] For our taste, Judah here gets a bit too excited about the honors extended to him by the *Sayyida.* But the early years of the boyish Sultan's reign had been disastrous for the country in general, and its Jews in particular, which explains why this public show of royal favor was taken as a sign that the general security situation had improved.

The recipient, Isma'īl b. Barhūn (in Heb. Samuel b. Abraham) Tāhertī appears in many Geniza letters and documents, which show him as a commuter between Tunisia and Egypt. His difficult character, alluded to here, is underlined in another letter.[3] His elder brother, Abu 'l-Khayr Moses[4] is mentioned in the opening paragraph of our letter as present in Egypt. Moses visited Jerusalem in, or around, 1022. Taking into consideration the various additional data provided for in nos. 11 and 12, it is reasonable to assume that our letter was written approximately at that time.

University Library, Cambridge, Taylor-Schechter Collection, TS 12.224.

(The first ten lines contain polite Arabic phrases, often rhymed, expressing hopes for quick reunion with the addressee.)

I have charged our brother Abū Ibrāhīm 'Ayyāsh, my brother-in-law,[5] may God support him, to take care of my affairs. Then I have sent him additional goods and asked him to deal with them as well, and to complete all the operations. I wish now that you assist and help him until everything is carried out in accordance with my instructions.

I have not charged you with this because I know your impatience[6]

[1] Mu'izz b. Bādis (1016-1062). In Bodl. MS Heb. d 65 (Cat. 2877), f. 17, l. 7. Judah alone was privileged to send goods in the Sultan's ship.

[2] Her name was Umm Mallāl. See Idris, *Zirides*, pp. 141-142.

[3] Bodl. MS Heb. d 65 (Cat. 2877), f. 9, ll. 15, 30, ed. S. Assaf, *J. N. Epstein Jubilee Volume*, Jerusalem, 1950, pp. 179-180.

[4] Moses (Mūsā) b. Barhūn Tāhertī is called Abu 'l-Khayr in TS 8 J 36, f. 2, a letter by our Judah b. Joseph to the three senior Tustarī brothers.

[5] See no. 11, n. 29. Ar. *ṣihr* could mean also *son*-in-law. But in that case the writer would have said "my son," "my child," not "our brother."

[6] Ar. *ḍīq khalqak*, lit., "the narrowness of your disposition."

and how busy you are. Therefore I did not wish to impose on you the care for these goods. I am content with your assistance through encouragement[7] and advice. For me this is worth as much as that, and even more.

I wrote to the agent of the ship 'Alī Abū Dhahab[8] and also to its captain that all you wished with regard to the transport of your goods, heavy baggage and other, should be carried out in accordance with your instructions; they should receive the goods from your brother and from the [. . .] and the friends and keep them and put them on the best place aboard. I strongly urged them to carry out their promises, so that the goods should not arrive too short a time before the sailing of the ships, but should be a support to you and strengthen your position.[9]

Letters from you should arrive here all the time to keep us assured of your welfare. For we are disquieted until we receive letters telling us how you have been and how you are. And Peace upon you!

(In the margin:)

All the boys,[10] Abū Sahl and his son, Abū Ibrāhīm, and the rest of the company, and everyone here send you kindest regards. (The end of the margin, which could have contained about sixteen words, is torn away.)

(P.S. on the reverse side:)

The favor of the Creator, may he be exalted and glorified, which never leaves us even for an hour or a minute, caused the Illustrious Lady[11]—may God make her glory permanent—to send me a dove-colored[12] mule from her [stable] with a beautiful, long saddle, and

[7] Ar. *ta'kīd,* insisting on a price demanded or offered.

[8] "The one with the gold," probably because it had a golden ornament on its bow. This ship belonged to the Sultan (TS 8 J 28, f. 9, l. 3, where, l. 8, our Isma'īl is mentioned, too). Judah b. Joseph obviously was an administrator of the Sultan's economic enterprises. See n. 1, above.

[9] Literally, "your heart." The goods were scheduled to be sent from Tunisia to Egypt early in spring. Their sale would take many months, sometimes years. But when they arrived in good time, their proprietor would be in a good bargaining position for buying merchandise to be dispatched with the convoys setting out from Egypt to the West in the fall.

[10] The writer's sons.

[11] See the introduction.

[12] Meaning: iridescent. Ar. *fākhitiyya,* from *fākhita,* ringdove.

beautiful robes of honor[13] for myself and a garment of honor[14] in the name of your brother, may God make [. . .] I am writing you this to make you happy,[15] so that you may give thanks to God for this together with me. [And Peace.]

(Address:)
To Abū Ibrāhīm, may [. . .],[16]
Isma'īl, son of Barhūn, (may he) r(est in) E(den).
From Judah b. Joseph.

13 A FREEDMAN ADDRESSES A MERCHANT PRINCE

Tunisia—Egypt, ca. 1020

The writer of this letter was Faraj, a former slave of Barhūn (Abraham), the father of the four Tāhertī brothers, about whom see no. 11, above. His master, whom he had certainly served as business agent, set him free, but he remained in some kind of family relationship with the Tāhertīs (a usage Muslim rather than Jewish; see *Med. Soc.*, I, 144-146). This is evident from a moving letter on his behalf, addressed to the merchant prince Joseph Ibn 'Awkal, by a brother-in-law of the Tāhertīs, who at that time, acted as the senior member of the family.[1]

By the time of our letter, the former slave had become a respectable merchant. He addresses the merchant prince with respect, but by no means in a way more deferential than that found in the letters of Ibn 'Awkal's correspondents born free.

[13] Ar. *khila'*.
[14] Ar. *kiswa*. This probably was destined for Moses Tāhertī, who at that time was in Egypt. See above.
[15] Text: *ltqr* [*'ynk*], lit., "so that your eye should be cooled."
[16] Two lines of blessings, totally effaced.
It was absolutely uncommon to address a distinguished merchant without any epithet such as "To the illustrious elder." This omission proves that the writer was far above the recipient in social standing.

[1] TS 12.175, ed. S. D. Goitein, *Tarbiz* 34 (1965), 169-174. About Ibn 'Awkal see no. 1, above.

The impact of the pilgrimage to Mecca, referred to twice, is noteworthy. It might have been possible to obtain fine pearls cheaply prior to the departure of the caravan from Cairo, probably because many pilgrims would sell their pearls for provisions and clothing needed on the way. And pearls would be abundant when the caravan returned—provided that there had been a good year for pearl-fishing in the Arabian Seas. Pearls as a lucrative article of trade, bringing up to 100 percent profit in Tunisia are mentioned in another letter to Ibn 'Awkal (no. 1, above).

Despite the dangers and difficulties, goods were sent on to countries where they might obtain a better price. Even our short letter contains an example for this golden rule of Mediterranean trade (Egypt-Tunisia-Spain).

Finally, as in no. 11, as against the products and manufactured goods of the East, the Muslim West provides gold.

University Library, Cambridge, Taylor-Schechter Collection, TS 8.12.[2]

My illustrious elder and master, may God prolong your life and make your well-being and happiness permanent, may he in his mercy always favor you and keep away from you all that is bad and hateful.

I am writing at the beginning of Shevat,[3] asking God to make it the most auspicious and blessed of all months for us and all Israel.[4]

I wrote you a letter, my master, with the first caravan[5] and informed you that the pearls with which you favored me have arrived. . . .[6] Thanks to God and thanks to you, my master, they brought profit and blessing. May God be praised.

The textiles in that consignment were sent by me to Spain, for they do not provide me with sustenance here this year.

[2] TS 8.12, ed. S. D. Goitein, *Tarbiz* 37 (1968), 164-166, trans. Stillman, *East-West Relations*, 287-292.

[3] Mostly January.

[4] At emancipation the slave became a full member of the Jewish community.

[5] At least three caravans set out from Qayrawān to Cairo during the winter season. See *Med. Soc.*, 1, 277, where the term *mawsim* for caravan is also explained.

[6] A blessing, not fully legible.

I have sent you, my master, . . . (with) Mūsā Ibn al-Majjānī,[7] may God keep him, a purse with 120 dinars in number and 118 1/2 and 2 qīrāṭs in weight, 5 of these dinars are in *rubāʿiyyas* (quarters). May God keep them in his mercy. I ask you now, my master—I know, I am imposing on you—to buy pearls, if they are good and to be had, prior to the departure of the people for Mecca and send them with the very first man setting out for here; and please send them by land.[8]

If pearls are not to be had, keep the money until the pilgrims' caravan returns from Mecca and God will give you opportunity to buy them.

If, God forbid, pearls should be scarce this year, buy pearls for one half of the sum sent, and for the other half *good indigo*[9] or . . . All this should be sent overland, if God wills. But you, my master, are alone competent to decide.

I ask you, my master—may God keep you—to be patient with me for I am a burden on you. So act, my master, in this matter in a way for which God will recompense you in this world and the world to come.[10]

Accept, my master, my most special regards, and greetings to my masters Abu 'l-Faḍl and Abu 'l-Ṭayyib[11] and also to all those encompassed by your care.

(In the margin:) I prefer everything to be sent by land.

(Address:)

To my master Abu 'l-Faraj—may God prolong his life—Joseph b. Jacob b. ʿAwkal[12] and to Abu 'l-Faḍl and Abu 'l-Ṭayyib, Hilāl and Benjamin, the sons of Joseph. From their[13] grateful Faraj, the freedman of Barhūn.

[7] Ibn ʿAwkal's representative in Qayrawān. See no. 1, above. Six words preceding the name are of doubtful reading and interpretation.

[8] That is, do not wait for the beginning of the seafaring season in spring.

[9] Heb., in order to keep this detail secret.

[10] Meaning that the writer would be unable to provide commensurate recompense. A frequently found polite expression.

[11] The recipient's sons. See the address.

[12] About this practice of separating the byname from the name see no. 11, n. 37, above.

[13] In the dual, probably caused by the reference to Ibn ʿAwkal's two sons. In later writings, the dual was sometimes used for the plural.

14 WRITING FROM ALEXANDRIA AFTER ARRIVAL FROM THE MUSLIM WEST

Ca. 1020

Many aspects of the Mediterranean trade are evident in this comparatively brief communication. The human relations: no less than twelve merchants, among them a Muslim, are connected with the writer and mostly also with the recipient. All the forms of commercial cooperation are present here: mutual help, partnerships of different sizes and combinations, and direct commission. Finally, the consignments sent from the West to Fustat contain a representative selection of Western goods: agricultural products, metals, minerals, and corals, but not the two staple exports: gold and silk.

The letter, like the preceding one (no. 13), is addressed to Ibn ʿAwkal, but this time by a man of his own rank and at an early time of his life, for only his eldest son is greeted. It is written on vellum and, as it often happens with this material, a hole cuts through five lines, and many words are effaced. But most of the missing parts can be restored.

University Library, Cambridge, Taylor-Schechter Collection, TS 12.291.[1]

Dear and beloved elder and leader, may God prolong your life, never take away your rank, and increase his favors and benefactions to you.

I inform you, my elder, that I have arrived safely. I have written you a letter before, but have seen no answer. Happy preoccupations —I hope.[2] In that letter I provided you with all the necessary information.[3]

I loaded nine pieces of antimony (kohl), five in baskets and four in complete pieces, on the boat of Ibn Jubār[4]—may Good keep it;[5]

[1] Ed. S. D. Goitein, *Tarbiz* 37 (1968), 74-77.

[2] Were the reason why you did not answer—a common phrase.

[3] Such as lists of prices in Sicily and Tunisia.

[4] Going from Alexandria to Fustat. I assume that *ā* is to be pronounced with Imāla (*ā* = *ä*) and that the name was actually Jubayr (Jubär), a rather common Ar. name.

[5] Ar. *qaṭāʾiʿ*, not yet found elsewhere in this meaning of a form of package. Later *qiṭaʿtayn* in the same sense.

these are for you personally, sent by Mūsā Ibn al-Majjānī.[6] On this boat, I have in partnership with you—may God keep you—a load of cast copper, a basket with (copper) fragments,[7] and two pieces of antimony. I hope God will grant their safe arrival. Kindly take delivery of everything, my lord.

I have also sent with Banāna[8] a camel load for you from Ibn al-Majjānī, and a camel load for me in partnership with you—may God keep you. He also carries another partnership of mine, namely, with 'Ammār Ibn Yijū,[9] four small jugs (of oil).

With Abū Zayd[10] I have a shipload[11] of tin in partnership with Salāma al-Mahdawī.[12] Your share in this partnership with him is fifty pounds. I also have seventeen small jugs of s[oap]. I hope they arrive safely. They belong to a man [called . . .]r b. Salmūn, who entrusted them to me at his own risk.[13] Also a bundle of hammered copper, belonging to [a Muslim] man from the Maghreb, called Abū Bakr Ibn Rizq Allah.[14] Two other bundles, on one is written Abraham, on the other M[. . .]. I agreed with the shipowner that he would transport the goods to their destination. I wish my brother Abū Naṣr[15]—may God preserve him—to take care of all the goods and carry them to his place until I shall arrive, if God wills.

Please sell the tin for me at whatever price God may grant and

[6] See no. 13, n. 7, above.

[7] Ar. *fajar* (cf. Dozy, *Supplément*, II, 242*b*), a common item in both the Mediterranean and the Indian trade. The opposite is *qaḍīb*, copper in large bars. See no. 43, n. 13, below (in Aden).

[8] A sailor, mentioned also below and in other letters. On Arab, as on Byzantine, boats sailors had the right to engage in the transport business on their own.

[9] A North African Jewish family name often found in the Geniza and still widely diffused. See Goitein, *Studies*, pp. 336-337.

[10] The captain of another Nile boat. See below.

[11] The shipload, *'idl*, comprised at that time about 300 pounds (see *Med. Soc.*, I, 335). Thus, Ibn 'Awkal's share was about one-sixth of the partnership.

[12] I.e., of al-Mahdiyya. Appears often in contemporary letters.

[13] Ar. *risāla.* About this term see *Med. Soc.*, I, 183-184.

[14] Typical Muslim names. Abū Bakr was the name of the first caliph.

[15] No doubt, this is Ibn 'Awkal's son-in-law, whose wife was older than her three brothers, for whenever they are mentioned together, greetings are extended to him prior to them. My suggestion (*Tarbiz* 36 [1967], 368) that this might have been Abū Naṣr Tustarī, the brother of Abū Sa'd (see no. 11, introduction, above), mentioned often in business letters, is, of course, only an educated guess.

leave its "purse" (the money received for it) until my arrival. I am ready to travel, but must stay until I can unload the tar and oil from the ships.[16]

I have no doubt that you have sent me a letter containing all the quotations.

I have learned that the government has seized the oil[17] and that Ibn al-Naffāṭ[18] has taken the payment upon himself. I hope that this is indeed the case. Please take care of this matter and take from him the price of five skins (filled with oil). The account is with Salāma.[19]

Al-Ṣabbāgh[20] of Tripoli has bribed Bu 'l-'Alā the agent, and I shall unload my goods soon.

Kindest regards to your noble self and to my master [. . .[21] and] Abu 'l-Faḍl, may God keep them.

(P.S.) Abu 'l-Faraj Marwān[22] sends you kindest regards and says to you: "I have with Alī Ibn Jubār[23] two baskets with liquid storax (?).[24] I ask you, my lord—may God protect you—to order one of your boys to receive them and [to transpor]t them to Abū Ja'far Ibn al-Mudallal,[25] the agent. I have not fixed the freight with him,[26] except that he would charge me what he charges others.

The textiles were taken by Ben Sārā,[27] for he . . . [. . .] and said

[16] The government had reserved for itself the right to buy these first. See below.

[17] Which arrived in Fustat.

[18] About this name see *Med. Soc.*, I, 85.

[19] See n. 12, above. This oil had been sent to Fustat on an earlier occasion.

[20] "The Dyer," a family name. The government agent would look the other way while the merchants would unload oil, tar, and other goods held back by the authorities. Although the merchants were recompensed for goods seized by the government, prices on the free market were higher.

[21] No doubt Abū Naṣr was greeted here. See no. 15, above.

[22] This name of two Umayyad caliphs was borne by many Jews in the eleventh century. Abu 'l-Faraj Marwān occurs also in other letters, e.g. no. 22, n. 27, and no. 41, n. 13, below.

[23] See no. 4, above.

[24] Ar. *sayyāla*, frequently mentioned in the Geniza, but not in the Ar. dictionaries. I take it as an abbreviation of *may'a sā'ila*, liquid storax, a plant used in medicine and perfumery, and a great article of export to the countries of the Indian Ocean.

[25] "The spoiled child," meaning: the one beloved excessively.

[26] With the captain of the boat. Freight was often paid after arrival.

[27] For *Ben 'Ayin Ṣārā*, "The man with the narrow eye," i.e., miserly. (This writer, as other Maghrebis, often writes *s* for *ṣ*); a Heb. nickname, occurring

to me: "I shall take care of the cost of the transport"—the soul knows what is in it.

Isma'īl Ibn Abī 'Uqba[28] greets you and asks you to receive a shipload of wax for him. It is in the boat of Abū Zayd and a quarter dinar has to be paid for its transport. It was loaded by Khallūf. "Ibn al-Shāma,"[29] and "Joseph b. Isrā'il b. Bānūqa"[30] are written on it. Give it (for sale) to any agent you see fit.

And peace upon you, may God preserve you.

(P.S., by the copyist:)[31] And I, Daniel Ibn al-Shāma, greet my lord and his boys—may God protect you.

(There follow two, mostly effaced, lines in another hand, presumably that of the sender of the letter. Then the first script resumes.)

Isma'īl Ibn Abī 'Uqba has a shipload of corals with Banāna, the sailor.

You also have four (?) *barqalūs*[32] of wax with Ibn Jubār.

(Another line and a short marginal note, both in the second script and mostly illegible, follow here.)

(Address:)

(To) my elder and master Abu 'l-Faraj, may God protect him, Joseph, son of Jacob Ibn 'Awkal.[33]

From his old friend[34] Abraham, son of Joseph, (may his) s(oul be at) r(est).

---

also in other letters. The purport of the only partly preserved passage: the man knew very well why he made such a generous offer.

[28] A son of Ibn 'Awkal's sister and in close business connection with his uncle.

[29] Not necessarily identical with the man from the Ibn al-Shāma family mentioned presently.

[30] Several members of this family were active in the Spanish and North African trade.

[31] It was common practice for merchants with bad handwriting, while on travel, to ask a business friend (sometimes a very distinguished one) to copy a letter. The writer, who would usually also know the recipient, would add his own greetings at the end.

[32] A shipload of smaller size than the *'idl*. See *Med. Soc.*, I, 335.

[33] See no. 11, n. 37, above.

[34] A weak rendering of Ar. *mu'attaq wuddih*, meaning: my love, like old wine, becomes ever stronger with age. I am inclined, however, to assume that the writer omitted a *d* (read: *mu'taqid*), "the one bound by the love of you," as in the contemporary letter TS Box K 6, f. 189.

15-16 LETTERS OF A COMMUTER

The Geniza has preserved at least seven letters, all addressed to Yūsuf b. Da'ūd b. Sha'ya (Joseph b. David, member of the prominent Isaiah family), by Mūsā b. Ya'qūb (Moses b. Jacob), called al-Miṣri, that is, "from Fustat." His family lived in that city, but being constantly on travel to Damascus, Tyre, Ramle, and the towns of Lower Egypt, he received this byname from his business friends abroad.

As was usual, Mūsā traded in many products of Syria-Lebanon, such as rose marmalade (a popular preserve), dried fruit (a great article of import to Egypt), oil, medical plants, and money coined in Syria-Lebanon. But the staple item exported by him from Damascus was paper. In a letter written from Tyre, Lebanon, in a year different from that in which the two letters translated here were dispatched, he acknowledges with satisfaction that the addressee had already sold in Egypt ten bales of the paper sent.[1] Here we read about twenty-eight camel loads (approximately 14,000 pounds), the mere transport of which cost 157.5 dinars, having a purchasing power of about $15,000.

The letters translated here were probably written in the third or fourth decade of the eleventh century.[2]

15 FROM DAMASCUS TO FUSTAT

University Library, Cambridge, Taylor-Schechter Collection, TS 13 J 15, f. 5.

I am writing—may God prolong the life of my lord, the elder, and make his honored position and prosperity permanent—from Damas-

[1] TS 13 J 17, f. 6, l. 5. Bale: *shikāra.*

[2] The approximate dating of the letter is based on these considerations: Ibrāhīm b. Da'ūd b. Sighmār, a letter to whom, enclosed in TS 13 J 17, f. 6 (see preceding note), is referred to in no. 17, below (1041-1042), and signed (TS 13 J 1, f. 12) in 1049. "The year of the plague," mentioned in TS 13 J 17, f. 6, refers perhaps to 1036, when the caliph al-Ẓāhir died of the plague. There were also plagues in the 1050s and 1060s. See Lane-Poole, *History of Egypt*, pp. 136, 143, 146.

cus on the second of Jumādā II.[3] I am well and prosperous, but God alone decrees.

I have written you before and informed you that I have issued two bills of exchange on your account to the amount of 250 dinars and given them[4] to Ibn Ḥazūr as a prepayment on paper with the trademark of Ibn Imām.[5]

Last week I turned over ten camel loads to Salāma b. Jaysh,[6] and today I shall turn over five loads to him, and I hope to send with him also the rest which God, the exalted, will enable me to buy.

The Illustrious Elder[7] instructed me to write you, my lord, and to ask you to buy sixty golden boxes of the best quality that can be had, without break / / (above the line) and without break / /,[8] only topnotch quality. Pack them in leather bottles and send them immediately with a warship,[9] with whomever God may let you find, to Ibn Abī Ḥaffāz.[10] Write me the price and also who will carry them. The matter is urgent.

I have also asked you to buy me a container with linseed oil[11] for any price and to send it as early as possible on a warship. You will oblige me very much if you favor me with carrying out these orders without delay and send me your letters continuously.

[3] See no. 16, n. 1, below.

[4] Ar. *dafa'tuh*. Such slips are common with this writer.

[5] Not a watermark in the paper (which is a later invention). It is likely, however, that the name of the manufacturer was stamped on a fly-leaf pasted to the beginning of each roll of paper, similar to the protocol-sheet that preceded all papyrus rolls. About the protocol (which simply means "first sheet glued to the role") see Grohmann, *World of Arabic Papyri*, pp. 32-42.

[6] The camel driver, i.e., head of the caravan (see next letter). The name Jaysh ("army") was already pre-Islamic.

[7] A notable, referred to by this honorific title.

[8] Ar. *maqṭa'*, or *muqaṭṭa'*. While making this repetitious addition the writer thought he had written something else before.

[9] About sending goods with a warship see no. 17, below.

[10] A representative of merchants in Tyre, Lebanon (see next letter). The boxes were to be sent by boat from Egypt to Tyre and from there overland to Damascus.

[11] Ar. *zayt bizr* (see *Med. Soc.*, I, 426, n. 28). Ar. *ẓarf* is a general word for container, but in the Mediterranean oil trade of the eleventh century it seems to have designated a (goat's) skin of standardized size.

Also inform me about the price of ox tongue.[12] I have sent the cover.[13]

And may your welfare increase.

(P.S.) I ask my lord to sell the containers with rose marmalade one by one.[14] By God, do not tarry.

(Address in Ar. characters:)
(To) my lord, the elder Abu 'l-'Alā Yūsuf b. Dā'ūd b. Sha'yā.
(From) one grateful for his favors, may I never be deprived of him.[15]
(To) Fustat, if God wills.
(Note of the forwarding mail agency:)
(To) al-Ḥusayn b. Ṭāhir.
(From) al-Ḥasan b. Muḥammad b. Ẓabyān.[16]

[12] This medical plant often appears in prescriptions, e.g., *Med. Soc.*, II, 267, 583, n. 37.

[13] Ar. *ghaṭā'*, of a vessel, certainly manufactured in Damascus, wherefore the cover to be replaced was ordered from there.

[14] In the letter cited in n. 1 mention was made that the rose marmalade could not be sold in Fustat wholesale.

[15] To remain anonymous was a sign of intimate friendship. The handwriting of Mūsā b. Ya'qūb is absolutely unmistakable. He writes his name in TS 13 J 18, f. 16, and 13 J 23, f. 6. His namesake and younger contemporary Moses b. Jacob, who wrote four letters to Nahray b. Nissim in a most beautiful hand, is not identical with him, as is proved by the content and tenor of these letters. (The script is not decisive here, because the Nahray letters were all sent from Jerusalem, where the sender might have used the services of a copyist. But of the letters of Mūsā b. Ya'qūb, two were written in Damascus, two in Tyre, and three in various Egyptian localities, and all are identical in handwriting, style, and personal touch.)

[16] See *Med. Soc.*, I, 293; Ẓabyān is spelled with *ḍ* = *ẓ*.

16 FROM TYRE, LEBANON

University Library, Cambridge, University Library Collection, ULC Or 1080 J 42

A. After arrival in Tyre, the paper was taken over by the representative of the merchants

I am writing to you, my lord, the elder—may God prolong your life and make your honored position and prosperity permanent—from Tyre on Dhu 'l-Qa'da 16.[1] I am well, praise to God alone.

I hope my letters have arrived and that you have read them. I informed you about what I had sent with Salāma b. Jaysh[2] and what I paid for the transport, namely 5 1/2 dinars per camel load, plus payments to the guard, 1/8 dinar per camel load. You are not unfamiliar with the security situation in Damascus and the whole of Syria.

When, by God's favor—may he be glorified—the camel driver arrived in Tyre, he was induced by Abu 'l-A'lā Ibn Abī Ḥaffāz to unload the paper, for the latter wished to get hold of his partnerships,[3] take the paper, and forward it on his own. A man from Aleppo, called Abū Muḥammad the Aleppan, traveled in the caravan with goods of the size of your partnership consignment—I do not know the exact number of the camel loads, but I have no doubt that he paid the same freight as I did, namely 5 1/2 dinars per load. He, too, left them in Tyre.

My lords, the elders in Damascus,[4] received a letter from my master Abu 'l-A'lā, the agent, informing them that he had received from Salāma b. Jaysh 15 dinars.[5] He had carried twenty-eight camel loads for us, seven for the partnership with Abū Naṣr, and twenty-one loads for our partnership. I wrote you, my lord, may God preserve your honored position, to get hold of Salāma b. Jaysh and sue him

[1] Five and a half months after the preceding letter.

[2] No. 5, n. 6, above.

[3] This representative of the merchants had a share in some of the paper sent from Damascus and intended to sell part of it in Tyre. See below.

[4] Those who had sent paper to Egypt in the caravan and had paid the entire or the major part of the freight.

[5] This was, of course, only a small fraction of the sums paid for the transport to Egypt.

for the balance. My lord, the elder Abu l-Ḥusayn[6] also wrote a number of letters to my lord and master Abū Naṣr.[7]

B. Defense against false allegations

When, however, I arrived in Tyre, two letters from my master Abu Naṣr Ṣadaqa arrived there which put me and him to shame. He writes that I had informed him that I had paid a freight of 4 1/2 dinars per load to Sālamah b. Jaysh. In another letter he says: "I know that the camel driver paid the entire freight due from him in Tyre." And this after I had written to him every week to get together with you, my lord, and to cooperate in suing the camel driver. Nothing has come out of this. He should have asked the camel drivers, he should have asked you, my lord, for how much his partnership consignment was transported, and then, if it was established that I had given too high a price, then let him suspect me.

Such behavior evinces little intelligence and piety. But nothing can be done. Everything is foreordained.

I paid to Salāma b. Jaysh 5 1/2 dinars per load for freight; to Tammām, 6; and to ʿAlā, the camel driver, 6.[8] He should have asked the camel drivers and the merchants about the freight before writing and casting suspicions.

On this very day a letter of his arrived to my master Abu 'l-Aʿlā Ibn Abī Ḥaffāẓ, in which he says: "Mūsā b. Yaʿqūb stays in Fustat for five years until he settles accounts with his partners and lists the purchase of merchandise belonging to them in Tyre thirty times, but he does not have money."

This is the talk of an irresponsible[9] person. If possible, please meet him and explain to him what is proper. Also, please sue the camel driver for the balance and be circumspect and exert yourself to sell

[6] One of the elders of Damascus referred to above. See nn. 4 and 11.

[7] While the kunya Abū Naṣr is extremely frequent, the combination Abū Naṣr Ṣadaqa has been noted by me only once: a man called thus and bearing the family name Shāmī (from Damascus or Syria in general) carried a letter from Qayrawān to Cairo in 1022. See Mann, *Texts*, I, 143, l. 13; S. D. Goitein, *Tarbiz* 36 (1967), 369.

[8] He wishes to stress that on earlier occasions the freight was even higher. The abbreviation *al-q.* cannot mean, as usual, *al-qinṭār* (100 pounds), since the average of a camel load was 500 pounds. It stands probably for *al-qīma*, "the price."

[9] Ar. *ghayr muḥassil*, intended to mean perhaps: who does not grasp things.

what I have sent either for our partnership or on my personal account, for, after my arrival in Fustat, I shall stay only a short time, if God wills. You will put me greatly in your debt by this and earn my thanks and good prayers. And act immediately.

C. Various business notes

A little over twenty bales of paper from a partnership of mine had remained in Tyre. I sent them to Ramle, and they have arrived there safely. I also have sent fifteen bales from a partnership with you and shall, God willing, carry all the merchandise with me.[10]

Kindly inform me whether you have received a letter from my lord, the elder Abu 'l-Ḥusayn,[11] stating that the rose marmalade and the lubricating oil[12] are on my private account.

Also, let me know what God has granted you to sell. Write me a letter every week, and in Hebrew script, please.[13] If you have any order to make, please honor me with it. *And may your well-being wax.*

(P.S.) If it is difficult to sell the paper or anything else by weight, and you prefer to sell it at retail,[14] do whatever your propitious judgment suggests to you. But, God willing, act without procrastination.

Kindly inform me, my lord, about the price of Nizāriyya *money*[15] coined in Damascus, for a friend gave me some to sell on my journey.

[10] These bales (the word indicates that the consignments were sent by boat) had remained in Tyre unsold. On his way to Egypt, the writer would first try to sell some of them in Ramle, Palestine.

[11] Of Damascus, see n. 4, above.

[12] Ar. *duhn,* oil used for ointments, painting, etc.

[13] Mūsā, as a widely traveled merchant, certainly knew Arabic script. But since the clerks writing Arabic often regarded illegibility as an expression of refinement, he preferred Hebrew script, which lends itself less to ambiguity than does Arabic, especially when the latter was written, as was customary, without diacritical marks.

[14] Ar. *bil-takhrīj,* lit., "by taking out," as opposed to "by weight," that is, selling entire bales or packages. In *Tarbiz* 37 (1968), 179 I was unable to explain the term (as found in ENA 3793, f. 7, l. 5), because, unlike here, it did not occur in an explanatory context.

[15] The Heb. word used here, *kesāfīm,* means lit., "silver pieces." But I learned from G. C. Miles that Nizār, that is, the Fatimid Caliph al-'Azīz (975-996), coined only gold in Damascus. The writer of our letter inquires about prices in Fustat in order to decide whether he should sell in Tyre, or Ramle, or wait until he came home.

Also the price of the rose marmalade.

My master Abu 'l-Barakāt al-Sharābī, who has lapis lazuli here in Tyre, has five loads of (dried) plums,[16] which find no buyer, in Acre. If plums have a good price (in Fustat), write me if he prefers to transport by land, in which case it will cost first 2 (dinars) per load from Acre to Ramle by sea and the total price to Fustat will come to 5 dinars, more or less. Kindly inform me what I shall do in this matter.

God alone suffices me.[17]

(Address in Arabic characters: same as in no. 15)
(Note of postal agency:)
(From) Najā al-Anṣārī
(To) 'Alī b. Muḥammad and his two sons Muḥammad and Ḥusayn
Please answer immediately.

17 PUBLIC APPEAL OF A MERCHANT

1041-1042

This piece is not a letter, but a speech, an appeal made to the rabbinical court of Fustat. But it contains all one expects from a good business letter: rich information on the movement of goods and a strong personal note, introducing us directly to the parties involved.

The plaintiff, Abu 'l-Faraj Jacob Ibn 'Allān, was a big merchant for his time—judging by the volume and value of his consignments

[16] Ar. *khawkh*, which is "peaches" in Egypt and "plums" in Syria-Lebanon. In *Med. Soc.*, I, 427, n. 3a I took it as "peaches," since our writer hails from Egypt. But I now prefer "plums," simply because dried plums (prunes) are common, while peaches are not, and our letter is written in Lebanon.

The proprietor was called *Sharābī*, seller of potions; he dealt in lapis lazuli, a half-precious stone serving as an ornament and also for medical purposes. But here he meddled in the difficult fruit trade—and without much success, it seems.

[17] This quotation from the Koran (e.g., 9:129) is occasionally found at the end of a letter.

—but he was unable to prevail against the powerful Majjānīs[1] of al-Mahdiyya, Tunisia, with whom he had many dealings. The Geniza has preserved a letter of the younger al-Majjānī (translated in no. 18, below), which refers to our lawsuit and which indeed throws an unfavorable light on its writer. On the other hand, the remark ascribed in that letter to the Nagid, or head of the Tunisian Jews, to the effect that our Ibn 'Allān was well known as an excitable person, prone to make appeals to the public, is borne out by our document. It is noteworthy that both the plaintiff here and Majjānī in his letter express the highest regard for, and their full confidence in, the integrity and justice of the Nagid and of the chief Jewish judge of Qayrawān, R. Hananel, who was also a famous scholar and author.

Our document—a long sheet containing 120 lines—is but the first leaf of a draft (in the hand of the court clerk Japheth b. David b. Shekhanya), with many words crossed out or added in the margin or between the lines. In addition, it is partly effaced and damaged by holes. Unlike other documents of this kind, which are either in Hebrew or in Arabic, this draft, at least in its first part, is a strange mixture of both languages. This probably represents the plaintiff's own use of words.

Bodleian Library, Oxford, MS Heb. a 3 (Cat. 2873), f. 26.

A. Address by the Plaintiff, Justifying his Renewed Appeal

This happened in our presence, we, the permanent court of Fustat, and the elders signing at the bottom, on the [ ][2] *day of the month of* [ ], *in the year 1353 of the era according to which we are accustomed to count in Fustat, Egypt, which is situated on the Nile River: Jacob, bynamed* Abu 'l-Faraj, *son of Abraham* Ibn 'Allān, *appeared before us and made the following appeal:*

"My lords. You remember well that I have appealed to you various

[1] A family name, derived from Majjāna, a town five days inland from Qayrawān, famous for its saffron. See no. 1, sec. F, no. 13, n. 7, no. 14, n. 6, above.

[2] The space for the day and the month was not filled in, so that the rough copy could not be used as a real document.

times against M. Yiḥye, son of Moses, Ibn al-Majjānī,[3] *who wronged me and robbed me of my money, not fearing God.* I appealed to you, as it is proper for *a Jewish man to appeal to the judges of the house of Israel and to the communities of Israel* to obtain redress of his long-standing grievances. I proved to you the injury done to me by this Yiḥye *with well-confirmed documents* and honest witnesses and asked you to kindly forward your findings to Qayrawān for the information of *the court of the h(onored), g(reat), and h(oly) M(aster) and T(eacher) Hananel, the Rav—(may the) All (merciful) p(reserve him)—and of . . . Jacob, the Nagid of the Diaspora . . .* (other titles). For I know their piety and *zeal for the cause of God,* and their custom—proved by experience—*of saving the oppressed from his oppressor, for Heaven's sake only.* Everyone knows that they do not show *partiality to any man, but fulfill the commandment which says: you shall hear the small as well as the great, you shall not be afraid of anyone.*[4]

"I had also thought that this Yiḥye would reconsider the affair and return to the right way . . . so that I would not be forced to make known his doings to *the communities of Israel in east and west,* and in particular to the community of Jerusalem[5] and the head of the high council there. I had hoped that he would spare me from disclosing my situation in *the meetings of the gentiles and to their judges.* You acceded to my request and wrote down your findings, and I dispatched them.

"When, however, the couriers arrived in recent days carrying with them the letters of this Yiḥye, I realized that he has not reformed, but persists in injuring me and argues that I am mistaken . . . Therefore, I have asked you—may God keep you—to make good your promise, to convene the court, so that I may be able to repeat my claims before you. Examine my proofs and draw up a document stating all that is to be established in court on the basis of *witnesses and documents,* so that I shall obtain my rights and *you will receive*

[3] In the margin there is an addition, legible only in part, to the effect that the complaint also involved the opponent's father.

[4] Deuteronomy 1:17.

[5] It was not so much the holiness of Jerusalem as the fact that almost every Jewish community in the world had its representatives there, which made an appeal to the public in that town particularly effective.

a reward from Heaven. I want to have several copies, so that I can send them both by land and by sea."

B. General Complaint About the Conduct of the Younger al-Majjānī, Including One Complaint Concerning a Former Partnership

Having heard M. Jacob's words, we acceded to his request, and he continued as follows. I have previously explained to you what this Yiḥye, son of Moses al-[Majjānī], has done to me. He sent me letters containing an account of my assets with him; however, when I filed a suit against him, demanding the payment of these assets, he sent me another account, different from the first, by which he misled my representative at the court of the Nagid of the Diaspora—a behavior which is indeed unworthy of a man adhering to the law of the Torah. He also influenced the man in charge of weighing in an illicit way . . . I have many claims against him, including one concerning a former partnership in a consignment of 160 bales of flax.[6] This time, however, I wish to confine myself to my claims in connection with his father, may God have mercy upon him.

C. Dealings with Majjānī, Sr.

First, there is a balance of an account which, according to his statement, amounted to 142 dinars. Then, in the year 429 of the era of the Arabs,[7] I sent him in the warship[8] sugar, sal ammoniac, nutmeg paste, nutmeg, violet blossoms,[9] rose marmalade, and . . . In the same year, in the Sheikhi[10] ship, which was bound for Tripoli,

[6] The scribe first wrote 120, which he later changed to 160, without striking out the first number. This was a very large transaction. As we know from other Geniza papers, a bale of flax would fetch between 150 and 250 dinars.

[7] The year 429 of the Muslim era began on October 14, 1037. Thus, the consignments referred to were sent four years prior to this lawsuit.

[8] Ar. *al-ḥarbī.* See Dozy, *Supplément,* I, 265*a*, and cf. ENA 2712, f. 17, an account containing the date 1059, *ḥarbī al-Mahdiyya* (twice); TS 16.244, l. 21 (here *markab al-ḥarbī*), and no. 15, n. 9, above. The goods were sent from Egypt in a warship because of the Byzantine naval attack on Sicily in 1038. See no. 18, introduction, below.

[9] An oil or ointment prepared from violet blossoms.

[10] Probably referring to the elders of the city of Palermo, known as Sheikhs, who took over control of their city at that time of the disintegration of the Muslim rule in Sicily (see Amari, *Musulmani di Sicilia,* II, 483).

but changed its course to al-Mahdiyya, I sent twenty-three bags of flax. There was another consignment, carried by Abū Isḥāq, in the ship of the Kuy (Pelican),[11] which also changed its course from Tripoli to al-Mahdiyya. This consignment, too, was delivered to him and I received letters, confirming that everything had arrived, namely brazilwood, "gazelle's dung,"[12] mastic, rose marmalade, violet blossoms, and other goods. I also received letters from him saying that he had sold everything and received its price, which was, after the deduction of the expenses, 37,428 3/4 pieces of silver and 15 1/2 gold dinars.

D. Goods Sent From Tunisia by Majjānī, Sr.

For this merchandise he bought and sent, in three bales, 200 brocade robes; 200 slips; a little over 50 mann of saffron (about 100 pounds); 3 1/3 qinṭārs of mercury; 264 pounds of cast copper; a crucible for melting copper, weighing 13 pounds; eleven cloaks (*kisā*); furthermore: 70 qinṭārs of antimony and a little over 20 qinṭārs of copper.[13]

All this was specified in his letters and in the account received by me, which I have asked you to examine and to validate by witnesses. The total value of the goods bought for me by the late Moses b. Yiḥye for the price of the goods sent to him by me, after the deduction of the expenses—forwarded in the three bales, as said before—was 37,115 1/2 dirhems and 160 gold dinars less 2 qīrāṭs.[14]

[11] Dozy, *Supplément*, II, 503*b*. Nickname, or a pelican was painted on the ship.

[12] Gazelle's dung boiled in vinegar was reputed to reduce the swelling when put on an edema (*Ibn al-Bayṭār*, trans. J. V. Sontheimer, Stuttgart, 1842, p. 237). But there was no need of importing it into Tunisia, where gazelles abounded. Therefore, "gazelle's dung" here must be the trade name of an Oriental product derived from its appearance.

[13] As this copper bears no other designation, it might have been hammered copper, as opposed to cast copper mentioned before. See no. 14, above.

[14] Thus, there remained a balance of 313 1/4 dirhems in favor of the plaintiff and of 2 10/24 dinars ((160 + 2/24) − (142 + 15 12/24)) in favor of Majjānī, Sr., which means that only about 5 or 6 dinars were owed by Majjānī. Such comparatively small sums were not paid in cash, but carried over to the following year's transactions.

E. Five Other Consignments, Sent From Various Ports, Some of Which Arrived in al-Mahdiyya after the death of Majjānī, Sr.

Then in the year 430 (began on October 3, 1038), I sent to the address of Moses b. Yiḥye al-Majjānī these consignments:

From Tripoli (Lebanon): Sixty-five pots of rose marmalade and two bales of lac.

From Alexandria: A wickerwork basket of sal ammoniac, in which was also a bag with mace; 12 qinṭārs of cotton; half a bale of lac, weighing 4 (qinṭārs) and some pounds, on my own account and the other half on account of my brother Abu Kathīr; three bales of yellow myrobalan, in one of which were flasks of musk;[15] thirteen bales of bandage flax, while Abu Is(māʿīl) took delivery of another two.

From Barqa, in the ship of Jabbāra:[16] fifteen bags of flax.

From Tripoli (Lebanon), carried by Abraham b. Isaac al-Qābisī:[17] five bags of flax.

Likewise from Tripoli: three bags of rose marmalade.

In the same year, namely 430, I sent from Syria, in partnership with Ibn al-Hītī:[18] seven mantles[19] made of cotton; two bales of tragacanth gum; one piece of sarcocol.

All these shipments arrived safely in al-Mahdiyya—thank God—after the decease of the aforementioned Moses. His son Yiḥye took delivery of them and sent them abroad with ʿAllūsh al-Majjānī who took care of their sale. Therefore, I claim from him the price of all of them in their entirety. First I claim the payments due to me from the transactions of the late Moses b. Yiḥye Majjānī, for I have letters from his son Yiḥye, announcing his father's death and specifying what the latter had bought for the money obtained from the

[15] Musk, a very expensive perfume, was traded in flasks or in little boxes. The word used here: *swk* is perhaps the Persian *sok* "ear of grain," or small flask. For myrobalan, a popular medical plant, see *Med. Soc.*, II, 367-368.

[16] The notorious pirate. See *Med. Soc.*, I, 327-328.

[17] A family name derived from the town of Gabes in Tunisia.

[18] A family name derived from Hīt, a town on the Euphrates in Western Iraq.

[19] The rare word *hudūm* is used. See Dozy, *Supplément*, II, 570*b*.

sale of the bandage flax, mentioned before, which was sent to him in the year (430).[20]

F. ATTESTATION BY WITNESSES THAT THE LETTERS FROM THE MAJJĀNĪS, PRODUCED IN COURT BY THE PLAINTIFF, WERE GENUINE

(In this section, which is only partly preserved, the plaintiff produces three letters, written in Arabic characters and dated according to the Muslim calendar. Four Tunisian merchants, known from other Geniza papers to have been active in Egypt at that time, testify that the handwriting of the first two was that of a person—according to his name, a Jew—who used to do the elder Majjānī's Arabic correspondence with the merchants. One of the four gives similar testimony concerning a third letter, also written in Arabic characters and dated according to the Muslim calendar, which was copied by another Jewish person for the younger Majjānī. In the last preserved line, reference is made to a fourth document produced by the plaintiff.)

18 IN HIS DISTRESS A MERCHANT TURNS TO HIS FORMER APPRENTICE AND PRESENT PARTNER FOR HELP

Ca. 1040

This letter is noteworthy both for the historical situation and for the personal circumstances which form its background. We are here in the years of the great Byzantine attack on Muslim Sicily, 1038-1042, which led to the fall of Syracuse, Messina, and other towns closely connected with the countries around the southeastern shores of the Mediterranean.[1] Because of the presence of the Byzantine navy the direct route on the high seas from Egypt to Tunisia

[20] Here there is a hole in the manuscript. Bandage flax was mentioned only in the consignment sent from Alexandria in the Muslim year 430.

[1] See Amari, *Musulmani di Sicilia*, II, 438-455.

was avoided, and merchants were generally reluctant to travel at all. The writer of our letter expresses the hope that at least the route through Barqa, Libya, could be used.

The dire situation of the Mediterranean trade was aggravated for the writer by his own misfortune. His father, once the representative in Tunisia of the merchant prince Joseph Ibn 'Awkal (see no. 1, sec. F, above), seemingly had fallen on bad times and, after his death, the son Yaḥyā (Ar. for Heb. Yiḥye, both meaning "may he live") was publicly accused of malpractices (see the preceding selection). In his distress Yaḥyā turns to his former apprentice and present partner in Egypt for help. To the reader of his epistle it appears that he expects a little bit too much from him.

Bodleian Library, Oxford, MS Heb. a 2 (Cat. 2805), f. 17.

A. The Addressee's Marriage and Decision to Settle in Egypt

I am writing to you, my dear brother—may God prolong your life and make permanent your well-being and honored state—from al-Mahdiyya, ten days before the end of the month of Elul (August-September). I am safe and well, thank God.

During last winter, I did not get any letters from you. But we learned about the shipwreck of the Nile barges. This troubled my mind, and some people held back payments they owed me.[2] Yet I put my trust in God. Finally, a courier arrived from Alexandria this week with your letter, dated "the middle of Sivan" (May-June) with a report about you and your well-being—may God make it permanent.

You mentioned that you married into a fine family—may God make this the most auspicious of all times for you. I have no doubt that your parents died fully satisfied with you, as God has let you attain such status. Your decision was the right thing to do. For the whole (Muslim) West is not worth a thing these days. I hope that God will make this the happiest and most blessed of times for you.

[2] The merchants in Tunisia feared that valuable goods belonging to our writer were lost in the shipwreck and that, as a result, he would be unable to meet his commitments.

I was happy for you, and so were all the people to whom I told the news.

B. About Copper and Antimony Going East, and Lac and Odorous Wood Going West

You wrote about the loss of part of the copper—may God compensate me and you, then—about the blessed profit made from the antimony and, finally, about the lac and the odorous wood which you bought and loaded on Mi'ḍād and 'Abūr.[3] (You mentioned) that the bale on Mi'ḍād was unloaded afterwards; I have no doubt that the other will also be unloaded. I hope however, that there will be traffic on the Barqa route. Therefore, repack the bales into camel-loads—half their original size—and send them via Barqa. Perhaps I shall get a good price for them and acquire antimony with it this winter. For, dear brother, if the merchandise remains in Alexandria year after year, we shall make no profit.

Only small quantities of odorous wood are to be had here, and it is much in demand. Again, do not be remiss, but make an effort and send the goods on the Barqa route—may God inspire you and me and all Israel to do the right thing.

C. About Flax Sunk Near the Isle of Jerba, Tunisia, and Other Sunk in the Nile

I tried to retrieve the two bales of Buṣīrī (flax) sunk in Jerba. We did not find one of them. (The other)[4] I treated and improved with the result that I saved seven qinṭārs, which I sent to Bona.[5] But until now, brother, I have not received a grain of its price. Abu 'l-Faḍl b. Jāwid (?) will confirm this to you. The three bales which sank in the Nile contained very inferior flax, one qinṭār being worth 60 dirhems. In addition, whenever bad news comes, the losses in the flax become even greater.

[3] Names of ships—the first meaning "a butcher's knife," so called perhaps because of its quick cutting of the waves, and the second, sirius, or dog star, the brightest star in the sky.

[4] One or more words must be lacking here. The letter is a copy on vellum made by a clerk.

[5] An important seaport in Algeria.

D. Request from the Addressee to Deal with Allegedly Unjustified Claims Made Against the Writer

By God, brother, I tried to procure 50 dinars for you, in order to buy you skins (containing oil) and send them to you, but I could not get hold of any, for I am harassed on every side. After the death of the old man (his father)—God's mercy upon him—and your departure, I was accused of things of which I had no knowledge and with which I had nothing to do[6] and which I did not commit. My mind became distraught, and I wanted to leave this world. Finally, I submitted the matter to my lord, the Nagid—may God keep him alive—and found that he knew the facts, which strengthened my heart. Then a letter of the elder Abu 'l-Ṭayyib[7] arrived at the house of Abu 'l-Faḍl b. Faraḥ, containing a power of attorney to bring action against me. At that time, Abu 'l-Faḍl was in al-Mahdiyya, and the letter fell into the hands of his brother—(or son)-in-law, Barakāt, who showed it to everyone. The people became agitated and hostile to me, and whoever owed the old man anything conspired to keep it from me. The receiver of that power of attorney submitted it to my master, the dayyān (judge)—*may the All-merciful keep him*, who validated it, whereupon the people approached him, but he did not disappoint (me) and stopped the affair.

My lord, the Nagid, intended to address a letter to the elder Abu 'l-Faraj,[8] but finally, he had no opportunity to write to Fustat this year at all. Instead, he asked Isḥāq b. Ḥabīb to convey his message to him, and when the latter, after all, did not want to go up to Egypt, he said to him: "By no means need you go up only for this affair." He then gave a similar message to the elders Abū Naṣr and Abū Sa'd[9] and, finally, to Shemaryah Ibn al-Maḥāra[10] also. Please, brother, meet all these people; keep an eye on what is going

[6] Text: "which I have neither eaten nor drunk."

[7] A creditor of the addressee, living in Egypt, and sending the power of attorney to Qayrawān, Tunisia, where the events described here took place.

[8] The writer's chief opponent, Ibn 'Allān, who had applied to the Nagid of Tunisia. See the preceding selection.

[9] Although these names were common, it is likely that these were the famous Tustarī brothers (junior) of Cairo (see no. 2, above). Since our letter states that no one in al-Qayrawān was eager to go overseas that year, it is probable that the three named last were Egyptian merchants.

[10] Oyster, a family name, which, no doubt, originally was a nickname.

on and report back to me with every courier coming here. Likewise, assure them under oath, in my name, that I have nothing to do with any of their claims and do not know anything about them, except for a claim concerning a transaction made many years ago. Do this for me; there is no greater service than this. By God, brother, my only wish is to be cleared and to get rid of this; if they want to sue me, I shall honor (the decision of the court) and do what is imposed upon me, for my only wish is to be cleared. Nor do I wish to lay my hand on that consignment from Syria.[11] As a matter of fact, the Nagid—may God keep him—and Abu Sḥāq admonished me saying: "As far as you are concerned, do not commit any wrong in this matter. For the people know these matters and remember them, and this is not the first time that he[12] has acted in such a way." I hope that I shall not be forced to do anything of the kind.[13]

E. Misgivings about the Addressee's Vilification of the Tunisian Nagid

In a letter, received here from Ibn Sighmār,[14] he accuses you of vilifying my master, the Nagid, which distressed me very much. I really cannot believe that you are capable of besmirching the honor of a noble man in his absence. We are obligated to revere him and to revere all those who serve him, and certainly not to do the opposite.

F. Request to Pay a Debt in Exchange for Merchandise to be Sent in Newly Acquired Spanish Ships

You wrote about the Shīrajī's[15] claim of 100 dinars. I also received a letter from him and from Ibn Budayr ("Little full moon"), which

[11] See in the document translated in no. 17, above.

[12] Ibn 'Allān. See no. 17, above.

[13] Namely, to apply to a Muslim court or another Muslim authority.

[14] The most prominent Jewish family of al-Mahdiyya, many of whose members commuted to Egypt or settled there. Here, no doubt, the reference is to Abraham b. David Ibn Sighmar, mentioned in sec. F of our preceding selection (only summarized there) and many other documents written in Fustat during this period.

[15] Seller or maker of sesame oil; here a family name.

caused me anguish and took sleep away from my eyes. Had I ready money which I could collect and send him, I would not care. The trouble is, my brother, that I have none at present, for something strange happened this year: not a single grain I earned remained with me, but everything went back to the merchants completely and in full. Now you wrote that you earned 100 dinars unexpectedly, through a tip I gave you. Will you, then, pay those hundred dinars for me as recompense, which will spare me trouble, for I explained the situation to you and you understand the hint.

For my part, I shall send you merchandise in these new ships, and I hope that it will sell well and bring us relief. During the whole of last summer I was in Qayrawān to arrange for the dispatch of the consignments belonging to M. Abu 'l-Faraj (Ibn 'Allān) and found that no one wanted to undertake an overseas journey this year. These new Spanish ships, however, were bought by the merchants and loaded, and I and everyone else hope for God's blessing —may he grant relief to me and to them. Now, brother, mind our friendship and the education given to you by me, and the bread and salt we have eaten together, for it was for a time like this that I took you on. Therefore, be my proxy everywhere and reply to every detail in this letter. Deal discreetly with this affair of Ibn 'Allān, both in person and through your friends, so that he may not encroach upon me, and I hope my lord, the Nagid, will do the rest and provide me with his protection.

G. Conclusion

Please convey my best greetings to M. Abū Ghālib, your brother-in-law, for I know him and his paternal uncles and know what pious people they are. May God strengthen you through each other; you have indeed attained a fine status.

Kindest regards to you personally, and regards to those under your care, as well as to everyone asking about me.

(Address:)
To my brother and master Abu 'l-Khayr—may God prolong his life—the dear Zakariyyā, son of Tammām—*(may he) r(est in) E(den)*

May God be his protector.

From Yaḥyā, son of Mūsā—*(may his) s(oul rest in) p(eace)*—Majjānī

His . . .

19 AN ENCLOSURE ON BUSINESS IN JERUSALEM

About Middle of the Eleventh Century

The form of the paper—a long strip (7 x 2 inches), folded twice lengthwise—as well as the arrangement of the writing, indicate that the text does not represent part of a sheet, but was an enclosure attached to a letter—most probably one dealing with public affairs. Only a few of such small-sized enclosures have been preserved.

Jewish Theological Seminary of America, JTS Geniza Misc. 15.

You inquired about *silk*. Here, black and sky blue are mostly in demand, and, indeed, all colors. Crimson, however, does not sell in Jerusalem, but it might be sold in Ramle or in Ascalon. Corals are weak in Jerusalem, for it is a poor town. In any case, bring them or a part of them, for success is in the hand of God. If Persians happen to arrive, they may buy them. And Peace upon you.

(It is characteristic of the medieval predilection for variety [*Med. Soc.*, II, 237] that in this small note Jerusalem is first called by its more ancient name *Bayt al-maqdis* ["The Temple"] and later by the one still in use *Al-Quds* ["Sanctuary"]. Many Persians, Jewish as well as Muslim, visited in Jerusalem or even settled there.)

20 WEAVING, EMBROIDERING, AND BLEACHING OF A THOUSAND GARMENTS

Tyre-Jerusalem, Eleventh Century

Yarn sent from Jerusalem was worked by Jewish craftsmen in Tyre, Lebanon, into clothes. A report about such work is contained in the letter translated below, which is reproduced here in its entirety with the exception of the usual introductory and concluding phrases. The yarn probably was of cotton grown in Palestine.

Mosseri Collection L 39*b*, as from line 5.

In my previous letter I have informed you about the arrival of the yarn. I was not remiss with regard to it, but, immediately after its arrival, I delivered it to a trustworthy Jewish craftsman. Earlier, I showed it to various craftsmen, who told me that it would make a thousand robes of the bazaar type and slightly more of the home-made kind. Among the rolls of yarn, there were four spoiled ones which were coarse and deformed. I also gave him (to the weaver) two robes of the bazaar type, in accordance with your instructions.[1]

After each roll[2] is finished, the craftsman is to receive 3 quarter dinars. The embroidering will require 1/6 dinar and 1/2 qīrāṭ, and the bleaching and pounding, 5 qīrāṭs, the total (for a roll) being 1 1/8 Nizāriyya dinars. The material is with the craftsman up to the present time. He will present it this week. I shall inform you how much of the yarn went into the weaving and how much remained.

The bleaching will not be completed until after Passover. For it is now winter, and God does not make bleaching possible in winter time, when it would not be as brilliant as during the summer. Had you sent the yarn a month before the (autumn) holidays, the whole work would have been easily completed in a short time.

21 PALESTINE'S IMPORTS AND EXPORTS

Middle of Eleventh Century

As in the previous letter we read here about yarn sent from Jerusalem, but this time processed in the city itself. In addition, mention is made of two other main products of the country in

[1] The clothes were given either as a model or as a present.

[2] Text: *maslak*, found in this sense also in other Geniza texts, e.g., TS 13 J 22, f. 30, l. 20-22; 10 J 7, f. 1, l. 21.

those days: oil and apples (see *Med. Soc.*, I, 121). Money in the form of donations and the main fabrics of the period: silk (see no. 19, above), flax, and Ṭabaristan brocade, reexported to Egypt (see below) were the main imports. A Christian moneylender is mentioned. In other Geniza letters from Jerusalem the Jews borrow from Muslims.

The sender, being in the Holy City and occupying himself with the pious work of support for its main religious institution, here uses the Hebrew form of his name. Details about him are given in the next selection. The clerk who copied the letter had a clear handwriting, but made many mistakes. The introductory phrases are omitted in our translation.

University Library, Cambridge, Taylor-Schechter Collection,
TS Misc. Box 28, f. 199.

I am writing to you . . . from Jerusalem on the 5th of Adar II (mostly February) . . . You instructed me to pay 1 dinar to our lord, the Head (of the yeshiva), one-half to our lord, the president of the court, and one-quarter to the Third.[1] I have done as you advised me, paying a total of 1 3/4 dinars. I also took a receipt for 15 dinars of full value from the Fourth, and also one for a dinar from the cantor Mūsā (Moses).[2] The receipts are enclosed, please pass them on to the donors.

I have already informed you that I bought you olive oil in two containers and sent them with Ibn al-Tuffāḥī[3] to Jaffa. I also bought the yarn and had it processed according to your instructions.

I have also written to you that, at the time of my travel from Ramle to Jerusalem, only four bags of the flax held in partnership[4]

[1] The yeshiva, or Jewish high council, of Jerusalem, was composed of seven members, the Gaon, or president, the chief judge of the high court, and five others, styled the Third, the Fourth, etc. Here the Fourth acted as cashier for the yeshiva. The reference is probably to Abraham, the son of the Gaon Solomon b. Judah (d. 1051), who was "Fourth" and in charge of the financial affairs of the yeshiva.

[2] The donor certainly had asked that prayers for the soul of a deceased relative should be said in Jerusalem. This explains why a cantor received the same special gift as did the head of the yeshiva.

[3] Wholesale trader in apples. From Jaffa the oil would be transported to Egypt by boat.

[4] Ar. *al-bāba,* "of that sort," as opposed to *al-ḳhaṣṣa.*

had remained unsold, and of the flax belonging to you personally—five bags. I have asked M. Abu 'l-Faraj, son of Salmān's[5] sister, to take care of this in my place if he happens to find a customer for this. He asked me to request you to kindly go to ʿAbdallāh al-Malaṭī[6] and ask him whether two bags with Ṭabarī cloth[7] which he had sent him have arrived safely. Take a letter from him and enclose it with your answer to me . . .

Give my regards to M. Abū Manṣūr b. Shuʿayb[8] . . . and inform him that Ibn Zurjiz (George) says: "He is making fun of me. He has not paid me a thing." Yes, this is what he said: "Ibn Shuʿayb has not paid me a thing." Please let me know which loan you have accepted from him.

Give my regards to Abū Saʿūd[9] b. Levi . . . and tell him that I am grateful to him.

May your well-being wax forever.

(Address:)

To my master and lord, Abū Jacob (!) Joseph, son of Nahum, *(may his) s(oul) r(est in peace).*

From Jacob, son of Samuel al-Andalusī, *(may his) s(oul) r(est in peace).*

To Miṣr, if God wills.

[5] A representative of merchants in Ramle; so called because he had apprenticed with his uncle Salmān.

[6] Misspelled *'l-'lmṭy.* From Malatia in Asia Minor.

[7] Presumably genuine Ṭabari(stān) fabric, imported from Iran and re-exported to Egypt.

[8] Mentioned twice in TS 8 J 38, f. 7, l. 1, and *verso,* l. 7, ed. E. Ashtor, *Braslavi Jubilee Volume* (Jerusalem, 1970), p. 482. The letter is in the hand of Israel b. Nathan, the same man who wrote the letter from Jerusalem to our Jacob b. Samuel. See next selection, n. 3.

[9] A rare name in those days with both Muslims and Jews.

22 A FAMILY PARTNERSHIP AT WORK

A Letter from Palermo, Sicily
Middle of Eleventh Century

Two Spanish merchants, brothers-in-law, had moved eastward during the early years of the turbulent eleventh century, one settling in the Muslim Middle West (Sicily-Tunisia) and one in Egypt. In a very detailed letter[1] Isma'īl, the father of the writer of our letter, Ya'qūb b. Isma'īl (Jacob b. Samuel), addresses his sister's son, Yūsha' (Joshua) b. Nathan, but refers all the time to the transactions of the "old man," his brother-in-law, who at that moment must have been traveling. Among many other things he mentions that he had a fine son who was entirely to the taste of the addressee and his father, and if the latter agreed, he would send the boy to serve as an apprentice in their firm. Whether this referred to the writer of our letter or to one of his two brothers (see below) cannot be made out.

By the time of our letter, in which Ya'qūb addresses his cousin Yūsha', both old men were dead. Here, Ya'qūb suggests that his own son and that of the addressee should start a partnership and thus continue the tradition of their grandfathers.

Besides the letter translated below we have five other complete and some fragmentary letters by Ya'qūb. One, TS 16.7, was written five days after this one and is almost identical with it. Two others were addressed to Nahray b. Nissīm (dated documents as from 1045), namely, one from Tyre, Lebanon, with an enclosure to our Yūsha', and one from Sicily, referring to the death of Maṣlīaḥ, the Jewish judge of Palermo (see below).[2] In his letter from Tyre Ya'qūb refers to his sojourn in Egypt, and we also have a lovely little letter to him from a relative reporting that Ya'qūb's family in Jerusalem, consisting of his mother, his "baby" (*ṭifla*), that is, young wife, and babies, were all well and happy. Thus it appears that the

[1] TS 20.127. In *Med. Soc.*, I, 376, sec. 28, this letter is (tentatively) misdated. It was probably written around 1030 and in Sicily. For the business cooperation expressed in it see *Med. Soc.*, I, 178, n. 41.

[2] TS 8 J 41, f. 2, *Nahray* 191; Bodl. MS Heb. c28 (Cat. 2876), f. 61, *Nahray* 190.

Andalusian merchant, while working in the East, settled his family in Jerusalem, which, in addition to its holiness, had the advantage of being inexpensive (as that letter states).[3] A letter by Jacob himself sent from Jerusalem is translated in the preceding selection.

The writer of our letter lived around the middle of the eleventh century, as can be established by the references to many persons mentioned in his letters who were active at that time. The addressee, Yūsha', was a prominent member of the community, as can be gauged from a document dated December 1046.[4]

As to the city from which our letter was dispatched the choice is between Palermo, Sicily, and Qayrawān, Tunisia, for mention is made of letters sent to al-Mahdiyya, the Tunisian seaport, to be forwarded to Egypt.[5] These considerations decide in favor of Palermo:

1. All the goods sent by the writer directly (secs. C and J.) are of the regular Sicilian type. See S. D. Goitein, "Sicily in the Cairo Geniza Documents," *Archivio Storico per la Sicilia Orientale*, 77 (1971), 9-33.

2. Typically Tunisian products, such as saffron, are sent not by him personally, but by business friends in Tunisia on his order (secs. F and J.).

3. He lives in a port city, reporting the arrival and departure of ships, but not in Mazara, the other Sicilian terminal for the trade with the East in those days (sec. E).

4. He is closely connected with Maṣlī'aḥ (b. Elijah), the Jewish judge of Palermo (secs. E and H).

The main text of the letter was written by a clerk, but the address and the long P.S. are in the peculiar hand of Ya'qūb, which looks like chicken scratches. TS 16.7, which is mainly a shorter version of our letter, is entirely in his hand.

University Library, Cambridge, Taylor-Schechter Collection, TS 20.76.

[3] TS 10 J 15, f. 12. "Inexpensive": *rākhī*, as in Tunisian Ar.

[4] TS 20.9, ed. Assaf, *Texts*, 137-140. Also TS 10 J 21, f. 1, where he bears an honorific title conferred on him by the yeshiva of Jerusalem, and where he is referred to as "Sefaradi," the Heb. word for Spanish.

[5] After the closing of the seafaring season, letters were dispatched in boats on the small stretch of sea dividing Sicily from Tunisia to al-Mahdiyya, from where they were sent on to Egypt overland.

A. Preamble

In your name.

My master and lord, may God prolong your life, make your well-being permanent, and be for you and with you as a protector and helper. I am writing from home on the first day of Elul (August), may God bring the month to a happy end for me and for you. I am longing for your dear countenance and asking God to unite us under the most auspicious circumstances.

Your letters containing the good news that you and your sons—may God keep them and augment their number—were well, have arrived. I am always eager to see a letter of yours; having one gives me the feeling that you are near to me, and merely looking upon it makes me happy. I ask God to let you always be well and never deprive me of seeing your face or your letters.

You say in your letter that you have not received any from me. I have written several letters to al-Mahdiyya with the request to forward them to you to Miṣr (Fustat).

B. Difficulties with a Muslim merchant[6]

You spoke of the trouble you had with Abū ʿAbdallāh Ibn Khafāja. I regretted this very much. Now, my lord, if, at the arrival of this letter, something is still owed, make accounts with him and take the balance from him, for your exertion is many times more valuable to me than this sal ammoniac. For the money received buy spices,[7] pack them in the wickerwork basket together with the sal ammoniac and send them as early as possible, if God wills.

[6] The addressee had been requested to buy sal ammoniac with the money owed the writer. But the Muslim merchant had delivered only part of the quantity paid for.

[7] *Saqaṭ*, pl. *asqāṭ*, extremely common in the business correspondence of the eleventh century, cannot have the usual meaning of "junk," "scraps," but denotes spices and seasonings. See, e.g., TS 13 J 29, f. 10, ll. 16-17: "All *saqaṭ* sell well: spikenard—25 (dinars); nutmeg—7 dinars; sugar—11; costus—25." In 12.693*v*, ll. 10-11, 14, pepper, cinnamon, and ginger are included. See below, at the end of the price list.

C. Goods sent (a) for the addressee, (b) on account of their partnership, (c) for the partnership with the writer's brother

I had sold seven out of the nine bales (of flax, sent by you). I added certain sums from my own resources to the price obtained and bought silk, *lāsīn*,[8] *farkhas*,[9] turbans, hides, and tin, and sent you everything by boat—may God ordain their safe arrival and unite me with you soon.

In the ship of Ibn al-Shawwā ("Mr. Cook") I sent you a bundle on account of our blessed partnership. It contains five bags of silk and lāsīn, and one of tin and copper. They are wrapped in twenty-five hides and two pairs of sacks and canvases. Three bags with silk and lāsīn for the partnership with my brother Elhanan are in the same bundle. The freight, completely paid in advance, amounted to 3 1/2 quarter dinars.

In the boat of Bū-gharwā Abdallāh b. Maymūn ("Greedy, Servant of God, son of Lucky") I sent you a bundle containing five bags with silk and lāsīn, twenty-five hides, and two pairs of sacks and canvases for the partnership with my brother Elhanan, and four bags with silk and lāsīn and one bag with tin in shells[10] for my partnership with you.

(Most of the seven subsequent lines were cut out. They speak about two bundles with cotton[11] (garments) and 106 quarter dinars "in number" [and presumably 100 in weight] sent. The corresponding passage in TS 16.7 states that the total value of the goods sent for the partnership in that year was 1,628 1/12 quarter dinars.)

This consignment, my lord, is the most profitable and blessed bought this year. Had I not dispersed[12] (agents) for buying lāsīn im-

[8] A specific Sicilian, cheaper sort of silk (see *Med. Soc.*, I, 102).

[9] The *farkha*, like the *thawb*, was both a sheet of cloth and a garment. A staple export from Sicily and Tunisia.

[10] Tin was traded in "tongues," *lisān*, and "shells," *maḥāra* (see TS 16.264, ll. 4-5). "Shells" of tin, mentioned, as here, in TS 13 J 19, f. 9, l. 13, DK XVIII, l. 8, *Nahray* 43.

[11] Egypt, today one of the great cotton-growing countries, imported cotton textiles during the Middle Ages from both East and West. See *Med. Soc.*, I, 105.

[12] Ar. *nufarriq*, a term found also elsewhere. Lāsīn, the popular Sicilian

mediately after my arrival, I would not have got a thing. As soon as your consignments arrive I shall take a loan[13] on them and buy with it merchandise with prospects of gain and send it on, if God wills.

D. Arrival of Shipments Sent by the Addressee

All the ships arrived safely, and also the bales transported by Nzlly,[14] son of the freedman of Ṣāliḥ.[15] One of the three bales was torn open and I sold them at the fair, for it was impossible to keep them any longer.[16] A hundred pounds (of flax) brought 24 (quarter dinars), and of the bale damaged by water, 14.[17] The bale of pepper and that of indigo held in partnership by myself and Abu 'l-Bishr ("Good Tidings") Salmān have also arrived safely, thank God, and I shall act according to your instructions.

E. Note on the Jewish Judge of Palermo and his Brother

You mentioned that you had given me a volume of legal opinions by Rabbi Maṣlī'aḥ, but I do not have it.[18] It is true that you told me I should have it copied and then return it to you, but when we parted, you did not hand me over anything. You will find it in your house. If this is agreeable to you, kindly give it to M. Abū Zikrī, the brother of R. Maṣlī'aḥ, for he traveled this year together with my brother Judah from Mazara, may God ordain them safety.

fabric was manufactured in countless little workshops, both in the city and in other places.

[13] It was August, and only a few weeks remained until the end of the seafaring season. Thus he could not wait for cash until he would have sold his partner's consignments.

[14] The name of this son of a former slave is written clearly, but I do not know how to pronounce it. Perhaps a European.

[15] Probably Ṣāliḥ b. Barhūn Tāhertī. For another case of a liberated slave of the Tāhertīs remaining in close contact with the family of his former master, see no. 13, above.

[16] At the arrival of a caravan or convoy of ships a fair was held, where the prices, naturally, were somewhat lower than usual. See *Med. Soc.*, I, 277.

[17] Reasonable prices under the circumstances. See *Med. Soc.*, I, 224-225.

[18] As far as I know, the book is lost, which is a pity, for we would have learned from it much about social and economic conditions in Sicily around 1050.

I need not counsel you with regard to him (the judge's brother): do not leave him without your effective guidance.

F. Saffron from Tunisia. Partnership between the sons of the writer and the addressee

My lord, I have instructed Abu 'l-Bishr Sulaymān b. Faraḥ al-Qābisī ("Good Tidings, Solomon, son of Joy, of Gabes [in Tunisia]") to buy saffron for 80 dinars from the sums he owes me and to send everything to you. In case he is unable to buy goods, he should send you the cash. If God ordains a safe arrival, take 25 dinars from it, add another 25 dinars on your side, and buy whatever God puts into your mind for the entire sum. This should be in partnership between my son Abū Ibrāhīm[19] and your son Abū Sahl,[20] as we have agreed, so that they should if God, the exalted, wills, follow in the footsteps of their grandfathers. On the goods bought by you "Isma'il b. Ya'qūb" should be written.[21] I shall make a similar arrangement for M. Abu 'l-Ḥasan,[22] if God wills.

For the balance buy whatever God puts into your mind and send it by boat together with the sal ammoniac and whatever you still owe me.

G. Some personal orders

Kindly buy me a holiday robe with its wimple,[23] made of fine linen, green with gold threads, worth between 8 and 10 dinars, made of dense fabric, so that it should be durable. Also (buy) two white wimples, six cubits long,[24] for 2 1/4 to 2 1/2 dinars, and a pair of . . . shoes.[25]

19 He was called Isma'īl, as was Ya'qūb's father, the kunya (honorific byname) of which was "Father of Abraham," Abū Ibrāhīm.

20 "Easy," connected with different names, probably given by the mother when delivery was smooth. Often paired with the Arabic equivalent of Nathan ("Gift"). Thus this boy, too, was called after his grandfather.

21 The name of the boy, not of the writer. See n. 19.

22 The addressee's second son. See below.

23 Ar. *wa-mi'jarhā*, the female turban wound many times around the head, then around the face, and finally floating down a shoulder.

24 Ar. *sudāsiyya.* A letter sent from al-Mahdiyya to Egypt in 1048 contains an order for a wimple 10 cubits long, *'ushārī* (TS 20.69, l. 38). For the length of turbans see no. 2, n. 17, above.

25 Orders sent to Fustat for shoes for personal use were common in the Geniza correspondence.

H. On a Consignment of the Jewish Judge of Palermo

My lord, a balance of 2 dinars in my favor had remained with M. Abū Sa'īd Dā'ūd b. Sha'yā (David b. Isaiah), of which, according to a note of his, he had spent half a dinar on a bag belonging to R. Maṣlī'aḥ. I had [asked] you to receive the bag and the balance from him, but you did not mention this in your letter. I hope you have, in the mean time, received delivery. Please give the bag, together with the other little bundles, to M. Abū Zikrī Judah, the brother of R. Maṣlī'aḥ, and assist him in their sale with your good advice. The purchase price was 60 quarter dinars.

I. Uninvited Shipments

I had asked you to tell M. Abū Sa'īd[26] what you have heard from my mouth, namely that he should not send me anything. But after all, you have not done this, for this year he sent me eight bales of flax. I have asked Abu 'l-Faraj Marwān[27] to accept delivery, to sell them, and to send him the price. He already has received them. Please tell him not to do this again—neither he nor anyone else—and inform him about the oath I have sworn in your presence.[28]

J. Conclusion

Kindest regards to you and to M. Abu 'l-Ḥasan, may God keep them,[29] and to your mother,[30] and all under your care. My son Abū Ibrāhīm sends you all kindest regards. Do not deprive me of your letters reporting about your affairs and your well-being and the well-being of your sons. I sent you with Abu 'l-Bishr Salmān b. Dā'ūd al-Barqī (of Barqa in eastern Libya) a jar of salted tuna fish, 15 [about twelve words missing]. And peace upon you. My trust is in God alone.

[26] See preceding paragraph.

[27] The bales were sent to al-Mahdiyya, and the writer of our letter asked the Tunisian merchant Abu 'l-Faraj Marwān (see no. 14, n. 22, above), to take care of them.

[28] Not to deal with merchandise sent to him against his instructions.

[29] The clerk had erroneously omitted the name of the elder son Abū Sahl.

[30] The mother is greeted, since she was old and the writer's aunt. It would not have been good form to greet the addressee's wife, who was still young enough to be expected to produce more sons. See above.

K. P.S. in the Sender's Own Hand

(The first two notes were occasioned by the arrival of a ship from al-Mahdiyya on its way to Egypt.)

Abu 'l-Bishr Sulayman b. Saul sent you in the bundle of Abu 'l-Faraj Mardūk (Mordechai) a chest with corals, for which no freight is to be paid, for he carried for him two chests with saffron. In this bundle of Mardūk I sent you a bag with shelled almonds, containing 25 pounds of almonds, receive them from him, also free of charge.

Abu 'l-Bishr Sulaymān b. Faraḥ[31] wrote me that he had bought 33 1/2 mann saffron, packed it in a bundle destined for his brother[32] and loaded it on the boat of Ibn 'Allān.[33] A rumor was spread that it was captured by the enemy. I ask God that this may be false and that we might be united in his mercy.

L. A Price List

You would certainly like to know the prices here (in quarter dinars per 100 pounds unless otherwise noted. Parenthetical question marks after some figures indicate that we cannot be sure that these prices are in quarter dinars).

Waddle flax[34]—22-33
Mālāl flax—18-20
Kirmānī indigo, first quality—200-350
Lawāḥī—100-300
Brazilwood (only one man in the town has it)—300
Cinnamon—110
Pepper, today—135
Myrobalan,[35] the yellow?—
Myrobalan, the Kābulī—1 din. per 1 1/2-1 2/3 pounds
Myrobalan, the Indian—1 din. per 8 pounds
Senna—50 (?)

[31] This refers to paragraph F, above. The quantity mentioned corresponds to about 70 pounds.

[32] Called Isma'īl b. Faraḥ, sender and recipient of many Geniza letters. See no. 31, below.

[33] Probably identical with Abu 'l-Faraj Ibn 'Allān (no. 17, above). See *Med. Soc.*, I, 309.

[34] For the types of flax see *Med. Soc.*, I, 456.

[35] A widely used medicine for intestinal troubles. Different varieties of it were on the market. See *Med. Soc.*, II, 267, where senna, too, is referred to.

Gum arabic—30 (?)
Nutmeg—18 (?) per 1 mann
Cardamom—4 (?) per 1 mann
Cubeb—1 din. per 4 pounds
Prunus Mahaleb[36]—25
Rose marmalade—43
Mace[37]—30 per 1 mann
Camphor—13 per 1 ounce
Musk—50 per 1 ounce

All spices are rare here and almost not to be had.

(In the price list of TS 16.7, which was written five days later, pepper had fallen from 135 to 120 quarter dinars, brazilwood from 300 to 200, but only 3 1/2 (and not 4) pounds of cubeb could be had for a dinar; see *Med. Soc.*, I, 219. In conclusion the writer greets the same persons as before and three others.)

(Address:)

To my master and lord Abu 'l-Surūr Yūsha, son of Nathan, (may he) r(est in) E(den), may God prolong his life and always keep him well and happy.

From his friend Jacob, son of Isma'īl the Andalusian, (may he) r(est in) E(den). To Miṣr (Fustat), if God, the exalted, wills.

23-26 A DIFFICULT PARTNER

Yeshū'ā b. Isma'īl ("Salvation," son of Samuel), like many Maghrebis, had settled in Alexandria, Egypt, where we find him first in the service of Mūsā Majjānī,[1] and later exchanging many letters with Nahray b. Nissīm.[2] His ramified correspondence reveals him as a difficult person, but frictions between partners were

[36] A drug against intestinal parasites and a pectoral (Maimonides-Meyerhof, p. 109, no. 220).

[37] Ar. *fisfāsa,* which I take as a variant spelling of *bisbāsa.* TS 12.251, l. 14, another price list from Sicily, notes mace with 50 quarter dinars per mann.

[1] Majjānī's letter to him (TS 12.566). For Majjānī see nos. 17-18, above.

[2] *Nahray* 13, 14, 17 (to Yeshū'ā); 86-90 (from him). For Nahray see ch. IV, below. *Nahray* 88 is translated in no. 34, below.

nothing exceptional. Khallūf, the senior partner, urged him to clear his accounts with him, since he was not eager to continue the relationship. It nevertheless went on for years, but was finally terminated when Khallūf sued him in court, a last resort normally avoided by respectable merchants. We know about this affair through the draft of a settlement carefully written in Yeshū'ā's own hand on the back of a letter to him by Khallūf's nephew Joseph Tāhertī, who had continued the partnerships of his uncle and father with him (see no. 25, below).

23 THE DISAPPOINTED SENIOR PARTNER WRITES FROM THE MAGHREB

Bodleian Library, Oxford, MS Heb. a 3 (Cat. 2873), f. 13.

A. The writer's disappointment

I am writing to you, my master and lord, . . . on the eve of the *New Year*, may God make it happy and blessed to its very end . . .

Your letter has arrived with the couriers[3] and I was happy with it, for it contained some apologies and promises, which reassured me somehow, for I was very much dejected because of all the losses I suffered through one for whom I exerted myself and worked here to no avail. Let us praise God for this very much.[4]

I had entertained the hope to derive some profit from our partnership this year. But when the ships landed and I learned which goods had arrived for me, I became very angry, but [. . .] and I thanked God, for I found that all merchandise arriving here this year brought no profit. Thus there was some consolation for me and [. . .]

In your letter you complain about how much trouble you had in the Rīf (the little towns and villages of the Egyptian countryside). I was very angry about this; as if *I* had chosen this for you! You have my letters from the beginning of our partnership; look

[3] It was September, the end of the seafaring season. Another letter, sent by boat, certainly was on its way. Couriers always went overland. See *Med. Soc.*, I, 284ff.

[4] Meant sarcastically. Religion commands to thank God for bad things as we naturally do for good ones (Mishnah Berakhot 9:5).

through them. Did I not advise you not to sell there even for a penny?! So, brother, this was your own choice, and there was no point in complaining to me about this, for, from this blessed undertaking of yours only losses came to me, namely, that my goods remained unsold year after year.

B. Previous Shipments

But the height of all is that you conjure me by God in your letter and call God as witness against me that I should not keep one dirhem of yours, except the goods not yet sold. As if you had had merchandise with me which I sold and whose price I retained! I showed your letter to people and then showed them the blessed goods you had here with me, namely, asarum,[5] cinnamon, clove, aloe,[6] *ḳhawlān*,[7] and another quantity of clove, about which I learned only this year that it belonged to you. I wrote to you about it at the beginning of the year, but you did not answer me. I asked my young man,[8] but he did not know a thing about it. Then, when I sold my own clove, I found that there was more of it than I knew of and asked Sulayman b. Saul[9] about the redundant quantity. Then, during this summer, I took out all your goods in the presence of a number of our friends and delivered them to Tammām,[10] who sold everything. I was about to write you and to enclose legal testimony that all this was sold only in the course of this year, so that you should be reassured.

Had I known how to sell other people's goods, I would have chosen first to sell my own and would not have entrusted them to one who keeps them unattended and does with them what he likes. But, brother, I do not argue with you, for you are excused; perhaps similar things have been said to you before and you have been fooled. Had I listened to what people say, I never would have en-

[5] Ar. *āsarūn*. A medical plant (used as an emetic), imported from the Orient (Maimonides-Meyerhof, p. 14, no. 21).

[6] Ar. *harnawa* (Maimonides-Meyerhof, p. 58, no. 113).

[7] See no. 25, n. 15, below.

[8] Ar. *ghulām*. He could have been a slave or freedman, or even a free employee.

[9] Mentioned in the P.S. of no. 22, above.

[10] The addressee's sister's son, who, as was usual, had apprenticed with him (TS 10 J 14, f. 20, l. 13, and *verso* l. 11).

tered into a partnership with you, but I am one who cannot be fooled. God calls to account every man for his deeds.

C. Transactions of the current year

All you have sent has arrived. I took delivery of eight bales of flax, seven of which had been torn open, and only one had remained intact. I sold them immediately after arrival. Together with Abū Abraham[11] I sold the one which was complete for 38-42 (quarter dinars per 100 pounds).[12] But when we were through with the sale and wished to collect the price there occurred here what you certainly have heard and the collection stopped. After great exertion and many interventions we were apportioned about 600 quarter dinars from its price, which Abū Abraham and I divided between us (for collection). But the money has not yet come in so that I could report about it.

I sold the ginger, for it was sought after here. Indeed, there was no other product which sold well.

The pepper, however, was dead. No one offered it (lit., cried it out). The price went down to 130, but still no one bought. Until the calamity occurred in the town, of which you know, whereupon all the foreigners either sold everything they had for 130-132, and regarded this as a boon, or bought and loaded. But my heart did not let me sell for such a price and I held it until the time when the sailing of the ships approached, in the hope it would rise. However, the slump got worse. Then I was afraid that suspicion might arise against me and sold your pepper to Spanish merchants for 133.

I bought you saffron, wax, and clothes, and packed everything together with what I had bought for my brother-in-law[13] in two bundles. I sent one in the small boat[14] and the other in the large

[11] Probably Isḥāq b. Barhūn (Isaac b. Abraham) Tāhertī, one of the writer's brothers-in-law.

[12] A bale weighing around 500 pounds often contained flax of different qualities. See *Med. Soc.*, I, 226.

[13] This one, of course, was in Egypt. His name was Mūsā (Moses). See no. 24, below. He was the father of Joseph, the writer of no. 25.

[14] Referring to the boat of the "Lady," one of the relatives of the ruler of Tunisia, while the large boat was that of the "Sultan" himself.

boat. The latter bears the inscription "for Mūsā b. Khalaf,"[15] in which you have four chests with saffron; the other, in the boat of the Lady, is inscribed "for Khallūf b. Mūsā"[16] and contains clothes, namely 112 broad *farkhas*, which I bought for a very low price such as no one has obtained: 50 quarter dinars.[17] Three hundred pounds of wax and all its containers are yours. You have another package with wax, well covered, in partnership in equal shares with Ya'qūb b. Azhar (Jacob son of 'Luminous,' Heb. Meir).

An account specifying all that has been sold and bought for you follows.

You will also receive a detailed account for last year's transactions copied from the original list. When I wrote the former account I was in a hurry and made a mistake in the addition. I am sending you also your own account book, so that you may check which goods you have sent to me and which have remained with you. For you have not charged me with the price of two bales of flax which arrived in al-Mahdiyya, neither last year nor this, and indeed do not list them at all.

D. Last-Hour News

Dear brother, while I am writing this letter—it is the night before the sailing of the ships—pepper has become much in demand, for the foreigners had sold all they had, while boats (with customers) arrived and only local people had some left. Thus it was sold for 140-142. I took collateral for the sale of my pepper at 140-142. But, brother, I would not like to take the profit for myself. Therefore I transferred the entire sale to our partnership. May God reward me for what I do for other people. I do not expect gratitude from men.

[15] "Moses, son of 'Substitute,'" with the family name Samarqandī (see no. 25, below), an old business friend of the writer of our letter.

[16] The writer of our letter. Khallūf is a form of endearment, common in the Maghreb, and means the same as Khalaf. See preceding note.

[17] This can only mean that a certain standard number, of, say, 10 farkhas, cost 50 rubā'īs. Compared with other quotations in the Geniza even this would be a very low price.

E. Various details

I paid Baruch 10 quarter dinars.[18]

The flax for your sister's son was taken by his mother. It did not reach me from her hand. Khiyār had delivered it to her.[19]

Those 10 quarters will be deducted from the additional pepper sold, and you will receive its account as soon as its price is collected, together with the balance from the sale of the flax.

For the price of the flax I bought for you 200 quarters. Thus, nothing belonging to you remains with me, neither goods nor cash, except what has to be collected from the balance of the price of the flax. I shall check everything which will come in, so that nothing should remain either on account of the partnership or your own account.

A letter has been received from Abū Sa'īd[20] saying that Mufrij's boat had arrived in Sfax[21] and that he would send for the lac and redirect it to al-Mahdiyya. I have no further information about this matter.

You admonish me in your letters to send you all goods ordered, as well as all cash received, and to make all the payments on which you advised me. All this has been done on my side and I ask you now to do the same for me. But, please, do not send me flax, for on those ships all flax gets ruined. (A few words written on the top of the sheet are partly effaced.) So, make an effort this year and leave one business for another (that is, do first things first), as other people do.

A green robe was in your bundle and I do not know whether it is for the partnership or on your own account and for what price you bought it before Ṭayyib[22] departed.

[18] See no. 24, end of letter, below.

[19] Tammām (see n. 10, above) then was in Egypt (see at the end of the letter). Several persons named Khiyār appear in the contemporary Geniza correspondence.

[20] Probably the writer's nephew who wrote no. 25. But Abū Sa'īd was a common kunya.

[21] In southern Tunisia. The boat carried lac sent by Yeshū'ā.

[22] See n. 8, above. Mentioned in Bodl. MS Heb. c28 (Cat. 2876), f. 61*v*, l. 23, *Nahray* 190, expressly as Khallūf's factotum. See also no. 43, sec. D.

F. Final Admonitions. Conclusion

You write that you have fixed 1 out of 10 dinars (from our partnership) for your sister's son. This is quite in keeping with your character.[23] But I shall not interfere with your actions.

You also charged the fare of 2 dinars for my employee to my account, although he traveled with your goods and for your affairs and you asked me to send him. I trust in God, but the decision is in your hand. Do what you deem fit.

Kindest regards. I wish not to say more about our mutual relations. I trust in your religiosity. Regards to anyone asking about me, especially, your sister's son. Your servants, my sons, send you regards. *And peace.*

G. P.S. i. In the Script of the Main Text

Please, with every courier leaving send me letters, for I am worried. I have received the price of the two bales. I shall buy for it additional saffron and turbans. *And peace.*

P.S. ii. In another script

You will receive with the Jewish sailor[24] a bag with fourteen pounds of silk. Give him a quarter. And peace.[25]

P.S. iii. In a third script

I ask you to settle my account with yourself and give the balance to my brother-in-law, for you are a very busy man. And peace.

(Address:)
To my master and lord Abu 'l-Faraj Yeshū'ā, son of Isma'īl, (may he) r(est in) E(den), al-Makhmūrī,[26] may God [. . .
From Khallūf, son of Mūsā, (may he) r(est in) E(den), Ibn al-Ṣā'igh ("Mr. Goldsmith").

23 Ar. *wa-ant ṣaḥīfat rūḥak.*

24 Because of the ever stricter observance of the Sabbath Jews had to give up the profession of sailor. The one mentioned here was an exception. See Goitein, *Jews and Arabs*, p. 108.

25 Here, and in the next P.S., "And peace" is in Ar. Before, it was twice in Heb.

26 The family name is half effaced here, but clearly written in TS NS J 145, where it occurs twice. *Makhmūr*, lit., "drunk," was taken perhaps in a mystical sense.

24 THE JUNIOR PARTNER RETORTS

This letter was written seven months after Khallūf's letter (translated in no. 23), but clearly refers to many details mentioned there. Yeshū'ā had sent other messages in between, but, because of the insecurity of communications, it was customary to recapitulate important details again and again.

University Library, Cambridge, Taylor-Schechter Collection, TS 12.389.

I am writing to you . . . from Fustat on the 8th of Iyyar . . . In my previous letters I wrote you about the serious illness which befell me during this blessed winter. Let's praise God for his favors, since the end was good and ask him to complete his gracious gifts in his generosity. *Amen.*

I had informed you about the safe arrival of your shipments, namely 111 broad *farkha*s (in your account you charge me with 112), four unbleached garments, two chests with saffron (you do not indicate their weight), three hundredweights of wax, fourteen pounds of silk, and, in partnership with Abū Joseph Jacob b. Azhar, six hundredweights less nine pounds of wax, twenty cloaks, and six coats.

When he (Jacob) arrived in Fustat, I was in a very serious condition, and he tried to take advantage of me. Our friends extricated the wax from him with difficulty. (Two damaged lines.) When he arrived in Alexandria, I met him, and he said "Yes," but put me off from day to day, until he was about to leave. Our friends informed me about his intention, and I went to see him with R. Nahray, but he said: "No, I do not yet pack." I believed that he spoke the truth, but people saw that he was packing, and away he went. I returned to his place, where his brother stood security for him to the amount of 2 dinars.[1]

[1] As far as can be made out from the damaged lines, Jacob delivered indeed everything, including the cloaks and coats (*kisā, 'abī*). The dispute was about the payment of expenses (freight and customs), a sum of 1 13/24 dinars being mentioned. Persons who take a light view of the property of others are inclined to get extremely excited at the slightest damage menacing them.

This is what happened to me with him. Please when he [arrives at your place], take from him what he still owes me. And when he says: "I have paid the expenses for the wax," our friends here are witness that he did not pay a penny for it. Only you can save me from him. You have entrusted him with the shipment, so you must save me from him.

I have notified you before that I have paid to M. Abū 'Imrān Mū[sā], your brother-in-law, 170 dinars, of which 100 are for you and 70 for him. God is my witness, that from this partnership (with you and your brother-in-law) people still owe me about 150 dinars. They try to take advantage of me and I could not collect the money from them. Therefore I had to pay these 170 dinars from my own resources, in order not to detain what is yours. Now, please check what you owe me. Perhaps you can buy me tin, either in "tongues" or in "shells"[2] and *lāsīn* silk from Isma'īl Ibn al-Andalusī,[3] or fine Spanish "pickups"[4] or fine *khazāsh* silk[5] or "carobs" . . .[6] Please do not detain what is mine, but act as I did, when I paid you from my own resources.

If God gives me health, I must leave the city (for the Rīf) in order to collect the outstanding debts. May God, in his mercy, unite us. Kindest regards to you and your boys, may God keep them.

Pay to Baruch 15 dirhems and to Ibrahīm 5 quarters. *And Peace.*

(Address:)
To my master and lord Khallūf b. Mūsā . . . "Goldsmith."
From his friend Yeshū'ā, son of Isma'īl, (may he) r(est in) E(den).
To the City of Sicily (Palermo), if God wills.

[2] See no. 20, above, n. 10.
[3] See no. 20, above.
[4] Ar. *iltiqāṭ*, "a silk yarn produced by combing and spinning waste silk." See *Med. Soc.*, I, 454-455, n. 53.
[5] Ibid.
[6] Nine letters partly effaced. "Carobs" do not denote here the well-known fruit, which is food for the poor, but something else. See Dozy, *Supplément*, s.v.

25 JOSEPH TĀHERTĪ OF AL-MAHDIYYA, TUNISIA, CONTINUES A PARTNERSHIP

Alexandria, Egypt

Ca. 1063

University Library, Cambridge, Taylor-Schechter Collection, TS 16.163.

A. The Addressee's Illness and Prospective Travel to Tunisia

I am writing to you, my master and lord—may God prolong your life and always keep you well and happy, from al-Mahdiyya on the 5th of Elul (August). I am well and prosperous, thanks to God, the lord of the worlds. Your letters, which were sent in the ships, arrived, and I was happy to learn from them that you were well and healthy, for which I thanked God. Only he, the exalted, knows what I felt when the courier arrived without a letter from you, and when R. Nahray wrote me that you were seriously ill. Then I saw a letter of Ibn al-Samarqandī[1] to Khallūf,[2] mentioning your illness, which worried me very much. Finally, your own letters arrived with the ships, whereupon I praised God and thanked him for what he had bestowed upon me[3] and you, and I am asking him to continue his beneficence to you, until you are restored to complete health. I was also glad to learn from your letter that you will be coming to us next year—may God ordain a safe journey for you and unite us under the best of circumstances in his grace and generosity.

[1] A family name, derived from the town of Samarkand in Central Asia. About this person see no. 23, n. 15, above.

[2] The writer's maternal uncle who sent no. 22, above.

[3] In accordance with the refined courtesy of the age, the addressee's restoration to health is a particular favor of God bestowed on his friend, the sender of our letter.

B. The Proposed Dissolution of Partnerships Shared by the Addressee, the Sender's Family and Others

I had, indeed, intended to make a list of all that arrived here from you and of what I had dispatched to you, and to send it on. When, however, your letter with the announcement of your coming arrived, I decided to leave it until you arrive. I intend to dissolve this partnership, insofar as it still exists, to settle the accounts of all concerned and to send them with the couriers. For I have refrained from going overseas this year only in order to clear up my accounts with everyone, and in particular with the daughters of my brother[4] —may God, the exalted, enable me to do so. You, too, with God's help, should dissolve what is in your care, buying and selling for whatever prices God may grant, and come down[5] with the first travelers. Do not tarry, coming with the last.

C. Acknowledgment of Goods Dispatched by the Addressee

The goods sent by you arrived safely through God's grace, namely: two *barqalūs* (small bales)[6] of pepper in the ship of the Sultan, four bales of flax in the ship of al-Jinānī ("Gardener"), and one bale of brazilwood, in partnership with R. Nahray, in the barge (*qārib*) of Mufaḍḍal.[7] The large boat (*qunbār*) of Ibn Yūnus ("Son of Jonah") arrived in Sfax with one bale of flax. [. . .] You wrote that you assigned a part of the four bales of Ṭamāwī flax[8] and of the two barqalūs of pepper to the sender of the 300 rubāʿīs (quarter dinars). One of the two barqalūs was damaged in the ship, and I had great trouble with it, for it was above wheat, and when I gathered it, it had become discolored with whiteness, and was therefore difficult to sell.

[4] Barhūn, our Joseph's elder brother, had died (see sec. G), and his heirs were entitled to his share in the family business. According to Jewish law—unlike the Muslim—daughters inherit the entire estate of their father in the absence of sons.

[5] Traveling from Egypt to the West was called "coming down."

[6] About this term see *Med. Soc.*, I, 335.

[7] About the types of boats see *Med. Soc.*, I, 305-308.

[8] An appellation derived from Ṭamā, a village in the Asyūṭ district of Upper Egypt.

D. Sale of Pepper in al-Mahdiyya in Foreign Currency (Sicily and Pisa)

The price of pepper this year is very low, a qinṭār being sold for 25 dinars, one half to be paid in rubāʿiyyas and the other in Pisan currency. On the former, there is an agio of half a qīrāṭ (approximately 2 percent) and on the latter of two-thirds. In fact, they charge more than a half for the rubāʿiyya dinars, and I have to make this allowance. Most of the discolored pepper was sold by me for rubāʿiyyas. . . . I changed all money I received into fresh Nizārī dinars[9] and sent them on with a detailed account. May God ordain their safe arrival and unite me with you.

E. Difficulties Owing to the Bankruptcy of a Big Muslim Merchant

The owner of half of the 300 rubāʿīs claimed his share of the pepper. I told him, however, that I was unable to fix the amount before our final account. The four bales of flax have not yet been sold, for Ibn al-Shiryānī is in arrears to the merchants with 4,000 dinars, and I had sold him a load of flax, in partnership with the elder Abu Ṣḥāq, for 100 dinars. The merchants complained to the Sultan, may God give him eternal rule, who decided that he was obliged to pay all that was due to the foreigners, while the local people should grant him a delay until the foreigners would leave. We obeyed the Sultan's ruling, but I was kept back from all my other work owing to my dealings with him together with the other merchants, and who knows what worries I shall have with this [. . .] He was required to leave one third, to accept responsibility for another, and to pay the rest (immediately), but up till now nothing definite has been done. I sent one of the four bales to Sūsa[10] and asked him to sell it, if there was a good market for it, and I shall send the rest there, if I am satisfied with the sales.

[9] Dinars struck under the rule of the Fatimid caliph al-ʿAzīz (976-996), whose personal name Nizār also appeared on his coins. Al-Mahdiyya was one of the towns where his coins were struck. Coins some eighty years old could remain "fresh" because they were kept in sealed purses.

[10] A seaport on the Tunisian coast, north of al-Mahdiyya. By "him" is meant a business friend of the sender active in Sūsa, who was also well known to the addressee.

F. Queries About Three Different Partnerships

You wrote that you had dispatched mastic attached to R. Nahray's shipment. I have no exact knowledge about this partnership, I mean, whether that item has remained in Alexandria, or was dispatched to Sicily. Likewise, I find in your letters that you have sent sal ammoniac attached to a cargo of M. Abū Zikrī Judah[11] and of Abū 'Imrān Mūsā b. Abi 'l-Ḥayy; of this, too, I did not hear anything last year. Please in your letters to me explain the situation with regard to these packages, for I am worried about them. Furthermore, you mentioned that you bought two bales of S.rq.nāwī flax and another two bales of flax in partnership with R. Joseph, of which I also have no knowledge.

G. About a Liability of the Sender's Late Brother

You noted that R. Nahray claimed from you the price of goods carried for him by my brother—*(may he) r(est in) E(den)*—out of the 100 rubā'īs paid to you by Ḥayyīm b. 'Ammār[12] on my account. He wrote me that he had assumed that the account was lost in the ship of Ibn Shiblūn,[13] but was informed by Judah b. [. . .] that it was in Sicily and that he would forward it to him as soon as he arrived there. I answered Nahray that he should take no action before the arrival of the account from Sicily, whereupon full payment would be made to him . . . , if God will. Therefore, in case you have paid anything to him, take it back.

H. Note About Market Conditions in al-Mahdiyya (Only Partly Preserved)

This year, the price of flax was very low in al-Mahdiyya and in Sicily. However, the spices sold well because of their rarity; likewise, nothing of the striped materials (*sanad*) and the fine linen (*sharāb*) came here either from Egypt or from Syria.

(In the damaged part, mention was made of goods which arrived at Qarqanna, an island ten miles off the Tunisian coast town

[11] Judah b. Moses Ibn Sighmār, the recipient of no. 28.

[12] Representative of the merchants in Palermo.

[13] Family name, derived from *shibl*, "young lion."

Sfax, and in this town itself and how they sold. The writer further remarks that the list of prices, to be given on the reverse side of his letter [sec. K, below] was not reliable, as it came from the "people," meaning the merchants, and not from authorized officials.[14] Finally, he states that he was unable to sell the *succus lycii* [*khawlān*], as it was believed to serve only as a medicament for eyes.)[15]

I. Discrepancies Between the Accounts of the Addressee and that of One of his Partners

I had informed you that the account of Abu 'l-Faḍl Baruch Ibn al-Shāma[16] was received by me, specifying what he had sold and what he had sent to you with each man. I compared it with your account, which was forwarded to me, and found that in the year 53,[17] he had sent you a purse worth 25 dinars and 2 qīrāṭs in the boat of Ibn Abī 'Aqīl.[18] You do not mention it however, in your account, either because you forgot to list it or because it has not arrived. Please let me know whether this purse has arrived or not, then I can write to Baruch and ask him to send me the name of the bearer, so that I can claim it from him.

(In the following, only partly legible, paragraph of this sec., are listed three other ships on which money was sent to the addressee by Baruch and also other seeming discrepancies between the two accounts.)

J. Purses with Dinars Sent to the Addressee and Through him to Others

I sent you three purses, containing a total of 300 dinars, in Mufaḍḍal's ship[19] with Ḥassūn Ibn al-Ghazzāl ("Spinner"), one of

[14] The reading of this word (nās), the first on the reverse side of the letter, is uncertain.

[15] A medical plant frequently mentioned in the commercial correspondence of both the eleventh and twelfth centuries. Actually used for eye treatment. ULC Or 1080 J 5*v*, margin.

[16] "Beauty Spot," a nickname which became the name of a family represented in the Geniza by many of its members.

[17] The Muslim year (4)53, which began on January 26, 1061.

[18] The qadi of Tyre, Lebanon. Often mentioned.

[19] Ar. *markab*, probably different from the same shipowner's barge, mentioned in sec. C, n. 7, above.

200 for Mūsā b. Abi 'l-Ḥayy, one of 50 for Nahray, and another one of 50 for Ibrāhīm. Likewise, three purses in Ḥiṣn al-Dawla's[20] boat with Ibn al-Shanṭanalī, one for you, containing 100 dinars, one for Nahray with 50, and one for Mūsā b. Abi 'l-Ḥayy with 60 less one-eighth . . . , all coins whose legend is arranged in lines.[21]

K. List of Prices in al-Mahdiyya[22]

The prices: Buṣīrī flax, first quality, from 18 to 16. "Bandages" (flax), from 7 1/2 to 6 1/2 [. . .],[23] Pepper 25, like Hell.[24] Brazil-wood 17 sells slowly unless one gets a Spaniard for it. Lac 40, because of its rarity. Sal ammoniac, 2 manns cost 1 dinar; its price has fallen by now. Mastic, 1 qinṭār, 25 dinars. Betel-nut = myrobalan, a mann as from half a dinar; yellow myrobalan, one qinṭār—10 dinars. Both are in small demand. *Succus lycii*, 3 1/2 pounds—1 dinar because of its rarity. The . . . are not to be had, likewise tamarind. Sweet costus is generally in demand, but does not have a good price. As far as the . . . are concerned, from *qāqulla* (cardamom) to *harnawa* (aloe) and nutmeg—buy whatever God puts into your mind.

(Two other, not clearly legible items are mentioned next. In the remaining three lines, which are badly damaged, the sender speaks about an account attached to this letter and about shipments forwarded by him in the ships of the Sultan and of al-Jinānī, mentioned above.)

(*Address*, as usual, written upside down on the bottom of the page:) To my master and lord Abu 'l-Faraj Yeshū'ā, son of Isma'īl —(*may he*) *r*(*est in*) *E*(*den*)—may God prolong his life, and make him always safe and happy.

20 Honorific epithet of the Ketāmī-Berber general al-Mu'allā b. Ḥaidara Ibn Manzū, who, during his governorship of Damascus (1068-1075), played a fateful role in the dismemberment of the Fatimid empire.

21 Legends on coins were arranged in concentric circles or in parallel lines. The difference did not affect the value, but could serve as an identification mark.

22 When not otherwise stated, the quantities are in qinṭārs, or 100 pounds. About the nature and significance of such lists see *Med. Soc.*, 1, 218.

23 The barely visible text seems to say that for this commodity, as in the case of pepper (see sec. D, above), an agio of 1/2 qīrāṭ had to be paid per dinar.

24 I.e., a very bad price.

From Joseph b. Mūsā, son of Barhūn, (*may he*) *r*(*est in*) *E*(*den*).

(The draft of the settlement, referred to in the introduction to nos. 23-26, above, is written in the space left blank between the end of the text and the address. The senior partner Khallūf b. Mūsā "Goldsmith," who is described here as Ḥamawī, that is, native of Ḥamāh in Syria, but still as resident in Palermo, Sicily, had made Moses Samarqandī [see no. 1, above] his attorney against Yeshū'ā. The matter came before the court of Mevōrākh b. Saadya, later Nagid, or head, of the Jews in the Fatimid empire, but was finally settled by "elders," who took the trouble to go through all the accounts and came up with a complicated settlement. Since the draft is in the hand of Yeshū'ā, we do not know, of course, whether this was the end of the story.)

26 WEAVING OF A *maqṭa'* CLOTH IN ALEXANDRIA FOR A BUSINESS FRIEND IN AL-MAHDIYYA

This note from a business letter sent by Mūsā b. Abi 'l-Ḥayy (see no. 25, sec. J) to Joseph Tāhertī, the writer of the preceding selection, no. 25, illustrates the personal services accompanying the overseas trade. R. Yeshū'ā, mentioned in the first line, is, of course, the recipient of no. 25, who had traveled to al-Mahdiyya as announced in that letter.

Alexandria was famous for its maqṭa's, and here we learn that they were woven from cotton and linen, or linen alone.

Bodleian Library, Oxford, MS Heb. c 28 (Cat. 2876), f. 34, l. 29, margin and top of page one.

From the threads belonging to R. Yeshū'ā I had two pieces of maqṭa' garments and one *baqyār* turban[1] woven. I took them from the weaver and handed them over to the blancher.[2] The rest of the (linen) thread is coarse, while the cotton is fine, so that it does not fit in with it. Therefore, if he wishes to have two maqṭa's made

[1] Large-sized turban. A baqyār, 25 cubits long, was made in Alexandria for Nahray b. Nissīm (TS 13 J 15 f. 19, l. 3, *Nahray* 108).

[2] "Whitening" or "blanching" was different from bleaching.

all in linen,[3] from the rest of the thread, let him inform me accordingly.

If he prefers, however, that I buy him some coarse linen to fit his thread, I shall have it made thus.

Together with the cotton he also had eight ounces of fine (linen) thread, which I did not notice when I gave them for whitening.[4] Thus, if he wishes, I shall buy, in addition to it, five or so ounces, which will make roughly two maqṭa‘s, the woof of which will be the cotton owned by him.

27 A DEDICATED PARTNER

From Tunisia to Egypt

This short letter of Nissīm b. Isaac Tāhertī, the cousin of Joseph (nos. 25 and 26, above) and brother of Barhūn (no. 30, below), is presented here partly as a contrast to no. 25 and partly as an illustration of the vicissitudes of prices and the total expenses for one single item. The recipient was the sender of no. 16, a prominent merchant, much of whose correspondence has been preserved.

University Library, Cambridge, Taylor-Schechter
Collection, TS 10 J 9, f. 3.

A. The arrival of a late boat

I am writing to you, my master and lord, . . . on the 25th of Elul (August-September)—may God bring this month to a good end for you, and accept these coming days from you and from me.[1] *May you be inscribed in the book of life, atonement and forgiveness, you, and I, and all Israel.*

My preceding letters have been sent to you in the boats, may God ordain their safe arrival. The boat of Ibn Mu'ajjir ("Lessor")[2] ar-

[3] Lit., linen by linen, i.e., both warp and woof being linen.

[4] This seems to imply that both the threads before weaving and the woven material were "whitened."

[1] That is, the prayers and the fast during the subsequent month of the High Holidays.

[2] A man who has apartments for lease. Such persons appear in the Geniza, but not the word in this form (could be read also *mu'jir*).

rived after they had sailed and he told us that the boats setting out from Alexandria had been forced to return.[3] Your letter arrived in the boat and I learned from it that you were well and in good health; may God keep you thus. The purse with pearls arrived, too, and Abu 'l-Ḥasan ʿAllāl[4] states in his memo that their price is 50 dinars. I shall, if God wills, make every effort to sell them well, as is incumbent on me. They should be sold only when demanded and with precaution.[5] I have given to you the account for the lac.[6]

B. Shipments with a Boat that had been Forced to Return

I had written you about the pitchers which I had bought in order to fill them with soap. A qinṭār (hundred pounds) then cost 2 1/2 dinars, but only the sultan was in a position to buy it.[7] After the sailing of the ships the price went down to 2 dinars less 1/8 dinar per qinṭār. Then that *khinzīra*-barge returned,[8] and Abū ʿAlī Ḥassūn[9] was in it. Therefore I asked God, the exalted, for guidance and bought (soap) to fill ten of those pitchers (which I had bought for you previously). A hundred of them cost 5 dinars less one quarter and now they are worth 8 dinars, for they are much in demand and are not to be had. I sold six of them for you for half a dinar and left the rest, which I might also fill, if God wills, when I shall have sold that purse of pearls and when the soap will be cheap and good this year because of the "redness."[10]

[3] By bad weather or enemy action.

[4] Perhaps a grandson of his namesake mentioned in no. 1, no. 30 (ʿAllāl = ʿAllān).

[5] See *Med. Soc.*, 1, 491, n. 7.

[6] Mūsā had forgotten that he had received the account and asked for it again in the letter sent in the late boat. The transaction is referred to again below.

[7] The "sultan" and his family, who were shipowners and participated in the overseas trade, made use of the pernicious "right" of preemption, later so strongly condemned by his Tunisian compatriot Ibn Khaldun.

[8] Probably forced by a leakage or a similar mishap which affected it alone. For the type of vessel called *khinzīra* see *Med. Soc.*, 1, 477, n. 13. Read *ra[j]ʿat.*

[9] Frequently mentioned as a commuter between Tunisia, Sicily, and Egypt.

[10] This technical term escapes me. The soap was a by-product of the great Tunisian olive oil industry. Olives would be collected only after the writing of this letter, and new soap would be available only months later.

I filled these ten pitchers with 745 pounds of soap, for a price of 2 dinars less 1/8 per qinṭār.

	Dinars
Total price: 14 din. less 1 qīr.	(13 23/24)
Add: Earthenware (the pitchers): 1/2 din.	(12/24)
Casing in two wickerwork baskets and fastening: a quarter	(6/24)
Filling, transport to the sea, and consideration for the sailors: a quarter and a *ḥabba*	(6/24, 1/72)
Freight: 3 din. & 1 1/2 qīr.	(3 1½/24)
All this has been paid in advance.	
Commission[11]: 1 1/2 quarters	(9/24)
Grand Total: 18 din., a quarter, an eighth, & a ḥabba[12]	(18 9/24, 1/72)

This sum will be retrieved from the balance of the price of the lac; what remains in my favor will be collected by me from the sale of the . . . and from your share in that purse (of pearls), God willing.

C. The Writer's own Shipments. Conclusion

I had written you before about two containers with olive oil, which I had sent on my own account. I hope God ordains their safe arrival. Now I am sending, again for my own account, five jugs with soap in this khinzīra-vessel with Abū 'Alī Ḥassūn, for which freight and everything else have been paid in advance. "Nissīm" is written on them with ocher, and "'Aṭā Tēhertī" with ink.[13] Kindly add their price to that of the oil and that of the three purses of gold sent with Raḥamīm[14] and buy for the total whatever you deem fit.

Regards to you and to those under your care.

P.S. Your letter destined for Sicily (that is, Palermo) has arrived and I shall forward it, God willing.

11 To the agent(s) who bought the oil for the writer.

12 The grand total seems to be short by 1/2 qīrāṭ (1/48 dinar).

13 'Aṭā, a brother of Nissīm, often mentioned in the Geniza, was to receive the shipment, while the addressee, the experienced local merchant, would handle the sale. Shipments usually were marked with ocher (red clay), not with ink (or sepia, *ḥibr*). "Tēhertī" is Tāhertī pronounced with Imāla (ē = ā). See the address.

14 "Mercy" (Heb.), a name frequent in the West.

"Mūsā" is written with ocher on the ten jugs.[15]

(Address:)

(To) my master and lord Abū 'Imrān, may God prolong his life, Mūsā (Moses), son of Abu 'l-Ḥayy, *(may he) r(est in) E(den)*, Khalīla[16]—God is his protector.

From Nissīm, son of Isaac, (may he) r(est in) E(den), Tēhertī.

(Since this letter provides exact information of the total cost of Tunisian soap at arrival in Alexandria, it is worthwhile to note the level of prices reached there. A qinṭār was sold throughout the eleventh century for 4 to 5 1/2 dinars.[17] Since the cost per qinṭār was here about 2 1/2 dinars, a comparatively high profit was assured. It is remarkable that no export duty was levied.)

28 COMMERCE DURING CIVIL WAR

The anarchy following the invasion of North Africa by the Hilāl bedouins in the late 1050s occasioned the rise of several small principalities warring with each other. Sfax, a seaport on the east coast of Tunisia, only about 80 miles south of al-Mahdiyya, made itself independent and remained so for about forty years (1059-1099/1100).[1] This situation is reflected in the Geniza papers. During this period, Sfax, instead of al-Mahdiyya, often served as terminal for boats coming from the East. When the "Sultan" of al-Mahdiyya actively fought the *qā'id*, or governor, of Sfax, he would seize the ships and confiscate the goods of the merchants of the rival city, and sometimes their very life was in jeopardy. The longest letter preserved in the Geniza, written in Mazara, Sicily, by Salāma b.

[15] Ar. *jirār*, referring to the ten pitchers, *qulal*, mentioned above. "Pitcher" was also a measure, as in English (cf. TS 8 J 25, f. 19, l. 20, *Nahray* 40: "a jug containing half a pitcher"). The medieval passion for variety in expression led to such inexactitudes.

[16] "Female friend," "mistress." See S. D. Goitein, "Nicknames as Family Names," *JAOS* 90 (1970), 521.

[17] Mosseri L-52, margin, ed. S. D. Goitein, *Tarbiz* 37 (1968), 50-51: 4 + dinars; TS NS Box 320, f. 2: 5 1/2; TS 8.25*v*, l. 3, *Nahray* 64: 4 1/2-5.

---

[1] Idris, *Zirides*, pp. 231, 251.

Mūsā b. Isaac ("Well-being," son of Moses) of Sfax deals profusely with these matters.[2] Salāma, who, like his father, was closely connected with the qā'id of Sfax, faced the executioner in al-Mahdiyya five times. Finally he recognized that life in North Africa had become unbearable; he bought a house in Mazara, Sicily, for 300 dinars and brought his family over. His partner in Egypt—and, as he wished, exclusive partner—was Abū Zikrī Judah b. Moses Ibn Sighmār, the brother of the Jewish chief judge of al-Mahdiyya (whose letter is translated in no. 33, below).

Salāma's extensive letter deserves to be edited in a separate publication. Here we translate a letter of his father, addressed to the same partner in Egypt, but showing us business as usual, with the slight qualification that the main carriers of goods and cash were Muslims, not Jews, probably because most of the greater Jewish merchants of Sfax had already left that city.

The time of our letter is defined by a reference to a ship of Nāṣir al-Dawla who was the actual ruler of much of Egypt during most of the years of terror 1062-1073.[3]

Bodleian Library, MS Heb. a 2 (Cat. 2805), f. 20.

A

I am writing to you, my lord and master—may God prolong your life and make permanent the days of your well-being, happiness, and prosperity—on Tuesday, 26th of the month of Elul (September). I am well and prosperous—praise to God in gratefulness—and longing to see you. May God bring us together soon.

I have sent you a number of letters from al-Mahdiyya and Sfax and hope they have arrived and you have read them. I informed you in them that I have dispatched two purses to you from al-Mahdiyya with Abū Ya'qūb Yūsuf al-Dūkī,[4] one for our partnership and one for my own account. The first contained 50 dinars eastern cur-

[2] Dropsie 389, 414. Facsimile of the opening in *Med. Soc.*, I, opposite p. 20. A P.S. to another letter sent by Salāma b. Mūsā to Judah Ibn Sighmār from Mazara to Egypt is found in INA D-55, no. 14.

[3] *Med. Soc.*, I, 310.

[4] Referred to in section G as "the Kohen al-Dūkī." Thus, this merchant from al-Mahdiyya was Jewish. Dūkī probably denotes a man having dealings with the Norman duke.

rency;[5] and also 57 mithqāls, gold ore and old gold, worth 50 dinars, totaling 100 dinars. I hope it has arrived. I also sent you 50 2/3 dinars eastern currency for my own account; furthermore, 63 Ḥasanī[6] dinars—may God ordain their safe arrival.

B

In the ship of the Amir Nāṣir al-Dawla I sent you thirty-one new large skins of oil, measuring sixty-two maṭars;[7] on their stoppers the names Salāma[8] and Judah are engraved. They are closed with small stoppers and fixed tightly with soaked palm leaves and parchment.[9] With them are two leather bags with soap, weighing five qinṭārs. The names Judah and Salāma are engraved on these as well. I hope everything will arrive. It is all in the hands of 'Abd al-Raḥmān b. Alī b. Ḥabīb Sfaqsī.[10] The balance of the amount advanced for the whole partnership comes to 1 1/4 dinar.[11]

C

In the same ship, I sent you two purses with 'Umar b. 'Uthmān al-Qa(z)dīrī Sfaqsī,[12] one for the account of the partnership, containing 20 Shaykhiyya[13] dinars, worth 18 1/3, and one for my own account, in which there are 20 dinars of full weight of eastern currency. Please add this to the first purse, sent with al-Dūkī.

Together with this letter, I am sending you for my own account

[5] Egyptian dinars, which were regarded as standard money, wherefore no weight is indicated here.

[6] Referring to the Fatimid Caliph Abu 'l-Ḥasan aẓ-Ẓāhir (1021-1036), whose coins were issued from various mints in Tunisia, Egypt, and other countries. Also in the account TS Box 8, f. 62.

[7] Derived from the same Greek word as our "meter." In Tunisia, it designates a measure for oil, which in modern times has a capacity of about 20 liters (see Dozy, *Supplément* II, 600*a*).

[8] The writer's son, who was the third partner. In Dropsie 389, ll. 31-32 (see n. 2, above), Salāma reports to Judah about a similar shipment of his father and adds "your name and mine are engraved on the skin."

[9] Text: *wa-salāmatuhā fuluḵ ṣighār wa-ḵhūṣ maṣbūgh wa-riqq.*

[10] A Muslim merchant, as his name indicates.

[11] Merchandise or money had been sent in advance from Egypt for the goods ordered in Tunisia.

[12] Qa(z)dīrī, a dealer in tin. Also a Muslim. His father 'Uthmān, did a similar errand in Dropsie 389, l. 51.

[13] Dinars or quarter dinars from Palermo.

a purse in which there are 44 Ḥasanī dinars, weighing 43 dinars, as well as large dinars of eastern currency, 56 in number, and Ḥākimī rubā'īs,[14] 20 in number, of a total weight of 60 dinars.

D

Please sell the Ḥasanī dinars of the two shipments for me and buy shining[15] flax of first quality for the dinars belonging to me, if possible, Māwī or Mīsārī,[16] unique in excellence, and if you find real Fayyūmī, knife-edge blades,[17] buy whatever you can—I ask God to inspire you with successful ideas.

E

For our joint business, too, make an effort and buy whatever you see fit of flax and spices. You will find a list of the prices of the spices in my letter to Ḥassūn.[18] Please make an effort and buy accordingly both for our joint business and for me personally. Success, however, lies in God's hands. Send everything at the beginning of the sailing season to Sfax. When you find an opportunity to send flax to Sicily, do so and address it to Isḥāq b. Khalaf.[19] Don't be stingy to write, but list in detail everything you received and sent, so that I shall be able to act according to your letters.

F

I asked you in my previous letters to buy me a flame colored robe, which should be short and well fitting of fine, not coarse, material; I would like to wear it first on the Day of Atonement.[20]

[14] I.e., quarters of a dinar issued under the Fatimid Caliph al-Ḥākim (996-1021). His coins were struck in Tunisia, Sicily (especially the quarters), Egypt, and other countries. Twenty quarters make 5 dinars; thus we see that 56 of the "large" dinars had the weight of 55 only.

[15] Ar. *munaqqil*. See Dozy, *Supplément* II, 716*a*.

[16] For the various types of linen, see *Med. Soc.*, I, 455-457.

[17] Meaning, probably, thin and strong.

[18] His full name Ḥassūn b. Yaḥyā in Dropsie 389, f. 39. See also no. 27, n. 9, above.

[19] Often referred to in Dropsie 389.

[20] The custom of wearing new clothing first on the Day of Atonement and not on the Feast of New Year, preceding it by ten days, is attested in other Geniza letters. Since this was a day of fasting which could not be honored with good food, one singled it out by new clothing. Talmud Bavli, Shabbat, 119*a*.

Likewise, a turban of fine *sharb*-linen, which should be short and of pleasant, not coarse, material. Send with this some odorous wood, flasks (of camphor) and perfume, with which I can appear before my lord, the qā'id—may God give him victory. Deduct everything from the sum due to me.

G

I sent you and to the elder M. Abu Sḥāq Ibrāhim,[21] with the Kohen al-Dūkī, 100 small sheets of . . . as "soap for your service."[22] They cost a little over 9 dinars; details are included in the letter sent with them. I hope everything will arrive.

H

I wrote to your brother in Tripoli[23] urging him to forward those Aleppan *shuqqa*-gowns which he had there in Tripoli. I hope he has got them.

I wrote this letter hurriedly; kindly excuse its form. Greetings to you, your boys, and brothers-in-law, as well as to everyone inquiring about me. *And Peace.*

(Postscript, written upside down on the top of the page:)

Regards to M. Abū Yaḥyā Nahray. Inform him that I sent him the balance due to him with the oil through 'Abd al-Raḥmān. I hope it will arrive.

(Address on the reverse side, otherwise blank:)

To my master and lord Abū Zikrī—may God prolong his life—
Ibn Sighmār—may God be his protector.

the dear, R. Judah, son of R. Moses, (*may he*) *r*(*est in*) *E*(*den*),
From his friend Mūsā, son of Isaac, (*may he*) *r*(*est in*) *E*(*den*)
Sfaqsī.

[21] Spelled thus. Probably the addressee's brother is meant, mentioned here in the next paragraph and in Dropsie 389.

[22] As an inducement to give good service. This was not a present, but a good bargain, sent by the writer to his business friends on his own initiative, without being paid for it in advance.

[23] Tripoli on the Lebanese coast is meant. There was no point in writing to Egypt for action to be taken in Tripoli, Libya, which is near Tunisia. In addition, the goods referred to came from Aleppo in Northern Syria, from where they were exported to the West through Tripoli.

Much support (to you from God!)

(In another script:)
Forwarded by Ibrahīm Ibn al-Iskandarānī.[24]

[24] A representative of merchants in Alexandria, who acted also as a postal agency. See *Med. Soc.*, I, 304, and nos. 72, 73, below.

CHAPTER IV

Merchant-Banker, Scholar, and Communal Leader

Nahray was one of those learned Jewish merchants of Qayrawān who in their youth commuted between Tunisia and the eastern Mediterranean and finally settled in Fustat for good. The first dated document of his career is the account of the transactions during his voyage to Egypt in 1045 (translated in no. 64, below), and the last a sickbed (or deathbed) declaration made on April 28, 1096 (Mosseri A 2). In 1098 he was dead.

Over three hundred letters, notes, and accounts, addressed to him or emanating from his hand have been preserved. This is the largest corpus of Geniza papers related to one person extant and it is all the more valuable as Nahray was active in many different fields. His variegated mercantile undertakings are succinctly described in *Med. Soc.*, I, 153-154 (see also the indexes to vols. I and II), while his banking activities form the main part of my article "Bankers' Accounts from the Eleventh Century A.D.," *JESHO*, 9 (1966), 28-66. Nahray was a central figure in the Maghrebi colony in the East; the yeshiva, or Jewish high council of Jerusalem, recognized his merits as scholar and communal leader by conferring on him the unique title "Senior, or most prominent, member of the yeshiva," and, finally, in no. 35, below, we find him at the head of the two Rabbanite congregations of Fustat.

Nahray's commercial activities are best studied through his accounts, translated in nos. 64, 66, 67, below. The brief selection of letters translated here intends to illustrate his career. By far the earliest item is the calligraphic memo no. 29. Despite its polite wording it says bluntly that, in Egypt, Nahray should act only according to instructions he would receive from the local merchant prince Abū Naṣr Tustarī. It is interesting to note that this writer, who reminds the young man of his apprenticeship with him, disappears entirely from the vast Nahray correspondence—also a sign of how early this memo must have been.[1] Letters 30 and 31 illustrate Nahray's rise to the status of a full-fledged overseas trader, while no. 32 is one of the shorter letters reflecting the esteem in which he was already held during his middle period. Selections 33-35 show him mainly in his capacities of scholar and communal leader.

Other letters to Nahray are translated in no. 5, above, and no. 72, below.

29 INSTRUCTIONS TO A BEGINNER

Mosseri Collection L 5

Memo from your friend who loves you, Khalfa b. Isaac, son of Menaḥēm, (*may his*) *s*(*oul*) *r*(*est in peace*).

My brother and master, Abū Yaḥyā Nahray, may God keep you and give you life. I sent you with my master, the elder Abu Sḥāq Barhūn b. Isḥāq (Abraham b. Isaac)—may God support him—two packages[1] with beads, 300 black units, 300 yellow units, and 400 green, red, and white ones. All these are mine. Those beyond this number (of 1,000 units) belong to the elder Abu Sḥāq Barhūn.[2]

I now wish you to remember the education I gave you and the interest in me of my master, the elder Abu Sḥāq Barhūn. Sell those beads to the extent and in the way you deem fit. No one will interfere with you in this matter. I wish, however, that you kindly inform my lord, the illustrious elder Abū Naṣr al-Faḍl b. Sahl al-Tustarī—may God make his honored position permanent—about the nature and the arrival of this shipment before you sell it and act in accordance with his advice. Likewise, after the sale, tell him

[1] But his three sons were Nahray's business correspondents: Joseph b. Khalfa (see *Med. Soc.*, I, 413, n. 46); Judah, in the account written by Nahray for the year 1058 (TS Box J 1, f. 1, l. 1), Ma'mūn, writing to him (DK 22, *Nahray* 194).

---

[1] Ar. *'ilāwa*, an appendage to a main load in a ship. See *Med. Soc.*, I, 337.

[2] For the value of this consignment cf. no. 64, sec. D, l. 19, below. About 1,600 dirhems or 40 dinars. A common item in both the Mediterranean and the India trade.

how and at what price you have sold and take his advice for further action.

May God guide you to the good and give success to you and through you to me.

And peace upon you, my brother and master.

(In the form of a flourish in Ar. characters:)

And God is sufficient for me and on him I trust.

(Additional Note in another hand:)

The total number belonging to Khalfa b. Isaac: 850 (units), for 150 were returned to him. The 850 (units) form a complete *'ilāwa* (package; see n. 1) and part of another one, the rest of which belonged to Barhūn and Nissīm, the sons of Isaac, as follows: 260 units, 24 units strung up,[3] 25 units loose, 16 bundles of "heaps."[4] Give this to 'Abd al-Raḥmān b. Khalaf, the goldsmith,[5] may God keep the shipment in his mercy.

(A note on the reverse side in Nahray's hand has nothing to do with this text.)

30 LETTER FROM NAHRAY'S MAIN MENTOR

"Buy from the Beggars!"
January 27, 1048

A memo, similar to the one just translated, but more detailed, in the hand of Nahray's main mentor, Abū Isḥāq Barhūn b. Isḥāq b. Barhūn (Abraham b. Isaac b. Abraham) Tāhertī, is contained in TS 13 J 14, f. 9, *Nahray* 205. These are last-minute instructions, sent from Qayrawān to al-Mahdiyya, where Nahray was about to embark on his voyage to Egypt. Again he is advised to follow the guidance of Abū Naṣr Tustarī, Barhūn's partner. The cooperation between the Tāhertīs of Qayrawān and the Tustarīs of Cairo, ob-

[3] Ar. *muzawwaja,* lit., "paired," as opposed to *mufrada.* The usual term for strung up beads in the Geniza is *manẓūma.* Richard Ettinghausen tentatively suggests "in double strings" for muzawwaja.

[4] MS. *ḳndlw,* cf. Persian *ḳindula.* (Doubtful.)

[5] Dealing in the same commodity with Nahray in no. 64, sec. B, l. 18, below. His son Abu 'l-Qāsim was a business friend of Barhūn b. Isaac, Nahray's mentor (TS 10 J 9, f. 5, l. 5, *Nahray* 171). Muslims.

served in selection 11, above, for the preceding generation, was even closer in the generation of Barhūn, his brother, and numerous cousins.

Another Cairene partner of Barhūn to whom Nahray is directed in that memo was the Muslim merchant Abu 'l-Qāsim 'Abd al-Raḥmān, whose name recurs again and again in the Nahray correspondence. Abū Naṣr and 'Abd al-Raḥmān are prominent also in the letter translated below. Thus we see that neither the Karaite sectarianism of the Tustarīs nor the Muslim creed of 'Abd al-Raḥmān impeded orthodox Jews living beyond the sea from cultivating strong and lasting business friendships with them.[1]

Barhūn, Nahray's mentor, must have been a very close relative of his, for in every letter, as in ours, he sends greetings "from *all* those who are with me," that is, all the females in the house. Weighing all the evidence available to me at present, I conclude that Barhūn was married to a sister of Nahray's father and expected that his nephew would marry a daughter of his and, one day, take over his firm. But the young man had other ideas. After several voyages to Egypt he decided to settle in that country, and married into a prominent family there, as others had done before and would do after him (see, for instance, no. 18, sec. A, above).

The date of our letter is fixed by the reference to the murder of Abu Naṣr's brother, the "vizier" Abū Sa'd, which occurred on October 25, 1047. The hope expressed in our letter that Abū Naṣr would be spared was fulfilled for only a short time. He was too rich to escape the caliph's henchmen.

Our letter, like the almost contemporary account translated below as no. 64, shows that the young trader Nahray had already proved his mettle. Yet he still receives much guidance from his old mentor. Barhūn died only a few years later. The account, in which his brother wound up his business with Nahray after his death was written in or around 1055. See *Med. Soc.*, I, 373, sec. 15.

University Library, Cambridge, Taylor-Schechter Collection, TS 20.180, *Nahray* 172.

[1] Barhūn asks Nahray to assure 'Abd al-Raḥmān of his *maḥabba*, lit., "love." TS 13 J 14, f. 9, l. 19.

A. Recapitulation of Previous Correspondence

I am writing to you, my dear brother and master, . . . on the 8th of Shevat (January 27, 1048) . . . I have previously sent you several letters with the couriers and again in recent days some with other couriers. I hope they have arrived. [. . .][2] I was about to travel, but it did not come off. I ask God that this may be to the good. [. . .] arrived in these days and also your letter, in which you informed me that you had gone up to Būṣīr and bought ten bales of flax, [. . . that you have packed] your goods and also bought the rest of your orders. You also referred to that consignment; may God give me and all others who have a share in it big success soon.

B. The Murder of Abū Naṣr's Brother

The couriers brought disastrous news, which terrified us. I ask God to set us at rest and to console everyone by keeping my lord, the elder Abū Naṣr, alive and by granting him safety. May we never hear bad news about him. This will be a comfort to all and calm our hearts with regard to you (pl.).[3]

C. Actions on the Writer's Side

I informed you in my letters what my brother had sold for you in Sūsa.[4] This week he again made good sales on your behalf at 235 and 210 (quarter dinars for a bale of flax of about 500 pounds).[5] But he was unable to obtain a loan on the price.[6] [. . .] He bought for you a hundred excellent garments of very fine quality.

This year a caravan, the like of which we have never seen, is in preparation, but I have not found anyone prepared to take with

[2] Here and in the two following lines two to three words are effaced in each.

[3] The writer dreaded the effects of the murder of the Jewish "vizier" on the Jewish population. See the introduction. One feels, however, that he did not appreciate the murdered vizier himself.

[4] The seaport Sūsa (see no. 25, n. 10), was also the great center of the Tunisian textile industry. In the memo referred to in the introduction Nahray is asked to buy first quality flax "good for Sūsa."

[5] *Med. Soc.*, I, 224ff. It was customary to mention the higher sum first (the opposite of what we do).

[6] The collection of the price from the buyers often took four months or more. The seller who was in need of cash took a loan on the expected sums.

him something for me, not even a hundred or so slips.[7] But I was not prepared to let that caravan go without sending something in it, for I know it will arrive in summer, when everyone burns to buy. Therefore I asked for God's guidance and sent you a purse for my partnership with you weighing 50 dinars in the caravan with 'Abdallāh al Bashqūrī,[8] another one, weighing 65 dinars, for my partnership with M. Abu 'l-Qāsim 'Abd al-Raḥmān, and with Khalīfa Ibn al-Munaghghaṣī ("Substitute, son of the Loathsome")[9] a purse with gold, weighing 50 dinars, for my partnership with you, and one of 65 dinars for my partnership with Abu 'l-Qāsim 'Abd al-Raḥmān, and for the latter also a purse with 1,000 silver dirhems. I also sent you, with his[10] companion Aḥmad Ibn Qāsim, a purse with gold weighing 30 dinars and a bag (of paper or vellum) with 1 1/3 pounds of Syracuse silk.[11]

In a previous letter I had written that I had sent you 1,000 dirhems with Abū Bakr al-Rashīdī,[12] but afterwards he declined to take them. Therefore I changed them into those 30 dinars (sent with Aḥmad).

I sent you with Abū Bakr a purse with 62,250 coral pearls on strings. I paid 25 dinars in advance for two units, but took only the amount noted, which costs 15 dinars per unit here.

D. Orders for Nahray

If you stay on, work on the purchase of four bales of good flax, but do not buy from the Ṭansāwī.[13] You have no strength for deal-

[7] According to quotations from the same period and place, the price for 100 ghilālas, according to quality, would vary from ca. 30 to 350 dinars (see TS 16.174, l. 27, *Nahray* 182, ULC Or 1080 J 79, l. 21, *Nahray* 229). The very fine ones were transparent (Dozy, *Supplément*, II, 809*b*).

[8] Sounds like an Egyptian place name. A Muslim.

[9] Also a Muslim. The nickname of the father was found also among Jews.

[10] The two Muslims mentioned first were known to the addressee. This one was introduced as the travel companion of Ibn al-Munaghghaṣī (who appears again, below).

[11] Either manufactured in Syracuse, Sicily, or made in the style of the silk woven there.

[12] A Muslim from Rosetta, the Egyptian seaport. As the continuation shows, he refused only to forward cash, but was prepared to carry goods.

[13] A Muslim flax merchant and shipowner (*Med. Soc.*, I, 311). The name is derived from that of an Egyptian village. Nahray obviously had written that he intended to buy from him next time.

ing with these great houses; you are better off picking up in person whatever you can from the beggars (the small merchants). You will see what serves best for your success. If the lac is good or if not much of it is to be had, try to buy it with the money you have at your disposal, and when the dinars and dirhems arrive with the early ships, buy well-aired indigo.[14]

If you travel, charge whomever you deem fit with buying flax or lac during the summer with the money at hand. Do not buy hastily. Buying in a hurry has no blessing. Except if you see goods that can be carried as light baggage, such as musk or lapis lazuli, which sells well here because only a little of it is on the market, or *'ḳhrāj*[15] pearls, if they are good. Buy close to your departure and try to get on the first boat setting sail. In short, do what God puts into your mind; may he guide you to good decisions.

E. Some personal requests

During the next few days a caravan from Sijilmāsa[16] is expected, which will continue its way shortly afterwards. If I find a suitable carrier, I shall send something additional with him. All shipments will be addressed to M. Abu 'l-Qāsim 'Abd al-Raḥmān.

I am worried about Abū Zikrī al-Ṭabīb,[17] from whom I have not seen any letter by couriers. I can imagine how he was affected by that terrible event. I ask God to let me hear that he and you all are well.

I had asked M. Abū Zikrī to buy me a *milḥafa* (cloak). If he has not found time for this, please buy me one and send it together

[14] Ar. *nafḍ al-nīl.* The word occurs in the Geniza in two meanings: the scutching, or beating of the dried flax in order to separate the seeds from the fiber, and the airing of cloths after they had been packed for a long time. About indigo see the Introduction, sec. 4.

[15] Meaning perhaps saddlebags. The trappings of riding animals of rich owners were richly decorated; if pearls were included they certainly were third class.

[16] The great caravan city in the south of Morocco which served as the terminal of the trade with sub-Saharan Africa. About the Sijilmāsa caravan to Egypt via Qayrawān see *Med. Soc.*, I, 279.

[17] "The Physician," a family name, one of the most prominent Jewish merchants in the capital of Egypt at that time and probably related to the Tustarīs.

with two Arjīshī robes. Do not be choosy, for here I have to purchase them for a very high price.[18]

Your letter did not contain any news from M. Abu 'l-Qāsim. I ask you always to report in detail about everything. Nor have I received a letter from him and do not know whether or not he has bought flax for me. I know, of course, that he is a dear one;[19] please convey to him my thanks and constantly remind him about my affairs.

F. Greetings to the Writer's Cousins and Friends

Give my best regards to M. Abū Isḥāq Barhūn, the son of my uncle Abu 'l-Faḍl, and to M. Abū Isḥāq Barhūn, the son of my uncle Isma'īl, and tell the latter how happy I was to learn about his safe arrival.[20] Best regards to M. Abū Ibrahīm 'Ayyāsh ("Long-lived") and tell him that I constantly remind his maternal uncle of his affairs.[21] As to M. Abū Sa'īd[22] I understand this letter will arrive only after his departure. May God unite me with him soon.

G. About the Sale of a Bible. Conclusion

In all my letters I have urged you to help 'Aṭā' ("Gift") Ibn Yijū with the books of the Bible he sent you. I hope you have done all you can for him in this matter, for you and I will thereby acquire a religious merit. Do not neglect his request.[23]

[18] Arjīsh, a town in Armenia, on the northern shore of the lake of Van, produced cotton textiles (see Le Strange, *Eastern Caliphate*, p. 183, Serjeant, *Islamic Textiles* x, 103). Since another letter, addressed to Nahray (TS 10 J 15, f. 5, *Nahray* 168, l. 4), states that Arjīshī robes used to be bought in Tripoli, Lebanon, from caravans coming from Aleppo, it stands to reason that these robes actually were imported from Armenia. The price of 1 dinar per robe, noted in the trousseau list in TS K 15, f. 99, col. III, l. 21, proves that the Arjīshī was made of cotton, and not of a more precious fabric.

[19] Ar. *annahū mā yufaddā*, "someone for whom one is prepared to offer oneself as a ransom." A common phrase, but one expects *man* instead of *mā.*

[20] Since boys were called after their grandfathers, it is not surprising that three cousins should be called by the same name Barhūn. There was a fourth one. A generation earlier, the fathers of these merchants are represented in the Geniza as traveling from Tunisia to Egypt.

[21] Two cousins bearing the name 'Ayyāsh appear in the correspondence of the Tāhertīs and of Nahray as closely connected with them.

[22] Abū Sa'īd Joseph b. Moses Tāhertī, also a cousin of our writer.

[23] Refers to the letter of 'Aṭā' b. 'Ammār b. Mevasser to Nahray in which he informs him that he was sending him a codex of the Bible which his father

Peace upon you. And all those who are with me[24] send you kindest regards, and so does my brother in Sūsa. I sent him your letter and have received his answer for you, which I forward to you together with my letter carried by Khalīfa Ibn al-Munaghghaṣī, who has the purses.[25]

And peace upon you, *and peace to the very end.*

(Address:)

(To) my dear brother and master Abū Yaḥyā, may God prolong his life, Nahray b. Nissīm, may God be his protector.

From Barhūn, son of R. Isaac, (*may the*) *m*(*emory of the*) *r*(*ighteous*) *be b*(*lessed*).[26]

31 COOPERATION BETWEEN SEASONED MERCHANTS

From Alexandria to Fustat
Ca. 1055

In this letter Nahray appears as a well-established merchant, although not yet occupying the position of authority which he later enjoyed. His correspondent, Isma'īl b. Faraḥ, a native of Gabes in southern Tunisia, but settled in Alexandria, was a close business friend, a friendship that was continued by the latter's son Faraḥ ("Joy"). Five other letters by Isma'īl addressed to Nahray have been found (*Nahray* 63-66, 249), and three by Faraḥ (*Nahray* 68-70), while Nahray addressed Faraḥ in three others (*Nahray* 3, 4, 246). Isma'īl must have been far older than Nahray, for in one of the letters of his son (*Nahray* 69), he is already dead, but he treats

---

had ordered for himself from the hand of the famous copyist Hilāl (Hillel). The dire economic situation in Qayrawān forced him to sell. The codex was the finest still remaining in Qayrawān (TS 10 J 20, f. 1, *Nahray* 200). His father 'Ammār is expressly called Ibn Yijū. See no. 14, n. 9, above.

[24] His wife and daughters. See the introduction.

[25] See above, sec. C, and n. 9.

[26] Something like "to Fustat" was added. The Arabic address is mostly effaced; but it is noteworthy because of the complete absence of titles.

Nahray as an equal (although he talks to him the way older people address younger men) and expresses warm admiration for him.

The time of the letter is fixed by the report that people were unable to leave Qayrawān, then the capital of Tunisia, for eight months. This must have been before November 1057—when the city was sacked and ruined by the Hilālī bedouins—and after April 1052, the decisive battle which opened the country to them. A letter from Qayrawān, written in August 1052 (TS 13 J 26, f. 9, *Nahray* 227) shows that the situation was already very serious, but not yet as bad as that described in our letter. Any time between 1053 and 1057 would suit the events reported here.

British Museum, Or. 5542, f. 9, *Nahray* 67.

A. Warm thanks and some suggestions

. . . 24th of Elul (August-September) . . . Your letter, transmitted by the courier Jacob[1] has been received, together with its enclosure of two letters by your friend and intimate Faraḥ;[2] may I never be deprived of your benefactions nor miss your kindnesses.

You mentioned the sale of the copper and the quantity still remaining in the *qaysariyya* (caravanserai).[3] May God enable you to sell well; I hope soon to receive the rest of the price of the copper which was sold. You further mentioned that Khalaf b. Ḥātim was on his way (to Būṣīr); please do not cease writing him so as to give him a boost and to encourage him to buy quickly; otherwise, he will keep his eyelids glued together[4] and not open his eyes. Have him buy flax of middle quality at current prices, and God will do the rest for you.

In your letter you mentioned that transaction which only a man like you was fit to carry through; may God reward you. Indeed, all

[1] Jewish couriers operated between Alexandria and Fustat.

[2] The writer's son, who was at that time in the flax-growing center of Būṣīr (see sec. D, below). It was a matter of delicacy in Arab letter writing to relate a person mentioned not to oneself, but to the addressee, even, when, as here, a father wrote about his son.

[3] See *Med. Soc.*, I, 191, 194.

[4] Ar. *yatalakhkhaṣ*, from *lakhiṣ*, having fleshy, swollen eyelids. The young man referred to never appears again in the Geniza correspondence known to me and clearly was not one from whose services the merchants expected much.

you touch with your hand makes other people happy, because it is profitable and done with pure intention.

B. Business in Maghreb in midst of turmoil and bloodshed

You wish to know the news from the West. Until now, four boats have arrived from the capital city of Sicily (Palermo), namely, Ibn al-Baladī,[5] Ibn al-ʿŪdī ("Trader in odoriferous wood"), Ibn al-Nushārī ("Sawduster"),[6] and Ibn al-Mufassir ("Koran-commentator").[7] I received a letter of my brother Sulaymān from Mazara.[8] He was carried out from Qayrawān as dead, for during eight months they tried to leave the city for Sūsa,[9] but were unable to do so. Finally, a group of Muslims and among them some [Jews??] left the city, but the Arabs (meaning: the bedouins) killed them, cutting their stomachs open and saying: "You have swallowed dinars." According to what I learned from our friends, al-Ashqar ("the Red-haired"), the son of Abū Sulaymān, the goldsmith, was one who died in this manner. But my brother Sulaymān said: "I do not leave the city in such a way." Had we not stored our goods in Sūsa, he would not have left at all. (Half a line in which three words, at least, are effaced).[10] The stores were plundered and so was the *funduq* (caravanserai) of Ibn Abī Miskīn, the large one. Qaṣr Ribāt[11] and Qaṣr Ṭāriq[12] were burned. That my brother escaped safely via Sūsa is a miracle. He carried with him purses of gold, two of which were for the Kohen (Nahray's brother-in-law). He gave one to Sidi Ibn ʿImrān, known as "Son of the Mule." I received it from him and it is here with me. He gave the other to Faḍḍāl

[5] Many localities were called or referred to as "Balad," place. Baladī could mean also "a man trading in local textiles."

[6] See *Med. Soc.*, I, 100, and 416, n. 4.

[7] All these ships are also mentioned in other Geniza letters, the last one as once transporting about 500 passengers.

[8] One of the boats mentioned before had called at this seaport on the southwestern corner of Sicily.

[9] A seaport on the northeastern coast of Tunisia.

[10] The ruler of the country is referred to with the Heb. word for "king."

[11] Probably identical with Qaṣr qaṣabat al-Ribāṭ, the castle of the fortress R. (Idris, *Zirides*, p. 565), which may be identical with Qasr Ribāḥ(?) of uncertain reading (ibid., p. 454), near Qayrawān.

[12] Near Sūsa (ibid., p. 446).

("Distinguished") b. Khalfa, "Son of the Slipper,"[13] and I received it from him together with letters and an account. I shall copy one letter and forward it together with this, my letter.[14] Likewise, if any goods should arrive for the Kohen, I shall not be remiss in taking receipt of them. In my eyes, my obligation toward him is like a religious duty, especially if the matter concerns his partnership (with you), for this is my part and my duty. Likewise, my master, if you will receive textiles[15] dispatched by him, send them on immediately, for they are much in demand, since many foreigners are here. I shall appreciate this greatly.

C. Reciprocal services in sales

You noted that you had sold the oil. May I never be deprived of your kindness. I, too, my master, shall recompense the benefaction and, if God wills, send you light silk,[16] silk, copper fragments,[17] and bundles with wax. I ask God to reward me and you, as is his good habit, and grant us safety for the shipment. When it arrives, sell what sells well and leave what is dull.

I have already sent you several letters, one with a Muslim, whom I asked to deliver it to Abraham, Son of the Scholar,[18] and a bundle with letters from Mardūk,[19] which I gave to another Muslim with the request to deliver it to ʿAbd b. Bishr ("Slave, son of Good Tidings").[20] In future, all letters I shall send with a Muslim shall be addressed: "To the house of ʿAbd." Please always inquire there.

[13] "Slipper," *babūsh* (spelled thus) was the nickname of his mother or of an ancestress. The Muslims were no less inventive in coining pejorative bynames than the Jews.

[14] After his brother's letter had survived so many dangers, the writer did not want it to be lost in a humdrum accident, such as falling into the Nile during the travel upstream. Copying letters before forwarding them was common.

[15] Ar. *matāʿ*. Same usage in no. 70, sec. C, below.

[16] Ar. *khazz* (see no. 2, n. 12, above).

[17] See no. 14, n. 7, above.

[18] This notable (see no. 5, n. 25, above) could be easily found by a Muslim, because he had his office in the "House of Exchange." See *Med. Soc.*, I, 238.

[19] One of the closest business friends of Nahray (see Mardūk's letters to him in *Nahray* 101-109, 245, 252-253). Other letters by and to Mardūk have been preserved.

[20] The proprietor of a *wakāla*, or warehouse, where business was also conducted. Thus our letter was sent to that place. See the Ar. address, below.

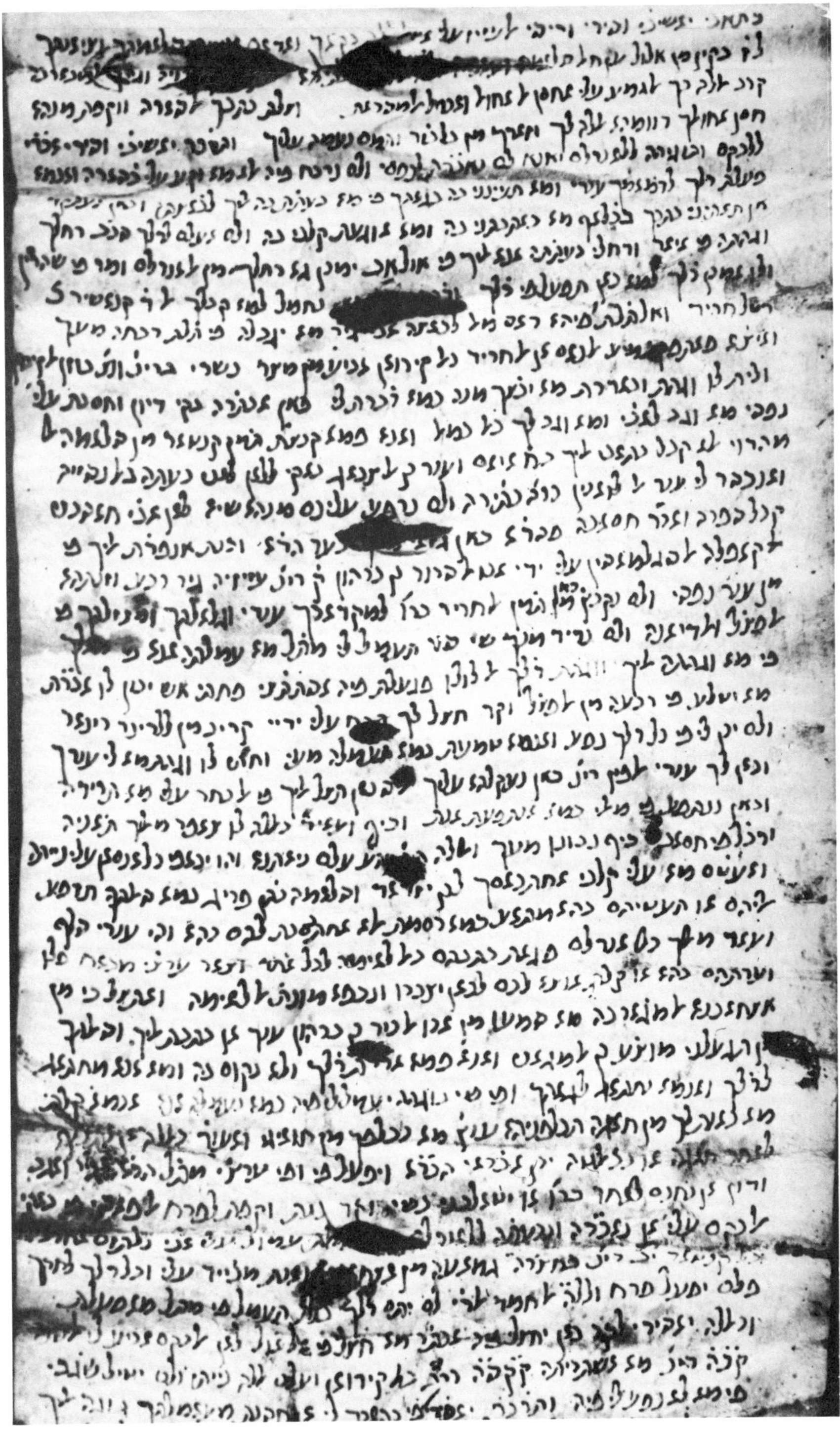

I. Beginning of letter no. I. Good example of the script of an eleventh century business clerk. From the David Kaufmann Collection, Budapest, Hungary.

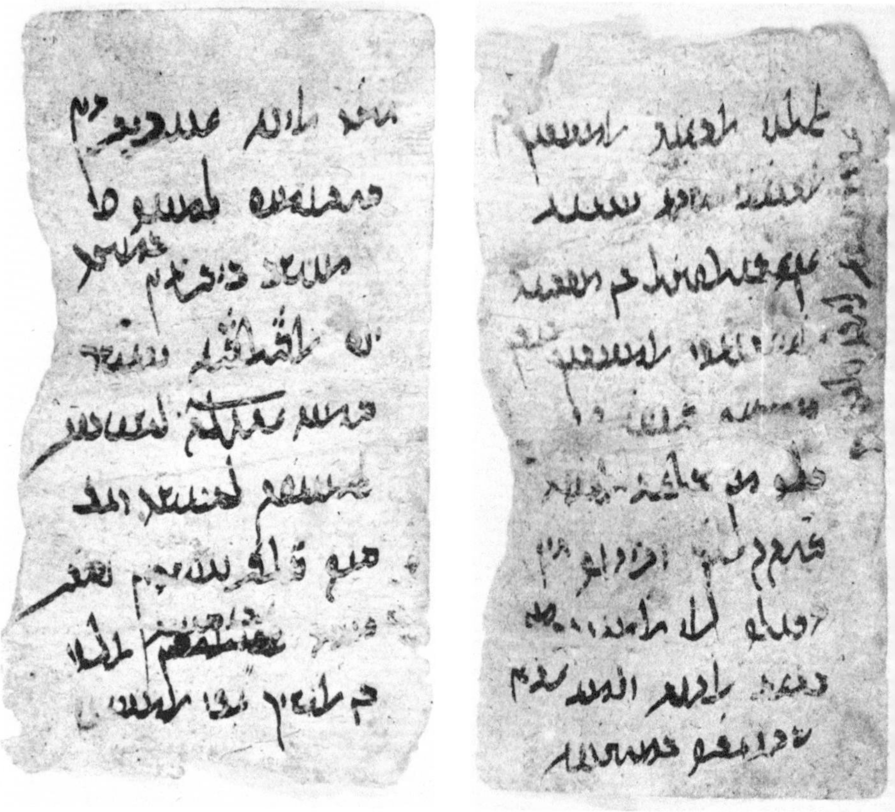

2a and 2b. Letter no. 46. Holograph of the Nagid Abraham Maimonides. Although born in Egypt in 1186, eighteen years after his father arrived in that country, his handwriting is in the Spanish style, probably because he had studied with a teacher from Spain. From the Taylor-Schechter Collection, University Library, Cambridge, England.

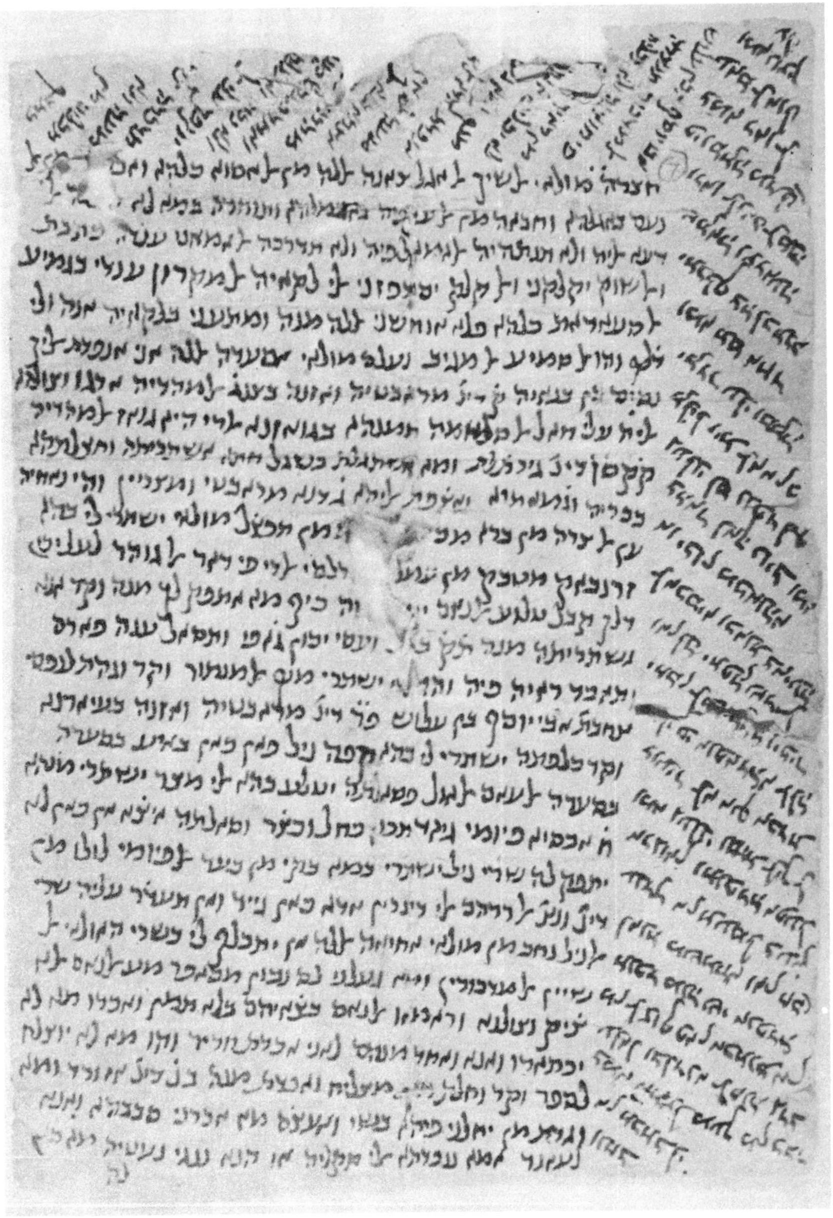

3a and 3b (over). Letter to ʿArūs (nos. 48-51). Script as used in books. A carefully written letter like this has the look of a carpet. The writer wrote from top to bottom, then in the margin from bottom to top, then, on the head of the page, from right to left, continuing overleaf only when needed. The reverse side had to be left at least partially blank since they used no envelopes. The recipient jotted accounts on the space left blank. From the David Kaufmann Collection, Budapest, Hungary.

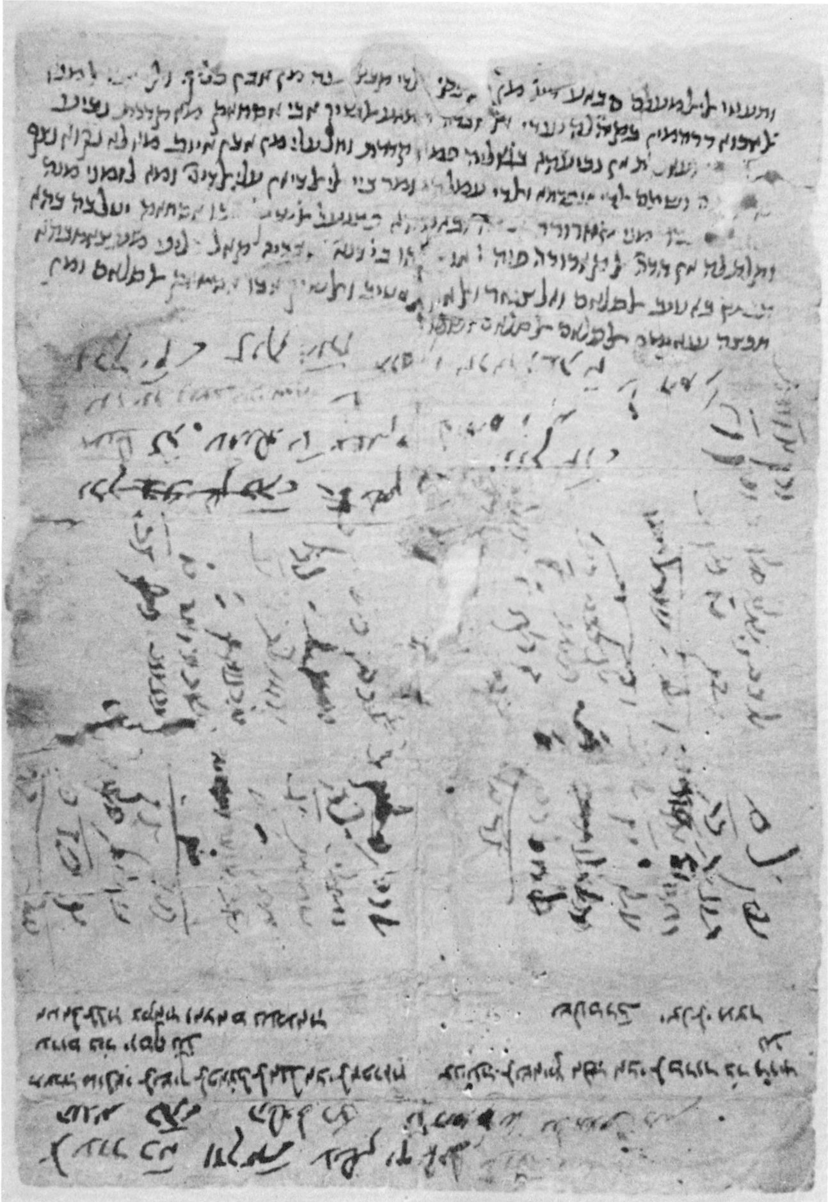

D. Cash for purchases

I asked God, the exalted, for guidance and sent you a purse containing 109 dinars, 40 of which are in a separate purse with Muhammad, the son of Shibl ("Lion cub"), the hazelnut trader. Kindly send these to your friend and intimate Faraḥ in Būṣīr.[21] Of the remaining 69 dinars, 64 were acquired by me from representatives of merchants, and they are the best money to be had in the town. Five dinars less one-sixth are broken quarters, of which 1 dinar is Rūmī (Christian, presumably Norman). Please sell everything and buy for them first-class, fine, and shining Shāmī (Syro-Palestinian) dinars and send them to me quickly.[22] Also write to me about the prices (in Fustat) of the goods sent from the Maghreb and from . . . (and) sal ammoniac. I shall appreciate this greatly.

E. Conclusion and a P.S.

The two purses of the Kohen[23] are of leather and sewn up. I shall weigh them together with the leather and write you their weight.

You write me about that Syro-Palestinian Jew. He lives in the (Jewish) quarter.[24] I shall go up to him and act in accordance with your instructions. But today is Friday, too short a day for this.[25] I shall go up to him after the Sabbath, if God wills. Best regards to you and to my lord, the elder Abu Iṣḥāq[26] Barhūn. *And Peace!*

(P.S.:) The dispatch of my letter has been deferred to Monday,

[21] See n. 2, above.

[22] The writer wished to order goods from one or several of the ports of Palestine, Lebanon, and Syria.

[23] See sec. B, above; "of," Ar. *matā'*, still rare in this period (see J. Blau, *Grammar*, p. 159, *d*). Thus in the same letter matā' has two entirely different meanings. See n. 15, above.

[24] A *ḥārat al-yahūd*, or Jewish quarter, in Alexandria is mentioned in TS 12.254, margin, *Nahray* 102, where Mardūk (see n. 19, above) complains that he could not find female help there after the death of his wife. Probably identical with *al-Qamra*, a predominantly Jewish neighborhood, often mentioned.

[25] A respectable merchant like the writer of our letter would not walk but ride (on a mule or a donkey). Sabbath, on which riding was prohibited, began on Friday an hour before sunset, approximately at 5:30 p.m. at the time and the place where the letter was written.

[26] Spelled with *ṣ* under the influence of *ḥ* and q. Nahray's mentor.

the 27th of Elul. The large ship of Ibn Abī ʿAqīl[27] has arrived; likewise, the barge of (Abu?) ʾl-Faraj, and that of the qadi of Tripoli, Syria.

My master Abu ʾl-Faraj Mardūk today received a bundle addressed to Elhanan and Joseph, the Kohen. . . .[28] I have explained to you what belongs to you (pl.) in this bundle in the copy of the letter which you (pl.) have received from my brother Isaac in Sūsa. Please buy 500 pounds of sugar and send them to me. *And Peace.*

(Address:) To my master and lord Abū Yaḥyā, Nahray, son of Nissīm (*may he*) *r*(*est in*) *Eden*—may God prolong his life and always keep him safe and happy.

From Ismaʿīl b. Faraḥ . . .

(In Arabic letters:)

To Nahray b. Nissīm

To the house of ʿAbd, the agent, if God wills.

To the house of ʿAbd, the agent.[29]

32 A LETTER OF THANKS AND APPRECIATION FROM JERUSALEM

Letters expressing gratitude to Nahray for his selfless help are legion. We have chosen this one for translation because it shows the personal style of Solomon b. Moses of Sfax (Salāma b. Mūsā), mentioned in the introduction to no. 28, above, as the writer of the longest letter preserved in the Geniza. Two other letters of Solomon to Nahray, both sent from Alexandria, show him in close and continuous connection with him, Nahray, as usual, not answering and

[27] The qadi of Tyre, Lebanon (see *Med. Soc.*, I, 296). The MS clearly has Abī (as correct), and not Abū, as usual. These ships came from the Syro-Palestinian coast.

[28] Elhanan b. Ismaʿīl al-Andalusī, the brother of the writer of no. 22, above, and mentioned there, sec. C. Appearing repeatedly as partner of Joseph ha-Kohen b. Eli of Fez. Merchants from Spain and Morocco operating together in Egypt were not uncommon in the eleventh century with its West-East movement of migration.

[29] Neatly written twice by way of emphasis.

Solomon, as was his habit, excusing him.[1] One of these letters refers to the death of a member of the Tāhertī family, who, in 1052, still signed a document in Fustat.[2] Our letter is from Nahray's middle period, ca. 1060.

University Library, Cambridge, Taylor-Schechter Collection, TS Box 25, f. 124, *Nahray* 185.

A. Arrival in Jerusalem

I am writing to you, my dear master—may God prolong your life and make permanent your honored position and your high and noble rank—from Jerusalem, the blessed—may God let me and you and all Israel see its rebuilding and establishment—on the 20th of Tevet (January). I am well and prosperous and full of gratitude to God who has let me reach this time and this illustrious view (of the Holy City). I ask God the exalted to grant me and all Israel remission in his mercy, as it is written: "*Come back to me, and I shall come back to you.*"[3] God is much-forgiving and merciful.[4]

I have written to you several times before from Abu 'l-Bays[5] and then from Ramle. I hope the letters have arrived, but I have not [received] an answer to any one of them. I hope that occupation with good things has kept you from answering. May you always be occupied thus, my lord, may God keep you, and in such a way that you are excused.

I arrived in Jerusalem safely and in good physical condition de-

[1] TS 10 J 4, f. 2, *Nahray* 184; Mosseri L 42.3 (IV-36). The latter is in the hand of Ibrahīm b. Faraḥ al-Iskandarānī, the Alexandrian representative of the merchants, but the name of the sender was written by Solomon.

[2] Mosseri L 42.3*v*, ll. 1-2. Barhūn b. Mūsā Tāhertī, a cousin of Barhūn b. Isaac, Nahray's mentor. See no. 30, above.

[3] Malachi 3:7. Muslims, Christians, and Jews regarded the hardships of a pilgrimage as a means for atonement. The quotation implies the additional meaning that the physical "return" to Jerusalem of the Jewish pilgrim induced God's "return," that is, forgiveness.

[4] A phrase extremely common in the Koran, a fact of which the writer was of course, ignorant.

[5] Usually called Bilbays, the town on the eastern border of Egypt, from which the caravans set out to Palestine through the Sinai desert. The fact that the writer was able to send several letters from there to Nahray shows that he had to wait a long time before he found a suitable caravan.

spite utmost exertion, as I was overtaken by snow on my way. The end was thus to the good, for he who hopes for the good will obtain it. God does not break his promise. I arrived safely on Thursday of last week in the middle of the month of Tevet.[6]

B. Return to the Maghreb

I intend, however, my master, to return and am preparing my travel to Ramle. I do not know how long I shall stay, for the city has already been gripped by heavy rain and snow for four days.

You have most kindly [honor]ed me in this matter of the purchase of three bales of flax. I have written you about this in my letter from Ramle and asked you to act—may God recompense you and help me to reciprocate, for at this time of the year goods are sold on credit, and he who starts first outruns others.[7]

Please buy these three bales of flax with the dinars you owe me and those to be received by M. Abū 'Imrān Mūsā,[8] son of Abu 'l-Ḥayy, (*may he*) *r*(*est in*) *E*(*den*), for twenty skins of oil. Take the balance from M. Abū 'Alī Ḥassūn, son of Yaḥyā, (*may he*) *r*(*est in*) *E*(*den*).[9]

Thus there remains nothing for me to do except to trust in God, the exalted, and in you. My travel (to the Maghreb) depends solely on God and on you. So, please do not be remiss, for I cannot know how long I shall be forced to tarry on my way; God ordains everything, and he will enable me to be united with my lord, my father, may God keep him, before he departs this world. By my father,[10]

[6] The Tunisian merchant sojourning in Egypt intended to use the quiet business season in midwinter for the pilgrimage to Jerusalem. His friends tried to dissuade him because of the rough weather conditions. But he persisted and states now that his optimism was justified.

[7] As the continuation shows, Solomon did not need credit. He wished to emphasize that buying during the low season was profitable, wherefore Nahray should now fulfill his promise.

[8] One of the most prominent Maghrebi Jewish merchants active in Egypt (see *Med. Soc.*, II, 445). Many of his letters have been preserved.

[9] A close business friend of Solomon and his father. See no. 27, n. 9; no. 28, n. 18, above; and, e.g., TS 10 J 4, f. 2, margin, *Nahray* 184, where he is in Jerusalem expecting an urgent letter from Solomon's father; or Dropsie 389, l. 39, where he travels from al-Mahdiyya to Mazara, Sicily. Here, he is in Fustat, of course.

[10] This is a popular oath in which the regular word for father, *ab*, is used. But in polite speech and throughout the Geniza letters, a father is referred to as *wālid*, "progenitor."

the purpose of my travel to the Maghreb, my lord, is solely to see my father—may God, the exalted, help me in this; business is at a standstill there.

C. Praise of Nahray

What you, my lord, have done will be rewarded in this world and the world to come, if God wills. (The continuation, written in the margin, about fifteen words, is lost. The writer seems to speak about something done for his father or someone unable to reciprocate.) He praises you everywhere. May God fulfill through you always the saying of the prophet: "*A good name is better than sweet-scented oil.*"[11] Thank God, my lord, for this good name, and do not care that man, as you will know, never obtains reward for his good deeds. May God never take this merit and all you have done for your friends and brothers and everyone else away from you and your children after you. And may you always be a refuge for everyone, as is befitting you.

D. The Illness of a Friend

I was sad to learn from your letter to my lord Abu 'l-Faraj Rabbi Abūn of Gabes[12] about what happened to my lord Abu 'l-Faraj Yeshū'ā.[13] May God accept this *as an expiation and atonement*, and, since the end was good, it should be regarded as a benefaction for which God should be praised. Please give him my regards.

E. Death in a Foreign Country

The passing away of Abū Zikrī Judah Ibn al-'Uṣfūra ("Sparrow")[14] affected me deeply. May God have mercy upon him and fix the Garden of Eden as his dwelling place and grant composure to his family. May he spare me and you[15] from death in a foreign

11 Ecclesiastes 7:1. The biblical verse means that the fame of good deeds is more pervasive than the scent of perfume.

12 Numerous letters of this native of Gabes in southern Tunisia to Nahray, all sent from Jerusalem, have been preserved.

13 Yeshū'ā b. Isma'īl. This grave illness may, or may not, have been identical with that referred to at great length in no. 25 A, above.

14 Female nickname which became a family name. Several persons bearing this name occur in the Geniza papers.

15 At the time of the writing of these lines, Nahray had lived in Egypt for at least fifteen years and was married to a local woman. Still, he was regarded as a Maghrebi.

country, for this, by my father, is hard. There is no escape from death; it comes sooner or later; may God prolong your life, spare you for your friends, and keep sorrow away from you.

F. Conclusion

By my father, my master, I am disquieted because of you and because of the absence of letters from you. May God let me hear good tidings about you soon. Perhaps you could send me a letter to Ascalon, in care of my lord Abū Isaac Abraham, the Son of the Scholar,[16] which would make my heart somewhat lighter and, together with it, perhaps a letter from M. Abū 'Alī [Ḥassū]n b. Yaḥyā[17] containing news and a report about goods arriving from the West; and perhaps a courier carrying a letter for me has arrived from there. (Two lines, written in the margin and concluding the letter, are lost. The top of the letter contains a note on an old woman, apparently a relative of Nahray, referred to also in other letters to Nahray from Jerusalem.)

(Address:)

To my master and lord Abū Yaḥyā, may God support and help him in his mercy.

Nahray, son of Nissīm, (*may he*) *r*(*est in*) *E*(*den*), God is his protector and helper.

From his grateful Solomon b. Moses, son of Isaac, (*may he*) *r*(*est in*) *E*(*den*), of Sfax. *Much support* (*to you from God*).

(In Arabic characters: Approximately the same text, but Solomon is called here Ḥassūn, either a misunderstanding of the clerk, or the Arabic name was temporarily changed. "To Fustat" is erroneously written twice. The sender is called "the Maghrebi from Sfax.")

[16] About this personality and his sojourn in Ascalon see *Med. Soc.*, I, 238-239. On his way back Solomon would stay and do some business in that seaport of southern Palestine.

[17] See n. 9, above.

33 FROM THE CORRESPONDENCE OF SCHOLARS

From al-Mahdiyya, Tunisia, to Fustat
1061

The writer of this letter was the Jewish chief judge of al-Mahdiyya. The judge, like a Muslim qadi, or the Christian patriarch of Alexandria, also engaged in business, and examples of the commercial correspondence between him and Nahray have been preserved. But this letter deals mainly, though not exclusively, with learned and legal matters. The scholar referred to in secs. A-D with such epithets as "Light of the World" or "Renewer of the Religion" was R. Nissīm b. Jacob, one of the greatest rabbinical authorities of all times (see no. 75, n. 10, below, where a book of his is copied in Messina, Sicily, ninety-two years later).

Our letter was written after 1057, the date of the ruin of Qayrawān, when R. Nissīm and other inhabitants of that city had found refuge in Sūsa, a seaport on the Tunisian coast north of al-Mahdiyya. R. Nissīm died in 1062 (see next selection). The reference to the Sicilian city whose male inhabitants were put to sword by the conquering Normans (sec. H) fits the fall of Messina in 1061.[1]

Institute Narodov Azii, Leningrad, D-55, no. 13.[2]

A. Nahray's eye disease

In Your name.

I am writing to you, . . . from al-Mahdiyya, at the end of Av (August), . . . The situation is well in hand,[3] thank God who dispenses all benefactions.

Your letters, my lord, . . . worried, disquieted, and troubled me, and scared the sleep from my eyes, because of the eye disease which had attacked you. I ask God to take care of you and to heal you and to never let me hear anything sorrowful about you and to accept me as a ransom for you. *May he send his word and heal you, heal you completely. Amen. May thus be his will.*

1 Amari, *Musulmani di Sicilia*, III, 71.
2 Ed. S. D. Goitein, *Tarbiz* 36 (1966), 56-72.
3 In contrast to the ruin of Qayrawān and the devastation of the Tunisian countryside.

I sent your letter to the [. . .], the Light of the World, and he wrote me how much he regretted to learn about your illness. He prayed for you, and I am confident his prayer will be accepted. I remained disquieted, however, until our friends arrived telling me that you were well and that your eyesight had been restored. But I shall not be completely quiet until I shall receive a letter from you to this effect. May God always let me have happy news from you.

B. The copying of R. Nissīm's works, interrupted by his illness

I wish to inform you, my lord, . . . that I asked a friend in Sūsa to buy parchment and to deliver it to a copyist. Unfortunately, they have only one copyist there, who also teaches children so that he can devote only a part of his time to copying.[4] He has already done sixteen quires, which have been compared with the original. The continuation had to be postponed because of what happened to our master, the great Rāv.[5] He was almost given up, and the community was grieved and disturbed, for he is *our solace in our misery, and under his shadow we live among the nations.*[6] But God looked upon us and did not afflict us and blind our eyes. He remained weak for some time. But recently I received his illustrious letter in which he breaks the good news of his complete recuperation. We praised God that he looked upon us and did not disgrace us, for the life of the master means progress for the nation, upholding of the Law, and renewal of the religion. I ask God to grant him life for us and for all the *communities* and accept us as a ransom from all evil destined for him.

C. A learned letter of Nahray lost

The master had taken notice of your criticism of a legal opinion by *our master* Hay[7] *of (blessed) m(emory)*. But he noted: "I know

[4] A common combination. See *Med. Soc.*, II, 189, 237.

[5] This shows that R. Nissīm supervised the copying of his works in person. Since much of his work has been found in the Cairo Geniza, this remark is not without importance.

[6] Referring in Lamentations 4:20 to "the anointed of the Lord," the king.

[7] The *responsums*, or answers to legal queries, by Hay Gaon (d. 1038) were eagerly studied long after his death.

that this legal opinion is open to objection, but I shall wait until Nahray's letter with the difficulties pointed out by him will arrive; then I shall explain the matter to him, for I have a fine solution for them." God, the exalted, however, ordained what happened to the letter on its way to Sūsa, which distressed our master very much.[8]

On the very day the copied quires arrived from Sūsa, I gave them to merchants from Damascus. But they said: "We have no proper place for carrying them." I shall send them to you in one of the boats.

The beginning of the commentary of our master on [. . .] was copied here, in al-Mahdiyya, on my order and I was about to have it bound and dispatched, when a beautiful and carefully corrected copy turned up.[9] I had the copying stopped.

D. A case of inheritance

I read what you have written concerning the affair of M. Israel[10] and have appointed an attorney in Sūsa, who informed me that he could not get more than 10 dinars out of Israel's brother, even after *our master* had talked to him. He wrote me himself, assuring me under heavy oath that Israel owed him over 100 dinars,[11] and asked me to let the matter rest until he would have written to his brother. After consultation with *our master* I issued him a certificate on the payment of these 10 dinars.

[8] The Writer had informed R. Nissīm of the point made by Nahray in a general way, to which the master had responded as reported here. But Nahray's letter was lost on the way between al-Mahdiyya and Sūsa, presumably in a case of robbery, about which the writer had reported in a previous communication.

[9] Probably looted during the sack of Qayrawān. My translation here corrects the version provided in *Tarbiz* 36 (1966), 61 and 69.

[10] A cousin and frequent correspondent of Nahray, whose brother, also called Abū Yaḥyā Nahray, sojourned in Sūsa.

[11] Very unlikely that the man would have paid even a penny if he was able to substantiate a claim on 100 dinars. Such exaggerated assertions were common at the beginning of a lawsuit.

E. Plea for the writer's brother

As to my words of excuse for my elder son and younger brother[12] —God knows that he is dearer to me than my own soul. In fact, no blame comes to him at all. Only because of my exaggerated love for him have I used some strong words against him. I ask God to protect my lord, . . . and now I am quiet that my brother has found a friend in such an illustrious man as my lord and I have no doubt that now he will be successful and well-guided.

F. A consignment sent with the qadi's "boy"

You noted what you had sent with the agent of the qadi, (may) G(od) in(spire him with right decisions).[13] He said, however, to Abū Lamtūna:[14] "The thing got lost in *Qnwn*; the councilmen[15] attacked us." I had written to my brother (the recipient) to send with him only a fixed, replaceable sum,[16] but not [. . .]. Now I had to prove the exact nature of the consignment. But they said: "Your brother likes us, why should he not confide his wares to us and we would carry them to you to your full satisfaction?"[17] When he comes to your place again, you will sue him, for he is [joining?] Abraham, the messenger, who travels to your parts this year, God willing.

G. Revival of Jewish learning in Egypt

I was much pleased to read in your letter about the dedication to the study of the Torah and the zeal for learning shown by the son of *our master* Nathan of (blessed) me(mory), the head of the

[12] The writer calls his younger brother Abū Zikrī Judah b. Moses, a prominent merchant from Qayrawān active in Egypt (see no. 28, above), "elder son," because he educated him. The words of affection are remarkable. In a previous letter, Labrāṭ had purposely used some harsh words while writing about his beloved brother.

[13] Interesting that a Jewish judge uses this blessing for a Muslim colleague in a letter addressed to another Jewish divine.

[14] Certainly the local Muslim representative of the merchants. A Berber.

[15] Ar. *shūrāwīn*. In the times of anarchy, towns made themselves independent under "councils," *shūrā*, which, as a sideline, practiced banditry. See Dozy, *Supplément*, I, 799.

[16] Read: *mithl maḥdūd*.

[17] The qadi's employee seems to emphasize that *force majeur*, not negligence on his side, was involved.

yeshiva.[18] May God keep his youthful zest[19] and support him. And may he protect the life of our lord, the *Rāv*,[20] may his honored position be permanent and may he always receive God's favors. For through him God has revived learning (in Egypt), illuminated the community and fortified religion. He must continue his efforts, knowing how much he has already achieved in those parts and how great his reward will be for this. May God keep him and multiply men like him in Israel. No doubt God pays special attention to this community, for he does not leave a generation without a man who revives what has become defective and teaches what might be in danger of being forgotten, for thus he has promised us: "*It will never cease from the mouth of their offspring.*"[21]

H. The Norman conquest of Sicily

You inquired, my lord, . . . about Sicily. The situation deteriorates constantly, and everyone is terribly disturbed about the progress of the enemy who has already conquered most of the island. The prices here go up, for this place must rely for its supply of grain entirely on Sicily.[22] Twelve families of our coreligionists have been taken captive,[23] and countless numbers of Muslims. May God protect all those of Israel who have remained there. [Messina (?) was conquered] by sword and a number of Jews died there. All these are matters which require attention.[24] May God look upon us in his mercy and hide us in the treasure houses of his forgiveness.

18 Nathan I b. Abraham served as head of the Jewish high council of Jerusalem for a short time only (1039-1042), but was president of its court for many years. His grandson and namesake served again in this capacity, while his great-grandson, compelled to leave war-ridden Palestine, was appointed judge in (New) Cairo. I cannot say which of the sons of Nathan I is intended here.

19 Ar. *tamm allāh shabābhu*, a phrase never seen by me.

20 About this personality in Fustat, who is referred to in countless letters solely with this designation "the Master," see no. 35, below.

21 Deuteronomy 31:21.

22 This astonishing statement had its immediate reason in the devastation of the countryside by the Arab bedouins, but the dependence of the Tunisian seaports on Sicily for their supply of grain remained a reality for centuries. See H. R. Idris, *JESHO* 4 (1961), 235.

23 The exact number of captives was known to the judge probably because he had to deal with their ransoming.

24 The care for the survivors. After all the terrors that had afflicted Tunisia

Please, never let me be without an illustrious letter of yours reporting your good health and any concern you may have so that I can deal with it to your satisfaction, . . . Kindest regards to my lord. Your servant Mūsā[25] sends to my lord kindest regards.

God is sufficient for me and in him I trust.

(Address:)

(To) my master and lord, the illustrious elder Abū Yaḥyā *M. R.* Nahray, *son of R.* Nissīm, (*may he*) *r*(*est in*) *E*(*den*), may God prolong his life and always protect him and keep him prosperous. (From) Labraṭ, *son of Moses,* (*may his*) *s*(*oul*) *r*(*est in peace*), Ibn Sighmār.[26]

(Nahray's address is repeated in Ar. characters. As destination "his home," obviously known to the courier, is given.)

34 DEATH OF THE MASTER

August 12, 1062

The writer of this letter, Yeshūʿā b. Ismaʿīl (see selections 13-16, above), and Nahray b. Nissīm had studied in their youth with R. Nissīm b. Jacob of Qayrawān.[1] Here Yeshūʿā informs Nahray of the death of their spiritual mentor a day after he had learned about it from travelers arriving from Sicily.

The date of the letter is established by the reference to the death of the Sicilian condottiere Ibn al-Thumna, who was killed in March 1062 (see Amari, *Musulmani di Sicilia*, III, 89).

University Library, Cambridge, Taylor-Schechter Collection,
TS 13 J 19, f. 20, *Nahray* 88.

---

recently, the judge looked at the Norman conquest of Sicily more from a practical point of view.

[25] Moses, the son of the judge. He might have been the copyist, who wrote this letter calligraphically.

[26] The non-Hebrew names are Berber, not Arabic.

---

[1] See no. 33, introduction, above.

A. Sad times[2]

I am writing to you . . . from Alexandria on the 4th of Elul (August 12, 1062) . . . My body is sound, but my soul is sore. But we must be grateful to God under all circumstances. "*He spoke, and so it was.*"[3] Your letter—may God make you honored—arrived after I had not seen a letter from you, nor heard from you, for a long time. Then your letter came, delivered by the courier Surūr ("Happiness"),[4] and from it I learned about your well-being; may God make it permanent. I thanked him, the exalted, for his benefaction. The worries expressed by you are shared by me. May God, the exalted, *hide us in the shadow of his wings*[5] *and not summon us to his court* in this time of *great tribulations.*

B. Death of the master

The gravest of all, however, that afflicted my heart is what I have to communicate you now:

The boat of Mujāhid ("Warrior in the Holy War")[6] arrived from Mazara (Sicily) after a passage of seventeen days. A number of our Spanish coreligionists traveled in it, among them Abū Jacob Joseph, whose son-in-law is in Miṣr (Cairo-Fustat). The boat arrived on Friday, the day of the new moon, but they were able to disembark only yesterday, on Sunday. I went to them and asked them about news from Sicily. They reported good and reassuring news, namely, that Ibn al-Thumna had been killed and that the situation in the place had become settled.

Today I was visited by M. Isaac, son of R. 'Ābid ("Devout," "Pietist")[7] and he relayed to me calamitous news from them "*which*

[2] The year 1062 marked the complete collapse of civil government in Egypt and its replacement by the anarchy of rivaling bands of mercenaries. In that year a pitched battle was fought between the Turkish and the black battalions of the caliph just outside Cairo, in which the former remained victorious.

[3] Psalm 33:9, which, however, refers to the miracle of creation.

[4] An equivalent of Heb. Simḥā. A Jewish courier. See no. 31, n. 1, above.

[5] Cf. Psalm 17:8.

[6] Mentioned as already being on its way from Egypt to Tunisia in 1046 and as sailing from Denia, Spain, to Alexandria, with no Jewish passenger on board in TS 8 J 20, f. 2, a letter by Isma'īl b. Faraḥ. See no. 31, above.

[7] His name was Nissīm al-'Ābid b. Isaac (TS 12.150, dated Fustat, 1005). Isaac and his sons Abraham and Moses were active as merchants. There were other families bearing this name in both the eleventh and twelfth centuries.

makes the ears of whomsoever hears it tingle"[8] and let me forget my previous worries. "*One disaster makes one forget the other.*"[9] The demise of our master Nissīm, (may his) m(emory) be (blessed).

I went to see them, and they told me that they were in Mazara when some Jewish people arrived from al-Mahdiyya and told them that he was buried on . . . in al-Mahdiyya.

When I heard this, I rent my clothes and took off my shoes,[10] *and cried out in the bitterness of my soul. I was like one whose beloved lay before him dead. I sat to earth appalled and tears burst from my eyes for the light of Is(rael) which has been extinguished because of our many sins. "The godly man has gone and the righteous one is no more."*[11] *For such a one I howl and lament and wail day and night, / for there is no cure to our affliction / and no one has compassion or pity. / Until the Mighty one will look forth / in mercy and indulgence / upon the dove without guile /*.[12] Before I said: *Praised be the true judge, all of whose decisions are just and right, and no one should censure his ways. Praised be he by whom no wrong is done.* How bitter is this cup, how heavy is this sorrow. *Would I had died in his stead. But "no man can redeem his brother nor give to God a ransom for him."*[13] *God is just in all his ways and merciful in all his deeds.* I ask him, the exalted, *to look at our tribulations, and not at our sins and have mercy and indulgence with the remnants of his people. Amen.*[14]

C. References to Nahray's letter

You wrote about the affair with Barhūn.[15] I showed him your letter and requested the account from him. He said: "Yes, I shall give it to you." I shall force him to do so, although he made the impression as if he did not know about that transaction. He is a very slow man, but I got all he owes me out of him, with only 2 dirhems remaining.

[8] Jeremiah 19:3.

[9] An imprecise reminiscence of Talmud Bab., Berakhot 13*a*.

[10] These customs of extreme mourning, permitted only at the death of a close relative, are prescribed at the death of one's main master.

[11] Micah 7:2, with change, discussed by me in *Zion* 27 (1962), 17, n. 38.

[12] The people of Israel. A rhymed piece from a dirge.

[13] Psalm 49:8.

[14] R. Nissīm was over seventy at the time of his death.

[15] Barhūn is Abraham. Impossible to say which one is meant.

I was sorry to learn about the hides. It would have been better if we had sold them at that time, but there is nothing to be done. Perhaps, when the people calm down, Sharaf will remember to ask for them.

D. Request to send the slave and business agent Ṭayyib

(Ṭayyib, Khallūf b. Mūsā's agent, had been lent by him to the writer of our letter—see no. 23, sec. F, and n. 8, above. But Ṭayyib had soon found out the unpleasant character of his new master and had left Alexandria for Fustat, Nahray's place.)

Kindly meet Ṭayyib and reproach him for what he has done to me. I have not treated him unkindly. Here are the letters of his master admonishing him and telling him that he should be at my disposal and never leave me, except if I wish to send him to Būṣīr (the center of flax-growing) or any other place. Now he has left me at the very time when I needed someone on whom I could rely. These tribulations came when I was through with the dissolution of the partnership[16] and intended to leave for the country (to collect debts). But everyone to whom I talked about this said: "Praise God that you were not in the Rīf when those troubles started, for people were destroyed there everywhere." Thus they calmed me somehow. If there was income there, it had gone anyhow. But man is covetous.

So, please make an effort and induce him to return and to be submissive. He could possibly come down to Fuwwa or to Malīj.[17] Perhaps God will grant me to retrieve (some of the money due to me). I need not urge you, my lord. You know best what is in my heart and how much I burn to retrieve that money. May God help me in this and let me choose the right thing, me, and you, and all Is(rael).

[16] Ar. *naqḍ*. Could mean also: demolition of a house. The addressee knew of course the matter alluded to.

[17] Places between Cairo and Alexandria. The writer wished to meet the slave half-way and then travel with him in the Nile delta to collect his debts.

E. Conclusion

As to R. Ḥalfōn, I talked to R. Mardūk and to R. Yeshūʿā, the member of the academy,[18] about this. We shall take up that matter with him and hope he will return what is due to you.

Whatever additional news arrive—I hope they will be good—I shall let you know. The boat of Mufaḍḍal ("Preferred") has arrived in al-Mahdiyya;[19] thus, all boats have arrived there safely, thank God.[20] *And peace.*

F. P.S.

Best regards to you and to R. Abraham,[21] R. Abū Naṣr, my masters your brothers-in-law, may God keep them, to all under your care and those who inquire about me. *And peace in plenty.*

R. Abū ʿAlī Ḥasan, the physician from Barqa, sends you kindest regards. He intended to travel to your place, for he is on his way to Jerusalem, may God rebuild it, and he insists on continuing the journey. When you write to me, mention him with greetings. He is a friend of yours and speaks of you all the time.[22]

(Address:)

(To) my master and elder R. Nahray, son of R. Nissīm, (*may his*) *m*(*emory*) *be* (*blessed*).

May God prolong his life and always give him honor and strength.

[18] Mardūk b. Mūsā (Mordechai b. Moses) was an intimate friend of Nahray's living in Alexandria (see no. 5, n. 15, above). Yeshūʿā (b. Joseph), the member of the academy, was Jewish judge and communal leader in the city. He was a Kohen, to mention which was absolutely *de rigueur*, but these words were scribbled in a narrow margin and the writer was stingy with his space.

[19] Mufaḍḍal of Haifa, Israel, was the proprietor of both a ship and a barge which commuted between Tyre, Lebanon, Alexandria, and al-Mahdiyya. The name was common among Jews and Muslims.

[20] This refers, of course, to the spring convoys. The fall convoys would sail in August and early September.

[21] R. Abraham, the Son of the Scholar. Many persons in Nahray's correspondence are called Abū Naṣr.

[22] The physician from Barqa, Libya, intended to travel to Cairo and from there to Jerusalem overland. Because of the anarchy prevailing in Egypt he would now wait in Alexandria for a boat going to Ascalon or Jaffa, Israel.

(From) his grateful Yeshū'ā, son of Isma'īl, (*may he*) *r*(*est in*) *E*(*den*).
Peace in plenty!

35 THE COMMUNAL LEADER

Ca. 1085

This short note shows us Nahray at the head of the two Rabbanite congregations of Fustat during a difficult period. The court physician and official head (*Rayyis*) of the Jewish community was temporarily in disgrace, and his adversary David, son of the late Daniel b. Azarya, who derived his origin from the kingly house of David and had been head of the Jerusalem Yeshiva, had usurped authority over the Jews of the Fatimid empire. David claimed to have obtained a ruling from the government that the name of the Rayyis should be omitted from the public prayer and excommunicated any synagogue dignitary who did not comply. This is the background of our note, which was written by the highest religious authority of the Jewish community of Egypt, who calls himself here by name, but is referred to in the Geniza throughout merely by his title "the Master" (*Rāv*).[1]

University Library, Cambridge, Taylor-Schechter
Collection, TS 12.657.

Judah ha-Kohen b. Joseph ha-Kohen[2]

[1] About the meaning of this title in those days see *Med. Soc.*, II, 211-212, 325-326.

[2] In short notes it was customary for the sender to write his name in the upper lefthand corner of the sheet. The identification of the sender is based on TS 20.83, dated March 12, 1066, and (partly) written and signed by Judah b. Joseph, the Kohen, who is referred to as "the Rāv" in the validation of the court. TS 8 J 7, f. 15 is also (partly) written and signed by him. His motto, tiny letters arranged in zigzag above and beneath his signature in both documents: "May something good be found in us" *ymṣ' bnw dbr twb*. A native of Palestine, as is suggested by his handwriting and by his origin from a priestly family of Jerusalem Gaons, he studied with R. Nissīm in Qayrawān (see no. 33, above), returned to his native country, where he must

In (Your) name, oh merci(ful).

His excellency, our lord, the illustrious *prince, the prince of all Israel,*[3] *may they in heaven guard, bless, and further him*, had ordered *the cantor* Hillel, . . .[4] to convey to *our master*, the *Senior of the Yeshiva*,[5] this information:

The prince had been informed that Joseph b. Elazar al-Ḥarīrī ("Silk-worker or merchant"), stationed in Tinnīs and known as "member" (of the yeshiva),[6] insisted on praying publicly and offering supplication for one, to mention whom as Rayyis the Sul[tan, may] God [give him glorious] victories, has prohibited, whereupon the prince had excommunicated him.

A request, however, was submitted to his excellency to examine this case again *for heaven's sake*, and he agreed to defer the matter until a letter sent to the aforementioned Joseph would have been received by him and his answer be known.[7]

Therefore, *our master, Senior of the Yeshiva*, . . . please order *the precentors leading the two congregations in prayer* to refrain from pronouncing the ban on that man, until his excellency will have made his decision. *And Peace.*

---

have incurred serious troubles (TS K 25, f. 244), and finally settled in Egypt. He is referred to as R. Judah, the Rāv, in ENA 2805, f. 9, l. 25, and TS Box 25, f. 106, l. 13. Further information in Mann, *Jews in Egypt*, II, 101, n. 2.

[3] David b. Daniel; see the introduction.

[4] Hillel b. Eli. See *Med. Soc.*, II, index, s.v.

[5] The honorary title conferred on Nahray by the yeshiva for his scholarship and communal activities. In his later years he was often addressed solely by this title.

[6] He was the spiritual leader of the Jewish community in that Egyptian seaport and signed as "member" (TS 20.103). But David did not recognize him as such.

[7] Most likely, the request was made by the writer of our note.

CHAPTER V

The India Traders

As FAR AS the information provided by the Geniza letters is concerned, the India trade was an extension and a branch of the commerce uniting the countries of the Mediterranean. The traders who left us their writings were, of course, all Arabic-speaking Jews, although Hindus are mentioned as close and reliable "brothers" and Abyssinians and other Christians as business friends. The leading Jewish family of Aden probably came from Iran, but its members had completely assimilated to the Arabic-speaking environment, or had used that language in writing when still in their Persian homeland, as had the writers of no. 2, above.

Over one-half of the commodities traded on the Mediterranean market, especially spices, perfumes, pharmaceuticals, dyeing stuffs, and certain textiles, were imported from India and the Far East, and this chapter (also no. 10, above) tells us how this was done. The West on its side sent copper, lead, and tin, as well as chemicals and a great variety of finished goods, but, in the main, the balance of trade was, as in Roman times, unfavorable: Western gold and silver were constantly flowing to the East (e.g., no. 37, sec. C; no. 38, sec. F). Silk is also mentioned repeatedly as an export to India, but only as a replacement for gold (no. 38, sec. E; no. 39, sec. E), as was often also done in the West (no. 71, n. 11), where a pound of silk had a standard price of 2 dinars.

In India, the Mediterranean man was a foreigner. The natural products of the country and its whole way of life were different. The little presents sent to India with practically every letter going there (e.g., no. 38, sec. F; no. 39, sec. F; no. 40, sec. B) provided him with the household goods to which he was accustomed (including writing paper, not to be had there) and items of food cherished or religiously required by him. Thus, the full grace, consisting of four

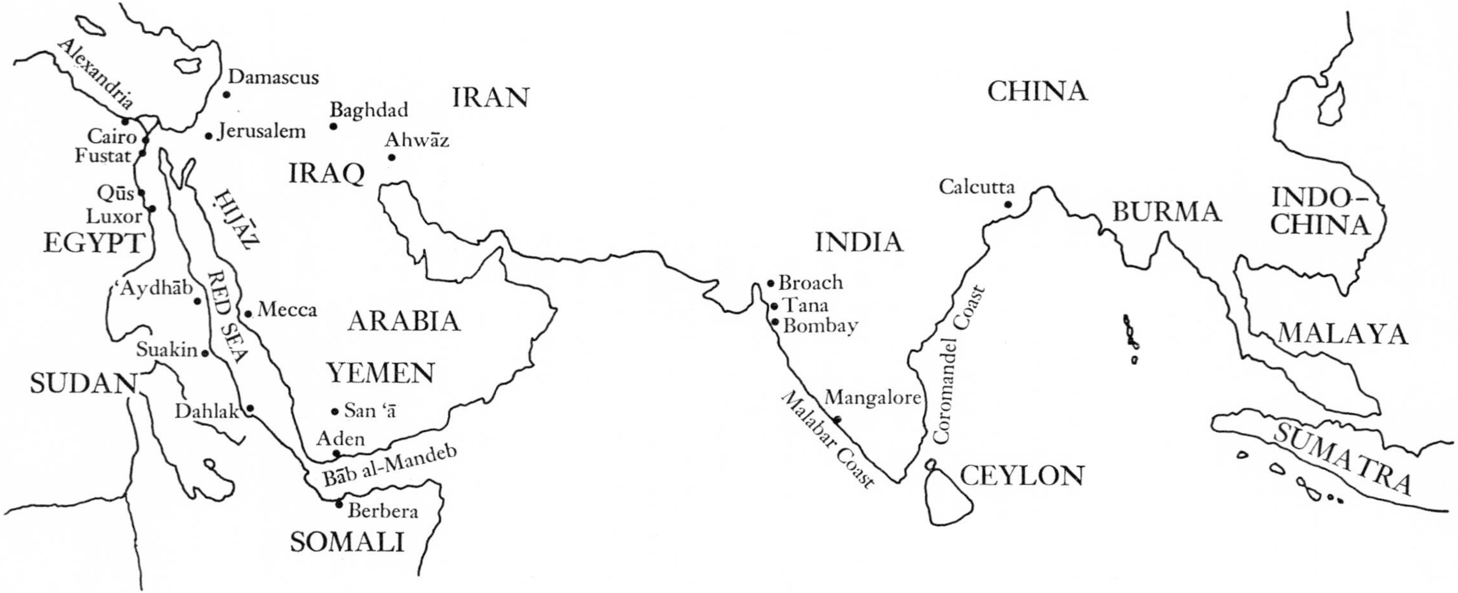

Map 2. The Route to India

benedictions, was said by Jews over bread baked of wheat, barley, or other Near Eastern grains, but not over the foreign rice, the staple fare of India (no. 38, n. 14). But saying grace was no less a necessity of life than taking food.

Three members of the leading Jewish family of Aden were shipowners, two of whom actually operated as such (no. 37, sec. B; no. 9); for the third see no. 38, n. 3. In the Mediterranean we have only one story about a Jewish shipowner, no. 76. For "the shipowner" and his son, mentioned in various lists of contributors to charitable collections in Fustat in the early decades of the thirteenth century (*Med. Soc.*, II, 508), are described with the Persian word *nākhudā*, which was used in Indian waters, not in the Mediterranean. Thus it seems that in the multinational countries bordering on the Indian Ocean it was easier for a minority group to gain prominence in maritime undertakings than in the Mediterranean area, where Muslims and Christians were poised one against another as powerful hostile camps. Maḍmūn (no. 37) was superintendent of the port of Aden, and a Muslim source reports that a Jew with the family name Khalaf, perhaps a relative of the writer of no. 38, drew up the customs tariff of that port.

With the exception of nos. 9, 10, and 79, the India papers are presented here as a group, and not dispersed chronologically between other material. This was done in order to convey to the reader an impression of the world of the India traders despite the comparatively limited space allotted to them.

36 THE VICISSITUDES OF THE TRADE

An India Trader, involved in lawsuits after his return to Fustat, writes to the Trustee of the Merchants in Aden, South Arabia
1097

The adventures and tribulations of Joseph Lebdi, the writer of this letter, are described in detail in my article "From the Mediterranean to India," *Speculum* 29 (1954), 191-195. His family name is derived from the town of Lebda on the Tripolitanian coast, the ancient Leptis Magna, whose magnificent ruins are among the most impressive remnants of the Roman presence in North Africa. He was a native of Tripoli, Libya, but later settled in Fustat.

Before setting out eastward to India, Joseph traveled westward to al-Mahdiyya, Tunisia, and collected goods from other merchants in order to trade with them on his way. He did the same, to a far larger extent, in Fustat. His trip to India, however, on which he was accompanied by the brothers of the trustee of the merchants of Aden, was marred by shipwreck and other misfortunes involving great losses. As is natural, he faced lawsuits after his return. Eighteen documents have been preserved on this affair, which provide us with much interesting information about the India trade at the end of the eleventh century.

The plaintiff against Joseph, who was a "trustee of merchants" in Fustat, had the same first name, but is always referred to here as Abū Ya'qūb al-Ḥakīm ("the father of Jacob, the Doctor").[1] Al-Ḥakīm entrusted Lebdi with textiles of various types, copper, silver vessels, drugs, chemicals, and corals, and instructed him to deliver one half to the trustee of the merchants in Aden for buying pepper on the Malabar coast of southern India and to take with him the other half to a place in the Gujarat province (in western India, farther to the north), where he should exchange it for lac. But Lebdi sold part of the goods on his way to Aden, and, with the best of intentions, deviated in other ways from al-Ḥakīm's provisions. Thus he became, at least in part, responsible for the losses.

Our letter was written at an early stage of the lawsuit, for which we have dated documents from November 9, 1097, through August 18, 1098. It is a draft written by the court clerk Hillel b. Eli in the record book of the court, because it was to serve as a piece of evidence in the lawsuit. It was addressed to the trustee of the merchants in Aden, Abū 'Alī Ḥasan (Hebraized as Japheth) b. Bundār, who had indeed bought fifty sacks of pepper, at a price of 5 dinars per

[1] In the Bible and in the Koran, too, Joseph was the son of Jacob. Since the first-born boy used to be called after his grandfather, a Joseph was given the honorific byname "father of Jacob" even while still in the cradle. "The Doctor" was the family name derived from the profession exercised by an ancestor. A grandson of this trustee of the merchants again became a physician.

sack, as instructed. Ḥasan-Japheth had noted all the transactions made in Aden in his account book, as is expressly stated in another letter by Lebdi, wherefore their knowledge is presupposed here. Fortunately, we know them because reference was made to them during the proceedings of the lawsuit.

Despite his bad luck on this trip, Lebdi was a prosperous merchant, as we know from other Geniza documents. He perished while traveling abroad, which did not deter his son from following in the footsteps of his father. We are able to trace the destinies of Lebdi's descendants until the middle of the thirteenth century, which is the more impressive as the known beginnings of the family go back to the tenth.

Bodleian Library, Oxford, MS Heb. d 66 (Cat. 2878), f. 66*v, India Book* 13.

In Your name, o Merci(ful).

My lord, the illustrious elder Abū 'Alī, (*our*) *m*(*aster and*) *t*(*eacher*) *Japheth, . . . the Prince of the Congregations,*[2] . . . my preceding letter to you relieves me from repeating here all its details.[3]

I am unable to describe to you—may God protect your honored position—the bickerings and quarrels I had to endure from the elder Abū Ya'qūb, the Doctor, with regard to the goods which I carried for him, part of which I left with my lord, namely:

Small silver vessels, seven in number; their weight is given in the aforementioned letter

A load of alcali, according to the Doctor weighing 400 mann (about 800 pounds)

Copper, weighing 110 pounds, according to him

Thyme, 10 mann, according to him

A small container with scammony

Things have happened between me and him which your excellency is too illustrious to hear from me. But those who will travel to your place will tell you. I had made him a prepayment of 100

[2] This title implies that the trustee of the merchants served also as head of the Jewish community in southern Yemen.

[3] A much corrected, and therefore not dispatched, version of this letter is contained in *India Book* 14 (69 lines preserved). Most interesting, but too much mutilated for consecutive translation here.

dinars on these goods until their proceeds would arrive. But after these settlements had been reached, we both began to argue and wrangle until the matter reached the courts. Finally, upright elders intervened, and today a settlement was reached to the effect that I should write you as follows:

Kindly list all the proceeds from the goods belonging to the elder Abū Ya'qūb, the Doctor, and also of the fifty sacks (of pepper), as far as they have been saved, on the payment of which my lord had given me respite,[4] for I had made up my mind that he should have fifteen sacks of them. Of the total received deduct the 100 dinars I have prepaid him here, plus 11 1/2 dinars I had paid for the goods,[5] and hand over the balance to your representative in accordance with your kindness to me at all times. I know well that all this causes you much trouble and I feel very badly about this, but it is not on my initiative that I write this letter. I am forced to do so. The account given to your representative should be *an official document*, signed *by the elders*.[6]

I wish to inform you also that it was established here *in court* that the total due me from my lord is:

100 dinars
11 1/2 dinars for the balance of the copper[7]
3 dinars for the additional expenses[8]
Fifteen sacks of pepper, 5 dinars per sack.

All that is above the total of this sum belongs to him and all that is less, to me, and he has no share in it and no responsibility; even if all has perished he is not obliged to return the prepayment of 100 dinars. This is stated expressly in *the record of the court.*

Now, my lord, exercise your usual circumspection—may I never

[4] Since Ḥasan-Japheth had goods of both Lebdi and the Doctor in his warehouse, he ordered pepper for them in India without demanding cash in advance, as was usual. While writing the letter referred to in the previous note, Lebdi did not yet know that most of the pepper, too, had been lost. This additional misfortune naturally exacerbated the situation.

[5] See n. 7, below.

[6] And not merely a report of the trustee of the merchants.

[7] The Doctor had sent hammered copper (*naḥās ḍarb*). In Aden it was found out that only cast copper (*ṣabb*) could be exported to India. Lebdi paid the difference, 11 1/2 dinars.

[8] The Doctor had given 20 dinars to Lebdi for expenses (freight, customs, etc.). But the total at reaching Aden was 23 dinars.

be deprived of you and never miss your favors—and examine with the light of God, the exalted, the case of those fifty sacks of pepper. Divide what has been salvaged in proper proportion between him and me. Originally, thirty-five sacks had been mine and fifteen his. So, divide the remains accordingly and explain everything clearly. The proceeds from the cast copper[9] belong to the elder Abū Ya'qūb, not to me. Please copy from your account book all that is due him after deduction of customs and commission and give a certified copy to your representative. Buy whatever you deem fit for my 100 dinars and send it with whomever you prefer. If possible, send pepper or lac. At the time of the sending of the shipment, please inform some of our coreligionists traveling here, at least two of them. *And peace.*

37 THE LEADERS OF THE INDIA TRADE

The Trustee of the Merchants in Aden writes to his counterpart in the capital of Egypt
Ca. 1130

This important and large fragment (69 lines preserved) lacks both the beginning and the end and consequently the address is also missing. But it is in the unmistakable, characteristic hand of Maḍmūn I b. Japheth, the son and successor (in his capacity of trustee of merchants) of the recipient of the preceding selection, no. 36. The graphological evidence is confirmed by many details, which also indicate that the letter was addressed to Maḍmūn's counterpart in Fustat, Abū Zikrī Judah Kohen b. Joseph, who also happened to be his brother-in-law (see no. 9, above).

This letter presents an excellent illustration of the activities of a Jewish trustee of merchants in a port city. He takes care of the estate of foreign traders who perished in shipwreck (sec. A) and collaborates closely with the most prominent Muslim merchant in town (secs. B, C). This man, Bilāl b. Jarīr, later became a general and ruler of Aden, a transition natural in medieval mercantile nations, such as the Arabs and Italians. Maḍmūn constructed a ship, presum-

[9] Called here *butrūh*, the term common in the India trade.

ably an especially strong one, for the route of 2,100 miles to Ceylon, the island near the southern tip of the Indian subcontinent, from which cinnamon and other Oriental products were imported. It is remarkable and perhaps not without interest for the history of minor arts that, besides merchants, three Jewish gold- (or silver-) smiths, one of them a Maghrebi, traveled in this new ship to Ceylon.

Bodleian Library, Oxford, MS Heb. a 3 (Cat. 2873), f. 19. *India Book* 32.

A. About the estates of two shipwrecked traders and a large gift to the family of one of them

My lord inquired about Zikrī b. Abu 'l-Faraj of Tripoli.[1] He arrived safely, sold, bought, finished his affairs, and returned home[2] in the same year.

The elder Nahray b. 'Allān[3] arrived with him, carrying a power of attorney from the son of Nissīm b. Benaya,[4] and Zikrī of Tripoli, too, had a power of attorney from the families of the two Maghrebis who perished in the boat of Ja'far. I took notice of the two writs. The two dead men had deposited with me 140 Maliki dinars.[5] With this sum the attorneys bought two bales of lac, containing 1,000 pounds, for 113 dinars, the expenses[6] for these two bales being 13

[1] One of the two traders who had a power of attorney to deal with the estates (see below). He is mentioned again as being engaged in the India trade in a letter written about ten years later by Judah Kohen, the surmised recipient of our letter (*India Book* 244*v*, ll. 3-4).

[2] Ar. *kharaj*. For this use see no. 43, n. 18, below. Normally, merchants who made this long voyage remained out on the India route for more than one year.

[3] A seasoned India traveler, repeatedly mentioned. An interesting letter of his is translated in no. 40, below.

[4] ENA 4011, f. 57*v*, dated June 24, 1129, shows him still active in Egypt.

[5] The exchange rate between this dinar of Aden and the internationally accepted Egyptian dinar varied in the Geniza papers from 1:2.2 to 1:4. The official exchange rate was 1:4.5 (see O. Löfgren, *Arabische Texte zur Kenntnis der Stadt Aden im Mittelalter*, 1936, glossary, p. 34). According to a communication of George C. Miles, the American Numismatic Society possesses a Maliki dinar weighing 2.33 grams. This would correspond approximately to the rate 1:2.2, provided it was not excessively debased.

The bulk of the dead men's possessions, their merchandise, naturally was with them in the shipwrecked boat.

[6] Customs and other dues in Aden plus freight Aden-'Aydhab. Our Maḍmūn was also *nāẓir*, or superintendent, of the port and as such able to know such things exactly.

dinars. They bought Qaṣṣī[7] fabrics for 14 dinars to cover the expenses of the customs in 'Aydhāb[8] and the freight for the way through the desert. This makes a total of 140 dinars.

The two attorneys agreed between themselves to put this shipment into the hand of Abraham, son of the *Reliable* Claimant,[9] in order, if God wills, to carry it to Fustat together with my merchandise. When all of them are there, the two attorneys will go to court and each one's right on this shipment will be established and he then will take it. Here in Aden there is no one who could decide this matter or even who knows the situation. I took a writ of release from each of them and no longer have any responsibility with regard to this.

I also gave two *bahārs* (sacks) of lac to Zikrī of Tripoli, as a gift to the family of the Nafūsī[10] in Tripoli, for I have heard that they are very poor. I believe this was the right thing to do.[11]

B. A partnership with the Muslim merchant prince Bilāl for the trade with Ceylon

After asking God, the exalted, for guidance I constructed[12] a boat in Aden and sent goods in it to Ceylon in partnership with the illustrious sheikh Bilāl. These of our coreligionists traveled in it: Sālim, the son of the cantor,[13] Ibn Ḥidāda ("of the art of smithing"), and al-Baṭīṭī ("maker of slippers"),[14] and the goldsmith, who had

[7] An Indian textile, which was one of the staple goods going West, mostly spelled with *ṣṣ* (not *ss*). See Serjeant, *Islamic Textiles*, XIII-XIV, 113-115.

[8] The great port on the Sudanese coast, now extinct, corresponding approximately to Port Sudan of today. From there one traveled overland to the Nile, and then by boat down to Cairo. See no. 10, sec. 14, above.

[9] A nickname probably given because of an incident during a lawsuit. The name appears elsewhere.

[10] Several merchants with this family name, derived from the Nafūsa region near Tripoli, were active in the India trade at that time.

[11] Two bahārs, averaging 600 pounds (see n. 25, below) were an exceptionally great gift, the like of which would never be sent even to the highest religious dignitary. We find gifts to the bereaved families of traders elsewhere, too, a kind of mutual insurance of merchants engaged in perilous undertakings.

[12] Ar. *anshaʾ*.

[13] Back in Aden in 1134 (*India Book* 87, ed. S. D. Goitein, *Sinai* 16 [1953], 231).

[14] These two merchants appear together in a letter to Judah Kohen (the

arrived here in his company, and the two goldsmiths, who came this year, Abū ʿAlī and the Maghrebi. All these traveled in the boat, may God ordain their safe arrival.

C. A partnership with Bilāl for the trade with Egypt

Again your servant asked God, the exalted, for guidance and sent sixty bales of lac, weighing 100 bahār, with the illustrious elder Nahray b. ʿAllān and with the elder[15] Abraham, son of Abu ʾl-Ḥasan, known as son of the Reliable Claimant, and through both,[16] in partnership with the illustrious sheikh Bilāl b. Jarīr al-Awḥadī[17] and eight bales of pepper, to be sold in ʿAydhāb for customs expenses and freight, and also 100 Qaṣṣī robes for customs in Suwākin[18] and other places. All this belongs to the partnership.

I am asking you now, relying on your favors, when this shipment, God willing, safely arrives, to kindly take delivery of one-half of the aforementioned bales and sell them for me for whatever price God will apportion and grant.[19] After the price is agreed upon, turn everything into gold and silver—nothing else[20]—and distribute it among various merchants, coreligionists, or others, if they are known as reliable,[21] and send it on.

---

surmised recipient of our letter) as commuting between al-Mahdiyya and Sicily (Bodl. MS Heb. c 28 [Cat. 2876], f. 60). See *Med. Soc.*, I, 332, n. 27.

[15] Not "illustrious." He was one of the many minor luminaries of the India trade. See also below.

[16] They were in charge of the actual transport.

[17] See the introduction and *EI*[1] under "Karam (Banu al-)." For al-Awḥadī, Löfgren, *Aden* (see n. 5, above), passim, always has al-Muḥammadī.

[18] Another Sudanese port, still operating.

[19] A Muslim trustee of the merchants would do the same service for Bilāl's share. But the final profits would be pooled together, as proper in a partnership.

[20] No merchandise, such as Lebdi carried with him on his way to Aden and India. See no. 36, above.

[21] This does not mean that non-Jews were regarded as generally unreliable, but the Jewish merchants between Spain and India, as far as they were of consequence, formed a kind of closed club, known to each other, certainly at least to the trustees of the merchants.

D. Instructions to the recipient and an order for household goods

Leave some money in the hand of the aforementioned Abraham, son of the Reliable Claimant, and if he has need for it, give him a loan of 100 mithqāls[22] in partnership with me, from which he might derive profit. Buy for him what he wishes[23] and let me know in your letter what you have bought for him.

I also ordered him to buy for me a wickerwork basket with china:[24] bowls, dishes, and cups, also for 4 mithqāls good rose marmalade, such as one prepares for the household. I gave him a memo, and please have him act accordingly.

On my own account I sent with him sixty bags of Sēlī (Ceylon) cinnamon, each bag weighing 100 pounds, which makes a total of twenty bahārs.[25] Kindly take delivery of one-half of this, too, and sell it for your servant for any price God, the exalted, may apportion. Please keep the account for this apart, since it is for me personally.[26]

(Here the manuscript breaks off. A short marginal note is incomplete and not connected with the text translated above.)

38 DAY-TO-DAY BUSINESS WITH INDIA

From Aden to the Malabar coast of Southwest India

1139

The writer of this letter, Khalaf b. Isaac b. Bundār, was a cousin of Maḍmūn b. Japheth (Ḥasan)—see no. 37—and closely cooperated with him. His correspondence, much of which has been preserved, is a valuable source for the India trade around the middle of the twelfth century. It shows that a very lively traffic connected India with the West; because of the tremendous risks the quantities

[22] Egyptian dinars.

[23] The Maghrebi merchant was not familiar with the Cairene market.

[24] Ar. *ghaḍār*, which could mean also fine pottery. Real china naturally came from the East and was sent by Maḍmūn *to* Cairo (*India Book* 33).

[25] Here the bahār is taken as weighing 300 pounds, which was indeed the standard at that time and place. But see no. 38, n. 2, below.

[26] And not in partnership with Bilāl. The other half of the cinnamon probably went farther west, e.g., to Palermo or al-Mahdiyya.

sent in each ship for each individual merchant were comparatively limited in size; losses were borne with remarkable equanimity; and a spirit of friendly cooperation prevailed between Jew, Muslim, and Hindu (also Christian, of course, although rarely mentioned), and between the free merchants and the bond-servants who served as their agents. Three of these slaves, acting as business agents, one with an Arab, one with a Persian, and one with a Hindu name, appear in this letter.

The recipient, Abraham b. Yijū, is the most important single figure of the India papers preserved in the Geniza. At least seventy items were addressed to him or emanated from his hands, including one which he might have written in his youth while still in his native city, al-Mahdiyya, Tunisia, namely, a poem in honor of the Jewish judge of that city, Labraṭ II b. Moses II (grandson of Labraṭ I b. Moses I, who wrote letter no. 33, above). The preservation of so much material related to one merchant finds its explanation in his life story. After a sojourn of at least seventeen years in India and an additional three in Yemen, he returned to Egypt and married his daughter and only surviving child to his nephew, who later became a judge with little interest, we may assume, for the mercantile and industrial exploits of his father-in-law (and even perhaps his poetical creations). Thus these carefully kept writings, which had been spared by the termites of India for so many years, then traveled by sea all the way from India to Aden, from there to a Sudanese port, then through the desert, and finally on the Nile down to Fustat, were heedlessly thrown away one day into the Geniza chamber. Nor did they remain there undisturbed. Most of the larger pieces are fragmentary, and the total of the material preserved clearly makes the impression of being only a small remnant of the original collection. Yijū was a calligrapher, as were several prominent correspondents of his, such as Khalaf b. Isaac, the writer of our letter. Merchants with a poor hand, such as Maḍmūn, usually had their letters copied by professional clerks. The synagogue compound, where the Geniza was located, also contained a school, and the schoolmasters, always eager to provide their more advanced pupils with examples of well-styled and beautifully written business letters, certainly plundered Yijū's files for generations. Yet what we do still have is priceless.

Khalaf's letter is translated here in full, because it is a comparatively short example of a completely preserved letter going from Aden to India. The calculation of the date is based on a comparison with several details found in other letters, to explain which would take us too far afield. Likewise, practically all the persons and ships mentioned here recur elsewhere. References to such occurrences are made only when they require comment.

University Library, Cambridge, Taylor-Schechter Collection, TS 24.64, *India Book* 56.

A. Introduction, the beginning in rhyme

In (Your) name, O Merci(ful).

The letter of your excellency, the illustrious elder, has arrived, [may God prolong your life /] and make permanent your honored position, and rank / highness, and loftiness / ex[cellence, and ascendancy /]. May he never deprive your dwelling-place and court of any good. / [May he bestow] upon you that which is most suitable of all he usually confers. / May he subdue those that are envious of you and crush your enemies, / and may all your affairs be completed successfully.

I was glad when I looked at your letter even before I had taken notice of its content. Then I read it full of happiness and, while studying it, became joyous and cheerful. For it was reassuring for me to learn from it about your well-being and your satisfactory state. Then I praised God for this very much and asked him to give you more of all the best in his mercy.

You mentioned, my master, that you were longing for me. Believe me that I feel twice as strongly and even more than what you have described; may God decree our coming together in the near future in complete happiness through his mercy, if God wills.

B. Shipments from India

I took notice, my master, of your announcement of the sending of "refurbished" iron[1] in the boat of the *nākhodā* (shipowner) Ibn

[1] Because of the perennial wars between Christians and Muslims, the Jews did not trade in iron in the Mediterranean. In the India trade, however, iron was a staple commodity rarely absent from any larger shipment leaving India. Four types are mentioned; "refurbished" translates *muḥdath*, lit., "renewed."

Abi 'l-Katā'ib. The shipment has arrived and I received from him two bahārs and one-third, as you noted.[2]

The nākhodā Joseph[3] arrived from Dahbattān[4] in the ship of Ibn al-Muqaddam and I received two basins, two ewers, and two basins for candlesticks from him.[5]

Likewise, I took delivery from my master, the illustrious elder Maḍmūn, of 30 raṭl cardamom from your bag and paid the customs duties for it, as you had written.

As to the covers,[6] which remained with you, my master, kindly send them.

However, my lord, I have not received a thing of the betel-nuts mentioned by you, for you wrote that you sent them with Jawhar, the slave-agent of Ḍāfir, but he has not arrived this year.

C. Shipwreck

As to your shipment, my master, forwarded from Fandaraynā[7] in the ship of Fatan Swamī[8] through the Sheikh Abu 'l-Ḥasan b. Ja'far:

His smaller ship arrived and I took delivery from it of one and a quarter and an eighth bahār of pepper, as was stated in your

[2] The *bahār* contained 300 pounds (see no. 37, n. 25, above). But the bahārs of different products sometimes differed in weight. See Hinz, *Masse*, pp. 8-10.

In *India Book* 26, Khalaf received 2 1/4 (not 2 1/3, as here) bahārs of iron. I observed similar phenomena elsewhere in the India trade. Should we assume that they had quotas for certain products such as iron?

[3] Certainly Joseph b. Abraham b. Bundār, another cousin of Khalaf active in the India trade. As the next selection, no. 39, shows, Joseph was especially interested in Indian bronze vessels.

[4] A port on the Malabar coast (still existing, under the name Valarapattanam), repeatedly mentioned, because Abraham Yijū had his brass factory there. See Muh. Husain Nainar, *Arab Geographers' Knowledge of Southern India*, Madras, 1942, p. 29.

[5] These basins, called here *ṭest sham'*, but today in Yemen *maghras*, serve as lampstand, flower vase (when turned upside down), and drinking cup.

[6] The covers of bronze vessels, often referred to. Obviously the vessels were standardized, so that covers could be ordered separately.

[7] Present day Pantalāyini, south of Cannanore, often mentioned since pepper was exported from there. See S. Maqbul Ahmad, *India and the Neighboring Territories, etc.*, Leiden, 1960, p. 83.

Note that one Jew sends a shipment to another with a Muslim on a Hindu ship. The same here, sec. H, and *India Book* 28, etc.

[8] Indian Pattani-svāmi, "Lord of the mart," chief of merchant guild in a port or market-town (communicated by Professor A. L. Basham).

memo to my master, the illustrious elder Maḍmūn, as well as of a bahār of *amlas* ("smooth)" iron.

The bigger ship, however, arrived near Berbera,[9] when its captain got into trouble with it until it was thrust against Bāb al-Mandeb,[10] where it foundered. The pepper was lost completely; God did not save anything of it. As to the iron, mariners were brought from Aden, who were engaged to dive for it and salvage it. They salvaged about one-half of the iron, and, while I am writing this letter, they are bringing it out of the Furḍa (the customs house of Aden) to the storehouse of the illustrious elder, my master Maḍmūn b. al-Ḥasan. All the expenses incurred for the diving and for transport will be deducted from whatever will be realized for that iron and the rest will be divided proportionally, each taking his proper share.

I regret your losses very much. But the H(oly one, be) he b(lessed) will compensate you and me presently.

D. Household goods ordered

As to the household goods ordered by you, my master:

You asked me to buy a frying pan[11] of stone in a case. Later on, its case broke, whereupon I bought you an iron pan for a *niṣāfī*,[12] which is, after all, better than a stone pan. I also bought you glassware for a niṣāfī: goblets, bowls and cups, namely sixty-eight goblets, ten bowls, and five cups; with the basket, which cost a qīrāṭ, it made exactly one niṣāfī; furthermore, five green bottles with their baskets for 11 qīrāṭ, the total being a dinar and 11 qīrāṭs.[13]

9 A town in the Somali Republic, Africa. The neighborhood was proverbial for its dangers for seafaring, but the town itself seems to be known only from literary sources over a hundred years later than the references in the Geniza. See *EI*² I, 1172, s.v. Berbera. See no. 79, below.

10 Up to the present day the name of the straits between the southern tip of Arabia and Africa. But in ancient times it was also the name of a place on that tip and this is what is intended here.

11 Called here *ṭājin*, which is Greek *teganon*, but referred to in *India Book* 60, which deals with the same matter, with the good Ar. word *miqlāt*. A Yemenite stone named *ḥaraḍ* is used for its manufacture and believed to give a specific, tasty flavor to the food.

12 Half a Maliki dinar. See no. 37, n. 5, above.

13 As indicated by the low price, all this must have been local glass, as the one manufactured in Lakhaba near Aden (*India Book* 61). Finer glass was ordered via Egypt.

As to the small pots, I could not get any separate, only in sets. The wheat has been made ready for dispatch to you by my master, the illustrious elder Maḍmūn.[14]

E. Silk sent instead of gold

I sent to you five mann[15] of good silk on my account, for I saw that my master, the illustrious elder Maḍmūn, had sent some to Ben 'Adlān and to others and it was reported in his (Ben 'Adlān's) name that it is selling well in Malabar. Therefore, I thought it was preferable to send, instead of gold, merchandise which might bring some profit. Thus, kindly sell it for me for whatever price God, the exalted, apportions and grants, and buy me whatever God, the exalted, assigns and send it to me in any ship, without any responsibility for any risk on land or sea. If there is an opportunity to buy betel-nut or cardamom, kindly do so, but you, my master, need no instructions, for you are competent. Indeed, I cause you trouble every year; but, you, my master, do excuse me, as it has always been your habit, past and present.

F. Request to intervene with a Muslim notable

Moreover, my master, last year, I sent to the captain Mas'ūd, the Abyssinian, 30 Egyptian mithqāls, to buy whatever God, the exalted, would apportion. When, however, he arrived at your place, the well-known misfortune befell him. He informed me that he had bought me two bahārs of pepper, which he carried with him, and that there remained for me 17 1/4 mithqāls, which were deposited with my master, the illustrious Sheikh Abu 'l-Ḥasan 'Alī b. Ja'far. Therefore, I, the captain Mas'ūd, and Bakhtyār, the slave-agent of 'Alī b. Ja'far, went to the illustrious Sheikh 'Alī b. Muḥammad Nīlī ("the indigo merchant") and he (Mas'ūd) reported the matter to him, whereupon I received a notification from Nīlī to 'Alī b. Ja'far about it. When you meet him, kindly greet him for me and ask him to buy

[14] The staple food of southern India was rice, not wheat. Wheat, which was frequently sent to Abraham Yijū, was needed for religious purposes. Grace was said over bread, not over rice.

[15] Approximately 10 pounds. Silk was traded in standard quantities of 10 pounds, costing 20 Egyptian dinars.

me for this sum what God, the exalted, apportions and to send it in any ship without any responsibility for any risk on sea or land, in this world or in the world to come.[16] I do not need to give you instructions on how to approach him: "*a hint is sufficient for a wise man.*"

May my lord receive the best greetings for his honored self and convey the best and most plentiful greetings in my name to my master, the noble scion,[17] and all whom your care embraces, and Bama.[18] *And Peace.*

G. Presents sent

(Margin:)

I sent what has no importance or value, namely a bottle of sugar and a good Abyssinian hide.[19] On the hide, there is written "Yijū" from outside and from inside on various places. Favor me by accepting this and excuse me, as has been your habit, past and present, and best greetings to you and sincerest regards and salutation. *And Peace.*

(Verso:)

I also notify you, my master, that the basket with the glassware and the five bottles are with the nākhodā[20] Aḥmad, the nākhodā of the ship of the Fadiyār; on all of them there is written Yijū in Hebrew script. The hide and the bottle of sugar are with the elder Abu 'l-Ḥasan al-Maḥallī, and the silk is with the elder Abū 'Alī b. Ṭayyib. Please, my master, take delivery of all this, which is in the Fadiyār's ship—may God ordain its safety.

16 This religious formula is not specifically Islamic. It is found in Heb. and Aram. Geniza documents.

17 The recipient's only son, who died on the way home.

18 Yijū's slave and business agent, a respected member of his household. In another letter (*India Book* 57), Khalaf calls him "Brother Bama." Bama, as I learned from Professor A. L. Basham, is vernacular for Brahma.

19 Probably for the dining room. See *Med. Soc.*, I, 111.

20 Nākhodā means literally "master of the ship" (in Persian) and usually designates its owner. But here it designates the man in command of the finances and other matters related to the passengers, i.e., the purser. The proprietor of this frequently mentioned boat was a Hindu, and the name, like Fattan Swamī (n. 8, above), was in reality a title.

May God, the exalted, unite me with you *in his mercy and compassion. And Peace.*

(Address, right side:)

To his excellency, the illustrious elder, my master Abū Isḥāq Abraham, *son of his h(onor), g(reatness and) h(oliness), R(abbi)* Peraḥya, *the scribe,*[21] son of Yijū; may God preserve his prosperous state.

(Left side:)

His servant, who is longing for him, Khalaf, son of Isaac; *(may he be) rememb(ered) for R(esurrection).*[22]

39 THE INDIAN BRONZE FACTORY OF ABRAHAM YIJŪ

A letter from Joseph b. Abraham, Aden
Late 1130s

Joseph b. Abraham b. Bundār, a cousin of Maḍmūn (no. 37, above) and Khalaf (no. 38), appears in most of his letters as a trader in products of the Indian bronze industry, although other Indian items, such as iron, spices of all descriptions, and textiles, are not absent from his correspondence. Abraham Yijū (see no. 38, introduction, above) ran a bronze factory in India, accounts of which have been preserved. From the West, that is Spain-Aden, copper, tin, and old bronze vessels were sent to India, while new or repaired vessels would return from there. Some of the items ordered here might have been for the use of friends or the writer's own household.

University Library, Cambridge, Taylor-Schechter Collection,
TS 12.320, *India Book* 51.

A. Losses and arrivals

In (Your) name, O Merci(ful).

The letter of your excellency, the illustrious elder, my master, has

[21] Thus Abraham had learned his beautiful handwriting from his father.
[22] This rare blessing is still used by the Yemenite Jews.

arrived. It was the most pleasant letter that came / and the most delightful message that reached me. / I read and understood it, etc. (another three lines).

You, my master, may God make your honored position permanent, wrote that you kindly sold the silk and sent goods for its proceeds and that you sent them in the ships of *Rāshmit*.[1] I learned, however, that *Rāshmit's* two ships were lost completely. May *the H(oly one, be) he b(lessed)*, compensate me and you. Do not ask me, my master, how much I was affected by the loss of the cargo belonging to you. But the Creator will compensate you soon. In any case, there is no counsel against the decree of God.

All the "copper" (vessels, *naḥās*), which you sent with Abū 'Alī,[2] arrived, and the "table-bowl" also arrived.[3] It was exactly as I wished —may God give you a good reward and undertake your recompensation (for only he is able to do it adequately).

B. Excommunication of a tardy debtor

You, my master, mentioned that you approached the *kārdāl*[4] gently in order to get something for us back from him. Perhaps you should threaten him that here in Aden we excommunicate anyone that owes us something and does not fulfill his commitments. Maybe he will be afraid of the excommunication. If he does not pay, we shall issue an official letter of excommunication and send it to him, so that he will become aware of his crime.

[1] For Rāmisht, a shipowner often mentioned in the Geniza papers. He died in 1140. See S. M. Stern, "Rāmisht of Sīrāf, a Merchant Millionaire of the Twelfth Century," *Journal of the Royal Asiatic Society* (1967) pp. 10-14.

[2] Abū 'Alī b. Ṭayyib al-Miṣrī (of Fustat), a Jewish India trader, introduced to Abraham Yijū as a novice in *India Book* 53, returning from India here, and again setting out eastward in no. 38, sec. G, above.

[3] Ar. *zīrkhuwān*, repeatedly mentioned in the Geniza papers, but otherwise unknown, is defined by the writer in *India Book* 219 as "a bowl (*marfa'*), decorated with network, which we call *z*." The word marfa' is still used in Yemen for (*a*) a drum made of copper, (*b*) a large bowl.

[4] For *kārdār*, "manager" (Persian). This affair is dealt with in greater detail in other letters. Our writer was a member of the rabbinical court in Aden. Ban as punishment for defaulting debtors already noted in the Talmud, Mo'ed Qaṭan 17*a*.

C. Various orders, especially for bronze vessels

The re(d) betel-nuts arrived, as well as the two washbasins[5]—may God give you a good reward. Please do not send me any more red betel-nuts, for they are not good. If there are any white, fresh betel-nuts to be had, it will be all right.

Please do not send me anything either betel-nuts or any other goods you acquire for me, in partnership with anyone, but specify each person and every item of merchandise.[6]

I am sending you a broken ewer and a deep washbasin,[7] weighing seven pounds less a quarter. Please make me a ewer of the same measure from its copper (or bronze, *ṣufr*) for it is good copper. The weight of the ewer should be five pounds exactly.

I am also sending 18 1/4 pounds of good yellow copper (*ṣufr aṣfar*, hardly "brass") in bars and five pounds of Qalʿī "lead"[8] in a big mold and a piece of Egyptian "lead" (in the form of) a shell. Please put the bars, the "lead," and what remains from the manufacture of the ewer together and have two table-bowls for two dishes made for your servant, each table-bowl being of seventeen *fil(l)*,[9] of the same form as the table-bowl you sent me; they should be of good workmanship.

[5] Ar. *jafna,* from which Spanish *jofaina* is derived.

[6] The Yemenites whose mores I studied are indeed very much opposed to partnership. (See Goitein, *Jemenica,* p. 39, no. 201.) But larger business was conducted in partnership. See no. 27, sec. B, above.

[7] Ar. *ḳarnīb,* from Greek *ḳhernips,* "gourd," regularly found in the lists of trousseaux.

[8] I put "lead" in quotation marks, for "Qalʿī lead" was a regular term for tin in the Muslim East (see *EI*[1] s.v. Ḳalʿī). Bronze is an alloy of tin and copper. The writer uses Ar. *naḥās* and *ṣufr* indiscriminately for copper, bronze, and brass, and for bronze or brass vessels. Even "yellow copper" (ṣufr aṣfar) here seems to be copper rather than brass, for brass is hardly traded in bars, at least when coming from the West. Richard Ettinghausen drew my attention to M. Aga-Oglu, "A Brief Note on Islamic Terminology for Bronze and Brass," *JAOS* 64 (1944), 218ff., who arrives at similar conclusions while discussing Islamic literary sources.

[9] From *India Book* 65 it is evident that the *fil(l)* was 1/100 of a *farāsila,* an often-mentioned Indian weight, which is given by Hinz (*Masse,* p. 9) as approximating 10-12.5 kg., and by O. Löfgren (*Aden,* glossary, p. 49; see no. 37, n. 5, above) as 10-17 kg. Thus a fil(l) would weigh at least 10 gm. The word might be connected with the Persian small coin *pul.*

D. Detailed description of a lamp ordered

Make me a nice lamp from the rest of all the copper (*ṣufr*). Its column should be octagonal and stout, its base should be in the form of a lampstand with strong feet. On its head there should be a copper (*naḥās*) lamp with two ends for two wicks, which should be set on the end of the column so that it could move up and down. The three parts, the column, the stand and the lamp, should be separate from one another. If they could make the feet in spirals, then let it be so; for this is more beautiful. The late *Abu 'l-Faraj al-Jubaylī* made a lamp of such a description. Perhaps this will be like it.[10]

E. Additional orders

This year, I did not succeed in sending gold[11] or silk. Instead, I am sending currency,[12] 20 Malikī dinars, old dinars of good gold. Please pay with it the price of the labor of the coppersmith and for the rest buy me a quantity of "eggs" (a kind of cardamom) and cardamom, and if this is not to be had, anything else which God, be he praised, makes available. And, please, send everything with the first ship sailing.

Please buy me two washbasins of middle size, somewhat larger than those you previously sent me, and a large washbasin, which holds two waterskins of water, measuring two *siqāyas*.[13]

F. Presents sent

I am sending you some things of no importance or value, namely two rubaʿiyyas[14] of white sugar; a bottle, in a tight basket, entirely[15]

[10] This lamp is similar to the "lampe d'usage domestique" (no. 39.85.2), which was kindly shown to me by Mlle. LeScour in the storeroom of the Musée de l'Homme, Paris, sect. Asie. It was acquired in Dindigul, north of Madura in southern India, not very far from where the recipient of this letter lived, but was made centuries after his time.

[11] Meaning Egyptian dinars.

[12] Ar. *sabīb*, meaning Adenese currency, Maliki dinars.

[13] "A measure, particularly for water or wine," Francis Johnson, *Dictionary, Persian, Arabic, and English*, London 1852, p. 705*a*; Wahrmund, *Wörterbuch*, I, 908*b*; but I was unable to find an exact definition.

[14] The weight of an Adenese "quarter" was about 10 kg.

[15] Because sometimes the bottles were filled half with raisins and half with sugar. These were presents for the children.

filled with raisins; and in a *mazza*[16] a pound of Maghrebi kohl, a pound of costus,[17] a pound of vitriol,[18] half a pound of litharge,[19] three ounces of *'ilk* gum,[20] and five sets of Egyptian paper; furthermore, in a little basket seven molds of "kosher"[21] cheese; five packages altogether. Furthermore, all the copper (*naḥās*) sent by me is in a canvas. This makes six packages. I wrote on each: "*Abraham Yijū*, shipment of Joseph," and sent the whole together with the 20 dinars with the Sheikh *Aḥmad, the captain, son of Abu 'l-Faraj.*

Furthermore, in a bag there are two linen *fūṭas*[22] for the children and two network veils dyed with carthamus.[23] Please accept delivery and forward them to the Sheikh *Abu 'l-Surūr b. Khallūf al-Ṭalḥī,*[24] as well as the letter destined for him. His name is on the bag.

My lord mentioned that there remained from last year copper to manufacture two bowls for drinking water. Kindly send them with the other copper.

Altogether there are seven packages with the bag of *Abu 'l-Surūr al-Ṭalḥī.*

May my master receive for his honored self the best greetings. And *upon you be peace!*

[16] Probably an earthen vessel. Denotes today in southern Yemen the clay receptacle for the water of the water-pipe used by the poor.

[17] This plant, the root of which has been used for fumigating since antiquity, is indigenous to Kashmir in northern India (see Sir George Watt, *The Commercial Products of India,* London, 1908, p. 980). That costus should repeatedly appear in lists of presents sent *from* Aden *to* the Malabar coast of India shows that the traffic between these two regions, separated by an ocean, was at least as lively as between northern and southern India. Costus was exported from Aden to the West in commercial quantities.

[18] Used as an eye salve (Maimonides-Meyerhof, pp. 68-69, no. 140).

[19] Served as an eye powder. Very frequent.

[20] Probably extracted from the Mediterranean pistachio tree. The chewing of the gum was intended to make the breath fresh and fragrant (Maimonides-Meyerhof, p. 148, no. 301).

[21] The term "kosher" was used in Europe, not in the East, where they said, instead, *ḥalāl* (Ar.), "religiously permissible." Then, as today, cheese was traded in molds and came in this form from Sicily and other places to Alexandria, from where it was exported to Aden, and from there to India.

[22] A sari-like piece of clothing.

[23] A yellow color.

[24] Probably called thus because he traded in Ṭalḥī paper (sent by Joseph as a present to Yijū in *India Book* 54).

(Address. Right side:)

To the honor of my lord, the light of my eyes, and the ornament of my neck, my m(aster) a(nd) l(ord) Abraham, the wise and the prudent,[25] *son of his h(onor), g(reatness) and h(oliness) ma(ster) Peraḥyā, (may he) r(est in) E(den), Yijū.*

(Left side:)

He that loves you and is proud of your good name, Joseph b. Abraham, . . .

40 A FATHER WRITES TO HIS SON IN ALEXANDRIA FROM THE SUDANESE PORT ʿAYDHĀB

Probably May 16, 1141

Nahray b. ʿAllān, the writer of this letter, was an India trader repeatedly mentioned as being on his way east- or westward at the time of Maḍmūn, representative of merchants in Aden, and Abū Zikrī Kohen, the latter's counterpart in Fustat (see nos. 10 and 37, above), both also referred to here. Nahray's father, ʿAllān b. Nahray, was domiciled in Alexandria,[1] and so, as the content of our letter shows, was his son, who, as usual, bore the name of his grandfather.

The exact date of the letter can be calculated on the basis of the following considerations. It was written on Friday, the 8th of Sivan, that is, a day after the Jewish holiday of Pentecost (Shavuoth), and the writer reports that he is embarking on the ship of al-Dībājī ("the brocade dealer"). Another India trader writes from ʿAydhāb that he will be traveling together with Nahray b. ʿAllān and another friend in one cabin[2] on that ship, and that they had already

[25] Genesis 41:39.

[1] Mentioned as such in letter no. 26, above (Bodl. MS Heb. c 28 [Cat. 2876], f. 34) in the section not translated.

[2] Ar. *bilīj*, a Malayan word, not exactly a cabin, but a place in a ship screened off by mats, where the merchants kept their wares, cooked, and slept. Frequently mentioned in the India papers. See Dozy, *Supplément*, I, 108*b*.

loaded their goods, and that they would sail immediately after the holiday. A line before, he announces that he and his friends had arrived safely in ʿAydhāb at the middle of the Muslim month of Ramaḍān.[3] All these chronological details make it almost certain that the travelers arrived in ʿAydhāb on or around April 24, 1141, and that our letter was written on May 16, three weeks later.

The main part of the letter is to be understood thus: a company of Muslim and Jewish traders sold part of their goods in ʿAydhāb, or rather, exchanged them for the products of the East. Since sailing time was near, the party split into two: the Muslims made their purchases in the pepper and brazilwood bazaars and the Jews in the lac bazaar, or took cash for their goods. This arrangement was made only for expediency's sake. The Jews, of course, traded in pepper and brazilwood as eagerly as the Muslims.[4] Our very letter makes mention of a shipment of brazilwood which Maḍmūn had sent to the writer from Aden to ʿAydhāb, and which he now forwarded to Fustat. There, the representative of the merchants would take receipt of all the shipments and distribute their proceeds to all those who had invested in that business venture.

British Museum Or 5566 D, f. 6, *India Book* 152.

A. The travel

My boy and delight of my eyes, may God prolong your life, keep and protect you, and not withhold his support from you. I have written several letters to you from Qūṣ[5] and also from ʿAydhāb before this one, in which I communicated some of my yearning for you and longing after you. May God in his grace and favor unite us under the most joyful circumstances, for he is generous and bountiful.

I am writing this letter on Friday, the 8th of Sivan. I am traveling in the boat of al-Dībājī. May God grant a safe passage in his mercy.[6]

[3] ENA 4020, f. 8, *India Book* 153, ll. 7-10. For Ramaḍān see no. 42, n. 21, below.

[4] On brazilwood see no. 1, n. 9, above.

[5] See no. 10, above.

[6] The casual way in which this boat is introduced shows that the seasoned trader had traveled in it before and that the family back home knew all about it.

B. Purchases in 'Aydhāb

Please take notice that I acquired 330 pounds of lac[7] out of the pepper, brazilwood, and lac available here in 'Aydhāb, for they sold the brazilwood and the pepper to the Muslims and took the price, but assigned to the Jews the lac and some cash ("gold"). I have not left cash for other shipments.[8] Two dinars went for packing, canvas, and ropes, [. . .] one-third for a sari, as a gift, and two-thirds [. . .].[9] One dinar was taken by the elder Abu 'l-Faḍl b. Abu 'l-Faraj al-Dimyāṭī[10] for the expenses for the lac. He carries the lac, a copy of the account, and the list of the distribution (to the partners). He will deliver all this to my lord, the illustrious elder Abū Zikrī Judah, the Kohen—may God make his honored position permanent.[11] He will kindly sell everything and deliver his share to everyone; he will send the balance to you, and you will also deliver his share to everyone. He also will send you the account.

C. Shipments from Aden

Likewise, my lord, the illustrious elder Yaḥyā b. Sar Shālōm ("Prince of Peace"),[12] may God make his honored position permanent, carries for you the shipment sent to me by the illustrious elder Maḍmūn, (*may his*) *Ro*(*ck*) *kee*(*p him*), consisting of two bales of brazilwood, weighing two bahārs[13] and 70 pounds, two bales of cowrie shells, measuring 1 *mudd*,[14] five manā[15] of ashbāh wood,[16]

7 The prices of lac fluctuated wildly. Taking the average I assume the writer intended that 330 pounds would bring 100 dinars in Fustat.

8 The writer took his main goods with him to Aden. See below.

9 A word is omitted here erroneously.

10 Family name derived from the Egyptian seaport Damietta.

11 One sees how intensely conscious of social rank those merchants were. Compare this with the way in which the carrier of the writer's goods mentioned before, was introduced.

12 Heb., Isaiah 9:5, a name with messianic connotations.

13 Ca. 600 pounds.

14 This cannot be the regular Egyptian *mudd*, which comprised about 2.5 liter, or about 5 pints, but was probably similar to the Jerusalem mudd which contained about 100 liter. See Hinz, *Masse*, p. 46.

15 Ar. *manā*, same as mann, about 2 pounds. Clearly spelled *kms t'mn'*, which proves that this twelfth century merchant with a good style and script already pronounced as modern speakers of Arabic do: *khames-tamnā* for *khamsat-amnā*.

16 A costly odoriferous wood (see Dozy, *Supplément*, 1, 725*a*), often mentioned. A manā cost 4 dinars in 1097. See *India Book* 19, l. 12.

and half a manā of old camphor.[17] Furthermore, ten Qaṣṣī robes for the expenses.[18] I asked him to make an account and, after deduction of customs and other expenses, to sell whatever he may deem appropriate and then inform you and await your instructions, whether you[19] would sell all these shipments or only part of them. As to the cowrie shells, if you think it best to send them to Spain,[20] do in all matters what God puts into your mind. May he choose the best for you and me in all matters.

D. The family

Receive the blessing of God for yourself and your boys, may God keep them and give you brothers to them. Regards to your mother, your wife, your maternal uncles and their sons, and regards to the sons of my maternal aunt. In several letters I had asked you about letters which I had forgotten to take with me, but you never replied to my queries. If you find them, keep them, for they contain accounts.

I need not impress on you to take good care of your mother, your wife, and your little ones; may God keep you for them and unite me with you.

E. Last minute thoughts

Know, my son, that this voyage will not bring much profit, unless God, the exalted, ordains otherwise.[21] I asked him for guidance and resolved to send 100 dinars from the proceeds of my goods with the ship of the elder Maḍmūn, may God keep him, to whatever place it might sail.[22]

[17] A mann of old camphor cost from 80 to 100 dinars. See *India Book* 193*v*, l. 16 (ca. 1130), 213, margin (ca. 1170).

[18] About these robes and the method of paying customs dues and other expenses with their proceeds, see no. 37, sec. A, above.

[19] I believe this is a slip of the pen and the writer intended to say: whether *he* should sell it. In Ar. this is only a difference between *t* and *y*.

[20] Cowrie shells served as amulets and ornaments for children and donkey saddles in the Muslim West, and in the Middle Ages also as an eye powder, in pulverized form, of course. See Maimonides-Meyerhof, p. 63, no. 127.

[21] During the weeks in ʿAydhāb the writer had opportunity to collect business intelligence from the merchants returning from India and Aden.

[22] About this ship see no. 37, sec. B, above. It was built about ten years before and the family knew about it from previous travels of Nahray b. ʿAllān

I have already instructed you to take one-tenth from all that will be received, after having put aside 15 dinars, leaving them until I come, and use them for whatever God may make profitable.[23] *And peace! (May your) l[ife be prolonged].*

(Address:)
(To) my son, the delight of my eyes,
'Allān b. Nahray (*may his*) *e*(*nd be*) *g*(*ood*).
(From) his father, may I be his ransom.
(In Arabic characters:)
[To Fustat],[24] to the elder Abu 'l-Barakāt b. Ḥārith.
Please forward [to Alexandria, to 'Allān b. Nahray].
From his father may he (!) be his ransom.

41 AN INDIA TRADER ON HIS WAY HOME

Abraham Yijū, after arrival in Aden, writes to his brothers and sisters "in al-Mahdiyya or anywhere else in Ifrīqiya" (Tunisia and neighboring districts)
September 11, 1149

This moving letter is remarkable for more than one reason. Yijū (see nos. 38 and 39, above) had been out of touch with his brothers and sisters for many years, as is emphasized in several

(cf. n. 6, above). The writer seems to say that this time he would not travel to India himself but make his purchases in Aden and send an agent to India with 100 dinars. Maḍmūn's ship was new and probably particularly seaworthy. See no. 37, introduction, above.

[23] The son's share appears to be surprisingly small. He is still regarded as his father's employee. I assume provisions had been made by the traveler for the household expenses of the entire family.

[24] The lower right-hand corner is torn away, but the instruction "please forward" shows that the letter was sent to Fustat with the request to forward it to Alexandria. Besides, the letter was addressed to a prominent merchant in Fustat known from at least five letters in the *India Book* alone. His father Ḥārith ("Ploughman," rare among Jews) bore the title "the elder of the congregations"; he himself is found in Spain in 1130 (*Tarbiz* 24 [1955], 145), and signing documents in Fustat around 1143 (TS 20.5, TS 12.706), where he calls himself of course with his personal name Abraham, not his honorific byname Abu 'l-Barakāt ("Blessings").

Geniza letters. The particularly strong upsurge of family attachment felt here had its source in the dire fate that had befallen Yijū's homeland, details of which must have reached Aden when he arrived there from India. The Normans, under King Roger II, had ravaged and occupied al-Mahdiyya and Sfax in 1148. Yijū's relatives, if alive at all, were now captives, or, at best, refugees. Indeed, we find them in Sicily, and not in their native country, as is expected here, and in a completely destitute state (see sec. C and no. 75, below). Now, Yijū's long years of toil in India made sense: the riches accumulated by him could put his relatives on their feet again.

There was another, more intimate, aspect involved in this relationship of Yijū with his family. His wife certainly was an "outsider," not, as usual, a cousin, or other more remote relative. Nowhere, not even here, is a reference made to her in his letters. In *Med. Soc.*, II, 20, I suggested that the (probably beautiful) Indian slave girl Ashū, whom Abraham Yijū manumitted in Mangalore on October 17, 1132, with so much ado, might have become his wife and the mother of his children. Now returning to the West and the social climate of his youth, he hoped that at least his daughter would marry into the family. In a later letter, sent from inland Yemen, he again emphasized that many were seeking her hand, but that he had only one wish: to have her married to her cousin. This wish was fulfilled: the Firkovitch Collection in the State Library of Leningrad has preserved a detailed list of her trousseau. She married her cousin, the writer of letter no. 75, below, in the summer of 1156, seven years after the writing of the letter translated here.

Abraham speaks in this letter to his brother Mevassēr ("Bearer of good tidings," a name with messianic undertones), because the latter had already visited Egypt and thus given a sign of life of himself. But the letter is in the first place addressed to the elder of the two, to Joseph, a father of three sons, while Mevassēr, as the extant correspondence shows, was unmarried.

University Library, Cambridge, Taylor-Schechter
Collection, TS 10 J 10, f. 15, *India Book* 68.[1]

[1] Ed. J. Braslawsky, *Zion* 7 (1942), 135-139. Since the editor had at his disposal only one item from Yijū's hand, while we have today over seventy, it is

A

My brother, I do not know what to write; so strong is my longing and so ardent my yearning. I ask God to unite us all presently in the best of circumstances.

This is to announce to you, my brother, that I have set out from India and arrived safely in Aden, may God protect it, with my belongings,[2] life, and children well preserved. May God be thanked for this. "*O that men would praise the Lord for his goodness and for his miraculous deeds with the children of men.*"[3]

Now I wish to let you know that I have enough to live on for all of us. May God, the exalted, let this money be a living for me and my children and be sufficient for you as well.

B

I have to reproach you, my brother, that you got as far as Egypt and did not come to Aden. I sent you to Egypt, with a shipment of my master, the elder Maḍmūn,[4] civet perfume worth 40 dinars, about fifty ounces of weight, carried by the elder Abū Naṣr b. Elisha[5]—may he be remembered with blessings. Afterward, I learned from the elder Abū Zikrī, the Kōhēn Sijilmāsī,[6] the brother-in-law of my master, the elder Maḍmūn, that the civet arrived duly in Miṣr (Fustat); however, as they did not find you there, my brother, they forwarded it to you to Sicily with a trustworthy Jew called Samuel, himself a Sicilian. I hope it has reached you.

---

natural that many of his readings, translations, and interpretations need qualification. No reference is made to these corrections.

2 The writer mentions his belongings first, because the aim of his letter was to invite his refugee brothers to share them with him.

3 Psalm 107:8, 15, etc. Always said after safe arrival.

4 See nos. 37-40, above.

5 A prominent India trader from Alexandria.

6 This is Judah b. Joseph ha-Kohen, the recipient of nos. 9 and 37, above. He was called Sijilmāsī (our letter has erroneously Silijmāsī) also in some other letters, probably because his father, or perhaps even he himself once had made the long voyage to the distant desert entrepôt Sijilmāsa in southern Morocco.

C

I also met the elder Sulaymān Ibn Gabbay [. . .][7] and he told me that you have been reduced to one single loaf of bread; therefore, I ask you, my brother, come to me under any circumstances and without delay; "*come down to me, do not tarry,*" "*and I will sustain you there.*"[8] I have a son and a daughter, take them and take with them all the money and riches—*may God fulfill my wishes and yours for the good.* Come quickly and take possession of this money; this is better than strangers taking it.

D

Also, find out who is the best of the sons of my brother Joseph or the sons of your[9] sister Berākhā, so that I may marry him off to my daughter. After your coming here, we shall live in Aden or Fustat or Alexandria, if it will not be possible for us to go to al-Mahdiyya or to Ifrīqiya, namely, to Tunis or Qayrawān.[10] Everything, of course, is in God's hand.

E

Please convey the best greetings to your brother Joseph and to his children in my name, and say to him: "Your brother Abraham says to you: By God, I shall not grudge you a thing; this money, which I have here, is at your disposal." Likewise, greet my sister Berākhā and her children and tell her the same.

I heard that Ma'mar, Yumn's husband died,[11] but was not sure

[7] *Gabbay*, "Almoner," is a common Jewish family name today, but is rare in the Geniza. It is likely that this Sulayman Ibn Gabbay is none other than the merchant bearing this name who accompanied the Spanish Hebrew poet Judah ha-Levi on his voyage to Egypt in 1140. See S. D. Goitein, "A Letter to Judah ha-Levi on the Collection of his Poems," *Tarbiz* 28 (1959), 345.

[8] Genesis 45:9-10. Joseph sending a message to his father Jacob.

[9] In sec. E he speaks of "*my* sister" and "*your* brother."

[10] Interesting is the emergence of the town of Tunis, which was of little importance in the eleventh century, and the revival of Qayrawān. In a few more years the whole region came under Almohad domination and was uninhabitable for non-Muslims.

[11] Ma'mar (or Mu'ammar), "Long-lived." Yumn, "Happiness, Good Luck." She must have been another sister of Abraham Yijū, for Abraham's granddaughter was also called by this name (*India Book* 80, top, l. 12), presumably because she had no offspring of her own.

about it. If it is true, may God comfort you all; however, by these lines, it is hard for me to write words of consolation on the death of anyone.[12]

Convey to my brother-in-law Marwān,[13] son of Zikrī, (*may he*) *r*(*est in*) *E*(*den*), Ibn Biḥār[14] the best greetings in my name—may God keep him alive and preserve him for you—and likewise to Abu 'l-Barakāt b. Qayyōmā the best greetings.

F

By God, and again by God, do not delay your coming here, take this dirhem, which I have earned, and buy and sell with it, if God will—saying less about this would have been enough. Would I try[15] to write all that is in my heart, no letter could contain it and no epistle could comprise it.

Written on the 7th of Tishrī, may God let you partake in the blessings of the month, of the year 1461 of the Documents (September 11, 1149).

G

Kindest regards to the cantor Moses, son of the cantor Abraham, . . .

(Margin:)

And Peace. And to my brother, his children and his wife special greetings. Likewise, to my sister, her husband Marwān, her sons and her daughter, special greetings. And to the daughters of my paternal uncle, their sons and their daughters greetings. To my maternal aunt and her ch[ildren] greetings. *Peace be upon you and peace on your house.*

[12] Abraham was shaken by the terrible news from his native country, to which he had intended to return, and was in general a tired man.

[13] This name of the founder of the second Umayyad dynasty was in use among Jews in Syria and Spain, countries formerly ruled by the Umayyads. See no. 14, n. 22, above.

[14] "The Seas," "An Ocean of Bounty," a family name still popular in many different forms with North African Jews.

[15] Ar. *ghazayt* for *ghazawt*.

H

I gave instructions that my letters to you should be in the hands of the elder Abraham b. Joseph, . . . Ibn al-Baqqāl ("Grocer")—may God ordain his safe arrival. And, by God, come as quickly as possible to Aden.

And kiss the soil[16] before my lord, *our teacher* Labraṭ, the *Dayyān (Judge), son of his honor, our master and teacher* Moses, *the Dayyān —may he rest in the garden of Eden* (and convey to him) the best greetings; and to all my friends *of my age class*, the best greetings. *And Peace.*

I

I heard what happened to the coastland of Ifrīqiya, Tripoli, Jerba, Qarqanna, Sfax, al-Mahdiyya, and Sūsa. No letter, however, from which I could learn who died and who remained alive, has arrived. By God, write exact details and send your letters with reliable people to soothe my mind. *And Peace.*

(Address, right side:)

This letter shall reach my dear brothers—may God prolong [their lives]—Joseph and Mevassēr, the sons of Peraḥya, . . . Ben[17] Yijū. God may recompense him that will be concerned to make an effort to transmit it into their hands, *and from the Lord he will receive good reward.*

Convey and get remuneration.

This is a deposit entrusted.

(Left side:)

Their brother, who is longing for them, may God unite him with them, Abraham, son of Peraḥyā, . . . Ben Yijū. To al-Mahdiyya, if God will, or anywhere else in Ifrīqiya.

[16] Used in reference to a judge, Muslim or Jewish. Yijū had no doubt studied under Labraṭ II (see no. 38, introduction, above), and was himself an accomplished talmudical scholar, as is evident from the many learned notes written by him on the reverse sides of letters received in his office.

[17] I leave here "Ben" (instead of "Ibn"), because Ben Yijū, especially in the French spelling Benichou, is still common among Jews of North African origin, of whom Paul Benichou, the author of *Morales du Grand Siècle* (6th ed., 1948) is particularly well known.

42 LETTER TO MOSES MAIMONIDES FROM HIS BROTHER DAVID WHILE ON HIS WAY TO INDIA

Ca. 1170

Tender love between brothers is one of the most attractive traits of the Geniza correspondence. (Several examples are included in my forthcoming book *Mediterranean People: Letters and Documents from the Cairo Geniza, translated with Introductions and Notes.*) This is what Moses Maimonides writes about eight years after his brother David drowned in the Indian Ocean.

> The greatest misfortune that has befallen me during my entire life—worse than anything else—was the demise of the saint, (may his) m(emory) be b(lessed), who drowned in the Indian sea, carrying much money belonging to me, to him, and to others, and left with me a little daughter and a widow. On the day I received that terrible news I fell ill and remained in bed for about a year, suffering from a sore boil, fever, and depression, and was almost given up. About eight years have since passed, but I am still mourning and unable to accept consolation. And how should I console myself? He grew up on my knees, he was my brother, he was my student; he traded on the markets, and earned, and I could safely sit at home. He was well versed in the Talmud and the Bible, and knew (Hebrew) grammar well, and my joy in life was to look at him. Now, all joy has gone. He has passed away and left me disturbed in my mind in a foreign country. Whenever I see his handwriting or one of his letters, my heart turns upside down and my grief awakens again. In short, "I shall go down to the nether world to my son in mourning" (Genesis 37:35).[1]

The letter translated below shows David in his relationship to his elder brother. The complete absence of any formal language as accepted in the epistolary style of the epoch even between closest relatives, shows the degree of intimacy prevailing between the two brothers. On the other hand, the authority of the firstborn was paramount. It was he who directed the movements of his younger

[1] *Responsums and Letters by Maimonides* (Heb.), Leipzig, 1856, p. 37*v*.

brother, wherefore David excuses himself again and again for deviating from his instructions. Maimonides had ordered him to travel as far as 'Aydhāb, the Sudanese port, and not to embark on the passage to India. But David, who had just successfully completed a daring feat, namely, crossing the desert between the Nile and the Red Sea, accompanied only by a fellow Jew, and who did not find in 'Aydhāb goods worthwhile buying, was bent on traveling to India in order to make his voyage profitable.

Was this the trip on which David perished? There can be little doubt about this. The letter is dated the 22nd of Iyyar, and it says that the boat would sail probably in mid-Ramaḍān, and at the time the letter would reach the addressee, most of the way to India would already have been covered. The Maimonides family arrived in Egypt in, or slightly before, 1168.[2] The only years in which the 22nd of the Jewish month Iyyar was reasonably near to the beginning of the Muslim month Ramaḍān were 1169-1171. As from 1172, through the next three decades, Ramaḍān *preceded* Iyyar, 22. In the passage translated above Maimonides says that he was incapacitated by illness for about a year after having received the news of his brother's death. In August 1171, he already had been appointed head of the Jews of Egypt, a position which he could have hardly attained while confined to bed. Thus 1169 or 1170 (preferably the first) are the only years coming into consideration for the writing of our letter; no previous India travel could have been referred to here. The foolhardy crossing of a waterless desert infested by brigands, without proper protection by the tribes inhabiting it, also betrays a novice in the India trade.

Three large and two smaller holes have destroyed large sections of the letter. Yet what has remained is still full of interest. See the notes.

University Library, Cambridge, University Collection,
ULC Or 1081 J 1, *India Book* 178.[3]

[2] At least we know for sure that Maimonides was already in Egypt in that year. See his own postscript to his *Commentary on the Mishnah*, ed. Joseph Qāfeḥ, Jerusalem, 1969, vol. 6, p. 738.

[3] The discovery of this letter is a fantastic story in itself. In 1954 I gave a lecture in New York on my *India Book* (which then comprised 130 pieces). Professor Saul Lieberman, who was present, remarked that it would be a fine thing if the Geniza could produce a letter from David, Moses Maimonides' beloved brother, who drowned in the Indian ocean. I replied that I could

To my beloved brother R. Mos[es, son of R.] Maimōn, (may the) m(emory of the) r(ighteous be) b(lessed).

David, your brother who is longing for you—may God unite me with you under the most happy circumstances in his grace.

I am writing this letter from 'Aydhāb. I am well, but my mind is very much troubled, so that I walk around in the bazaar and do not know—by our religion—where I [am . . .], nor how come that I did not imagine how much you must worry [about m]e.

This is my story: I reached Qūṣ[4] and after Passover[5] I booked for 'Aydhāb in a caravan. (Five lines almost entirely lost. Luxor, famous today for its ruins, and "the desert" are mentioned twice. The writer must have explained here why he separated from the caravan.) So we traveled alone out of fear of him. No one has ever dared to embark on such a disastrous undertaking. I did it only because of my complete ignorance. But God [saved] us after many frightful encounters, to describe which would lead me too far afield. When we were in the desert, we regretted what we had done, but the matter had gone out of our hands. Yet God had willed that we should be saved. We arrived in 'Aydhāb safely with our entire baggage. We were unloading our things at the city gate, when the caravans arrived. Their passengers had been robbed and wounded and some had died of thirst. Among them was Ibn al-Rashīdī, but he was unharmed[6] [... ... ...] We preceded him only slightly and there was only a small distance between us and those who were robbed. We were saved only because we had taken upon ourselves those frightful experiences. All day long I imagine how you must feel

write a story about him, but would not dare to invent a letter. Back in Cambridge, England, I suggested to the Librarian of the University Library that I examine the so-called University Collection, that is, the Geniza papers acquired before Solomon Schechter's trip to Egypt in 1897, which had never been classified, let alone catalogued, and select from them all the documentary material. The Librarian kindly acceded to my request, and the results were the collections now bearing the marks ULC Or 1080 J, and 1081 J (J meaning "Documents"). The very first item fished out from those crumbling papers was this letter, which, therefore, bears the number 1081 J 1. Naturally, I recognized its real nature only after close study. What attracted my eyes immediately was the name of the Sudanese port 'Aydhāb.

[4] City on the Nile in Upper Egypt, where the caravans to 'Aydhāb set out from, a trip of seventeen days. See no. 10, above.

[5] About a month before the writing of this letter.

[6] "Of Rosetta." The man was personally unharmed, but robbed. See below.

when you hear about 'Aṭā' Allāh ("God's gift") Ibn al-Rashīdī, how he was robbed (lit., "eaten"), and you believe that I was in his company. Then God comes between me and my reason.

To make a long story short: I arrived in 'Aydhāb and found that no imports had come here [. . .] at all. I found nothing to buy except indigo. So I thought about what I had endured in the [des]ert [and how I was saved;] then it appeared to me an easy matter to embark on a sea voyage. I took Manṣūr as my travel companion,[7] but not Ma'ānī, for all my troubles came [only from him; *you know*] *the man and how he behaves*.[8] Once, if God will, I shall tell you [all that happened between us] on our way from Fustat to 'Aydhāb.

My company[9] in the Mala[bar] sea will be [. . . ,[10] . . .], Sālim, the son of the (female) broker[11] and his brother's son, Makārim ("Noble character") al-Ḥarīrī ("Silk merchant") and his b[rother], and the brother of Sitt Ghazāl.[12] But Ma'ānī[13] embarked, together with Ibn al-Kuwayyis ("Nice") on another ship, and Bu 'l-'Alā remains in Dahlak,[14] since the ship in which he traveled foundered, but he was saved and absolutely nothing of his baggage was lost. Ibn 'Aṭiyya ("Gift"), however, was in another boat,[15] together with Ibn al-Maqdisī ("The Man from Jerusalem"). Their boat foundered and only their din[ars] remained with them.[16]

Now despite of all this, do not [worry]. He who saved me from

[7] About the institution of the travel companion (*rafiq*) see *Med. Soc.*, I, 347-348.

[8] II Kings 9:11.

[9] Merchants normally traveled in groups. But only two were rafīqs. See n. 7, above.

[10] In the hole there was space for two names. One of them might have been Manṣūr. See above.

[11] Female brokers were common. See *Med. Soc.*, I, 532, index, s.v.

[12] "Lady Gazelle," a name frequently found. Perhaps identical with the donor of the house mentioned in *Med. Soc.*, II, 419, sec. 36, dated 1184, and mother of the donor of a dinar called "Son of Lady Gazelle." Ibid., 481, sec. 30.

[13] David's earlier companion, mentioned above.

[14] An island off the coast of Eritrea, Ethiopia, in those days a great harbor, as nearby Massaua is today.

[15] Ar. *jalba*, a type of boat, used in the Red Sea, repeatedly mentioned in the relevant Geniza papers. Again here, below.

[16] Altogether, twelve merchants are referred to here as David's original travel companions. Ibn al-Rashīdī—for whose name there is no space in the hole (see n. 10, above)—would be the thirteenth.

the desert with its [. . .], will save me while on sea. (Five lines lost, in which the word "desert" recurs once, and "sea" twice.) And, please, calm the heart of the little one[17] and her sister;[18] do not frighten them and let them not despair, for *crying to God for what has passed is a vain prayer.*[19] (Two lines, marred by holes.) I am doing all this out of my continuous efforts for your (pl.) material well-being, although you (sing.) have never imposed on me anything of the kind. So be steadfast; God will replace your losses and bring me back to you. Anyhow, what has passed, is past, and I am sure, this letter will reach you at a time when I, God willing, shall have already made most of the way. "*But the counsel of God alone will stand.*"[20] Our departure will probably be around the middle of Ramaḍān.[21]

I shall trav[el with . . .[22] Tell this] to his uncle, and also that he is fine. Abraham is fine. [Best regards to you, to][23] Bū 'Ali[24] and his brother, to the elder Bū Manṣūr and his brothers,[25] to my sisters[26]

[17] Ar. *al-ṣaghīra.* A young wife is always referred to thus, as opposed to *al-kabīra*, the old, or great one, meaning the grandmother, who was in command of the house.

[18] I can explain this only by the assumption that Moses Maimonides was married to the sister of David's wife. Maimonides' own sister was married to his brother-in-law Abu 'l-Ma'ālī.

[19] Mishnah Berakhot 9:3. See what follows.

[20] Proverbs 19:21.

[21] *Ramaḍān* is the Muslim month of fasting (and feasting) and had (and still has) a tremendous impact on the economy. Therefore it is often referred to in the Geniza letters, although these (like our letter) were mostly dated according to Jewish months.

[22] Probably a person mentioned before, and referred to here again in the section dedicated to greetings.

[23] David had arrived on the very bottom and had to use the margin for regards to persons other than his brother.

[24] The husband of one of Maimonides' sisters, who are greeted later.

[25] Another brother-in-law of Maimonides. Maimonides' wife had five brothers (see Mann, *Jews in Egypt*, II, p. 319, with my corrections on p. xxxv). Our text has *akhawayh*, which would mean "his *two* brothers," but they used the dual for the plural and vice versa.

[26] In classical Ar. this would mean that at least three of his sisters had come with Maimonides to Egypt, but in middle Ar., as explained in n. 25, dual and plural were not strictly differentiated.

Miriam, a sister of Maimonides, had remained in the Muslim West and wrote him from there. See S. D. Goitein, *Tarbiz* 32 (1963), 188-191, where her letter is edited.

and the boys,[27] to all our friends, to the freedman,[28] and Maḥāsin ("Favors").[29]

Written on the 22nd of Iyyar, while the express caravan[30] is on the point of leaving.

43-44 TROUBLES IN ADEN, SOUTH ARABIA

43 FORCED CONVERSION OF THE LOCAL JEWS, BUT BUSINESS AS USUAL
August 1198

Only the lower part of this interesting letter, still containing 59 lines, has been found thus far. The events described in its first section were preceded by a long period of crisis. Muslim religious propaganda had become extremely aggressive, while the Jews feverishly expected the immediate coming of the Messiah, and a simple-minded, pious man had indeed declared himself messiah and found followers.

In this period Moses Maimonides wrote his famous "Yemenite epistle," or rather epistles, in order to strengthen the faith of his brethren, but also to unmask the futility of their expectations.[1]

Things came to a head when the eccentric nephew of the great Saladin, al-Malik al-Mu'izz Ismā'īl, ruled Yemen (1197-1201). He had the audacity to style himself "caliph," although a caliph sat on the throne of the Abbasids in Baghdad at that time. His unorthodox

[27] Meaning the children of his sisters.

[28] The family had brought with them a slave whom they liberated, but who remained in the household.

[29] Probably also a factotum in the extended family of Maimonides.

[30] Text *kj'r*, which I take as Turkish *kaçar*, "running," designating either special couriers or an express caravan, which would carry only mail and light, but precious goods, such as pearls.

---

[1] Scientific edition by Abraham S. Halkin, with an English translation by Boaz Cohen, New York, 1952. Halkin, following others, thought that the "Epistle to Yemen" (as he calls it) was written in 1172.

ways are also evident in the forced mass conversions described in our letter, for Islam regards such conversions as illegal and invalid.

Mosseri Collection, L-12.[2]

A. Forceful conversion of the local Jews

[. . . to] Aden. Immediately after his arrival [he was brought before the caliph?], who said to him: "Become a Muslim, or you will cause the death of [your] brethren." [. . .] He cried bitterly, but there was no other way for him [. . .] except to embrace Islam. Before his arrival in Aden, all those who were with him on the mountains had *apostatized*;[3] the physician (known as) the Efficient, and everyone on the mountains apostatized; only the Jews of Aden remained. But the elder Maḍmūn[4] accepted Islam on Wednesday, the first of Dhu 'l-Qa'da.[5] On Friday, the third, the bell (of the market-crier) was rung: "Community of Jews, all of you, anyone who will be late in appearing in the audience hall[6] after noon, will be killed." None of the Jews remained, all went up to the audience hall. Moreover, he (the caliph) ordered that anyone returning to the Jewish faith would be killed. Thus all apostatized. Some of the very religious, who defected from Islam, were beheaded.

B. The foreign Jews

As to us, do not ask me what we felt, witnessing horrors the like of which we had never seen.

But with us God wrought a miracle and saved us, *not through our might and power*, but through his grace and favor. For when we went up with them to the audience hall, the foreigners assembled separately, and the caliph was consulted about them. God put these

[2] *India Book* 348. The part dealing with the forceful mass conversions was edited, with omissions, by Bernard Chapira, "Lettre de Maimonide aux Juifs du Yemen," *Cahiers Juifs*, vol. 2, 3d year (1935), p. 58.

[3] The Heb. term used here, and in the Geniza in general, is *pāsha'* (not *rāsha'*, as in Chapira's text; see n. 2), lit., "to renounce one's allegiance." See *Med. Soc.*, II, 300.

[4] Maḍmūn b. David, the head of the Jewish community, who wrote no. 44, below. See ibid., n. 1.

[5] Corresponding to August 25, 1198.

[6] Ar. *manẓar,* in Yemen a room on the upper floor, open to the fresh air.

words into his mouth: "No foreigner should be molested."[7] He ordered that everyone should pay a third of the poll tax.[8] We disbursed this and he dismissed us graciously, thank God. This is the upshot of what happened. But, by the great God, I am really not able to convey to you even part of what happened, for witnessing an event is one thing and hearing about it—quite another.

C. New impositions on visitors to Aden

The merchants were outraged by the new impositions promulgated. Finally, however, God, the exalted, helped. (The caliph) had ordered that 15 out of 100 dinars should be taken from everyone both at arrival and departure, but God helped, and he ordered that this Kārim[9] should remain unchanged with no rise in tariff. But everyone coming later would have to pay 15 out of 100 dinars from all goods, and also from gold and silver, from wheat and flour,[10] in short, from everything. Such will be the earnings of anyone coming here next year.

D. Prices in Aden

Pepper, a sack—sold for 52, later went down to 45
Cinnamon, a sack—45
Brazilwood obtained different prices:
  Good Āmiri, a sack—18
  Middle quality—16
  End pieces (*ṭr'f*), a sack—16
  The long variety, a sack—18
Indian Indigo, a piece—70 din.
Clove—not to be had; the mediocre—45
  the [. . .]—44, 10 (mann, or double pound)

[7] This shows that, at that time, the Jewish India traders must have been still of considerable importance for the economy of Aden.

[8] The poll tax of the non-Muslims was to be paid at their permanent residence. Thus, this imposition was illegal. But the travelers were content to buy their religious freedom with this price.

[9] This use of the term Kārim in the meaning of the totality of India travelers operating during one year is very remarkable. See S. D. Goitein, "New Light on the Beginnings of the Kārim Merchants," *JESHO* 1 (1958), 175-184, where the previous literature on the topic is cited.

[10] Meaning that even from the provisions of the travelers 15 percent had to be turned over to the ruler of Aden.

Celandine[11]—not to be had
New camphor—8 1/2 a mann
The odoriferous woods are of middle quality and expensive.
The price of the copper was—[12]
Copper in fragments,[13] first—72, later—85;
in bars—70; later it attained 90
Tin—70
Corals—11
Antimony (kohl) of Shalwadh,[14] a sack—17
of Madrid,[15] a sack—25
The "gray" perfume,[16] a sack— . . .
Cinnabar[17]—10 (mann) 18
Mercury—10 (mann) 17
Please take notice of this, my lord.

E. Conclusion

I asked God for guidance and am traveling home in the boat of Ibn Salmūn, the same in which I made the passage out.[18] May God bestow safety upon it. My brother Abū Naṣr[19] will be traveling with me. I am kissing your hands and feet.[20]

[11] Or swallowwort (which is an English rendering of the Greek word), a plant of the poppy family, serving as a tonic. See Maimonides-Meyerhof, p. 120, no. 241.

[12] Up to this point, our lists show goods imported from India or other eastern countries, which would be carried to Cairo and other places west. Here begins the list of imports from Spain and other western countries, which had been brought by these merchants.

[13] See no. 14, n. 7, above.

[14] A locality in Spain. Yāqūt 3, p. 316, says that kohl was produced there from lead.

[15] Reading doubtful.

[16] Ar. *al-ṭīb al-shayba*. Maimonides-Meyerhof, p. 10, no. 11, and Dozy, *Supplément* 1, 808*a*, probably refer to another product. I have not seen this expression elsewhere.

[17] Since Roman times a precious export of Spain.

[18] In the language of the India traders *dakhal*, to enter (namely, the Indian waters), designates the way out, and *kharaj*, to come out (from the Indian ocean), means going home.

[19] No identification possible. My India card index, still incomplete, notes twenty-five persons of this name.

[20] One kisses the hands of a senior relative and the feet of a judge. The writer might have been a relative of the judge Isaac b. Sāsōn, who was the

(A P.S. of four short lines, referring to several of the goods mentioned before, is too much effaced to attempt translation.)

44 MURDER OF THE SELF-STYLED CALIPH AND RETURN OF JEWISH LIFE IN ADEN

July 1202

The sender of this letter, Maḍmūn b. David, was the head of the Jewish community of Aden. He is referred to in TS 8 J a, *India Book* 183, ll. 4-8, as the Adenese counterpart of Abraham Maimonides, the head of the Jews in Egypt. Thus he is identical with the Maḍmūn of the preceding selection.[1] The Hebrew equivalent of Maḍmūn, which means "protected by God" was Shemarya, and under this name, namely, Shemarya b. David, "the Nagid (leader) of the Land of Yemen," he appears both in Hebrew literature and in Geniza documents.[2]

The aforementioned letter, TS 8 J a, contains also the name of the recipient of our letter, *al-Muwaffaq*, "the Successful," a title which had become a proper name. He had another title *Amīn* (*al-Dawla*), "Trustee (of the Government)," the like of which would be given to a Jewish representative of merchants. The two titles are contained in the untranslatable honorific epithets of the introduction, so characteristic for the artificial style of this late period.[3] Fortunately, the main text of the letter is in straightforward language.

As far as I am able to read between the lines, the Jews were permitted to return to their religion only after the murder of the self-

---

Jewish chief judge of Cairo and a close associate of Maimonides, but also very active in the economic field. See next selection.

---

[1] No. 43, n. 4, above. Maḍmūn I b. Japheth (d. 1151; see no. 37, above) probably was his great-grandfather.

[2] TS NS J 242, *India Book* 311; TS 6 J 2, f. 10, *India Book* 310. The famous Spanish Hebrew poet Judah al-Ḥarīzī dedicated to him his masterpiece, Taḥkemoni (or, rather, a copy of it). See Mann, *Jews in Egypt*, II, 338.

[3] For instance, instead of the title Trustee of the Government, the introduction has: "Your Trusteeish Excellency."

styled caliph. This is clearly alluded to in the remark that the Feast of Weeks was celebrated "*in the proper way*," which makes no sense in normal times. The writer did not mention the change of religion expressly because his action of leading the community into even temporary apostasy, although eminently reasonable, was religiously not without blemish. The P.S. of the writer's namesake, perhaps a cousin, is even more outspoken.

University Library, Cambridge, Taylor-Schechter Collection, TS 28.11[4]

In the name of the Merciful.

A

Your servant Maḍmūn, son of David, (may the) s(pirit of) G(od) g(rant him rest),[5] sends regards to his high and lofty excellency . . .[6]

B

I received your distinguished letter in which you report about the trouble you had with the pepper carried with you. God knows that my intention in this matter was only to be useful to you. God, the exalted, will support you and grant you success. Amen, Amen.

C

I should like you to share this with your servant: the troops killed al-Malik al-Mu'izz, who claimed to be caliph. He is succeeded by al-Malik al-Nāṣir Ayyūb, the son of the Sultan Sayf al-Islam,[7] who is still a boy, and his Atabeg (guardian and regent) is the Sultan Sayf al-Dīn Sunqur.

[4] Ed. D. H. Baneth in *Epstein Jubilee Volume* (Jerusalem, 1950), pp. 205-214, with an excellent introduction and most instructive notes. With one exception, deviations from Baneth's interpretation are not noted expressly.

[5] For this blessing see *Med. Soc.*, II, 551, n. 14.

[6] Eight lines of introduction.

[7] "The victorious king, Job, the son of the Sword of Islam," a younger brother of the murdered "caliph." The Sword of Islam was a brother of the famous Saladin.

D

After his government had become settled, your servants submitted your case to him.[8] He referred it to the administrative court. But your servants declared that this was a case belonging to the religious court. We obfuscated the matter before the divines and paid the poll tax.[9]

E

All this happened in the month of Sivan, one day before the eve of *Pentecost.*[10] We celebrated the feast in the proper way, in *happiness and joy.* Some *Jewbaiters* formed menacing groups, but could not do a thing, thank God, the exalted. All that happened to us has come through the blessings of our lord, the Rayyis Moses—*(may the) m(emory of the) r(ighteous be) b(lessed)*[11]—and the blessings of our lord, *the pious man, our master* Isaac,[12] and through your blessings, may God, the exalted, grant you good reward for your liberality.[13]

F

Your distinguished letter, containing several orders, has arrived. Your servant hopes to be able to carry them out. I do not doubt that

[8] Since a reference to the poll tax follows presently, I assume the case involved goods for which foreigners, but not local people, had to pay high customs dues. By paying the poll tax, the Cairene merchant, who had just visited Aden (see sec. B, above), and probably had done so often before, became a permanent resident there.

[9] The Muslim divines, like their Jewish colleagues, were local and merchants. The administrative court was in the hand of officers from the foreign mercenary troops, with whom little contact existed. Matters affecting non-Muslims were indeed the domain of the religious court.

The editor, to my mind, misinterpreted this passage by taking *al-mamālīk,* which simply means "your servants," as "Mamluks."

[10] Corresponding to May 27, 1202. The Heb. word used here is not "Feast of Weeks" (Shevuoth), as common today, but *'aṣereth,* as in the Talmud, which is identical with the Christian word for Pentecost, *'anṣara,* used all over the Middle East.

[11] Moses Maimonides the Rayyis, or head of the Jewish community in Egypt. The blessing following his name was normally said over a dead person, but in Yemen occasionally also over one alive, especially an eminent divine.

[12] The chief Jewish judge of Cairo. See no. 43, n. 20, above.

[13] See n. 16, below.

you—may God make your honored position eternal—love me and are concerned with my well-being. May God, the exalted, help me to satisfy your wishes, as is my duty, if God wills.

G

I renew my reliance on you for having the two pieces sent with you co[llated] and a third copy made in good script and on fine paper.[14] And have the medical writings of my lord the Rayyis copied for me. And please buy for me any fine copies of useful books you can lay hands on and kindly send them to me—may I never be deprived of you and never miss you.[15]

H

(P.S. by a bystander:) Your servant Maḍmūn b. Jacob, . . . present at the writing of this letter, sends his best regards to his excellency, my master. Thanks to [God? . . .], the affair with all *those Arabs*, ended happily in this *salvation*. We were not worthy of this, but *the H(oly one, may) h(e be) b(lessed)* did what he is worthy of, *for the sake of his great name*, and brought relief to the Jews in the entire country of Yemen. Relief was brought first, slightly before us, to the people of the mountains. Finally the Sultan came to us, and the relief became complete, *by the help of God* and through your success.[16] "*They thank God for his lovingkindness.*"[17]

Kindest regards to his excellency my lord and to all under his care, *and to all connected with him and subordinated to him a million greetings of peace.*

[14] Most probably a reference to parts of Maimonides' legal code. The writer, like some other readers, had doubts with regard to many passages and wished his copies to be collated with a reliable text. The other members of the rabbinical court needed a copy as well.

[15] The writer may, among many other things, have dealt in books, as did Nahray b. Nissīm before him. But since this letter, certainly purposely, does not mention any business detail, I prefer to think that the head of the Yemenite Jews simply was a lover of books—as Yemenites are now.

[16] Again a reference showing that the recipient had been substantial in the turn of the fate of the Jews in Yemen (see sec. E). He, together with Maimonides and the Jewish judge of Cairo, had intervened with the Muslim authorities in that city. The allusion to his liberality means that the arguments based on Islamic law had to be fortified by "presents" to the proper persons.

[17] Psalm 107:8, to be cited when saved from a danger.

Written on 17th Tammuz[18] *1513 of the Documents* (July 9, 1202).
Salvation is near.
Two copies were made and sent by way of the Ḥijāz.[19]

45 AN INDIA TRADER WRITES TO HIS WIFE

Ca. 1204

A voyage to India necessitated an absence of two years at least, but often of many more. When the trader, as happened frequently, suffered shipwreck, or was plundered by pirates, he had to work first to replace the capital entrusted to him by others and, of course, his own, and then to make gains which would make his toilsome and dangerous trip rewarding. Years would pass in this endeavor. So long an absence put an intolerable strain on the trader's wife, a situation reflected in a number of Geniza documents. The letter translated here was selected because of its personal tone, the like of which is rarely found.

The writer was closely connected with another India trader whose son is mentioned, as traveling to India also, in a document from the summer of 1226 (see sec. F). The letter opens with a condolence on the death of Judge Manasse. In a deed from January 1214, reference is made to a house "formerly known as the home of the late Judge Manasse."[1] Section B reveals that the family back in Fustat was

[18] A day on which fasting is obligatory. I have found many letters written on that fast in July: perhaps the merchants were too exhausted to do much business and passed the time in letter-writing.

[19] Overland, and not, as usual, by sea, probably because all the ships of the season had already sailed.

This note makes sense only if we assume that what we have is the original draft which was destined to be retained in Maḍmūn's office. The manuscript gives the definite impression that this is indeed the case. It is written with utmost carelessness and the main letter lacks any conclusion. This draft found its way to Fustat as scrap paper: on the reverse side the Jewish calendar for the years 1207-1212 is jotted down. Someone who used that calendar took the paper with him to Egypt. After it had lost its practical value, he threw it away into the Geniza.

---

[1] TS 13 J 4, f. 14, ll. 9-11. This judge was active in the time of Moses Maimonides. Another judge Manasse, most probably his grandson, was a member of the court of Abraham, Moses' son. *Med. Soc.*, II, 124 and 514, sec. 27, are to be corrected accordingly.

saved "from the great terrors, the like of which have not been experienced for many generations," no doubt alluding to the famine and plague which ravaged Egypt in the years 1201-1203. Thus the summer of 1204 is the most likely date for this letter.

No address is found on the space destined for it. The writer might have had second thoughts about his own frankness (see sec. E) and not sent the letter off after all. In view of the poor state of preservation, some omissions, always indicated, have been necessary.

Jewish Theological Seminary, New York, E. N. Adler Collection, ENA 2739, f. 16, *India Book* 176.

In (Your name!)

A. Death of the judge

Just is the Lord in all his ways, etc. (Psalm 145:17)
The righteous man has gone, etc. (Isaiah 51:1)
Comfort, comfort my people, etc. (Isaiah 40:1)
From their father who is yearning after them,[2] Solomon, son of Japheth, (may he) r(est in) E(den).

I am able to express only a fraction of my grief over the passing away of my lord, the illustrious leader, *(his) h(onor), g(reatness, and) h(oliness), our master and teacher Manasse, the wise and prudent judge, whose demise has hurt the hearts and caused pain to the souls. (May the) m(emory of the) r(ighteous) be b(lessed).* How deeply was I afflicted by his death and by his being taken away from those who relied on him. May God assign him *a place with the saints*, may he grant consolation to his mourners and heal their wounds and comfort them *in his great mercy*.[3]

[2] Decency required that a husband should not address his wife in a letter, a piece of paper which could fall into anyone's hand. Most Geniza letters destined for wives are addressed to another relative. Our letter, which is entirely directed to the writer's wife, starts in the third person plural masculine, continues in the second person plural, but ends in the second person feminine singular. The reader will be alerted on the transition to the latter.

[3] The judge was also a spiritual leader and as such his death was felt by the community like that of a father (see no. 34, above, and no. 60, below). The remarkable thing is that our writer, who had been away from Egypt for years and was facing manifold adversity, should express himself in such a way.

B. Escape of the family from the plague

Would I try to describe the extent of my feelings of longing and yearning for you all the time, my letter would become too long and the words too many. But He who knows the secrets of the heart has the might to bring about relief for each of us by uniting us in joy.

Your precious letters have arrived; I have read and scrutinized them, and was happy to learn from them that you are well and healthy and that you have escaped from those great terrors, the like of which have not been experienced for many generations. Praise be to God for your deliverance and for granting you respite until you might be recompensed in a measure commensurate with your sufferings.

C. The dedicated husband

In your letters you alternately rebuke and offend me or put me to shame and use harsh words all the time.[4] I have not deserved any of this. I swear by God, I do not believe that the heart of anyone traveling away from his wife has remained like mine, all the time and during all the years—from the moment of our separation to the very hour of writing this letter—so constantly thinking of you[5] and yearning after you and regretting to be unable to provide you with what I so much desire: your legal rights on every Sabbath[6] and holiday, and to fulfill all your wishes, great and small, with regard to dresses or food or anything else. And you write about me as if I had forgotten you and would not remember you had it not been for your rebukes, and as if, had you not warned me that the public would reprove me, I would not have thought of you. Put this out of your mind and do not impute such things to me. And if what you think or say about my dedication to you is the product of your mind, believing that words of rebuke will increase

[4] This seems to show that the letters had been written by the trader's wife herself. In a letter dictated to a clerk or a relative she would not have gone to such length.

[5] Every time third person plural masculine, but I feel it would be odd to translate here "them" instead of "you."

[6] A Jewish scholar is bound by law to visit his wife once a week, namely on the night of the Sabbath, that is, Friday night (Talmud Bab. Ketubot 62*b*). For other occupations other rules are set, but our India trader and his wife clearly regarded themselves as belonging to the learned class.

my yearning—no, in such a way God will not let me reach the fulfillment of my hope, although in my heart there is twice as much as I am able to write. But he is able to have us both reach compensation for our sufferings and then, when we shall be saved, we shall remember in what situation we are now.[7]

D. Travel beyond the Coromandel coast

You rebuke me with regard to the ambergris.[8] You poor ones!!! Had you known how much trouble and expenses I have incurred to get this ambergris for you, you would have said: there is nothing like it in the world. This is the story: After I was resurrected from the dead and had lost all that I carried with me I took a loan of [. . .] dinars and traveled to countries beyond al-Ma'bar.[9] I checked my accounts[10] and found [ ] with "the decimals."[11] I took them and paid to one of our coreligionists who traveled back from al-Ma'bar to Aden . . . . . . and for it he bought for you . . . (Three lines and the beginning of the words written in the margin damaged.)

E. Drunk but pious

This was my way of life from the moment I left you until I arrived in Aden (and from there to India) and from India back to Aden:[12] Day and night I was constantly drinking, not of my free will,[13] but I conducted myself in an exemplary way[14] and if any-

[7] I am not sure that I have correctly understood the last two sentences.

[8] A highly valued perfume and medicine, one variety coming from the Indian ocean and one from the Atlantic (see *EI*², s.v. *'Anbar*). The wife was not satisfied with the quality or quantity of the ambergris sent.

[9] This is the Coromandel coast of south-*east* India. Very few of the thousand or so Jewish India travelers mentioned in the Geniza went as far as the Coromandel coast, but *beyond* it next to none. Our traveler had to take this exceptional trouble in order to replace his losses.

[10] An Arab proverb says: "When a Jew is broke, he checks his grandfather's old accounts," meaning that he always finds someone owing him something. This seems to be the situation alluded to here.

[11] Ar. *deqāt*. A counting machine, it seems, derived from Greek *deka*, ten. See S. D. Goitein, "Side Lights on Jewish Education from the Cairo Geniza," *Gratz College Anniversary Volume*, 1971, p. 98, n. 62.

[12] It seems that our letter was written there.

[13] But because of the grief over the separation from his beloved wife.

[14] No slave girls or whores.

one poked fun in foul speech in my presence, I became furious with him, until he became silent, he and others. I constantly fulfilled what God knows, and cured my soul by fasting during the days and praying during the nights. The congregations in Aden and in India often asked me to lead them in prayer,[15] and I am regarded by them and regard myself as a pious man.

(Here begins the reverse side; the twenty-four first lines are damaged beyond repair. Maḍmūn, meaning no doubt Maḍmūn b. David the trustee of the merchants in Aden, [see nos. 43 and 44, above] and a shipment of clove are mentioned.)

F. As to divorce—the choice is left to the wife

Now in one of your letters you adjure me to set you free, then letters arrived from the old man[16] saying the same. Later Maʿānī ("Eloquent") b. al-Dajājī ("Seller of Fowl")[17] met me and told me that you[18] came to his house before he set out on his travel. You had given him nutmeg paste as a collateral[19] on a loan of 100 dirhems, but he released 20 dirhems to you. Please let me know whether this is correct, in which case I shall return this sum to him. He reported also that you had asked him to return to you letters which your late father—may God have mercy on him—had sent with him, but he had said to you: "I have already packed them away on the boat."[20] Then you said that these letters were not written with your consent and you asked him not to deliver them to me. On this Maʿānī had replied: The judge might have meanwhile sent a message demanding something from the elder,[21] in which case the delivery of these letters might be useful to him.

[15] Distinguished guests were often given this honor. See *Med. Soc.*, II, 161-162.

[16] Her late father.

[17] See no. 46.

[18] From here to the end of this section she is addressed, as natural, in the second person singular feminine.

[19] Text: *duhn*, which can mean many different things. But since this is the wife of an India trader, I assume that here (as often) *duhn bān*, nutmeg paste, is intended.

[20] From Cairo-Fustat up to Qūṣ (see no. 42, n. 4, above) one traveled on the Nile.

[21] The writer of our letter.

Now, if this[22] is your wish, I cannot blame you. For the waiting has been long. And I do not know whether the Creator will grant relief immediately so that I can come home, or whether matters will take time, for I cannot come home with nothing. Therefore I resolved to issue a writ which sets you free.[23] Now the matter is in your hand. If you wish separation from me, accept *the bill of repudiation* and you are free. But if this is not your decision and not your desire, do not lose these long years of waiting: perhaps relief is at hand and you will regret at a time when regret will be of no avail.

And please do not blame me, for I never neglected you from the time when those things happened and made an effort to save you and me from people talking and impairing my honor. The refusal[24] was on your side, not on mine. I do not know whether this[25] is your decision or that of someone else, but after all this, please do not say, you or someone else: this[26] is our reward from him and our recompense. All day long I have a lonely heart and am pained by our separation. I feel that pain while writing these lines. But the choice is with you; the decision is in your hand: if you wish to carry the matter through, do so; if you wish to leave things as they are, do so. But do not act after the first impulse. Ask the advice of good people and act as you think will be the best for you. May God inspire you with the right decision.

G. Greetings, errands, gifts

(The concluding part is very much damaged. It began in the margin, much of which is lost, continued in the main part of the page, and returned to the margin, but was never completed. Clearly the letter was not dispatched; see also the introduction. Only continuous sentences are translated.)

22 Meaning a divorce.

23 A conditional bill of repudiation, which becomes valid as soon as she agrees.

24 To accept a divorce offered by him before when his absence from home became too protracted.

25 Demanding a divorce.

26 The dispatch of the conditional bill of repudiation.

[Best regards to my sister][27] and her husband, the illustrious elder Abu 'l-Faḍā'il, the scholar, to Ma'āni, the scholar (?), and his son. I have exerted myself for him to a degree that only God knows. The elder Abu 'l-Khayr ("Mr. Good") agreed to pay him 10 mithqāls (Egyptian dinars), which the elder Abu 'l-Makārim ("Noble Character") will deliver to him.[28]

Convey my greetings to the elder Abū Isḥāq, the son of your paternal uncle, to his mother, to the elder Abu 'Imrān and his children, to [. . .]j, the daughter of your paternal uncle, and to all those whom you[29] know, my most sincere regards.

I sent you 7 1/2 mann of nutmeg, which is better than anything found in the Kārim[30] and worth more than other sorts of it by 1 dinar; 11 mann of good galingale;[31] two fuṭa cloths for the children; 2 1/2 of celandine and 25 of odoriferous wood; fourteen pieces in number.[32]

(Repetition of some greetings and other matters from above. The end of the story can be restored with a high degree of probability. The letter was not sent, but reached Fustat nevertheless, which can only mean that the writer succeeded in coming home. I do not believe that he would have returned to Fustat had his wife accepted the repudiation. He then would have stayed in Aden and married there. Thus the long years of suffering had not been in vain. The India traveler was finally united with his wife.)

[27] See below.

[28] Probably a case of inheritance of a merchant who had died in Aden. Abu 'l-Khayr was in Aden and Abu 'l-Makārim in Cairo-Fustat.

[29] Feminine singular!

[30] The goods going from India to the West. See no. 43, n. 9, above.

[31] Ar. *khawlanj*, from which the English word is derived; a plant from the ginger family serving as an aphrodisiac or as a constituent in narcotics.

[32] These quantities of costly Oriental products were not really "gifts," but destined to be sold and to serve for the upkeep of the family.

46 DEATH IN MALAYA

July 7, 1226

This and the following short piece are not letters, but are translated here in order to alert the reader to the fact that countries from which we do not have a single letter still were visited by traders who belonged to the same group of people who have left us hundreds of letters in the Geniza. It was not customary to send letters over very great distances. Almost no letters sent from Iran to Egypt or from Spain to Egypt have been found despite the manifold and close relations connecting these countries (see no. 2, above). Likewise, in the India trade one would write from India to Aden and from there to Egypt, but rarely, if at all, directly. The medieval seafarer needed a month to reach Malaya or Indonesia from India.[1] He would send a message from there to the southeastern coast of India, as is implied here, but not farther. Thus it is natural that no letters from those distant parts have found their way into the Geniza.

The document translated below is a draft containing the gist of a court record and is written on both sides of a tiny piece of paper measuring 4 x 2 1/2 inches. It is in the hand of the Nagid Abraham Maimonides in his most cursive style, which we are able to read safely only because so many of his holographs have been preserved. A court clerk would write out a complete record, or rather two, one of which would be written in Arabic characters, to be submitted to the government office of inheritances.[2] These copies, of course, would be signed by witnesses.

University Library, Cambridge, Taylor-Schechter Collection, TS Arabic Box 30, f. 42, *India Book* 322.

We, the undersigned members of the court, were assembled *in a session of the court,* in Miṣr (Fustat) on Tuesday, 10th of Tammuz, 1537 of the Documents, corresponding to the 10th of Rajab of the year 623 (July 7, 1226), when Abū Sa'īd, the Levi, son of the elder

[1] See Jean Sauvaget, *Relation de la Chine et de l'Inde, rédigée en 851*, Paris, 1948, pp. 8-9, 43.

[2] For this purpose the Muslim date was added here.

Abu 'l-Ma'ānī, the Levi, the merchant, known as al-Dajājī[3] appeared before us and deposited his testimony that Abu 'l-Faḍl b. Mukhtār ("Chosen") al-Iskandarī ("Of Alexandria"), known as Ibn [. . .] died in Kalah,[4] which is in the country of. . . .[5] He checked and verified this when he visited al-Ma'bar[6] in the country of India. After he had deposited his testimony in our presence, we confided it to writing so that it should serve as a title of right and a proof.

47 DEATH IN INDONESIA

This is the upper left-hand corner of a query submitted to the Nagid Abraham Maimonides.[1] It is translated here for the same reason as the preceding selection.

Fanṣūr, a port on the island of Sumatra, Indonesia, was famous for its export of camphor and is mentioned as such not only by Muslim writers, but also by the famous Venetian traveler Marco Polo. The Fanṣūrī camphor was the best to be had both according to the Geniza documents and the later European sources.[2] No wonder that Jewish traders, too, made the long way from Cairo to Fanṣūr, requiring four months at least.

Jewish Theological Seminary, New York, E. N. Adler Collection, ENA 4020 I, f. 55 (?), *India Book* 233.

[3] About this man and the meaning of his names, see no. 45, sec. F, above. It is noteworthy that the son, although already having returned from a trip to India, is not yet styled "the elder."

[4] Kalah (today Kedah) on the west coast of present day Malaysia, is frequently mentioned by Muslim geographers as the main port for the export of tin, but also of camphor, aloe, and other Oriental products. See the extensive article in *EI*[1] s.v., also Sauvaget (cf. n. 1, above).

[5] Partly effaced, which is a pity, for the medieval Arabic name of the Malayan peninsula has not yet been established with certitude. I am still working on the identification.

[6] The Coromandel or southeastern coast of India. Only the upper part of the last three letters of *'l-M'br* has been preserved, but no place name in India beginning with 'l-m other than al-Ma'bar is recorded in the Geniza.

[1] Not contained in Abraham Maimuni, *Responsa*, Jerusalem, 1937.

[2] See Heyd, *Commerce du Levant*, II, 592-594.

[What is the legal opinion of . . .   .] our illustrious master and teacher Abraham, the paramount Rav [. . .   . .], the leader of our generation, the light of the world—may his glory be enhanced—about this: a man has traveled to the land of India and remained there for about fifteen years. [Before setting out he had appointed] his wife as his legal representative. She maintains herself and her two daughters by work. [. . .   . .] Recently a Jewish man has arrived from Aden [and was questioned by another] Jewish man[3] who asked him [about that man who had traveled to India]. The Jew who had arrived from Aden said: we have heard [that he traveled to Fanṣūr and] died in Fanṣūr and that the ruler of that country [had taken his property (?) . . .]

Can the wife on the basis of this testimony [. . .   . .]. (Rest of lines visible. The question was not only whether the wife could marry again, but how much of the property of her late husband she was permitted to take for herself. According to Jewish law, the daughters, not she, were the heirs. But since she had maintained herself [and the children] for fifteen years, which was the duty of the husband, she was clearly entitled to remuneration of the living costs for this long period.)

[3] Many queries were styled in such a general way (without mentioning names) in order to emphasize the purely legal character of the problem.

CHAPTER VI

Twelfth Century and Later

THE LETTERS OF the India traders form a consecutive sequence from the end of the eleventh century to the beginnings of the thirteenth. The same cannot be said of the letters of the merchants who were active during the same period in the Mediterranean. There are not many of them during the first half of the twelfth century and even fewer during its second half. From the thirteenth we have next to none.

Various causes might have contributed to this uneven distribution of the Geniza material (see *Med. Soc.*, I, 148-149). Fustat was eclipsed and finally replaced by Cairo as the economic center of Egypt, and the Geniza chamber, we remember, was in Fustat. But the scarcity of documents seems to reflect an actual situation. The ascendancy of the Italian city-states and the preponderance of their fleets no doubt were decisive factors. And literary sources, too, seem to indicate that by the beginning of the thirteenth century Jewish overseas trade in the Middle East, as far as it was still in existence, had switched from the Mediterranean to the India route.

Our selections in this chapter open with four letters addressed to a distinguished craftsman (or perhaps we should say, industrialist), a purple-dyer whose father had immigrated to Egypt from Tunisia. The second group is formed by four letters written by a Persian silk merchant who had settled in Alexandria and occupied an honored position in the community there. The third are letters by a well-educated man from a family from Baghdad, whom we find doing business all over the Mediterranean area. A stray letter (no. 52) by Maghrebis working in Egypt is destined to show the reader that there is still much material in the Geniza which has not yet been related to cognate sources. The twelfth century selections conclude with two letters exchanged between Spain and North Africa, but these two, like all the others mentioned before, were written before 1150. The two letters from the thirteenth century (nos. 61 and 62) were sent within Egypt. Selection no. 8 is the only example in this book of a letter referring to Mediterranean business in the thirteenth century.

48-51 FOUR SHORT LETTERS TO 'ARŪS B. JOSEPH, THE PURPLE-MAKER

Abu 'l-Afrāḥ 'Arūs ("Happy Bridegroom") b. Joseph, whose father had emigrated from al-Mahdiyya to Fustat, is known from many letters as well as from documents dated May 1088 through October 1116.[1] He had a hand in the India trade[2] and handled many commodities of both the East and the West, but was mainly a purple-maker and was called thus (*arjawānī*). A detailed account on the cost of the transport of purple from Fustat to Tunisia, presented to him, is discussed in *Med. Soc.*, I, 339-343.

'Arūs used to write accounts on the reverse sides of letters or other communications received by him, and many of these notes, easily recognizable by his erratic hand, have been preserved. He was a much respected and beloved man, but most of the letters addressed to him and expressing these feelings refer to unconnected details and do not lend themselves easily to translation.

48 PURPLE FROM ALEXANDRIA, EGYPT, TO ALMERIA, SPAIN

Two letters referring to the same shipment have been traced. The first lacks the beginning, and with it the address on the reverse side, and is damaged by holes and torn-off margins. But it presents a more complete picture than the second letter, which is preserved in its entirety, but, as natural, presupposes the knowledge of what

[1] TS 13 J 1, f. 20; Gottheil-Worrell, *IB*, p. 10; *India Book* 144*a*.
[2] *India Book*, ch. v, sec. b.

has been said in the first. The two comparatively short letters are translated here in order to show the reader that the completeness of a Geniza paper does not necessarily make it valuable, while a much damaged piece might prove to be much more instructive. The letter presented here first was identified by me more than ten years after I had copied the second.

The material sent from Egypt to Spain is described as "dyed purple" or simply as "wool." Here a qinṭār, or a hundred pounds, cost 6 dinars, while the purple sent by ʿArūs in the account discussed in *Med. Soc.*, I, 339-343, was worth about 14 dinars. Thus probably old purple renovated by additional dyeing is intended here.

The two letters were written by the same pleasant hand and both were sent from Alexandria, although this is said only in the second letter whose beginning is preserved. The writer, Hilāl ("New Moon," corresponding to Hebrew Hillel) b. Joseph might or might not be identical with a man bearing the same name who in 1099 bought ninety-one jugs of wine (Bodl. MS Heb. e 101, f. 16), for these were common names.

The purpose of this letter needs a short explanation. Pious people and respectable merchants avoided giving an oath under any circumstances (see also no. 51, n. 6). Therefore our writer consented to enter into a business connection solely if the other party agreed never to demand an oath from him, or, in legal parlance, to accept his word as valid as the testimony of two trustworthy witnesses, accepted by a court.

University Library, Cambridge, Taylor-Schechter Collection,
TS Arabic Box 30, f. 255.

. . . [Everyone] of our friends [knows] that I am *trustworthy* [never giving an oath] and that I do not accept *responsibility* for risks on voyages.

I shall be traveling on the Spanish boat, and we shall load, if God will, on the 1st of Nisan (March)[3]—may God let me and you partake in its blessings.

You wrote that you would send other wool. Do not send anything

[3] Most of the spring convoys recorded in the Geniza sailed in May. Either the lading took a long time or the Spanish boat was stronger than the ships going to Tunisia and Sicily and dared to brave the freaks of spring weather.

of the kind, for dyed purple is not worth a thing in Spain. During my absence on the land[4] someone came to Khiyār[5] and told him that dyed wool was not worth a thing there; so please do not send any.

Send money for the freight and customs and write me who has the papers of the shipment, namely, the paper for the Mānak (customs) house,[6] and that for the commission, for no goods can leave (the city gate for the harbor) unless they have a sign that they are cleared;[7] otherwise one has to pay the dues again. The purple-maker 'Abd al-Raḥmān[8] said he had no papers, except the 2 dinars less one-sixth which you (or, I) have received from Ibn Mu'allā.[9] He said that the wool was worth 6 dinars per Egyptian qinṭār and that it weighed five qinṭārs, which makes 30 dinars, to which will be added the sum you will send for freight and customs. 'Abd al-Raḥmān asked me also to write to you in his name to pay to Ḥasan 1 dinar and 2 qīrāṭs for the packing.[10]

When you have done what I am asking you to do in this letter, write to 'Abd al-Raḥmān to deliver the wool to me and send me the testimony. For he said to me: "Take the wool as a commenda."[11] I answered: "I shall not accept anything before I receive an answer to what I am writing to him." This is what impeded my accepting delivery from him: I have sworn that I shall not enter into any agreement with anyone in the world unless he makes a legally binding declaration that I am *trustworthy*[12] and that I am free from any *responsibility*. I notify you of this. God is my witness that, had I not given such a binding oath, I would not have written you anything of the kind, for between the two of us there is more trust

[4] Ar. *al-barr*, meaning perhaps the Egyptian *Rīf*, or countryside.

[5] Of the various persons bearing this name this one probably was Khiyār b. Zikrī, for his son Zikrī b. Khiyār wrote the letter ULC Or 1080 J 54 to 'Arūs. Another contemporary was Khiyār b. Jacob (TS 10 J 28 f. 12 [dated 1100]).

[6] A customs house of Fustat, where exports were cleared.

[7] Text: *mā yaqdir yakhruj illā* [*mar*]*sūm*. See next letter.

[8] A Muslim colleague of 'Arūs, who had carried that "dyed purple" together with his own goods to Alexandria.

[9] The meaning of this clause is not evident.

[10] Text: *tglyg*, which is a scribal error. I assume that *tglyf*—i.e., *taghlīf*—is intended.

[11] Text: *iqriḍ*, referring to the term *muqāraḍa*.

[12] Meaning not obliged to give an oath under any circumstances.

than exists in the whole world, and I know well that you are more trustworthy than I am myself.

You still owe me 2 gold qīrāṭs, balance of the price of the [. . .] which I sent you. The son of your sister, 'Allān,[13] wrote to Hilāl[14] to pay me these 2 qīrāṭs, but he has not done so.

Best regards to you and to those under your care. And most respectful regards to your partner Sibā' ("Lion").

God alone is sufficient for me.[15]

49 A LATER LETTER ON THIS SHIPMENT

TS NS J 197.

I am writing to you . . . from Alexandria. . . .[1] Your letter with the testimony has arrived. Had I not been under oath, I would not have troubled you with this. Our friends will convey my excuses to you, namely, that I do not carry a thing for anyone except with this arrangement.

I loaded the wool, although I did not have the exact weight. 'Abd al-Raḥmān said that it weighed five qinṭārs and was worth 30 dinars. I took the expenses for the canvas, the ropes, and the freight from Abū Mūsā Hārūn ("Aaron, father of Moses") Ibn Shammār ("Trader in fennel").[2] I had great trouble in getting the shipment out to the harbor, for its papers had been lost. The two additional pieces which arrived with Hārūn[3] are already on board. The total

13 Often mentioned in 'Arūs' correspondence. Since 'Arūs had no male offspring, he groomed his sister's son (who probably was married to a daughter of his) as the prospective heir of his firm.

14 Most likely Hilāl b. Binyām (Benjamin), proprietor of a drugstore in Alexandria, given as an address in no. 50, n. 4, below. Drugstores, then as today, served as landmarks and small bourses. See *Med. Soc.*, II, 261.

15 This phrase from the Koran was mostly used by Jews from the Maghreb. See above, passim.

---

1 Seven short lines of the usual phrases.

2 In TS 8 Ja 1, f. 5 (middle of the eleventh century) a man with this family name lives in al-Mahdiyya.

3 The aforementioned Aaron, it seems. When mentioning him first the writer had to be exact, since he charged the addressee with a debt to this man.

freight: 6 dinars; I paid here 3 dinars, and the remaining 3 dinars will be paid in Almeria after safe arrival. Please take notice of this. Best regards to you and your partner Abu 'l-Waḥsh ("Father of the wild animal").[4]

God alone is sufficient for me.

(Address, on the otherwise blank verso:)

(To) my master and lord Abu 'l-Afrāḥ, 'Arūs b. Joseph, . . .

(From) his grateful Hilāl b. Joseph, . . .

(As usual, the blank space is filled with lists in 'Arūs' hand, but this time obviously referring to a collection for a public appeal.)

50 SPANISH SHIP SEIZED BY THE EGYPTIAN GOVERNMENT

Ca. 1100

Here again two letters refer to the same shipment, but there is no need to translate both, for they were sent more or less simultaneously because of the urgency of the matter. Some details contained in the letter not translated here (Bodl. MS Heb. c 50, f. 19, referred to below with "Bodl.") are used in the comments.

The Egyptian government ordered the Spanish ship to be emptied in order to use it for naval operations in case of necessity, most likely in the war with the Crusaders, who had just arrived on the scene. As was assumed above (no. 48, n. 3), that ship probably was larger and stronger than the other Muslim boats anchoring at that time in Alexandria.

University Library, Cambridge, Taylor-Schechter Collection, TS 13 J 27, f. 9.

(Upside down:) Written in the night after the holiday.[1]

(Six short lines of the usual opening phrases.)

[4] Identical, of course, with "Lion" of no. 48.

---

[1] Meaning Pentecost (Shavuoth), in May when the ships set sail.

I have just received your note in which you inform me that you have bought a bahār of lac and packed purple. But I must tell you that I cannot take anything from you with me. For when I took leave from you, I was planning to travel to Spain, but when I arrived here, I found that the Andalusian ship was completely emptied on written order from the Sultan.[2] Therefore I boarded a ship going to al-Mahdiyya. If you intend to send your goods to al-Mahdiyya, please send me a message and instruct me before we sail, since I do not think it would be proper on my part to carry your things with me unless you tell me so expressly in your letter. And be not late in writing, for the al-Mahdiyya boats are ready to sail; they have no further business here.[3] Otherwise, your goods might get stuck in Alexandria. Do not send your letter with anyone who you are not sure will deliver it. The best thing is you send it with a mukārī (donkey driver) to the store of Hilāl b. Binyām.[4]

(Short greetings and a note on the recipient's cousin, not completely legible in both letters.)

(Address in Ar. characters:)
This letter should be brought to the Colonnade[5] to the store of 'Arūs.[6] Deliver and be rewarded.
(In Heb. characters, upside down:)
To the illustrious elder 'Arūs, son of R. Joseph, . . .
From his "son" Zikrī, son of R. Hananel.

51 THE FRUSTRATED JOURNEY OF A BUSINESS FRIEND

The letter is written in the beautiful and regular hand of a trained scribe. Unlike other letters, where the address is put on the

[2] Bodl.: *al-markab al-andalusī qad ta'aṭṭal bi-kitāb min 'ind al-sulṭān wa-furrigh jamī' mā fīhā.*
[3] Bodl.: *al-marākib al-mahdawiyya qad rājū*, an expression I have not seen before specifically in this sense.
[4] A drugstore. See no. 48, n. 14, above.
[5] Ar. *al-ṣaffayn.* See *Med. Soc.*, I, 194.
[6] Clearly a landmark known to the muleteers.

top of the verso, here it is arranged as a broad band almost in the middle of the completely blank reverse side, creating an aesthetic effect similar to certain artistic Iranian dishes from the same period.[1] Such care for the outward appearance of the letter shows the esteem in which 'Arūs was held by the writer. He was called Ḥalfōn ha-Kohen b. Judah, and describes himself as the recipient's friend (*muḥibb*). I have not yet traced him elsewhere.

University Library, Cambridge, Taylor-Schechter
Collection, TS 10 J 13, f. 4.

(Six lines of the usual introductory phrases.)

I was leaving you with the understanding that I would travel overseas. But on the way[2] I had an accident, all my things were drenched, and the sugar was spoiled in its entirety; by these lines, not more than about twenty pounds were saved.[3] I was overcome by a great depression and refrained from going abroad.[4] I dispatched my things, but the boats are still in the harbor. May God—be he praised and exalted—grant them a smooth passage.

Now to the story of Abū 'Imrān Mūsā ("Moses, Father of Amram"). He arrived, and people tried to arrange a settlement between us. He swore solemn oaths that he did not owe me more than those 100 dinars.[5] I thought, even if I forced him to give an oath in court,[6] he would not concede more than this. Therefore I made a settlement with him and took from him those 100 dinars and issued him a release. Please take notice of this. May God never deprive me of you and your kindnesses and keep you for me and for all

[1] A similar, and even more artistic, arrangement in TS Box K 6, f. 189, a letter from Jerusalem addressed to Abū Naṣr Faḍl al-Tustarī. See no. 30, B, above.

[2] From Cairo to Alexandria.

[3] One traveled on the Nile, and goods often fell into the water. See *Med. Soc.*, I, 297ff.

[4] The wording seems to mean that it was not the material loss, but the depression that induced the writer to give up his travel plans. He perhaps took the accident on the Nile as a bad omen.

[5] He had already conceded on a previous occasion that he owed this debt.

[6] Giving an oath in court was a very serious matter and regarded as damaging to one's reputation. Respectable merchants avoided it, if possible (see *Med. Soc.*, II, 240). Conceding part of a debt entailed an oath expressly provided for in the Torah.

other people who need help.[7] May he give you *male children studying the Torah and fulfilling commandments in Israel. May your well-being increase and never decrease. Amen, in eternity, Selah.*

Kindest regards to you and the elder Abu 'l-Waḥsh[8] and to all under your care. *And peace be upon Israel.*[9]

52 A STRAY LETTER

Business During an Epidemic
Ca. 1080-1100

The letters of traders translated thus far make the impression that they are all preserved in groups. This impression should not be generalized. The mass of unconnected material is very considerable. But the translation of an unrelated letter often requires much guesswork and lengthy comments, which are better left for a full-fledged edition of the original. The letter presented below, which is roughly contemporary with, or slightly preceding those addressed to ʿArūs (nos. 48-51), is such a case. The persons mentioned in it might or might not be identical with others found in approximately contemporary letters or documents, but the weighing of the pros and cons would be time-consuming without being rewarding. Despite this drawback the letter translated here is by no means without interest.

Abu 'l-Faraj Nissīm ("Miraculous Delivery"), the recipient of this letter, was an India trader, against whom, while in India selling precious Western textiles and mercury, a power of attorney was issued in Fustat.[1] The date of that document is not preserved, but the names of the signatories, known from other sources, put it around 1090. The sender of the letter shared with him the family

[7] Clearly ʿArūs had been influential in inducing the debtor to concede that he owed 100 dinars.

[8] See no. 49, n. 4, above.

[9] This quotation from Psalm 128:6, often found in the mosaic pavements of ancient synagogues, was not used as conclusion of a letter, but refers here to the peaceful settlement of the lawsuit.

---

[1] TS 12.19, *India Book* 163.

name, and since he writes in a style possible only among close relatives, he was most probably his nephew. Both clearly were Maghrebis; therefore, their family name must be read as al-Ruqqī, derived from a little town in Tunisia named Ruqqa, and not al-Raqqī, from Raqqa, the ancient city on the Euphrates in northern Mesopotamia.[2]

The letter was sent from Fustat to Alexandria, for the writer refers to goods brought by him from North Africa ("the West"), but still remaining in the town of the receiver of the letter (sec. D). Many other details in this letter tally with this assumption. The writer most probably left Alexandria on a Thursday and passed the Sabbath in Fuwwa, where he embarked on a Nile boat; or he could have made the whole journey on a boat, using the Khalīj canal, which connected Alexandria with the Nile. See *Med. Soc.*, I, 298-299.

David Kaufmann Collection, Budapest, DK 3.

A. An uneventful Nile voyage

I am writing to you, my lord and master—may God prolong your life and grant you permanent well-being and happiness—to inform you that I arrived on Friday, after an eight days' journey, and unloaded my cargo on Sunday, the day I am writing this. Everything which I carried with me arrived completely intact.[3]

B. Confusion on the money market

Now, what you wish to know: Business here is slow and practically at a standstill. For there is much confusion in the rate of exchange and, at the present time, 50 dirhems are to be had for 1 dinar, more [or less]. An epidemic[4] is raging in the environs of the town,

[2] For Ruqqa (from medieval Latin *rocca*, from which also English *rock* is derived?) see Idris, *Zirides*, p. 446. This family name was quite common in the Geniza. It is found also in a Muslim document from the eleventh century. See Idris, ibid., n. 366.

[3] The Sabbath begins an hour before sunset on Friday afternoon. The writer explains that not enough time remained to unload on Friday. In view of the accident on the Nile reported in no. 51 (paralleled by many Geniza letters) one understands the express remark that everything arrived safely.

[4] Ar. *byh*, derived from *wabā'*. An epidemic ravaged the capital of Egypt in 1111-1112. Bodl. MS Heb. 75, f. 13.

and because of this, the flow of good dirhems has been cut off so that everyone is having difficulties with his business.[5]

C. The Western imports: textiles and oil

As to the textiles: The reddish material,[6] first class, is worth 4 1/2 (dinars) at most; other qualities, less than 4. Unbleached saris (*fūṭa*) 7 1/2,[7] but the red ones are selling poorly; Abu 'l-Surūr informed me that he sold for you ten red saris for 7 (dinars) and 10 qīrāṭs, on one month's credit. The cloaks (*malāḥif*) are selling very poorly. As to the small pieces of reddish material and the fine saris, I do not know the situation, for I did not sit on the market.

Oil is being sold 25 pounds for a dinar; so I am holding my oil back, in the hope that the situation will improve a little.

D. The representative of the firm in Fustat

I met with the elder Abū Sa'd ("Fortunate") with regard to Salmān and learned that Salmān had gone to Palestine. He, Abū Sa'd, will write you a letter to be sent simultaneously with my letter, for I told him that you were very much upset about this matter and took a very serious view of it.

I talked to him about the textiles which I had brought with me from the West; he said that he had sent a letter with instructions to bring them here, but the letter had crossed me on my way. Therefore, my lord, if someone can be found to transport them, please do so; for he has no way of explaining to you what happened, as he does not write with his own hand, and there is someone staying in his house, in whose presence things cannot be discussed.[8]

[5] This seems to mean that the city was dependent for its silver money on the environment (Ar. *jihāt-hā*), which is rather unusual.

[6] Ar. *shuqra.*

[7] Meaning, as the continuation shows, that *ten* saris cost 7 1/2 dinars.

[8] This rather obscure paragraph seems to imply that the Fustat business correspondent recommended bringing the Maghrebi textiles to the capital despite the poor market situation.

E. Arrangements with a partner

Al-Shayyāl ("Porter")[9] received what was sent for you and will inquire as to what was lost and what remained. He requested me to ask you whether this involved the partnership. As to his own merchandise—whether (textiles) from Sicily or Majorca, or oil—whatever has been sold of this, he will receive the price agreed upon. As for everything else, after it is sold, each partner will get his share in accordance with his investment. Please take notice of this, my lord.

F. Some business intelligence

The silk (*khazz*) robes do not fetch a thing, one robe being worth less than 4 (dinars). Please inform Abu 'l-Ḥasan accordingly. Likewise, Joseph al-Fāsī (of Fez) asked me about this. Please also tell Abu 'l-Ḥasan Ibn al-Shāmī (Syro-Palestinian) not to move with his oil; he will only regret it.

My master, the elder Abū Sa'd informed me that the elder Abu 'l-Bishr ("Good tidings") sold his silk (*ḥarīr*) to the government and received its price. However, I was in no mood today to ask him how he sold it. I shall sell what I have with me, for I do not see that there is much hope (for a better price).

My lord, the elder Abū Sa'd talked to me about the textiles, namely, which of them had not been sent and had been left with him. I understood that he wanted to get rid of them; so I said perhaps he could find someone to send them with and get them out of his sight.[10]

G. Urgent request: send the receipt for the poll tax

My lord, I left my cotton robe, which I used to wear above my iridescent[11] robe; in its pocket there is the tax certificate together with a paper bag in which there are some dirhems and a letter

[9] A family name still common among Muslims in Egypt. But in the Geniza period many Jews were porters; the term used mostly was *ḥammāl.* An Ibn al-Shayyāl is in a list of poor people of the eleventh century. See *Med. Soc.*, II, 467, sec. 108.

[10] Probably textiles for which no market could be found in Fustat. Perhaps cotton fabrics coming from India.

[11] Ar. *fākhitī*, having the color of the ring-dove or wood pigeon.

given to me by Salāma, the agent of our master, the Nagid—(may his) R(ock) p(reserve him). Please send me the tax certificate as soon as you have read this letter, for I have given a bail bond on it until it arrives.[12]

H. Conclusion and a P.S.

Whatever needs you have, please write me about them. Please write me in detail about the price of oil at your place and how things are, for I am very much worried. May God let me receive good tidings, as is his bountiful custom.

Accept my best greetings, and likewise, my best greetings to the elder Abu 'l-Ḥasan; if he needs anything, let him write me about it. Greetings to Rachel[13] and her mother and to everyone in the house. Greetings also to Abu 'l-Ḥasan,[14] to the son of my paternal aunt, and his sons. *And Peace. And may your life be prolonged!* And look for the storax[15] for me, for I did not find it in the package.

(Address, written upside down, as usual:)
(To) my lord, the elder Abu 'l-Faraj Nissīm, son of Solomon, (*may he*) *r*(*est in*) *E*(*den*)—may God grant him permanent well-being and happiness—Ruqqī.
(From) his "son" and protégé Solomon, son of Abraham, . . . Ruqqī.

[12] No Christian or Jew could travel without carrying with him a certificate proving that he had paid the poll tax.

[13] Jewish women in Egypt did not have biblical names. But among the learned Jews of the Maghreb female Hebrew names were common. Rachel, no doubt, was the writer's wife and the addressee's daughter. She is greeted before her mother, referred to as *sitt-hā* "her mistress." Good form required that the lady of the house be greeted as mother of her children, not as wife of the recipient.

[14] This is a member of the family. The Abu 'l-Ḥasan greeted before was a merchant, probably identical with one of the two mentioned in sec. F above.

[15] Ar. *m'h*, for *may'a*, storax, much used in medicine and perfumery and frequently mentioned as exported on the India route.

53-56 LETTERS OF ISAAC NĪSĀBŪRĪ, A PERSIAN RESIDING IN ALEXANDRIA

Isaac b. Simḥā ("Joy," Heb.) of Alexandria was not only named Nīsābūrī (from Neyshābūr, as it is spelled today, in the most remote northeastern corner of Iran), but certainly was a man whose mother tongue was Persian. Persian, like English, is an Indo-European language. Therefore Isaac, while writing Arabic, incurs difficulties similar to those that are familiar to American students trying to learn that Semitic language. He has troubles with the sounds specific to Arabic, makes many mistakes, and, in particular, always mixes up masculine and feminine. For Persian, like English, but unlike Arabic, has no feminine endings in nouns, adjectives, and verbs. Not rarely is his syntax blurred and sometimes one must try to retranslate his Arabic into Persian in order to find out what he intends to say. But his letters are worth reading.

A short description of Isaac Nīsābūrī's variegated business is provided in *Med. Soc.*, I, 153. More extensive letters of his, such as DK XI and Bodl. MS a 3 (Cat. 2873), f. 23, cannot be translated here because they contain too many details requiring lengthy comments. But it is hoped that the first selection from his correspondence presented here gives a fair idea of his mercantile enterprises.

The first three specimens translated are addressed to Abu 'l-'Alā' Ṣā'id ("Topnotch," in Heb. 'Ullā) ha-Levi b. Joseph, almoner and trustee of the court, the Damascene, in the capital of Egypt (mainly Fustat). The nature of the communal offices and the business activities of this man are explained in *Med. Soc.*, II, 78. I should add here that Jews from Damascus and Aleppo often appear as bankers (and, of course, merchant-bankers) in Egypt and the West, and appropriate individuals among them were therefore appointed as trustees of the courts, to whom the property of orphans and widows and collateral deposited with the courts were entrusted. This position of confidence gave them approach to the leading men of the community, in which capacity we find indeed the recipient of the letters translated below.

The writer of the letters belonged to a slightly lower stratum of the society, but since he dealt with communal matters in nos. 45 and 46, I assume he occupied a leading position in the "Iraqian," that is, "Eastern," Jewish congregation of Alexandria, of which he, as an Iranian, probably was a member.

One letter (no. 54) contains the date 1117. The merchant Abu 'l-Faraj ("Delivery") Ḥamawī, that is from Ḥamāh in Syria, whom we find here in the Maghreb, was about ten to fifteen years later active in the India trade. Taking the whole correspondence of Isaac Nīsābūrī together, it should be attributed to the period 1100-1130, approximately.

53 WESTERN AND EASTERN GOODS AND FRIENDS

March 1119

University Library, Cambridge, Taylor-Schechter Collection, TS 13 J 22, f. 30.

(Five lines of conventional introductory phrases.)

A. Standstill of the silk trade because of bad sailing conditions

As to the silk. At the arrival of the Spanish ship, all business stopped, no one sold and no one bought. After some days, small quantities were sold at the price of 21-22 (dinars) per ten (pounds).[1]

When, however, all the ships tarried in coming, the merchants were eager to buy, but those who had silk kept it. Today it is thirty-three days that only one ship has arrived and only one ship has sailed. Now there is much confusion and worry about the ships. For today it is twenty-three days from the Feast of the Cross[2] and

[1] The standard price for silk in Alexandria was 20 dinars for 10 pounds. See *Med. Soc.*, I, 222.

[2] The Coptic Feast of the Cross, meaning the rediscovery of the Cross, corresponds to September 26 or 27 of our calendar (see E. W. Lane, *The Manners and Customs of Modern Egyptians*, Everyman's Library edn., p. 547). It was a great date for seafaring, and is often referred to as such in the Geniza. "*From* the Feast of the Cross" must mean, to my mind, *before*, because the Maghrebi ships normally set sail for the return westward slightly before the *'Īd al-ṣalīb*. Sometimes people are warned *not* to travel in the *marākib ṣalībiyya*, which does not mean "Crusaders' ships," but ships setting out shortly after the Festival of the Cross.

not a single ship has arrived from the Maghreb, nor has any news come from there.[3] The winds are adverse, neither east nor west. On this very day they paid for coarse silk 23 dinars. No one sold or will sell until it is known what will be. So please, do not move with the silk except in the event that trustworthy unravelers are available to whom you might give a small reel to unravel, good only for the countryside.[4]

B. Sale of Oriental and western products in Fustat

As to the cubeb,[5] if it reaches a quotation of 6 dinars, to be sold on credit, sell it, don't leave it.

I have instructed the elder Abu 'l-Khayr Salāma ("Solomon, the Good")[6] to sell the ambergris if it is worth 1 1/2 dinars. Otherwise, he should leave it.[7]

C. Three business friends

I wrote to his excellency, my lord Abu 'l-Riḍā, and did not receive an answer, which surprised me, since it concerned one of his own affairs. But you understand that I cannot send him a reminder.[8]

When any news or letter arrives from Shām (Syria and Palestine), kindly inform me.[9]

[3] When ships were sighted off the coast of western Egypt runners were sent to Alexandria to alert the merchants, for in fall ships were often kept back by east winds.

[4] Meaning that these *naqqāḍa* would pick out the inferior silk which was good only to be sold in the Egyptian Rīf. See *Med. Soc.*, I, 104.

[5] The *fāghira*, a spicy berry of the pepper family, coming from the East Indies and used in medicine and in cooking. Often mentioned in the Geniza (see Maimonides-Meyerhof, p. 151, no. 307). The unit traded, as suggested by other texts, probably was 10 mann (slightly over 20 pounds).

[6] The name Salāma was common. Of those noted by me, the son of the writer of no. 28, above, would best fit the time and the circumstances.

[7] Probably the Atlantic variety of ambergris is intended. In no. 6, above, the Alexandrian merchant Abu 'l-Barakāt b. Khulayf, a friend of our writer (see no. 54, n. 7, below) carries ambergris from Alexandria to Fustat.

[8] Abu 'l-Riḍā Solomon b. Mevōrākh was a son of the late Nagid Mevōrākh and brother of the incumbent Nagid Moses and representative of the merchants in the Egyptian capital. The writer politely requests the recipient to talk to the great man and to remind him.

[9] Travel from Palestine to Cairo by land was as common as the voyage

I received a letter from Abu 'l-Faraj al-Ḥamawi[10] from the (Nafūsa) Mountain.[11] He is now in 'Ānāt and they expect to cross the sea soon. May God ordain safety for them.

I received also a letter from Isaac Nafūsi,[12] and your honor, too, mentioned this in your letter, namely, that he is in a hurry to get what he has ordered from me in his memo. But in order to be properly executed, this order requires proceeding slowly, for here there is plenty of cash for buying, but little to buy. Moreover, the holidays are another impediment: in this week there are only two business days.[13] Notwithstanding, most of the things ordered are already in and the rest will be acquired soon. I shall send them with someone who travels there.[14]

What you asked me to buy for you, he had already asked.[15] I do not take any remuneration from anyone and do not want people to say that this travel of mine is only for my own business.

D. Corals and conclusion

Loose corals[16] are being sold on this very day in the customs house[17] for 11 1/2 dinars and some even for 8 dinars, while my

by sea from Alexandria to the eastern shores of the Mediterranean. Mail especially was sent overland.

10 For this traveler to the West and on the India route see the introduction. His personal name was Hiba ("Gift").

11 The Nafūsa mountains southwest of Tripoli, Libya, as is indicated by the place name 'Ānāt, following immediately (see Yāqūt 3, p. 594). See next note.

12 I have the impression that three different Isaac Nafūsīs appear in the Geniza papers of this period. (We had above four cousins bearing the uncommon name Barhūn Tāhertī.) Here the India trader bearing this name is probably intended.

13 The writer clearly refers to the year 1119, when the Muslim "Great Festival" (which coincided with the pilgrimage to Mecca) was celebrated on March 24-26, and the Jewish Passover on March 29-30.

14 He would not carry them himself, although he intended to travel to Cairo, so that people should not say that he charged his own expenses to his business friends whose goods he carried.

15 'Ullā traded in both western and eastern goods.

16 As opposed to corals on strings. Text: *marjān turāb*. I assume the correct Arabic word escaped the writer. But this might be a term not otherwise found in the Geniza.

17 Ar. *ṣn'h,* which I take as *ṣinā'a,* the customs house of Fustat, which served also as bourse. The term might have been used by that time also in Alexandria since the European word *arsenal* is derived from it.

corals are worth 20 dinars, and none have arrived thus far either from Europe[18] or from North Africa.[19]

Kindest regards to you and to all the friends.
And may your well-being wax indefinitely.

Two P.S.'s: Textiles from Alexandria

The scarfs[20] are with the bleacher. God willing, I shall send them as soon as they are ready.
(In the margin:)
I am sending three brocaded robes with the muleteer Kāfūr ("Camphor").[21] They are for Isaac Nafūsī. Give them to him.

(Address, right side, five short lines:)
(To) his honor, my lord, the illustrious elder,
Abu 'l-'Alā Ṣā'id), (*our*) *master,*
Joseph, *the almoner, the trustee,*
the Friend of the yeshiva,
may God make his honored position permanent.
(Left side, four lines:)
(From) his grateful Isaac *ha-Levi, son of Simḥā al-Nīsābūrī,* (*may the*) *m*(*emory of the*) *r*(*ighteous*) *be b*(*lessed*).
(*I*) *h*(*ope for your*) *s*(*alvation, oh*) *G*(*od*).[22]
(Third P.S. beneath the address:)
Do not move with the silk. Leave it as it is, unless you find . . .
. . . . . .

[18] Ar. *Rūm.* Corals are found especially on the shores of Sardinia.

[19] He seems to say that his corals were of a particularly fine quality.

[20] Ar. *radda.* My card index of textiles contains about sixty entries of this item from Geniza lists of trousseaux, but the word seems not to be mentioned elsewhere. Its meaning can be established through the combinations in which it appears. One of many which might be of interest here: "An Alexandrian cloak, *milḥafa,* with a *radda*—6 dinars." Bodl. MS Heb. f 56, f. 48, l. 15.

[21] A slave or freedman, as his name indicates. Transport by land was regarded by our writer as safer for precious textiles than the treacherous voyage on the Nile.

[22] This use of the verse Genesis 49:18, abbreviated *LQI*, must have been common to "Easterners," for the Baghdadi who wrote the selections 47-49 follows the same usage. In later centuries it became customary to write *LQI* on the top of a letter, and many Oriental Jews still do so.

54 PROVISION FOR THE FAMILY OF A MERCHANT ABROAD

When a merchant traveled abroad for a prolonged period, he did not leave cash for the maintenance of his family, for cash in those days did not mean paper, but gold and silver, the supply of which is limited by nature and therefore possessed an incomparably higher purchasing power than our so-called money. Even a well-to-do merchant set his gold working all the time and carried very little with himself even for his own needs (see *Med. Soc.*, I, 200). The requirements of the family were provided for through monthly payments by a business friend, often fixed in an official document made out by a notary before the husband would set out on his journey. The business friend would take care also of additional needs of the family, often also foreseen in the legal instrument safeguarding its well-being. In addition to a fixed sum the family often was provided with such basic requirements as wheat, oil, and firewood. Several such notarial documents have been preserved. Our letter shows how the arrangement worked in practice.

Our Isaac Nīsābūrī of Alexandria took care of the family of Abu 'l-Faraj al-Ḥamawī, who traveled in the Muslim West (see no. 53, n. 10). Ḥamawī remained there for two winters at least, for our letter refers to provisions for three periods of five months each. The payments were made twice by bookkeeping arrangement and once by sending gold. The family lived in Fustat where it was looked after by the addressee, who was an important merchant, but also an almoner and trustee of the court. The accounts were made with Abu 'l-Riḍā, representative of the merchants (see no. 53, n. 8).[1] But he could not be bothered with such matters as payments to the family of a merchant abroad. This was left to a man one rung lower on the socioeconomic ladder.

University Library, Cambridge, Taylor-Schechter Collection, TS 13 J 21, f. 26.

[1] A document referring to a commenda of 300 dinars given by this man to three partners traveling to Yemen "and other countries" is contained in *India Book* 156. It is dated January 1118, that is, during the period of our nos. 53 and 54, here. The document, pieced together by me from four different fragments, is the longest referring to the India trade, but is still not complete.

(As from l. 4.) In a previous letter I had written to you about the family of our friend, the elder Abu 'l-Faraj al-Ḥamawī—may God ordain him safe travel—namely, that you should take from his excellency, my lord, the elder Abu 'l-Riḍā 2 dinars every month,[2] as from the new moon of Iyyar (April). This is on his private account, not on that of his warehouse, for I paid expenses for the goods he sent to the Maghreb.[3] I have written to him about this and communicated the account to him. I paid for him 10 1/8 dinars. Thus, this is for five months, from the new moon of Iyyar to the first day of Tishri (August 30, see below).

He also credited me[4] with 10 other dinars, this time on account of the warehouse. I also sent the other letters.[5] Thus they have now 2 dinars every month until the 1st of Tishri, 1429 (August 30, 1117), complete.[6]

I sent with my lord, the elder Abu 'l-Barakāt b. Khulayf ("Blessings, son of little dear substitute")[7] a purse with 10 dinars in number and 10 in weight for another five months. Please take it from him and pay them 2 dinars every month until the new moon of Adar (mostly February). When this will be finished, I shall send more.

For the balance of the price of the cloak[8] buy wheat for them, and when the al-Mahdiyya ships arrive, I shall send them [. . .], and if they wish something else [. . . a line and a half lost . . .] in the Kārim[9] . . . [three lines lost] and send me the news from

[2] The standard minimum monthly budget of a middle-class family. Here they receive wheat, in addition.

[3] The warehouse, *dār al-wakāla*, was often kept in partnership, in this case probably with a prominent Muslim. See *Med. Soc.*, I, 188-189.

[4] Text: *rf' 'ly.* To the best of my knowledge, this can only mean: he charged me. The Persian writer seems to mean: he asked me to pay for him.

[5] He had forwarded before letters by Ḥamawī to his family and business correspondents.

[6] The first of Tishri is the Jewish New Year. The writer closes here the accounts for the year preceding August 30, 1117; in addition to the five months referred to above, payments had been due for another five months.

[7] Called "the Alexandrian" in a note to him from his brother (TS 16.244). See also no. 53, n. 7, above, where he is also on his way from Alexandria to Fustat.

[8] An Alexandrian *milḥafa* (see no. 53, n. 20) was sent to the recipient with a request to buy for the family other items requested by them.

[9] He wishes to receive information about the goods that arrived that year "in the Kārim," that is, from India. See no. 43, n. 9, no. 45, n. 30.

Shām (Syria and Palestine).[10] (Three damaged lines with the conventional phrases of conclusion. In the margin, the writer's son Simḥa kisses the hand of the recipient, and greetings are extended to his brother Abū Sa'd and the latter's son. The address, on the otherwise blank verso, is as in no. 44. The Heb. Shālōm ["Peace"] is added in the upper lefthand corner; see no. 45.)

55 INVITATION OF A SCRIBE FROM EUROPE

The father of the recipient is called here not by his Hebrew name Joseph as in the two previous letters, but its Arabic equivalent Munajjā ("The rescued," namely, from the pit in the biblical story, Genesis 37). The medieval writers delighted in such variations.

The invitation of a scribe from Europe at a time when many local scribes were available in Alexandria should not be understood as an indication that the Jewish copyists of "Rūm" were in general superior to their Egyptian colleagues. The Geniza material on this question needs further study. This and the following selection are presented only to show that the merchant Isaac Nīsābūrī had concerns other than his business.

Bodleian Library, Oxford, MS Heb. d 66 (Cat. 2878), f. 43.

I am writing from the port city Alexandria, may God protect it, . . .

A. Mats ordered in Alexandria

Abu 'l-Ḥasan Caleb[1] b. Nathan arrived some time ago and told me that he had carried with him a note with the measurements for the pair of mats which your honor had ordered to make; he had lost it and also did not remember the measurements. I expected a

[10] See no. 53, n. 9.

[1] The biblical name Caleb was popular among Byzantine Jews, probably because of Caleb's connection with the Land of Israel (Numbers 13-14; Joshua 15:14-18) and among Arabic-speaking Jews because it sounded much like the Arabic name Khulayf (see no. 54), which was sometimes used as its equivalent.

letter from you in this matter carried by Barakāt al-Ja'farī;[2] he has arrived, but no letter of yours was with him. Please honor me with your letter whenever you have any need or concern.[3]

B. The Scribe

I ask you also to meet with R. Abraham the Rūmī, *the scribe*, who wrote a *Torah scroll* in Tinnīs,[4] and this year, too, I have heard that he wrote two others in Fustat. Formerly we did not have here in Alexandria a Torah scroll on *parchment*.[5] But now, with the support of the *Creator*, we have obtained parchment and are resolved, with the help of the H(oly one, be), he p(raised), to carry this matter through. Therefore I ask your honor to meet with the aforementioned R. Abraham and make an agreement with him regarding his remuneration and all his expenses. He should come here as early as possible. Here are many *scribes*, but our endeavor in this matter is that the scroll of the *congregation* should have the very best script.[6]

I intend to go up to Fustat, but wait for the answer to this letter of mine and the arrival of that man. Immediately afterwards I shall travel to Fustat where I have many things to do. So please have this matter done quickly.

Kindest regards to you and to all who inquire about me. I have learned what you have done to extricate that load of brazilwood.[7] May I never be deprived of your kindness. *Peace in plenty.*

(Address is on the otherwise blank verso, as in the preceding selections, with the variation indicated in the introduction. *Peace in plenty* is repeated.)

[2] His full name was Abu 'l-Barakāt Berākhōt ("Blessings," in Ar. and Heb.) b. Nathan. *Ja'fari* was a type of paper, in the manufacture or sale of which he specialized (TS 16.207).

[3] Mats were one of the main products of Alexandrian industry. They were exported overseas to Sicily and Tunisia.

[4] Once a famous center of the linen industry on an island east of Damietta. Very often referred to in the Geniza. See, e.g., the indexes of *Med. Soc.*, I-II, s.v.

[5] This translates Heb. *gewīl* (spelled by Nīsābūrī gevīl), which is written on the side of the hair, not on that of the flesh.

[6] Torah scrolls usually were donated by private persons, often by women, and donations naturally are not always of the best quality. The congregation (the biblical word *'ēdā* is used) made a special effort.

[7] Probably from the customs in Fustat after arrival from India.

56 REQUEST FOR GOVERNMENT INTERVENTION IN ALEXANDRIA

Late 1110s

The first part of this letter (ll. 6-36) deals with a partnership in a boat, in which the writer, the recipient, the representative of the merchants Abu 'l-Riḍa Solomon (see nos. 53 and 54, above), and several other persons, one of them already dead, were involved and on which the Nagid himself was expected to make a decision. The fact itself is interesting, since the Geniza is surprisingly reticent about partnerships in boats (see *Med. Soc.*, I, 309). But the details provided refer to a pending lawsuit not otherwise attested and do not sum up to a meaningful complete unit worth translating.

The second section, translated below, is concerned with a topic of vital importance to the Christians and Jews living under Islam, namely, whether they were permitted to regulate their matters of inheritance according to their own laws or had to refer them to Muslim courts. The Geniza contains much material on this question (see *Med. Soc.*, II, 394-399). The passage presented here is of some specific interest since it shows that the government had no "policy" in this matter; rather, it acted when a community, and each local community separately, took the appropriate initiative.

The addressee was a *nā'ib*, or deputy director of some government office. Such people usually conducted their correspondence in Arabic script, wherefore there was no reason to deposit its remnants in the Geniza. Thus far I have not found any other item referring to him.

University Library, Cambridge, Taylor-Schechter
Collection, TS 18 J 4, f. 6, as from l. 38.

A very serious matter occurred here, which should not be passed over in silence or slackness. A foreigner, a teacher, died here and left some gold. One of our coreligionists took it, but there was some dispute about it, and one of our fellow Jews went to the qadi and to the director of the (Muslim) office of inheritances and informed them. The qadi sent five policemen, who took the money.

In the times of our lord the Nagid (*may the*) *m*(*emory of the*) *r(ighteous) be b(lessed)*,[1] a decree was obtained from the lord of lords, al-Afḍal[2]—may God give him victory and make his government stable—to the effect that no one was permitted to interfere in the affairs of a dead Jew and that these were to be settled by the Jewish authorities.

Now, if those people here in Alexandria are successful in this matter, the community will perish. For people here are not like those in Miṣr (Fustat): if they get their hands on something, it is lost to them completely.

Therefore it is imperative that you meet with his high excellency, the Ra'īs,[3] and with his excellency, my lord, the illustrious elder Abu 'l-Mufaḍḍal[4]—may God make his honored position permanent—and deliberate on this affair. A new decree should be issued declaring the action taken here as unlawful and forbidding the like of it in the future. You will do this because of your concern for the whole of Israel[5] and because this is a meritorious action rewarded in this world and the world to come.

Not long ago the Christians here obtained a decree in the same matter, namely, that no one should interfere in their affairs. I have also heard that similar decrees were issued for Upper Egypt, Tinnīs, and Damietta,[6] namely, that no one should interfere in their affairs. Similar action should be taken with regard to the Jewish communities.

Kindest special regards to your honor and please convey my service and greetings to his excellency, my lord, the illustrious elder Abu 'l-Mufaḍḍal, may God let his prominence endure. Kindest regards to my lord, the illustrious elder, your father.

Please answer this letter quickly and if you have any concern, please honor me with it. *May your well-being increase forever.*

[1] The Nagid Mevōrākh b. Saadya (died March 30, 1112).

[2] The viceroy and actual ruler of Egypt al-Malik al-Afḍal (murdered 1121).

[3] The official head of the Jews of Egypt, Moses, the son of Mevōrākh. See n. 1, above.

[4] Chief Jewish judge in Cairo (not Fustat) and, like the Muslim qadis, also a great merchant (see *Med. Soc.*, II, 442, sec. 16; 477, sec. 18, 478, 503, sec. 119). The same kunya, or byname, was also borne by a nephew of the Nagid Mevōrākh. See ibid., 478.

[5] And not only your own community in the capital of Egypt.

[6] All these were regions with large Christian communities.

(The address is in the same style as in the previous letters. The recipient: Ṣadaqa ("Alms"; namely, given by God), son of R. Yaḥyā, *(may his) e(nd be) g(ood)*,[7] the Deputy.)

57-58 LETTERS FROM SA'DĀN BAGHDĀDĪ

A Trader Active in Spain, North Africa, and Egypt

Sa'dān b. Thābit ("The two auspicious stars," that is Jupiter and Venus, son of "Steadfast") was another Easterner who had settled in the West. In a letter not translated here we find him in Spain, in our first selection his home is Tripoli, in the second Alexandria, and from that city other letters of his were dispatched. His father, Thābit b. Sa'dān, is already mentioned as being in the West, whether as a visitor or on a more permanent basis is not evident. Sa'dān's script and style are beautiful and his letters have mostly a fine human touch. They may be dated around 1130.

57 SA'DĀN'S SON ELICITS A PROMISE OF OVERSEAS TRAVEL

The thirst for adventure is innate in man. At a time when the art of war was exercised solely by foreign mercenaries it was the noble profession of the overseas merchant which quenched that thirst for those who felt it most strongly. In the Geniza letters we see repeatedly sons urging their fathers to send them abroad. Our letter shows in particular how a father, caught by a promise given while drunk, proceeded to introduce his boy into the mysteries of the overseas trade.

Our letter was never sent, certainly for the same reason as that assumed with regard to no. 45, above. The reference to the drinking

[7] This strange Aramaic blessing, *S(āfēh) Ṭ(āv)*, is to be understood in the spirit of Job 8:7: "Though your beginning was small, your end (that is, your latter days) will be great."

bout was introduced in order to explain why the writer could commit such a folly as to send an unexperienced youth abroad. On second reading it was felt that such a detail was not commensurate with the dignity of an "illustrious elder."

University Library, Cambridge, Taylor-Schechter
Collection, TS 10 J 16, f. 19.

(The seven lines of introduction are much damaged. The letter is sent from "my home, Tripoli.")

[. . .], *son of our master and teacher Joseph,* (*may the*) *m*(*emory of the*) *r*(*ighteous*) *be b*(*lessed*), arrived this year by boat[1] and told me much about you, my lord, about your exertions for your friends and your noble character traits, all of which, of course, I knew before. I ask God to grant you fame for your virtues and merits and to let you never lose that *good name*. May he bless you with *a male child*, who will be like you or even better[2]—Amen, oh Lord of the universe.

I wish to inform you, my lord, that it so happened that, while I was drinking, my boy asked me to let him travel overseas. I swore to him that he would travel this year unless no ship set sail.[3] But God, the exalted, had willed that there was one. Thus I sent him and ordered that at arrival in Miṣr (Fustat), he should follow in everything the instructions of my lord, and ask you to guide him with your good advice. If a bahār of lac which had fallen into the water comes your way, buy it for him. In case it does not, and the boy goes down to Alexandria, kindly advise him to leave with you the money for such a buy, until the occasion for it arises. Then you will buy it and send it to him. Naturally, you will act according to your own judgment.[4]

[1] Interesting, because it shows that travel overland had again become common. During the half-century following the invasion of North Africa by the Arab bedouins, travel had become practically confined to the sea.

[2] The wish that the addressee's children should become better than he himself is somewhat strange to us, but natural in a society with strong family affection. The same occurs in no. 11, n. 12, above.

[3] Remarkable that such a possibility was taken into consideration. The Geniza mentions a case when no boat sailed from Alexandria to Tripoli. One had to take a boat to Palermo and from there back to the Libyan coast.

[4] The father wished the boy to come home with a big sack—a bahār normally comprised 300 pounds—but he did not want to spend much money on

Buy him also two mann of clove bark.[5] If it is expensive, buy one. Also a quarter mann nutmeg, and a quarter mann odoriferous wood of middle quality, for the family. Kindly do me this favor—may I never be deprived of you, and may God keep you for your friends. (Some greetings.)

58 SHIPPING CARAWAY FROM ALEXANDRIA TO FUSTAT

The Gaëta Boat

Bodleian Library, Oxford, MS Heb. c 28 (Cat. 2876), f. 55.

(Conventional but beautifully styled introduction, seven lines.)

A

I congratulate your high excellency on these noble days of festivals approaching you.[1] May God let you reach similar ones for a long time and during many consecutive years. *May you be blessed to behold the beauty of the Lord and to visit constantly in his Temple.*[2]

B

In your precious letter to Abū Isḥāq Ibrahīm you asked that I send you the bale of caraway.[3] I acted in accordance with your instructions, asked God for guidance and loaded it on the boat of

---

that venture. Therefore he asked to buy lac damaged by water, which had little value.

[5] This fragrant spice was often sent as a present and is intended as such here, too, as is expressly said. The father wanted to train his son also in this important task of a traveler: selecting presents for those at home. Three qualities of clove are mentioned in the Geniza: "heart of clove," "cleaned clove" (namely from its bark), and "the bark," which is the meanest.

---

[1] They were approaching the writer as well. But all good things had to be related to the recipient.

[2] Psalm 27:4. A common wish for those feast days, like Passover or Pentecost, with which a pilgrimage to Jerusalem was connected.

[3] Caraway seed (the English word is derived from the Arabic) came from Spain or North Africa.

the Ḥajj (Mecca pilgrim) Ibn Dunyā.[4] I canvassed its ends and bound it, for it had loosened. Until it was on board I paid for it 34 1/2 (dinars).[5] In the customs house and at the Sidra gate[6] I paid 1/2 and 1/3 less 1/8 dinar;[7] for the canal,[8] 16 dirhems. For freight I have made an agreement on 15 dirhems, which you will pay him after its arrival, with God's will, glorified be his might. Please take notice of this.[9]

C

By God, the discontinuation of your letters to me, while they reach others, hurt me much. But your honor is excused, may God keep you well and allot me again your favors.

D

I need not tell you what happened to the boat from Gaëta and about its final arrival. The elder Abū Isḥāq has written you a detailed letter about this and all other matters.[10]

E

I am eager to meet with you after the holidays, if God wills. I extend to your honor my humble and most sincere greetings and

[4] "Man of the World," but meaning: despising worldliness.

[5] In the approximately contemporary TS 12.290*v*, margin, the price asked for 100 pounds of caraway in Fustat was 3 1/2 dinars. Even if we assume that this bale, *'idl*, comprised 600 pounds, we would arrive at a sum of only 21 dinars. Thus, there must have been different qualities. Dirhems cannot be intended here, for the next line no doubt refers to dinars.

[6] A city gate of Alexandria at which goods destined for Cairo or the countryside were charged with a toll. Often mentioned.

[7] That is, $12 + 8 - 3 = 17$ (out of 24) qīrāṭs, approximately, three-quarters of a dinar.

[8] The usual word for the canal connecting Alexandria with the Nile is Khalīj. The word used here and at the end of the letter is *khawr*, designating a gulf largely formed by a river, especially in India. The use of this word here is perhaps owing to the increase in the India trade.

[9] This complete report about one shipment shows again that customs and the cost of transport, compared with the value of the merchandise, were not oppressively high; 31 dirhems were less than 1 dinar at that time. See *Med. Soc.*, I, 380, secs. 50-52.

[10] A Jewish merchant from Egypt, writing from Spain in the spring of 1137, intended to come home on the boat of "the man from Gaëta." (see *Levi Della Vida Jubilee Volume*, Rome, 1956, pp. 403-404). Here it is called *al-markab al-gyṭ'ny*, "the Gaëta boat."

ask you to kiss for me the eyes of your noble issue, your boy, may God let you see the fulfillment of the hopes you have for him. If you will honor me with the favor of your letter containing a report about your doings and your well-being, this will be the finest present I ever received. *And may your well-being increase.*

F

My lord, ask Hazzūn[11] b. Rajā' ("Hope"), how much he paid for the bale on the canal. If it was less than they took (from me), deduct the balance from the freight. And peace!

59 FROM ALMERIA, SPAIN TO TLEMÇEN, ALGERIA

Probably July 10, 1138

The recipient of this letter, Abū Sa'īd Ḥalfōn b. Nethanel ha-Levi, was a great traveler. One year we would find him in Aden and India, and the next in Spain and North Africa. About eighty Geniza items refer to him. He used his extended travels for meeting scholars and poets and for searching after interesting books. He was rightly characterized as "the center of all the leading personalities of his time." His intimate friendship with the Spanish Hebrew poet Judah ha-Levi was the cause of the preservation of five holographs and a good number of other items related to this great writer: they were kept with Ḥalfōn's papers and, one day, deposited in the Geniza with them. Here we find Ḥalfōn in Tlemçen in present-day Algeria, after he had traveled there from Fez, Morocco. Shortly afterwards a letter was addressed to him to Lucena near Granada, Spain.

The writer, Isaac b. Baruch, although of a somewhat lower social rank, belonged to the same circle of merchants who combined busi-

[11] I have not met this name elsewhere. Certainly a Muslim. This was the captain of the boat which carried the caraway, while the proprietor was the Ḥājj. The toll for the use of the canal was not levied in Alexandria, but somewhere on the way. The captain had received the sum of 16 dirhems in advance, but could not know exactly how much he would have to pay.

ness with interest in literature. The charming poem of Judah ha-Levi on the occasion of the circumcision of his grandson and namesake, and even more the longer one celebrating the birth of his own first-born, show the esteem in which he was held.[1] His domicile was Almeria, the port on the Spanish east coast. A letter addressed to him there by Ḥalfōn b. Nethanel has been preserved, as well as several other letters sent by him to Ḥalfōn.

As for the date of our letter: Sunday, July 10, 1138, can be assumed with great probability. The poet Judah ha-Levi (see sec. B) left Spain for good in the summer of 1140. In a famous poem written in that year he speaks of Ḥalfōn's dedicated friendship which had become particularly intimate "these last two years." Ḥalfōn visited Spain in 1128, 1130, 1135, and 1138, but only in the last of these four did the last day of the Jewish month of Tammuz, given as the date of the writing of the letter, fall on a Sunday. Thus the last day of Tammuz which corresponded to July 10, 1138, is the almost certain date of this letter. This is made even more likely by *India Book* 115, where a person with whom Ḥalfōn had concluded a partnership in Fez in January 1138, carried a letter of his from Tlemçen to Almeria.[2]

In Spain, even a humdrum business letter like ours was preceded by a carefully worded introduction, mostly in rhymed prose. The superlative epithets contained in it can be rendered in English only very imperfectly.

Bodleian Library, Oxford, MS Heb. d 74, f. 41, *India Book* 104; partly edited *Tarbiz*, 24 (1955), 134-138.

(In the upper left-hand corner:) Your admirer and glorifier Isḥāq (Isaac) Ibn Baruch.

A. Introduction

My most exalted master / and highest support, / my strongest resort, / most abundant resource, / most liberal help, / and Fate's finest gift to me, / may God, the exalted, prolong your life / and

[1] *Diwan des . . . Jehuda ha-Levi*, ed. H. Brody, Berlin, 1894, 1, 120, 189.

[2] Details in my paper "The Biography of Rabbi Judah ha-Levi in the Light of the Cairo Geniza Documents," in *Proceedings of the American Academy for Jewish Research*, vol. 28, New York, 1959, 41-56.

fulfill your hopes to your satisfaction. / I am writing these lines, may God exalt you, out of esteem of your worthiness / and admiration for your greatness. / May God keep you and remove all adversities from your domains.

B. Large payment to the poet Judah ha-Levi, Ḥalfōn's silent partner

I received your esteemed epistle carried by Abū Jacob Ibn al-Naghira,[3] my master and your admirer, may God keep him, in which you asked me to pay you 20 1/2 mithqāls (dinars). I shall carry out your instructions.[4]

I am writing this letter on Sunday, the last day of Tammuz. Four days ago I received from Tlemçen, with Abū Jacob Ibn al-Minna, ("Present," made by God to the mother)—may God keep and console him[5]—[100][6] 1/2 and 1/3 mithqāls for the burnished copper.[7] You wrote in your letter that I should send 150 mithqāls out of the sum received from Tlemçen; but only 100 have arrived. Anyhow, I shall carry out your orders, contribute a part of the sum myself and send it to R. Judah Ibn Ghiyāth,[8] my most high support, may God keep him, who will forward it to R. Judah, the Levi, my most high support, may his honored position be permanent.

C. Changing market conditions in Almeria

I have already informed you that I have received the 100 mithqāls you sent from Fez. You instructed me to buy silk for it. Silk sold indeed for a reasonable price. Therefore I bought it for 50 mithqāls.

3 This man concluded a contract of partnership with Ḥalfōn in Fez, Morocco, in January 1138 (see *India Book* 115). Abū Jacob, that is, the Heb. instead of the Ar. form, odd as it sounds, was Maghrebi usage.

4 As is stated at the end, the payment was made to this partner of Ḥalfōn.

5 A period of mourning has occurred in this man's family.

6 See what follows. The writer omitted at the beginning of the line the letter q = 100.

7 The best quality. See below.

8 A sum of 150 dinars, on which a middle-class family could exist for six years, was no gift. Judah ha-Levi, who was a successful physician, had invested a part of his capital in Ḥalfōn's business ventures, on what conditions we cannot know. Here, he gets his investment back, no doubt with considerable profit. Ibn Ghiyāth ("Present," often wrongly pronounced Ghayyāth) himself a poet, was closely connected with Judah ha-Levi, and the latter addressed to him several poems. See e.g., pp. 53, 60, 151, 174, in his *divan*.

But when the time of the sailing of the ships approached and it became clear to me that you would spend the rest of the summer in Spain,[9] I desisted from further action: I did not buy and left the money. But between the time I bought and today the mithqāl lost some of its value and the goods are today more expensive, namely:

D. A price list[10]

Peeled *khazāj* silk	. . . mithqāls
First class (khazāj)	5; the best 6; today, to 4[11]
The very coarse	3-2 1/2
Khazz silk[12]	9 1/2-9.[13]

As to the cash being paid today for silk, it is permissible to pay (only) one-third in the present currency, the difference between the current mithqāl and the Ḥammūdī mithqāl is a *thumānī* (1/8).[14]

Good, "burnished" copper	8
Cast copper	7
Good wax of Fez	8 1/2 per 100 pound
Pepper	27-25 per 100 pound

(Three damaged lines)

E. Smaller items and conclusion

The 20 1/2 mithqāls will be paid by me to Abū Jacob from the

[9] And not sail back from North Africa to Egypt directly.

[10] Another price list, sent by Isaac b. Baruch to Ḥalfōn only a few weeks later (*India Book* 202) shows a very considerable additional rise in prices, occasioned, of course, by the imminent departure of the last convoy of ships to the East.

[11] They used to mention the higher quotation first.

[12] For the various types of silk see *Med. Soc.*, I, 104, 418, and, esp., 454-455, n. 53. See also no. 2, n. 10, above.

[13] The quantity was standard and therefore is not indicated. In *India Book* 202, l. 16, it is referred to with *al-wazna*, "a weighing," a term used in different countries and periods. See Dozy, *Supplément*, II, 800*b*; Hinz, *Masse*, p. 35.

[14] Very interesting, but extremely surprising. The Ḥammūdīds were a small Berber dynasty which ruled various Spanish cities, especially Malaga, for a short time (until 1057), and which had an extremely poor record as far as their coins are concerned (see Harry W. Hazard, *The Numismatic History of Late Medieval North Africa*, New York, 1952, pp. 96, 236-237). The passage must wait for parallel sources.

balance remaining with me.[15] For the (price of the) spices I shall buy pure khazāj silk, as you have ordered, if God wills.

Kindest, best, and sincerest regards to my master and support, expressing the extent of my yearning for you—may God ordain our reunion, if God wills. Reiterated greetings of peace be upon my high support and the mercy of God, the exalted.

I beg to inform you that a time was set for the sale of the myrobalan.[16] I sold half a pound for 1/2 mithqāl; then I noted that you had fixed its price as 1 1/2 mithqāl per pound, whereupon I left it. I had not sold more than that half pound of it. The turpeth[17] costs today 1 mithqāl per two pounds.

F. About ships expected from Egypt

A day after the completion of this letter a barge arrived from Alexandria, which had been on its way sixty-five days. Muslim merchants, who had traveled in it, said that they had left behind them two ships ready to sail for Almeria. But they have not seen the ships sailing from Spain, nor do they have any information about them.[18] Kindest and best regards to my highest support. May God's mercy be upon him. I have paid to Abū Jacob the 20 1/2 mithqāls as ordered by you. And peace.

(Address:)[19] From the admirer of his worthiness—may God exalt him—Isaac, son of Baruch, (*may he*) *r*(*est in*) *p*(*eace*).

[To] the illustrious merchant, the noble and generous elder Abū Sa'īd ha-Levi, son of Nethanel[20] ha-Levi, *m*(*ay his*) *s*(*oul be*) *b*(*ound up*) *in* (*the bundle of*) *l*(*ife*).

15 See n. 4, above.

16 A widely used Oriental medical herb for intestinal troubles. "A time was set," i.e., the market price was announced.

17 Ar. *tirbid* (from which the English word is derived), an emetic made from a plant cultivated in Ceylon and other Oriental countries. See M.A.H. Ducros, *Le Droguier Populaire Arabe* . . . , Cairo, 1930, p. 28, no. 50.

18 *India Book* 105, which was sent on August 8, 1138, reports that these two ships arrived on Friday, August 5, and that Jews traveling in one of them told that Ḥalfōn's brother, who served as judge in Cairo, and all friends in Egypt were fine.

19 Note that in this letter the sender is mentioned first.

20 Spelled *Nt'l* instead of *Ntn'l*. Not a mistake, since this spelling is found also in other letters.

60 FROM FEZ, MOROCCO, TO ALMERIA, SPAIN

Written at the time of the Almohad menace
December 1141

Joseph Ibn Migash (Megas, "Great"), the spiritual leader of the Jews of Spain, whose death is referred to in section D, died in Sivan (May/June) 1141.[1] Our letter was written between the 20th and 30th of December of that year, as noted in section E. It is translated here because of its historical significance. It took another five years until Fez, the city in which this letter was written, fell into the hands of the Almohads.[2] But here we see that the merchants were fully aware of the imminent danger: business had come to a standstill in the capital, although the Sūs, the region referred to here, is in the utmost southwest of Morocco, while Fez is situated in its northernmost part. To be sure, the term Sūs comprised in the Middle Ages more than it does today, when it denotes the plain between the Atlantic Ocean, the Great Atlas, and the Anti-Atlas mountains.[3]

The beginning of the letter and the address on the verso are lost. Script and style are not those of the Spanish intellectuals, as found in no. 59, written by the merchant Isaac b. Baruch of Almeria, who is mentioned here also (sec. B). The writer was either a native of an eastern Mediterranean country or belonged to a class of people in Spain otherwise not well known to us. His script and style, although not remarkable in any respect, are regular and pleasant. They are similar to those of no. 7, above, but not quite identical. The two letters might have been written by the same man, but at different periods of his life (see also n. 15, below). Our translation begins on line 5, where the first consecutive sentence is discernible.

University Library, Cambridge, Taylor-Schechter Collection, TS 13 J 21, f. 12.

[1] TS 10 J 24, f. 4*v*, l. 9, *India Book* 121, ed. S. D. Goitein, *Tarbiz* 24 (1954), p. 33.

[2] See *EI*², I, 79, s.v. *'Abd al-Mu'min* (the Almohad caliph), and II, 818-819 (s.v. *Fās*).

[3] See *EI*¹, IV, s.v. *al-Sūs al-Akṣā*.

A. Order of wedding robe for a bridegroom

S[ell] the hundred pounds of [. . .] and take 20 mithqāls (Spanish dinars) from the price for yourself. With the balance buy a silk robe from the master who made the ʿattābī (tabbi)[4] for the elder Abū Zikrī[5] for 3 1/2 mithqāls approximately. It should be tailored.[6] If you cannot get it ready made, have it made quickly, dye it pistachio green,[7] and have it ironed in the very best way. Send it on quickly with the mats for Abraham, for the robe is also for him and he needs it for his wedding. Please be not slack in this matter.

B. The conquest of the Sūs by the Almohads: Various business notes

Please inform R. Isaac b. Baruch, (*may his*) *R*(*ock*) *p*(*rotect him*), that I paid to Aaron Ibn al-Barjalūnī ("the man from Barcelona, Spain") the 2 mithqāls that he, Isaac, owed him, when he, Aaron, set out for Sijilmāsa.[8] Please take them from Isaac without delay.

My heart burns because I have assembled gold and have found no one with whom I could send it. So I must send it with David, which does not make me happy at all.[9] But "*trust in God*."[10] I shall also send copper, as much as I can get, with him.

Take notice that lac remained on its original market (price) for only a short time. From the day when the usurper[11] occupied the Sūs, a general depression set in.[12] Five bales have still remained with me. Baruch has been hitherto unable to sell the quantities I gave to him and I am upset about this more than about anything else. The entire lac is with me in my apartment.[13] Had I not been

[4] The English is derived from the Arabic.

[5] Many persons with this byname are known from that period.

[6] Ar. *tafṣīl*. For *thawb* designates not only the standard robe, but a piece of cloth needed for its tailoring.

[7] The color worn in Paradise.

[8] The desert entrepôt in the deep south of Morocco.

[9] Who will travel later (see end of letter). They hated to let money lie idle.

[10] Psalm 37:3.

[11] Ar. *al-khārijī*. The Almohad is intended, as is indicated by the place and the date.

[12] Ar. *ḍarab bi-rūḥih al-arḍ*.

[13] Ar. *ḥujra*. Respectable merchants did not live in a caravanserai, but hired

concerned about the other goods you had entrusted to him, I would not have given him a thing, so that it should not be said that my goods were with him.[14] May God, the exalted, turn everything to a good end.

Do not think that anything keeps me back here in Fez except that I must await what will happen with Baruch. For most of the things which Ibrahīm[15] has taken, he has managed to sell.

You asked me about the price of brazilwood. A pound and one-half can be had for 1 mithqāl.

C. Order in Almeria of scales and weights for a goldsmith in Fez

I mentioned in a previous letter that a Jewish goldsmith here is very helpful to me in the collection and payment of debts. He wishes to have a pair of scales and a set of weights, and has already given to me the entire price of this. In addition to my letter to you in this matter, I have also written to the scales maker[16] directly. Please do not neglect this matter.[17]

The arrival of your note has been acknowledged by me several times.

D. Expression of grief over the death of the spiritual leader of Spanish Jewry

I am unable to describe to you my unhappy mood[18] here in Fez. This was increased by the great disaster, the terrible catastrophe, the death of *our master* Joseph, *the great Rāv,* (*may the*) *s*(*pirit of*)

---

an apartment for themselves when they stayed in a foreign city for a more protracted period.

[14] This Baruch was a local merchant. The writer did not wish to become suspect of evading customs by declaring his own merchandise as belonging to a local man. See no. 7, above.

[15] The bridegroom Abraham mentioned above (cf. n. 23, below). He might have been identical with the Abraham referred to in no. 7 above.

[16] Ar. *mayāzīnī.*

[17] What astounds me in this paragraph is (*a*) that the great industrial center of Fez did not have a maker of scales, a common commodity, but one had to order them from far-away Spain; and (*b*) that seemingly the weights used by the goldsmiths in Fez and Almeria were identical.

[18] Ar. *ḍīq ṣadr* "narrowness of the breast," which sometimes corresponds to "depression."

G(od set him at) p(eace). I am unable to give you an idea about my feelings in this matter. Had God willed that I had remained in my previous state, I would have sought his company and made his personal acquaintance. Never in my life have I felt a sadness more bitter than this.[19]

E. Shipments of alum sent from Morocco to Spain

Please take notice that in the shipment of alum which I sent you there are seven bales of particularly good quality, each qinṭār costing more than the regular price by 1/4 mithqāl. The remaining quantities are of different values,[20] but the whole purchase was at a low price. Before its official announcement,[21] a qinṭār rose by 1/4 mithqāl. You may either sell each quality by itself or mix them, you know the market better and are able to act in accordance with the situation. Sell also all the containers; each one is worth 1 dirhem. The entire weight of the alum belonging to you is 45 1/2 qinṭārs, small measure. May God, the exalted, grant success. Had I had courage, I would have sent you 100 qinṭārs. But I did not dare, since there was a great demand for it.[22]

Be under God's safeguard and protection. Best regards and greetings to you and yours. Written in a hurry, while the bearer is on the point of leaving. *May your well-being wax.* Written during the last ten days of Tevet (December 20-30, 1141).

Do not neglect to send me letters. The bearer of this letter is the packer who was present when the alum was packed. He knows which is the good quality and which the excellent one. I have lent him my small saddle. When he arrives, take it from him. With

19 The news of the Rāv's death had reached our writer several months before, and then, of course, he wrote a letter of condolence in the style of nos. 34 and 45, above. Here he expresses regret that he had not continued the studies pursued in his youth, which would have given him the opportunity to be near to the late master (who resided in Lucena, near Cordoba). The *lām al-ta'ḳīd* is spelled here as a separate word: *la.*

20 Later he goes on to say that the packer would arrive and tell which bale was of which quality.

21 Ar. *qabl ḳhurūjih.* The writer bought at a lower price before the official market price was made public.

22 The writer was afraid that many Spanish merchants would send alum to Almeria, and its price would fall.

Dā'ūd[23] I shall send you various letters specifying all you need to know. *And peace!*

61 A NOTE FROM THE COUNTRYSIDE

Short letters dealing with local business and having the form of notes (see no. 35, n. 2, above) are typical for the Geniza correspondence of the thirteenth century.

The recipient of this letter was a banker, who, together with another investor, had a partnership with the writer, which was most successful. For a profit of 60 dinars for each of them, as mentioned here, was unusually high under any circumstances. Like all citizens of the Egyptian capital, the writer hated to travel in the countryside, but his telegraph-style note is cheerful and bears the imprint of a personality.

University Library, Cambridge, Taylor-Schechter
Collection, TS 13 J 13, f. 18.

Your slave and servant
In (Your name). Ibrahīm b. Abu 'l-Surūr, . . .

I yearn for my lord and master, the illustrious elder Abū Naṣr—may God prolong his life and crush his enemy. Another matter: my lord, I parted from you, without having been satiated with the pleasure of your company, which I regret very much. Another matter: Your letter arrived. I kissed it before reading it and took notice of its content. The spices[1] and the silk arrived, may I never be deprived of you and never have to miss you. But the spices, may God punish him who packed them. No profit will come from them. By my head, I shall not see a dinar from them. Had I been in the store, as I intended, I would have found that they are not of full weight. The rose marmalade is thin and does not bring relief to a person in

[23] Identical with David, sec. B, above. See n. 15, above.

[1] That is, all an *'aṭṭār*, or perfumer, used to sell. Later, *ḥawā'ij* simply meant "spices." The partnership no doubt concerned only the silk, while the "spices" had been ordered by the writer on his own account. Otherwise, he would not have used such strong words against the sender.

illness.[2] The tragacanth gum is not worth a penny. A God-fearing man does not do such a thing.

My lord, I sent you beekeepers, scrapers of honey,[3] with Ibn Ḥāja ("Son of Something"),[4] also a basket with half a *wayba* of sifted caraway seed, a quarter for you, and another for the elder Maʿānī.[5] This is for your kindnesses; no payment is required. Each of us has made a profit of 60 dinars. I gave him (the basket) and was extremely happy for having been able to do this. I am coming to town. Only the debts owed me keep me in the country. The end will be good for you; trust in God and extricate yourself. The seeking of sustenance spurns a man as does the seeking of glory. So make an effort and extricate yourself. (Greetings to the sons of his maternal uncle and three other persons.) Kind regards. The answer to this letter should be sent to Alexandria. Would I try to describe to you how much I am eager to get out of the countryside, a letter would not suffice for this. And peace.

(P.S. on the first page:) And send me the alcali quickly. Put it in a jug and secure its . . . .[6]

(Address:)

To Fustat, to be delivered to the elder Abū Naṣr, (*may his*) *e*(*nd be*) *g*(*ood*), son of Abu 'l-Karam, (*may he*) *r*(*est in*) *E*(*den*).[7]

[2] Rose marmalade was widely used for the alleviation of illness.

[3] The honey scrapers (see *Med. Soc.*, I, 125, 429, n. 71) were fellahs, who would not have made the journey to the city alone.

[4] A nickname, derived from the phrase *lī ḥāja ilayk*, "I want something from you," too often used by an ancestor or ancestress. There is also a nickname *Ibn al-Ḥājja* "Son of the Female Pilgrim" (with article and double *j*).

[5] Abbreviated from Abu 'l-Maʿānī ("Eloquent"), a common name in that late period. A man bearing this name contributed to the same appeal as the recipient (see n. 7, below, and *Zion* 7 (1942), 143, col. 11*b*, l. 10).

[6] Text: *shs-hā*, "its opening"?

[7] Contributed to the public appeal discussed in *Med. Soc.*, II, 488-490 (see Bodl. MS Heb. c28 [Cat. 2876], f. 47, ed. E. Strauss-Ashtor, *Zion* 7, p. 142, col. 1*a*, l. 19). There he is described as *ṣayrafī*, banker.

62 BUYING PALM BRANCHES

Letter to a Qadi

The Islamic *dār wakāla*, or warehouse, like the Roman basilica, was a hall where goods were traded and stored and where judges and notaries had their seats for the settlement of disputes and arrangement of formalities connected with business transactions (see *Med. Soc.*, I, 187-189, and here, introduction, sec. 3, above). Even a small town like Qalyūb (northwest of Cairo) possessed such a semipublic building.

Palm branches are frequently mentioned in building operations, and in our letter this type rather than the one used for religious purposes is intended. It is interesting that the permission of the chief of the police was required, probably because payment of a tax was involved. The letter is written in beautiful, clear Arabic characters, in many cases even equipped with diacritical marks.

University Library, Cambridge, Taylor-Schechter Collection,
TS Arabic Box 40, f. 126.

(*Verso*:) To the warehouse, to be delivered to the illustrious and excellent qadi Ṣadr al-Dīn,[1] who acts there as a notary,[2] may God always give him success.

(*Recto*:) God is the best of helpers.

Your servant Omar b. ʿIwaḍ[3] serves the high seat of our master and lord,[4] my master Ṣadr al-Dīn, may God let him prosper all his days, and informs him that your servant went to Qalyūb, but did not find the chief of police. Then your servant met with the "Learned and Practicing" sheikh[5] and he kindly settled the matter after great

[1] A title, not a name. "Leader of Islam."

[2] Ar. *shāhid.*

[3] "Long-lived, son of Substitute," not necessarily a Muslim. Other derivatives of the root *ʿmr*, "life," such as ʿAmmār and ʿUmayr, were very frequent Jewish names.

[4] Thus a judge is officially addressed ("*our* master").

[5] Ar. al-ʿālim al-ʿāmil, a title, which around 1200 became extremely popular. This man was the local *faqīh*, or juris consultant, who, like everyone, engaged also in business. Since he was a public figure, he could sell without waiting for permission.

exertion. We did not find any waxed palm branches, and the green branches are sold for 70 (dirhems) a thousand. I paid the *waraq* dirhems and he took a few branches from each orchard.[6] I paid him 60 dirhems, on condition that he transport the palm branches to the (Nile) river. But when I arrived again in Qalyūb, he still had to bring them to the river, and there they had only a small boat able to carry just a few victuals. I am sending now a messenger to my lord, and ask you to send him to the sheikh "The Learned" with a request that he deliver the palm branches to you, and you will keep them for your servant in Qalyūb.

(The verso contains also the beginning of the draft of a petition in Arabic language and Hebrew characters of the dyers in Qalyūb. The words are crossed out, probably because the clerk realized that the sheet would not be sufficient for the text dictated to him.)

The servants, the dyers in Qalyūb, kiss the ground and announce that they perish because of the high price of the wheat, the scarcity of work, the heavy license fee,[7] and the rise of the exchange rate . . .

(On the same page there is also a calligraphic trial of the pen: "Said the Khazarī." "Said the scholar." This shows that in this little town there was a scribe who tried to copy the theological *magnum opus* of the Spanish Hebrew poet Judah ha-Levi. Learned scribes were often found in small towns, where life was less expensive than in the big cities. See *Med. Soc.*, II, 239.)

[6] No palm branches cut some time earlier and preserved by being covered with wax were available for sale. Therefore they had to be cut wherever possible, and fewer than a thousand were brought together. The low-value silver coin of the Ayyūbid period was called *waraq*. See *Med. Soc.*, I, 384, 388.

[7] Ar. *ḍamān*, meaning the sum they had to pay to the tax farmer.

CHAPTER VII

Accounts

ACCOUNTS often accompanied letters and were produced and accepted as evidence in court. The examples translated below were selected with a view to provide a fairly representative cross section of the material preserved. Letter no. 63 shows how the import of raw material from Egypt and the export of finished textiles from Tunisia were handled by a Tunisian family business. Number 64 is the account of a young Tunisian trader detailing his variegated sales and purchases in Egypt for his employer back home and for himself, as well as his living and personal expenses, the former being charged to the employer, the latter borne by himself. Number 65 is a typical account for a single partnership venture. Number 66 is a report on actions for a relative taken during his absence. Number 67 demonstrates how a banker deals with cashier checks, promissory notes, and specie of different types. Finally, no. 68, formally the opposite of 67, shows a merchant settling accounts with his banker, and like 67, evidences to how great an extent Fatimid Egypt had become a paper economy.

The forms of the accounts are also not without interest. Some of them go back to antiquity, others are preserved to our own day. But a discussion of such details is better left to an edition of the originals.

63 SHIPMENTS TO AND FROM TUNISIA

Summer of 1024

This account is carefully written on vellum, each sheet measuring 7.5 x 7.5 inches. Two pages specify the sales of twenty-three bales of flax imported from Egypt, while the third page lists the textiles exported there from Tunisia. Thus, our account is an excellent illustration of the role of Tunisia as an industrial center, and of Egypt as the provider of the main raw material (flax, not cotton, in those days!).

The bales have an average weight of 350 pounds, which must have been the standard at that time. With the exception of those in no. 1, all bales are divided into two sections of differing quality and price. The differences are small (3/4 to 2 1/2 percent), but this method of keeping even slightly differing varieties distinct must have greatly simplified trading procedures and is expressly recommended in one letter (see *Med. Soc.*, I, 457, n. 71). Moreover, practically every bale also contained a quantity of flax damaged by water. This was sold each at a flat rate, no price per 100 pounds being agreed upon as in the case of the other qualities.

The details for the first ten bales are translated here. The lower part of the manuscript is largely lost and with it most of the accounts for bales 11, 12, 21-23, and the totals at the bottom of the second page. The prices are given in *rubā'īs*, or quarter dinars, as was usual in Sicily and Tunisia at that time. According to this account the silver coin, the dirhem, then was worth 1/24 of a dinar (see the calculation in *Med. Soc.*, I, 369, sec. 3). The total price obtained for the first ten bales was 1,381 quarter dinars and 63 dirhems; for the total shipment, about 3,400 quarters or 850 dinars. This was a very large sum in those days, corresponding in purchasing value to about $100,000.

Of the textiles destined for Egypt only the numbers, prices, expenses for their packing and transport, their carriers, and the ships in which they were sent, are indicated. Descriptions were given in bills of lading or in letters, or both. From the price obtained from the sale of the flax, only 674 pieces of cloth were bought, while 1,374, which means twice as many, were sent. This reflects a business practice discernible in many Geniza papers. Local goods were bought, as far as possible, during the off-season, in winter. During seafaring time, when the markets teemed with European Christians and with merchants from all parts of the Muslim world, prices usually went up (unless the bazaars were choked with goods, which also happened not infrequently because of poor communications which made business intelligence haphazard).

The total amount spent on the textiles sent to Egypt after the arrival of the current year's shipments was approximately[1] 3,025 quarter dinars, not much less than the price obtained from the flax, but their value was about twice as much. Clearly, the balance was taken from the proceeds of the preceding year.

Our account was rendered in Tunisia for Isma'īl (Samuel) b. Barhūn (Abraham) of the Tāhertī family, about which see the introduction to no. 11, above. He and his brother Isḥāq (Isaac), and at least another one, if not all the three of his brothers were then in Egypt. Their permanent domicile was Qayrawān, then the capital of the country today called Tunisia, but the temporary sojourn of each of the four Tāhertī brothers in Egypt is attested by other Geniza documents.

University Library, Cambridge, University Collection,
ULC Or 1080 J 291.

Account [for my lord] Isma'īl b. Barhūn.

A. Arrived in the year 415[2]

(For the convenience of the reader the details are arranged in the form of a table, below, p. 276. In the account book a line is drawn under the entries for each bale.)

B. Exports from Tunisia

This was bought with God's blessing and support:

674 pieces of cloth, price 2,560 quarters. Additional cost for cleaning, scraping, mending, and embroidering:[3] 202 quarters. Purchase costs 27 quarters.[4]

With this material 6 bundles were packed. Cost of ropes, threads, wrapping material, cotton, cotton carder, and packer for 6 bundles: . . . .

[1] The bottom of page 3 is badly damaged, with some details about the last item and the totals gone.

[2] The Muslim year 415, which began on March 15, 1024. Our account was no doubt written before the sailing of the autumn convoys from Tunisia to Egypt (approx. August).

[3] Ar. *qiṣāra maḥakka, raf', ṭirāz.*

[4] Ar. *ḥaqq shary mushtarā,* which should not be translated as "sales tax." I assume, payments to middlemen.

			QUALITY I			*QUALITY II*		*SPOILED BY WATER*		
Bale No.	Total weight	Price per 100 pounds	Weight (pounds)	Total price rub.[b] dir.[c]	Price per 100 pounds	Weight (pounds)	Total price rub.[b] dir.[c]	Weight (pounds)	Total price rub.[b] dir.[c]	For whom
1	305	34								Isma'īl
2	345	37	170	62 3/4	37	145	52.3[a]	30	9.3[a]	Isma'īl
3	343	39	171	66.3[a]	38 3/4	162	62.5[a]	10	3	Isma'īl
4	339	43	174	74 3/4	43	152	65.1 1/2[a]	13	4	Isma'īl and Isḥāq
5	349	35 3/4	150	53.2[a]	35	190	67.3[a]	9	2 1/2	Isma'īl
6	339	42	140	53.4[a]	42 1/2	156	66	43	15.3[a]	The two brothers
7	346	37	170	62.5[a]	37	166	61.1[a]	10	3.2[a]	Isma'īl
8	347	45	167	75	44 1/2	180	80		1	The two brothers
9	350	37	188	68.5[a]	36 1/2	156	56.5[a]	6	2	Isma'īl
10		44 1/2	150	75.3[a]	44 1/2	152	67	23	3 1/2	The two brothers

[a] 66.3 = 66 quarters, 3 dir.
[b] rub. = rubā'īas, or quarter din. (gold)
[c] dir. = dirhems

Purchase of 84 canvases, 64 double Ḥumaydīs, and 20 single large ones. Price: 168 quarters.[5]

With this material a bale was packed, containing 4 bundles

2 for you, containing 220 pieces

2 for your brothers,[6] containing 240 pieces

Onto this, 14 canvases belonging to you were fastened, namely, 8 double Ḥumaydīs and 6 large single ones.

I loaded this bale on the boat of Ibn 'Amīd[7] with the goods of 'Allūsh al-Ḥabība ("Little dear Mr. Lamb").[8] Cost of ropes, threads, packer, transportation of the bale (to the harbor), weigher, and "consideration":[9] 1 quarter, 1 dirhem. Freight paid in full:[10] 7 quarter dinars less 1 quarter (of a quarter) of full weight, at a rate of 1 1/2 quarter dinars.[11]

I also packed a second bale with 4 bundles

2 for you, containing 215 pieces, and

2 for your brothers, containing 202.

On this 14 canvases were fastened, namely, 10 double Ḥumaydīs and 4 large single ones.

I loaded this bale on the boat of Ibn Jumhūr ("Mr. Multitude")[12] with the goods of Abu 'l-Faḍl b. Faraḥ ("Nobility, son of Joy"). Cost of ropes, threads, . . . packer, weigher, and "consideration":

[5] This packing material served for all the goods listed in this document (see what follows). All the eighty-four canvases were sent. See also n. 13.

[6] Ar. *ikhwatak*, which, in this period, might designate two or more.

[7] Abbreviated from *'Amid al-Dawla*, "Support of the Dynasty," an honorary title.

[8] Mr. Lamb had a number of bales on that ship and probably supervised them in person. For reasons of safety the single bale for the Tāhertīs was stored together with his. Evidently, no remuneration was demanded for this service. On another occasion, the Tāhertīs would reciprocate with a similar favor. 'Allūsh, lamb, is common in the Geniza and is still a widely used family name among North African Jews. "The little dear" (fem.!) is a nickname.

[9] Ar. *frtyl*, meaning *birtīl*, a small consideration given to the sailors.

[10] Usually, part of the freight was paid after arrival.

[11] Per 100 pounds, I assume. Since the bale contained as many as 460 *shuqqa*, or pieces of cloth, each large enough for a gown, these Tunisian materials must have been rather fine and light.

[12] A name expressing the mother's wish that the newborn may become "a father of a multitude of nations" (Genesis 17:4). *Jumhūriyya* is the modern Arabic word for "republic."

1 quarter, 1 dirhem. Freight paid in full: 7 1/2 quarters at a rate of 1 3/4 quarters.

I also packed a bale with 2 bundles, one for you with 150 pieces, and one for your brothers with 138 pieces. On this, 32 double Ḥumaydī canvases were fastened and a large single one.[13] Cost for this bale, namely, ropes, threads, packer, porter to the embarking space, weigher, and "consideration": 1 quarter, 1 dirhem. Freight paid in full: 8 quarters at a rate of . . . I loaded it on the boat of Ibn Ja'far[14] with the goods of Dā'ūd Ibn al-Rakhīṣ ("David, son of Mr. Inexpensive").

[I packed still another bale . . . . . .]

. . . for you 119 pieces and your brothers 90, with 19 large double canvases. Cost of porter, weigher, and "consideration": 4 dirhems. [. . . . . for freight . . . . . .] at a rate of 2 quarters [. . . . . .].

I sent it to you with Abu 'l-Faḍl b. [Faraḥ].

(Another four pages of this account book, containing details for about 120 bales of flax costing 1,278 1/4 dinars and 32,421 dirhems is preserved in TS Box J 1, f. 54.)

64 ACCOUNTS OF AN OVERSEAS TRADER FOR HIS EMPLOYER

1046

Barhūn (Abraham) b. Isḥāq (Isaac), to whom this account is addressed, was the son of Isḥāq, one of the Tāhertī brothers mentioned repeatedly in no. 63. The account is in the beautiful and unmistakable hand of Nahray b. Nissīm. See nos. 29-35, above.

In no. 30, above, which was written two years after this account,

[13] The canvases were needed in Egypt for packing the flax. In this bale, with only two bundles of textiles, more of the heavy canvases could be carried than in the two bales listed first.

[14] Repeatedly used by the writers of Geniza letters, e.g., TS 13 J 17, f. 11, l. 22, ed. S. D. Goitein, *Tarbiz* 36 (1967), p. 387.

we find Nahray as a partner of Barhūn. Nothing of such a relationship is mentioned here. On the contrary, he appears as Barhūn's employee or agent, *ṣabī*, "boy," in Arabic, whose living expenses are paid by his master, while the latter retains all the profit for himself. Even the expenses for Nahray's sister, who had accompanied him on his journey to Egypt, no doubt as a housekeeper since the young trader was unmarried, were charged to Barhūn, but not Nahray's personal expenses, such as clothing, gifts, and drugs.[1] On the other hand, the "boy" was free to do business for himself, a privilege Nahray availed himself of copiously, although not always with success. This relationship is usually described as *risāla*, "shipment," that is, carrying a shipment for someone else. See *Med. Soc.*, I, 183-184.

Our document has to be understood as follows:[2] The writer presents his account for Jewish calendar years, which were more practical for bookkeeping than the Muslim year since the Jewish New Year falls in September, which was the end of the seafaring and business season. After the previous account had been sent in the preceding year with the autumn convoy of ships sailing from Alexandria to Tunisia, some additional sales had been effected before the New Year in September 1045. These are listed in sec. A. The charges to the employer are listed in sec. B. The account is balanced by a debt owed the employer while the writer was still back home in Qayrawān. This method of "closing the account"[3] every year is attested in many other Geniza documents.

Section C contains the personal account of Nahray and does not form part of the document submitted to his master. But since Barhūn, as we have surmised in the introduction to no. 30, above, was his uncle, he might have sent him these details for his information.

Sections D and E list sales, purchases, and other payments made for the employer during the current year 1045-1046, but one sheet is missing between D and E. The balance of the transactions made by

[1] My remark on opium in *Med. Soc.*, II, 270, has to be corrected accordingly.

[2] The correct sequence of pages is: fol. 65*a*, 64*a-b*, 65*b*. This does not reflect in any way on the eminent scholar who catalogued these manuscripts. Naturally, a busy keeper of hundreds of manuscripts cannot devote to the study of each as much time as a student specializing in its subject matter.

[3] This Arabic expression might have been the origin of our own relevant phrase.

Nahray for Barhūn during that year amounts to about 500 dinars (see n. 50, below), a very substantial amount. On the other hand, the variety of goods handled by him still was comparatively limited: finished textiles, raw silk, hides, kohl, and large amounts of corals and beads. An account written to him by Barhūn only two years later (TS 20.69*v*) already reflects that great variety of goods which characterizes Nahray's business in general.

For easier reference, the lines of the original are indicated in the translation.

Bodleian Library, Oxford, MS Heb. e 98, fs. 65*a*, 64*a-b*, 65*b*.

I (f. 65*a*)

[1] In the name of the great God.[4]

Account submitted to my lord Abī (2) Isḥāq Barhūn, son of Isḥāq, (*may the*) *m*(*emory of the*) *r*(*ighteous*) *be b*(*lessed*), in the year [4]806 (September 14, 1045–September 3, 1046), when the ships sailed.[5]

[3]

REMAINDER OF THE ACCOUNT FOR THE YEAR 805

A. CASH IN THE HANDS OF THE AGENT

[4]	This was sold after the sailing of the ships:	
[5]	Two baskets with antimony (kohl) weighing 3 (hundred pounds)	11 1/3 din.
[6]	Less expenses for the kohl which was on your private account, excluding what Salāma charged me	5 din., 5 qīr.
		Balance: 6 1/8 din.
[7]	Short shawls,[6] less commission, 9 din. less 1/8 of these,	

[4] This superscription is uncommon. A representative of merchants in Alexandria, Ibrahīm b. Farāḥ ("Abraham, son of Joy"; see *Med. Soc.*, I, 304), used it. Nahray, who wrote in Alexandria, might have taken it from him.

[5] Could also be translated "with the ships," meaning, that various copies of this account (and accompanying letter) were sent in different ships of the fall convoy sailing from Alexandria to al-Mahdiyya.

[6] Ar. *'awāriḍ*, which I take as a (wrong) plural of *'arḍī*, shawl, an extremely

[8]	2 1/4, 1/8 din. were kept back. They will be listed when collected	
		Balance: 6 1/2 din.
[9]	331 linings, less commission and discount	16 1/2 din.
[10]	Collected from the price of the other 300 (linings) sold previously in the Colonnade[7]	1 1/2 din.
[11]	Leather mantles[8] used as covers for the beads	1/2 din.
[12]	1 1/4 units (of corals) on strings, less commission and discount	3 din.
[13]	Collected by me in Qayrawān before leaving:	6 din.
	in number; in weight	6 din. less 1/6
[14]	Obtained, through God's bounty, for the silk which I bought in al-Mahdiyya[9]	19 din. less 2 qīr.
[15]	Hide good as cover for baskets[10]	1/2 din.
	500 single[11] (coral) strings	1/3 din.
[16]	Received from Surūr b. al-Ḥaṭib ("Joy, son of the stick")[12] 193 1/2 (dirhems), exchange rate 33 1/3[13]	6 din. less 5 qīr.
[17]	Received from his brother in al-Mahdiyya	50 (din.) 1/6, 1/8
	Paid 50. Balance for you	1/6, 1/8
[18]	Grand Total	65 1/2, 1/4 din., 1 qīr.

B. DUE FROM THE EMPLOYER

[19]	From this is to be deducted:	
	Balance (in my favor) of the previous account, submitted (l. 20) in the year 805 (1044-1045	39 1/4 din.

---

common item of export from Tunisia-Sicily to the East. Ar. *'awāriḍ* means "crossbeams," but nowhere do we find that these Tunisians traded in timber.

7 About this locality for business transactions see *Med. Soc.*, I, 194.

8 Ar. *anṭā' jalābīb.*

9 The silk was brought to this Tunisian port either from Sicily or from Spain.

10 Ar. *maḥāmilī.* Cf. Dozy, *Supplément*, I, 328*b*.

11 Corals were often sold in *double* strings. See col. III, l. 18, below.

12 Tall and thin, which was regarded as an indication of stupidity (see Goitein, *Jemenica*, p. 175, no. 1362). The same in classical Ar. and other Ar. dialects.

13 That is, dinar:dirhem = 1:33 1/3.

II (f. 64*a*)

[1] Expenses for the packages of (coral) beads carried by me 9 1/2 din., 2 qīr.
[2] Expenses for the prepaid shipment[14] which arrived in the Shāmi[15] boat 1 1/4, 1/8 din., 1/2 qīr.
[3] Balance due for my late sister—may God have mercy upon her—for her passage[16] 1 din., 1 1/2 qīr.
[4] Expenses for the porcelain beads which you
[5] charged against me for Alexandria and Miṣr (Fustat) and which I actually paid[17] 16 1/4, 1/8 din.
[6] Living expenses for fourteen months from Elul to Tishri (July/August 1044-September/October 1045) 22 1/2 din.
[7] Grand Total 90 1/6 din.
[8] Owed by you and covered by what I owe (you) in your house[18] 24 din.[19]

[9] C. MY PERSONAL ACCOUNT FOR THE YEAR 805 (1044-1045)

[10] Half an Arjīshī gown[20] and its tailoring from the perfumed bolt 1 din., 1/2 qīr.
[11] Present for the wedding of the son of the judge[21] and expenses on my account 2/3, 1/6 (din.)
[12] Seeds and opium[22] 1 1/4, 1/6 din.
[13] Mending a coat, cotton and tailoring 1/8 din.

14 Normally, part of the freight was paid after arrival. In this case, the whole freight had been prepaid, and the junior partner had to pay only customs and smaller expenses such as payments to the porters, etc.

15 Belonging to a proprietor living on the eastern coast of the Mediterranean.

16 See the introduction.

17 Barhūn had asked Nahray to pay the customs and tolls in Alexandria and Fustat with his own money.

18 Meaning: for transactions made in Qayrawān prior to his journey.

19 90 1/6 din. — 65 1/2, 1/4 din., 1 qīr. = 24 din., 1 qīr. Such rounding up was common, although not always applied.

20 Ar. *thawb*. For Arjīshī see no. 30, n. 18, above.

21 Heb. *dayyān*. Probably the Jewish judge of al-Mahdiyya is meant, and the "expenses" refer to the cost of the transport of the present.

22 Served as medicament, but perhaps also for other purposes.

[14] A bale of flax, including all expenses, loaded
on Mujāhid's boat[23] 15 1/6 din., 1 qīr.
[15] Two bags of cornelians for R. Joseph,
sent with al-Qābisī[24] 1 1/2 din.
[16] A small package of linen (or: flax) for
my mother and . . .[25] for it 1/2 din.
[17] Total 20 1/3, 1/4 din., 1/2 qīr.
[18] Received from ʿAbd al-Raḥmān[26] for
ten hundred pounds of beads belonging
to me (l. 19) after I had made account
with him concerning the ambergris deal[27] 17 din. less 1/3
[20] Debit on my personal account 4 din. less 1 1/2 qīr.

III (f. 64*b*)

(Note in small script near the upper edge of the page, written from the middle to the left end:)

[1] These are the details of the account which I submitted in 806.

[2] Account for the year 806 (1045-1046)

May God bestow upon us its blessings.

[3] D. SALES

[4] 98 pieces of *ṣāfiya* ("shining") cloth,
less commission 174 din. less 1/3
[5] 2 *ṣāfiyas* left in the bazaar until
their price is collected
[6] 52 scraped off[28] hides, less commission 19 din. less 5 qīr.

[23] Frequently mentioned; a Muslim.

[24] That is, from Gabes in southern Tunisia. Many persons with this family name occur in the correspondence of the eleventh century.

[25] Ar. *w-mhr ʿanhā*. The package was sent from Egypt to Qayrawān, where his mother lived.

[26] A Muslim business friend of the Tāhertīs and later of Nahray himself. See no. 20, introduction, above.

[27] One word is corrected here and not clearly legible.

[28] Ar. *nukhāliyya*; *nukhāla* is the bran of grains or the scrapings of a metal. I have not seen the word in connection with hides. The same term in TS 20.69*v*, l. 7.

[7]	1 silk cover,[29] less commission and discount	12 1/4 din.
[8]	Another cover, small, of the class of the gowns, less commission and discount	6 1/4 din.
[9]	14 silken gowns, less commission and discount	
[10]	11 pounds and 28 dir. weight of Spanish silk	17 din. less 1/4
[11]	3 covers, less commission	3 din., 1 qīr.
[12]	19 pounds of "peeled off" (silk),[30] less commission	24 din. less 5 qīr.
[13]	57 pounds of "unraveled" silk, less commission	69 1/4, 1/8 din.
[14]	. . .][31] pounds less 1 ounce lā[sin], less commission	4 1/6, 1/8 din.
[15]	Collected from the price of the Spanish silk which[32] was . . . ; details later	50 1/4 din.
[16]	37 units of Tabrūrī ("hail" corals), less commission	3 1/4 din., 1 1/2 qīr.
[17]	205 colored units (of coral beads), less commission and discount	12 1/3, 1/8 din.
[18]	4,200 double strings and 5,700 single strings (of coral beads), less commission	9 din. less 1/6
[19]	10,000 chick-pea beads, less commission	1/3 din.
[20]	300 single strings (of beads)	5 qīr., 1 ḥabba
[21]	Grand Total	472 din.,[33] 2 qīr.

E. PURCHASES AND OTHER PAYMENTS MADE FOR THE EMPLOYER IN 1045-1046

(The sheet with the purchases and probably other payments is lost. What follows is the end of the list of payments.)

[29] Ar. *kisā'*, may serve as a garment or a bedcover. See next line.

[30] About this and the following types of silk see *Med. Soc.*, I, 104.

[31] According to the grammatical form of the word "pounds," the lost number must have been between 3 and 10.

[32] Written between the lines and mostly effaced.

[33] The figure 472 is correct, but the second sign looks like 40 rather than 70.

(Col. i)

[1]	Exit permit[34]	3 (dir.) less 1/4
[2]	Toll stations[35]	3 dir.
[3]	Transport[36]	20 dir.
[4]	Sales agents and weigher	8 1/2
[5]	[37]	1 1/2 din.
[6]	Expenditure for the bundle:[38]	
	Toll stations	3 dir.
[7]	Canvas	5 dir.
[8]	Transport to al-Mahdiyya	38 dir.
[9]	Porters in al-Mahdiyya	2 1/2
[10]	Packing[39]	5 dir.
[11]	Petitions[40]	4 dir.
[12]	Messenger of the customs house[41]	4 1/2, 1/4
[13]	Dues of the caravanserai[42]	1 1/2

(Col. ii)

[1]	Night watch (for the goods)	1 dir.
[2]	Eastgate and caravanserai toll[43]	2 1/2
[3]	Toll for the exit to the port for two *'ilāwas* (attached packages)[44]	8 dir.

[34] This and the following four items refer to a shipment described on the lost sheet. Exit permit: from Qayrawān for the shipment concerned.

[35] Ar. *marāsid* for *marāṣid*, common in Tunisian speech.

[36] Overland from Qayrawān to al-Mahdiyya.

[37] Sign consisting of a circle followed by a stroke, alluding perhaps to a gratuity given to a government official for permitting the export of that particular item, mentioned on the lost sheet.

[38] Ar. *rizma* (from which English *ream* of paper is derived), a large bundle, usually containing many different goods, but different from the standard "bale" and "load."

[39] For the sea voyage.

[40] Against exaggerated customs dues. See n. 41, below.

[41] Ar. *dīwān*, from which French *douane*.

[42] The writer certainly stayed with friends. But the goods were left in a caravanserai. See n. 43, below.

[43] Ar. *bāb qibla wa-funduq*. This caravanserai is not identical with the one inside the city, but formed part of the customs house. While leaving the city and entering the customs house one paid a toll, here as elsewhere.

[44] Some of the goods carried for the employer were packed in two 'ilāwas, packages attached to a larger one and therefore requiring less freight. See *Med. Soc.*, i, 337.

[4]	Freight for two ʿilāwas, one attached	
[5]	to the ʿilāwa of my cousin[45] and one attached to my own	6 (quarters?)
[6]	7 bags[46]	3 1/4 (dir.)
[7]	Packing (of the ʿilāwas)	4 1/2 (dir.)
[8]	Customs dues	50 dir.[47]
[9]	Threads and canvas	2 less 1/4 (dir.)
[10]	For the captain[48]	a quarter (din.)
[11]	Porters to the sea	3 dir.
[12]	Freight[49]	4 1/4 din.
[13]	This makes 176 din. and [2 1/2 qīr.] . . .	

Grand total owed by you:
In gold: 176 din. and 2 1/2 qīr.
In silver: 10,663 dir.[50]

65 ACCOUNT FOR A PARTNER

Summer 1057

This short fragment is a telling illustration of the working of a partnership. The whole tenor of the account, which *alludes* to the items concerned rather than specifying them, and the fact that very personal orders, such as shoes, are included as well, prove that these merchants were old friends, if not relatives. But the partnership is a yearly venture. The writer contributes exactly the equivalent of his friend's yearly balance, down to a ḥabba (1/72 of a dinar), and

[45] Two cousins of Nahray are known, one called Nahray (b. Nathan), like himself, and one Israel. See no. 23, sec. D, above.

[46] Ar. *jawānī*, sing. *jūniya*, especially for the transport of corals. Known to me only from the Geniza.

[47] Clearly a flat rate on which agreement was reached after the writer had protested.

[48] It was usual to pay such a consideration to the captain and the crew. The freight went to the proprietor of the boat.

[49] This must refer to the bundle listed in col. IV, 1, l. 6.

[50] Since the exchange rate of dinar:dirhem was at that time 1:33 1/3 (see col. 1, l. 16, above), the dirhems here would be worth approximately 324 dinars, and the total transactions about 500 dinars.

then proceeds to buy merchandise for the partnership. It should be noted, however, that not all partnerships were conducted in this way.

Only the end of the account for the preceding year is preserved. The items are divided from one another by lines, as in no. 63, above, and there is another detail interesting for the history of the technical aspect of bookkeeping: in some cases a stroke connects the end of an item described and the sum written at the end of the line. For the convenience of the reader the text is arranged in the form of a table.

University Library, Cambridge, Taylor-Schechter Collection, TS Misc. Box 8, f. 65.

A. PRECEDING YEAR

1. CREDIT

Price of 8 1/2 manā[1] rose marmalade for R. Joseph	1 1/2, 1/4 din.
Price of 4 Maghrebi kerchiefs (mindīl)	1 1/2, 1/4 din.[2]
Total Credit	129 din. less 1 ḥabba

2. DEBIT

What I paid to Ibn Rajā' ("Hope [fulfilled]")[3] for the lac which I bought from him	100 1/4, 1/8 din.
What you advised me to pay to my lord, the Rāv[4]	2 din.

[1] About 17 pounds. Rose marmalade (see no. 51, n. 2 above) was an eastern product, not sent from the Muslim West. This item certainly appeared in a previous account on the debit side; meanwhile R. Joseph, the buyer, had paid for it.

[2] Unusually low price. On *mindīl* see Franz Rosenthal, *Essays on Art and Literature in Islam*, Leiden, 1971, pp. 63-99. For the rich Geniza material on the topic, see Y. Stillman's Ph.D. thesis, "Female Attire in Medieval Egypt," University of Pennsylvania, 1972.

[3] A Muslim judge and keeper of a caravanserai and bourse, *dār wakāla*, anonymously referred to in *Med. Soc.*, I, 190, 447, n. 18.

[4] The highly honored religious leader who wrote no. 35, above. This was a present, a standard sum regarded as sufficient for a month's living cost of a modest middle-class family.

Price of shoes[5]	1 din.
Price of a Ṭabarī[6] robe	1 din., 2 qīr.
Price of an Ascalon robe[7]	1 din.[8]
. . .	1 din., 14 qīr., 1 ḥabba
. . .	1/2, 1/8 din.
Silk and felts brought by al-Bunnī[9]	9 din. less 2 qīr.
Price of wimpels,[10] (paid) to Ibn al-Tammār[11]	9 1/2, 1/8 din.
Paid to 'Uqbān	1/4 din.
To Ibn al-Majjānī[12] returned what he had taken from him personally	2 1/2, 1/4 din.
To the same for 40 *waraq* dirhems worth	1 din.
To Ibn al-Tammār additional payment for a shawl[13]	1/4 din.
To Ibn Abu 'l-Ḥayy[14]	2 1/2, 1/4 din.
Total Debit	134 din., 5 qīr.
Debit Remaining	5 din., 5 qīr., 1 ḥabba

[5] Egypt must have been famous for its shoes. Although Sicily and Tunisia exported hides to Egypt in great quantities, one often finds records of shoes ordered from Egypt for private use in both countries.

[6] Made of Tabaristan cloth, not genuine, of course, but imitated in Egypt. Tabaristan is a district in northern Iran south of the Caspian Sea.

[7] Ascalon, then the great port of southern Palestine, was also an industrial center. Its robes are listed also in TS NS J 127*a*, l. 5; its *maqṭa'*s (see no. 16, above) in TS 13 J 25, f. 14, *Nahray* 129. In TS 10 J 16, f. 10, *Nahray* 156, ll. 10-11, it is said that Ascalon was the best market for Egyptian flax in the whole of Palestine and Syria.

[8] Again the impressive *standardization of prices*. Cf. *Med. Soc.*, I, 229: the *thawb*, or robe, the main piece of male clothing, had an average price of 1 dinar.

[9] Spelled here *bwny*, elsewhere often *bny*. Could be derived from *bunn*, carp (pickels), or *ra's bunn*, a place in Tunisia.

[10] Ar. *ma'ājir*, the standard headcover for women, as the turban was for men.

[11] "Trader in dates," often mentioned, but always as a textile merchant.

[12] This is Yiḥye al-Majjānī. See nos. 7 and 8, above.

[13] Ar. *talthīma*, a shawl around the lower part of the face worn by women and judges (see Dozy, *Supplément*, II, 516*a*). In a document dated 1172 (ULC Or 1080 J 142, col. 1, l. 10), it was yellow and consisted of three parts. For Ibn al-Tammār, see n. 11, above.

[14] The writer of no. 16 above. See also no. 15, sec. J.

B. CURRENT YEAR

Sent by him in the year 49[15] with Ḥassūn:[16]	
A purse weighing	107 1/3 din., 1/2 qīr.
Expended from this:	
Against a collateral redeemed	7 1/8 din.
To Nissīm b. Sāsōn[17]	10 din., 2 qīr.
Debit remaining from the account submitted above	5 din., 5 qīr., 1 ḥabba

C. THE PARTNERSHIP

Balance from the purse noted above	85 din. less 2 qīr., 1 ḥabba
Added by me	85 din. less 2 qīr., 1 ḥabba
Total for the partnership	170 din. less 1/6 din., 2 ḥabbas
Bought for this:	
Two units of lac weighing 700 pounds, price per (camel's) load 28 din., total price	39 din., 5 qīr.[18]
Transport and . . .	9 qīr.
Price of a Laythī[19] qinṭār of flax	6 din., 1 dir.
Price of two-thirds[20] of the borax, 93 mann	12 1/2, 1/4 din.
All this was packed into one bale, which required for the payments made in Miṣr (Fustat)	3 1/3 din.
Retained for the customs dues in Alexandria, rent of storerooms there, toll into, and out of the city, readying of the shipment (for the transport by sea), and freight	5 din.
Total [of the lac etc.]	67 din. . . .[21]

(The continuation, like the beginning, is lost.)

15 The Muslim year 449, which began on March 10, 1057.

16 Probably the one mentioned in no. 15, sec. J, above.

17 "Miracles, son of Joy" extremely common names (both Heb.); therefore difficult to identify.

18 This shows that in 1057 the camel's load was reckoned in Fustat as containing 500 pounds.

19 About this weight and this price, see *Med. Soc.*, I, 227, 361.

20 A third partner participated in the borax (which used to be exported to Sicily).

21 Correct addition of the items acquired for the partnership enumerated thus far.

66 ACCOUNT FOR A BROTHER-IN-LAW

Ca. 1066

Abū Sahl, the man for whom this account was written, was a money changer, who specialized in high value silver dirhems and old and exotic gold currencies. No other Geniza account contains so many references to *nuqra* silver, called here also by the strange name "golden silver," as this one (see n. 3). Money-lending must have been another line of Abū Sahl, and one of considerable dimensions, as is proved by the valuable securities deposited with him. He had sold them either because the persons concerned had renounced them or perhaps had left the city altogether. Their price was paid during his absence. A bucket worth 74 dinars deserves particular attention (col. II, ll. 1-2). This must have been a bronze vessel inlaid with figures or other decorations in silver of the type we still admire in our museums. Orders of payment coming in for Abū Sahl or issued by him are also noted. In addition, he traded in a great variety of goods.

Commodities as different as wool, tin, and hazelnut—the first exported from Egypt, the second coming from Spain, and the third imported from Syria—were traded by him in considerable quantities.

The account was written by Abū Sahl's brother-in-law, Nahray b. Nissīm, whom we have repeatedly met in nos. 29-35, above, and also as author of account no. 64. Nahray took care of his brother-in-law's accounts during a short absence (cf. col. I, l. 2: "The purses he *left*" and col. IV, l. 10: "Debited after his arrival"). From col. III, ll. 2-3, where Nahray pays rent to his brother-in-law for two and a half years, one might derive the erroneous conclusion that our account was concerned with such a long period. Fortunately, we are informed about this detail from another source. After his marriage, Nahray, who was a native of Tunisia, took up residence in the family mansion of his brothers-in-law in Fustat. After some years the young couple needed more space than that provided by the share of the house left to his wife by her father (it was one-sixth of the house). Therefore, Nahray agreed to pay to his brothers-in-law, on whose premises he encroached, a monthly rent of 1 dinar.[1] The payment listed here is from the time of that agreement and to be understood as retroactive.

The period for which our account was made must have been short, four to five months, for people used to travel during summertime and there is only one item for the purchase of wheat and none for that of grapes (for the preparation of wine), an item appearing regularly in letters and accounts around August, and, above all, the account contains no date. Had it concerned more than one year, references to preceding years could not have been absent.

The account is written on a sheet forming four pages of small book size (5 1/2 x 4″), as Nahray used in his commercial papers.

University Library, Cambridge, Taylor-Schechter Collection, TS Arabic Box 30, f. 215.

A. Credit

(Col. I)

[1]	To my lord, the elder Abū Sahl, "the son of the Kohen"[2]—may God make his honored position permanent.	
[2]	Price of all he left in 6 purses	68 1/3, 1/4 din.
[3]	Price of 94 1/2 golden silver pieces[3]	5 2/3 din.
[4]	Price of 103 given to Abū 'Alī[4] (5) of which I have received the price of 65 dir., namely	4 din.
[6]	Balance to the debit of Abū 'Alī	38 dir.
[7]	To his debit also	20 dir.
[8]	Same, first payment through his paternal uncle	200 dir.
[9]	Same, balance of	272 dir.
	Total	710 dir.[5]

[1] TS 8 J 11, f. 18, dated 1066. The information was conveyed to Abū 'Alī, Nahray's other brother-in-law (see below). The house was *mushā'*, "undivided," i.e., the various shares were numerical, not physical units.

[2] This was the family name, "Mr. Cohen."

[3] Text: *fiḍḍat dhahab*. This "golden silver" must be identical with *nuqra*, or full, silver, as the identical exchange of 1:17 proves. It cannot correspond to *electron*, since this coin alloy contains far more gold than warranted by the price indicated here. See below, col. I, l. 15, and col. II, ll. 6-7.

[4] Nahray's other brother-in-law. See n. 1, above.

[5] Total of the last four lines.

[10] Total weight 869 1/2 dir.[6]
[11] Debit on Abū 'Alī through Ibn al-Sukkarī[7] 17 dir. for 1 din., 1 din.
(one line left free)
[12] Price of the collaterals deposited by the Preacher[8] 18 1/3 din.
[13] Balance of payment for two pots of 'Alī 7 1/3 din.
[14] Price of 438 silver dir., after the loss of two dir., which had
[15] fallen off.[9] Price 17 dir. per din. 25 1/2, 1/4 din.
[16] (Torn away) . . . 2/3 din., 3 qīr.

(Col. II)

[1] Price of the bucket 67 din., ⟦2/3, 1 qīr.⟧
[2] Balance from the sale of the bucket 7 din.
[3] From my master Abū 'Imrān 17 din., 1/2 qīr.
[4] ⟦Balance of an account⟧[10]
[5] A pair of anklets 20 din., less 1/4
[6] Sale of 94 dir. nuqra
[7] from the rest of the silver
Price 17 1/2 dir. for 1 din., 5 din., 11 qīr.
A t?rsymh[11] remained from it.
[8] For 208 din., 5 qīr. Nizāriyya[12] 219 1/8 din.

[6] Total of ll. 3-9.

[7] "Sugar merchant." Here and in the following line about four partly effaced words were added, it seems in another pen.

[8] This Muslim preacher, *wā'iẓ*, gives real sermons and is different from the *khaṭīb*, who reads the more formal *khuṭba*, or address, during the public Friday prayer. A khaṭīb was among Nahray's customers.

[9] The sum concerned had been 440 dirhems, but there had been a *nafḍ*, a kind of small loss not yet identified, amounting to 2 dirhems.

[10] Crossed out probably because this balance had been settled elsewhere.

[11] *Tarsīm* is a fine to be paid for delay in the payment of a bill of exchange. But none is mentioned here and the suffix *h* does not refer to any preceding word. One can hardly assume that Nahray intended to write *tarmīsa*, the old *tremissis* (or one-third of a gold piece), whose Greek-Latin loan word is normally found only in Hebrew texts.

[12] Coins minted under the caliph al-'Azīz (975-996), i.e., about eighty years before our account. See above, passim.

[9]	There remained a bag of them to be exchanged with the elder Abū Sa'd[13]	
[10]	Received from Ibn al-Sukkarī for the wool[14]	131 1/4 din.
[11]	From Sulaymān, the Spanish goldsmith	1 din. less 2 ḥabba
[12]		Total 619 din., 5 qīr.
[13]	In number[15] 9 din., 1 qīr., and 4 fragments. Remaining.	
[14]	⟦Price of hazelnuts	37 din.⟧[16]
[15]	Purse of Ibn Nājiya for the sale of the purses with (16) the exotic[17] din. and those with intricate script	28 din., 1 qīr.
[17]	For a note from Ibn Bahlūl[18]	22 din.

(Col. iii)

[1]	Profit from the tin	5 din.
[2]	Two-and-a-half years' rent in the house	30 din.
[3]		Total 713 din., 7 qīr.
[4]	Debit, as summed up[19]	133 2/3 din., 1 qīr.
[5]	Balance in his favor	579 1/3, 1/4 din.

[13] Text *kīs*, which is not normally used in the Geniza documents of this period for "purse" (called *ṣurra* in the Mediterranean area).

[14] As the specification below, col. iii, ll. 12-16 shows, the money for this very large sale of wool did not come in at once, but arrived through different channels, presumably from a number of customers. If we assume that the price of wool here was approximately the same as in TS Arabic 30, f. 255, l. 10 (which was slightly later), namely, 6 dinars per qinṭār, over 20 qinṭārs were sold by Abū Sahl.

[15] All the entries in this account are according to weight. This payment, which contained fragments of dinars, was only counted. Since there were no coins of 1 *qīrāṭ* (or, at least, we do not know of any), we must assume that certain fragmentary dinars were traded as such.

[16] See col. iv, ll. 5, 18. Abū Sahl first had given an order to pay for this item and then withdrew the order.

[17] Text: *al-jānn*, it seems, a term for "exotic." The coins of this period, both Fatimid and Murābiṭ, bore legends in monumental Kūfī characters. There were, however, Sijilmāsa quarters, minted under the Murābiṭ ruler Yūsuf b. Tashfīn (1087-1106), which were half in Naskhī and might have looked rather intricate (cf. Hazard, *Numismatic History of North Africa*, p. 103, no. 91, and Plate 1). Perhaps coins with such script were minted also by Yūsuf's predecessor.

[18] The bottom of the page and with it the lower parts of the name and the number are torn away. But the restoration is safe.

[19] In a previous account.

B. Debit

[6]	For the house behind the synagogue[20]	1 din.
[7]	For the poll tax[21]	1 din.
[8]	Price of half a mann of spikenard[22]	10 qīr.
[9]	His promissory note to Abū 'Alī	20 din. less 2 qīr.
[10]	⟦Note handed to Isma'īl for a purse of the Treasury	30 1/3, 1/4 din.
	Loose gold	20 din.⟧
	(one line left blank)	
[12]	Specification of the sale of the din. received from Ibn al-Sukkarī[23]	
[13]	Through Abū 'Imrān 17 less 1/2 qīr.	18 din.
[14]	Through myself 12 less 1 1/2 qīr.	12 2/3
[15]	Through Abū 'Alī 96 1/2, 1/8	95 din., 2 qīr.
[16]	Through (torn away)	5 din.
[17]	(Torn away) half a din.	Total 131 1/4

(Col. iv)

[1]	For the poor for the poll tax	1 din.
[2]	⟦Price of two cloaks for Umm Abī . . .	1 1/2 din.⟧
[3]	⟦For the rent of a store room	1 din.⟧
[4]	For two sacks[24] of wheat and their transport	2 din. less 1/3
[5]	For 3 loads of hazelnuts in the house of al-Anṣārī[25]	34 din.
[6]	and for the "boys" (officials)	6 dir.
[7]	Commission and weigher ⟦included in⟧ in addition to the price	1/2, 1/8 din.

[20] Alms given to people living there and promised by Abū Sahl before his departure.

[21] Poll tax of a poor person, given to him as an act of charity.

[22] This drug, which comes from the mountains of Nepal, was used against fits of hysteria and epilepsy. Ducros, *Droguier*, p. 74.

[23] This refers to col. II, l. 10 (see n. 14, above). The first two items (ll. 13, 14) refer to dinars which had a slightly higher value than the standard dinar in which this account is made, the third one (l. 15) concerns an opposite case.

[24] *Tillīsayn.* This is a sack made of palm leaves and containing 150 pounds of wheat (see Hinz, *Masse*, p. 51) which were needed for the household.

[25] This Muslim, who appears repeatedly in Nahray's accounts kept a place for the sale of fruit imports.

[8]	Rose-water and Chinese rhubarb[26]	1/4, 1/8
[9]		5 1/2 qīr.
[10]	After his arrival through my master Abū 'Imrān:	
[11]	Purse of the House of Blessing	50 din.
[12]	Purse of Ibn Muhadhdhib al-Dawla[27]	38 less 1 1/2 qīr.
[13]	Purse of the Treasury	15 1/3, 1/4
[14]		Total 103 1/2 din., 1 1/2 qīr.
[15]	Purse of Hiba al-Khashaba ("Mr. Gift Wood")	51 1/2
[16]		Total 155 din., 1 1/2 qīr.
[17]	Handed over to him purse of . . . (torn away)	
[18]	Balance from the price of the hazelnut . . .[28]	

67 A BANKER'S ACCOUNT

Ca. 1075

This account, like nos. 64 and 66, is in the hand of Nahray b. Nissīm, who acts here merely as a banker, as he did in the later years of his life. Abū Zikrī al-Ṭabīb ("The Physician," a family name), for whom the account was made, was one of the most prominent merchants in Fustat, always spoken of in the highest terms of reverence and closely connected with the Tustarīs (see nos. 2 and 11, above), as the passage about him in no. 20, sec. E, above, clearly indicates. One Geniza source shows him in contact with the government, probably as a representative of merchants.

The structure of the account is highly interesting. It starts out with the big items, the *suftajās*, or bills of exchange of the customer,[1] deposited by him with Nahray (sec. A). This is followed by two self-contained units, each showing approximately balanced credits

[26] Chinese rhubarb, a drug coming from Northwest China or Tibet, served as a popular tonic and purgative and frequently appears in the Geniza, as it does here, in small quantities, i.e., used for the household, not for commercial purposes (see Ducros, n. 22, above, p. 61). Rose-water was added to many medicines.

[27] An honorary title given by the government to Muslims and others.

[28] Published first in *JESHO* 9 (1966), 57-62, but thoroughly revised here.

[1] About this important instrument of commercial operations see *Med. Soc.*, I, 242-245, and no. 70, n. 18, below.

and debits (secs. B and C). The final and largest section shows the payments in cash, that is, purses with gold coins, made to the customer, and the cost of some minor, personal purchases made for him by Nahray (sec. D). The total here corresponds *exactly* to that in sec. A. A note in Arabic characters saying that the entire account was transferred to large sheets (for the convenience of the recipient) proves that these bookkeeping practices were not confined to Jewish merchants. Our account itself is written on a sheet folded so as to form four pages of small size (5 x 3 1/2″), the last of which remained blank. Everything was crossed out, as was done after the transfer to the account book and to the letter destined for the customer.

The account does not contain any charge for the banker's services, nor, of course, interest for money deposited. About the banker's earnings see *Med. Soc.*, I, 247-248. From sec. A it seems to appear that "bills of exchange" were traded.

University Library, Cambridge, Taylor-Schechter
Collection, TS Miscellaneous Box 24, f. 39.[2]

(Page *a*)

A. Large credits: the customer's bills of exchange

[1] For my lord, the elder Abū Zikrī, "The Physician,"
may God make his honored position permanent:
[2] Suftaja of Salmān[3] 40 din.
[3] Suftaja of "the Son of the Alexandrian"[4] 25 din.

[2] I copied this account from the original manuscript in the University Library, Cambridge, England, on August 21, 1968. In August 1971, while in Jerusalem, working feverishly on the photostats from a private collection, I was alerted by my former student, Dr. Mordechai A. Friedman, to look at the microfilm of that manuscript. Since I was not sure whether I had copied the text in its entirety, I transcribed it again. Comparing the two transcripts I realized again (as on several previous occasions), how vital it is, at least for the purposes of editing, to work with the original and not with a photostat or microfilm.

[3] Several merchants with this name are known from that period. See, e.g., no. 42, sec. D, above.

[4] Abraham or Ibrahīm b. Faraḥ, representative of merchants and postal agency in Alexandria (*Med. Soc.*, I, 304, and no. 54, n. 4, above).

[4]	From R. Nathan[5]	20 din. less 1 qīr.
[5]	For suftaja of Abū Ghālib ("Victor")[6]	26 2/3, 1/8 din.
[6]	For suftaja of Joseph b. Khalfa[7]	200 din.
[7]		Total 311 1/2, 1/4 din.

B. Credits balanced by promissory notes

[8]	To him from "The Son of the Scholar"[8] for eight	
[9]	camel loads[9] and 422 pounds of flax	132 1/2 din.
[10]	To him commission for 11 bales of Qāsim[10]	2 din. less 1/6
[11]	To him one half of the 17 din. less 1/3[11]	8 1/3 din.
[12]		Total 142 2/3 din.
[13]	Debit: his promissory note no. 1 to "the Kohen"[12]	100 din.
[14]	Another promissory note	42 din.
[15]	Balance in his favor	2/3 din.

C. Small credits and debits

[16]	Credit: 1/2 of 1/6 of a camel load of flax	
[17]	costing 15 din. per load, a remainder from	
[18]	the flax of Ahnās[13]	1 1/4 din.

(Page *b*)

[1]	Credit from half a suftaja of 10 din. from Ahnās	5 din.
	(space of about four lines left blank)	

[5] Probably Nathan b. Nahray, a cousin of Nahray b. Nissīm living in Alexandria.

[6] Common Jewish (and Muslim) name.

[7] About the commercial activities of this man see *Med. Soc.*, I, 413, n. 46, also chapter IV, introduction, no. 1 above.

[8] Abraham, "Son of the Scholar," banker and judge. See *Med. Soc.*, I, 238-239, and no. 5, n. 25, above.

[9] 4,000 pounds. See no. 55, n. 18, above.

[10] A Muslim merchant, repeatedly mentioned. The representatives of merchants received a commission for their sales. See *Med. Soc.*, I, 186.

[11] The recipient of the account knew which item was meant.

[12] One of Nahray's brothers-in-law (see no. 56, above). One of the two probably had died meanwhile.

[13] A place in the flax-growing district Bahnasā south of Cairo (see *Med. Soc.*, I, 459, where, however, Ahnās is not listed). See Yāqūt, I, 409, Ibn Duqmāq 5, p. 5.

[2]	Debit for the honey	(not filled in)
[3]	Debit for a Bible codex	5 1/2 din.[14]

D. Payments made by the banker

[4]	Due me for half of my payment to	
[5]	the finance director (*'āmil*) of Ahnās[15]	5 din.
[6]	Price of a codex of the Mishna[16]	1 1/2 din.
	(space left blank for another 8-10 ll., but the items are carried over to page *c*)	

(Page *c*)

[1]	For a turban[17]	3 1/6 din.
[2]	An unbleached bolt[18]	1/2, 1/4 din.
[3]	Ibn al-Majjānī[19]	1/2, 1/4 din.
[4]	A purse	40 din
[5]	For 20 (din.) less 5 qīr. new coins	21[20] less 5 qīr.
[6]	Price of a hide brought by Salāma	2/3 din.
[7]	Purse of Ḥasan b. 'Alī, guaranteed by "the Kohen"[21]	103 din.
[8]	Purse of the "boy" of Dubādib[22]	50 din. less 2 qīr.
[9]	Purse of the Treasury	50 din.

[14] The total of the credit in this section would be (together with the balance from sec. B) 6 11/12 din. Thus the price of the honey would be 1 5/12 din. The item was not filled out probably because the bill referring to it was not at hand.

[15] Payment of a sale's tax to the government in the flax district. See n. 13, above.

[16] Much cheaper than the Bible because the text contained mere letters without signs for vowels and cantillation. No doubt both the Bible and the Mishna codices were only parts of the entire books.

[17] This and the next item were sent by Abū Zikrī.

[18] Ar. *farkha*, see no. 22, n. 9, above.

[19] Not necessarily the one mentioned in nos. 7-8, above.

[20] This number is correct, as is proved by the addition. The number 20 at the beginning of the line is probably a lapse.

[21] The man was a money changer (see no. 56, above), and officially entitled to certify the true value of a sealed purse.

[22] An onomatopoeic nickname for "a fat man talking with a loud voice." Repeatedly mentioned in Nahray's banking accounts. See *JESHO* 9 (1966), p. 45.

[10]	Purse of Ibn 'Awkal[23]	20 din.
[11]		Total 289 din., 1 qīr.[24]
[12]	From "the Kohen"	22 2/3 din., 1 qīr.
[13]		Grand Total 311 1/2, 1/4[25]
[14]	Settlement complete[26]	
[15]	(In Arabic characters:) Transferred to long sheets	

68 A GREAT MERCHANT SETTLES ACCOUNTS WITH HIS BANKER

1134

A new aspect of medieval business practices is reflected in this account, which was written about sixty years after no. 67. Here the customer submits the account to his banker. This strange procedure might have had its origin in the specific relation between the two persons concerned, as revealed by many items from the Geniza. The account is in the unmistakable handwriting of Abū Zikrī Kohen, a representative of merchants of Old Cairo and prominent India trader.[1] It refers to his dealings with the banker Khiyār b. Nissīm in the year 1134. In November 1131 the two concluded a partnership for the duration of one year in a banking business with Abū Zikrī as senior partner, who alone was entitled to grant loans.[2] There exist also twenty orders of payments, ranging from 1 1/4 through 100 dinars given by Abū Zikrī to Khiyār in the month of Av (July-August) 1140, one from 1138, and one from 1141.[3] At that time, Khiyār had become Abū Zikrī's main banker through

[23] Probably a grandson of Joseph Ibn 'Awkal (nos. 3-4, above).
[24] I find 289 *less* 1 qīrāṭ. But I assume Nahray is right.
[25] See page *a*, l. 7.
[26] Ar. *wa-huwa 'l-wafy*.

[1] See no. 9, above.
[2] *India Book* 325.
[3] Ibid. 137, 229*d*, Mosseri VII-189, 1.

whom he conducted his day-to-day business, although he also had dealings with other bankers.

Columns I and II contain Khiyār's debits, i.e., Abū Zikrī's payments to him or made for him; cols. III and IV, his credits. Since the latter naturally consisted mostly of smaller sums, this list was longer and continued on consecutive pages which are lost. As far as it has been preserved, the account should be read in the following order: col. I, ll. 1-14, lists Abū Zikrī's first series of payments, which totaled 125 1/6 dinars. Unlike the usual routine, the amount is not indicated here, but appears on col. IV, l. 10, where Khiyār's credits are provisionally summarized as amounting to 96 1/2, 1/3, 1/8, less 1/144 dinars. The balance of 28 dinars, 5 qīrāṭs (specified here as 1/8 dinar, plus two qīrāṭs), and 1/144 dinars, is listed again in col. I, ll. 15-16, where it heads the second series of payments by Abū Zikrī. The second total of Khiyār's debits amounts to 102 3/4 dinars, less 1/72 (col. II, l. 4), to which a single item of 7 dinars is added. Here, a balance was carried over from the part of the credit account lost to us (col. II, ll. 7-8), followed by a third series of payments by Abū Zikrī, this time not in cash—as in the two first series—but all in promissory notes drawn on him by Khiyār. Whether Abū Zikrī made these payments for Khiyār in cash or by book transfer is not evident.

Promissory notes of 3, 5, or 7 dirhems should not surprise the reader. Silver money was scarce. Day-to-day transactions, as we have noted above, were largely made by paper. See *Med. Soc.*, I, 245.

Our account seems to show that Abū Zikrī, despite his highly honored position in the merchants' community, refrained from making overdrafts. He was also careful not to let his money idle, obviously depositing payments received immediately. It must have been customary to settle accounts at short intervals, perhaps once a month.

University Library, Cambridge, Taylor-Schechter
Collection, TS NS J 321, f. *7a, India Book* 316

A I. Payments to the Banker in Cash

FIRST SERIES

(Col. I)

[1]	The Elder Khiyār b. Nissīm	
[2]	Balance to his debit after all	
[3-4]	accounts to the 10th of Sha'bān (5) (June 6, 1134)	
[5-6]		75 1/6 din.
[7]	Other debits	6 1/2 din.
[8]		20 less 5 qīr.
[9]	Through his son-in-law	9 din.
[10]	From me	5 1/8 din.
[11-12]	From the elder Abu 'l-Faḍā'il	5 din.
[13]	From Zikrī	3 din.
[14]	From the same	1 din., 10 qīr.
	(The total of 125 1/6 din. is not indicated here, but one line was left for the purpose)	
[15]	28.5 (in Coptic numerals)	
	Balance to his debit[4]	28 din., 5 qīr., 1 dāniq[5]

A II. Payments to the Banker, Mostly in Cash

SECOND SERIES

(Col. I)

[16]	From me in gold	17 1/4, 1/8
[17]	In silver	11 din.
[18]	Gold and silver	20 din., 13 1/2 qīr.
[19]	Also in dir.	1 din.

(Col. II:)

[1]	From me in gold	22 din., 2 qīr.
[2]	Promissory note	1 1/2 din.
[3]	From my cousin	1 din.

[4] Transferred here from col. IV, l. 12 (see the introduction). The Coptic numerals for 20 and 8 are written in one line and that for 5 a little higher up, but between the two.

[5] A *dāniq* was 1/6 of a qīr. and 1/144 of a din.

[4]	(In another, thick, pen: Balance)	102 1/2, 1/4 din. less 1 ḥabba
[5]	Debit beginning: his note on	7 din.[6]
[6]	(In small letters: Total)	109 2/3 din.
[7]	(In small letters:) Balance of debit	14 din., 1 qīr.
[8]	(In bold letters:) Balance, debit	14 din., 1/6[7]

A III. The banker's promissory notes

[9]	His note	100 din.
[10]	His note	66 din., 9 qīr.
[11]	His note	36 din.
[12]	His note	30 din. less 1/6
[13]	His note	26 din.

(the rest of the page, about 8 lines, left blank)

B. The banker's credits

(Col. iii)

[1]	The Elder Khiyār b. Nissīm[8]	
[2]	Credit beginning: a note	9 1/2, 1/8 din.
[3]	Paid to Abu 'l-Munā	1 din.
[4]	Note to Abu 'l-Munā	4 din.
[5]	To our lord[9]	15 din. exactly
[6]	Note to Joseph	10 din. exactly
[7]	Price of . . .	9 2/3, 1/4 din.
[8]	To the ḥazzān[10]	17 (or 16) qīr.

[6] See the introduction.

[7] The slight difference between ll. 7 and 8 is to be explained best by the fact that Abū Zikrī first wrote the number out of his memory, but looked through the account before beginning his new series of entries.

[8] The Arabic letter *d*, followed by a curved stroke, appears here, it seems an abbreviation for *dāmat 'izzuhū*, "may his honored position be permanent."

[9] The Gaon Maṣlīaḥ, who was the head of the Jews in the Fatimid empire 1127-1139, and had his seat in Cairo. This was not a personal gift, but a contribution for his school.

[10] "Cantor," referring to Ḥalfōn b. Manasse, who was also the court clerk and received payment for the writing of legal documents.

[9]	To the Nezer[11]	1 din.
[10]	Credit	19 qīr.
[11]	Credit	23 dir.
[12]	To the ḥazzān	1 din., 7 qīr.
[13]	Balance of (the price of) the slave girl	1 din.
[14]	To Musallam	7 dir.
[15]	Note	1 din.
[16]	Note	10 din. exactly
[17]	Price of wheat[12]	140 dir.
[18]	Note to Ibn al-ʿAbd	3 din.
[19]	To al-Qasṭallānī	3 1/4 din.
[20]	Price of grapes[13]	5 din., 1 qīr.
[21]	To Musallam	120 dir.
[22]	A note	4 din., 2 qīr.

(Col. iv)

[1]	Note	2 1/3 din.
[2]	Note	1 din., 13 1/2 qīr.
[3]	Note	5 dir.
[4]	Note	3 dir.
[5]	To me	1 din.
[6]	Note	109 1/2 dir.
[7]	Through Musallam	2 din.
[8-9]	Total	96 1/2, 1/3, 1/8 less 1/144
[10-11]	To his debit	125 1/6 din.
[12]	Balance to his debit[14]	28 din. 1/8, 2 qīr. 1/144

[13] ⟦My note on 70 din. He has cashed it.⟧

[11] Honorary title, borne at that time by the judge Eli b. Nethanel. A judge, when writing out documents, also received a remuneration.

[12] The banker did not procure the wheat or the grapes, but in the order of payment it was stated for what purpose it was made, as is proved by the orders preserved.

[13] Certainly not for trade, but for home consumption. Many used to make their wine at home (employing servants). The quantity listed here is very large. Wine was consumed daily.

[14] See col. 1, l. 15, above, and the introduction.

[14]	Credit against this	15 qīr.
[16]	Credit two notes for four payments	
[17]	of poll tax	6 din., 10 qīr., 2 ḥabba, and 4 dir.[15]
[18]	Note on	35 1/2 dir.
[19]	Paid to me	30 din., yellowish ones[16]
[20]	For customs duties	10 qīr.
[21]	⟦Note to the Rayyis[17]	5 din., cancelled⟧
[22]	Note given to Musallam	10 din. exactly
[23]	Note	7 qīr., less 1 dāniq 1/144 din.
[24]	Credit	30 dir.

(All four columns are crossed out by one vertical stroke drawn over each of them. This may denote that all accounts were settled, or that they were transferred to "the large book," the ledger referred to in other accounts similarly crossed out.

Abū Zikrī usually writes numbers in words, wherefore one number of his sometimes occupies two lines. For the sake of quick information all numbers are rendered here in numerals.[18])

[15] The dirhems were paid to the officials who collected the poll tax.
[16] About the discoloring of the dinars see *Med. Soc.*, I, 378, sec. 35.
[17] The Gaon. See n. 9, above.
[18] Published first in *JESHO* 9 (1966), 62-66, but thoroughly revised here.

CHAPTER VIII

Travel and Transport

TRADERS mostly were travelers, at least during a major part of their lives; and a traveler invariably was a carrier of goods, who had to keep an eye on his own merchandise and often also on that of someone else. Since travel and transport constituted the daily routine of a trader, mention was made of them in letters only if there was a special reason to do so. Otherwise, accounts and bills of lading took care of most of the factual information needed by a business friend.

The whims of nature often caused utmost discomfort to the traveler, upset his dispositions, or even endangered his life, as may be learned from nos. 3, 5, 8, 27, 36, 39, 42, 45, 51, 53, 60, above, and nos. 70, 72, 74-76, below. Enemy action and pirates constituted another menace (see nos. 4, 9, 27, 28, above, and 69, 71, 73, 74, below).[1] Against the former, the seafarers sought protection by taking refuge in ports or roadsteads on their way, as is illustrated so vividly in no. 72, below, or, if they had not yet traveled far, returned to the port of embarkation, an exceedingly frequent occurrence (see, for instance, no. 72, n. 18). Both expedients caused much delay and often great losses. Enemies and privateers were kept off by naval escorts, as in nos. 69 and 70 (see also no. 9, above). Such escorts, naturally, accompanied only large convoys carrying the shipments of the great merchants and persons of high standing. The convoy attacked in no. 73 clearly lacked such protection.

Only a few bills of lading have found their way into the Geniza.

[1] See also *Med. Soc.*, I, ch. IV, "Travel and Seafaring," in particular, secs. 8, "On the High Seas," and 9, "Piracy, War, and Other Man-made Dangers"; S. D. Goitein, "Glimpses from the Cairo Geniza on Naval Warfare in the Mediterranean, etc.," in *G. Levi Della Vida Jubilee Volume*, pp. 393-405; id., "Two Eyewitness Reports on an Expedition of the King of Kish (Qais) against Aden," *Bulletin of the School of Oriental and African Studies* 16 (1954), 247-257.

Since a copy had to be deposited with the captain or, rather, the proprietor or bursar of a ship, no doubt most of them were written in Arabic characters and no need for their preservation was felt. No. 77, below, is an example of a small shipment, probably attached to the bale of a business friend, for whom the bill of lading was written in Hebrew characters.

Although an ancient Arabic proverb has it that of the good things of this earth Muslims enjoy most sex, Christians—money, and Jews—food,[2] the Geniza letters contain very little information about culinary matters in general and provisions on travel in particular. The short note translated in no. 78 arouses rather than satisfies our curiosity: how were those roast chickens and quails preserved?

A business trip in the Mediterranean area required an absence from home for at least one summer; one on the India route, for at least one year, but often far more. Naturally, such long separations imposed great hardships on married couples, as is eloquently brought home in no. 45, above. Unfortunately the religious and learned middle-class traders, who left us their writings in the Geniza, were as tight-lipped about sex as we are bubbling over with it. The whole problem has been dealt with by me in the forthcoming third volume of my book *A Mediterranean Society*. Here, two specimens touching on it are translated, one from the India route (no. 79), and one from the Mediterranean (no. 80).

69 LAST-HOUR ARRANGEMENTS FOR DISPOSITION OF PRECIOUS SHIPMENTS

Alexandria to Fustat
Ca. 1023

As repeatedly emphasized in the letter, this is a hurriedly written apology explaining why it was impossible to carry out instructions received from the addressee. Details (such as the names of the travelers entrusted with the care for the shipments) would follow later.

The shipments involved were very large, especially if one con-

[2] Discussed in Goitein, *Studies in Islamic History*, p. 251.

siders that the time of their dispatch was one of warfare and great perils. Eighty-five bales of flax,[1] containing about 30,000 pounds, about 140 pounds of pepper, and one bale each of finished textiles and lac, and a camel load of myrobalan,[2] had a value of well over $300,000. The proprietor living in the capital had received intelligence of the war situation in Tunisia and had given last-minute instructions to divert all shipments destined for Qayrawān, then the capital of Tunisia, to Palermo, the capital of Sicily. But it was too late; moreover, good news from Tunisia meanwhile had reached Alexandria, where this letter was written.

The addressee, Abū Naṣr Tustarī, the son of Sahl, the recipient of no. 11, above, was one of the leading merchants of the Egyptian capital during the first half of the eleventh century until he was liquidated, shortly after his brother Abū Sa'd had been murdered in October 1047.

The writer, Ṣadaqa b. 'Ayyāsh ("Charity," son of "Long-lived") was the son of the brother-in-law and representative of the leading Jewish merchant of Qayrawān around 1000, who has been met by us in no. 11, n. 29, and n. 5, above. Ṣadaqa is praised by his uncle for his efficiency in a letter to his father 'Ayyāsh (Taylor-Schechter Collection 13 J 23, f. 14). The ease with which he addresses the great Abū Naṣr Tustarī shows that the two belonged to the same social class.

Bodleian Library, Oxford, MS Heb. d 66 (Cat. 2878), f. 15.

(Five lines of introduction, containing the date: second half of Iyyar [May], and acknowledging letters received.)

As to your order, may God preserve your honored position, to send everything to Palermo: I had asked God, may his name be glorified, for guidance, and, in accordance with your prior instructions, loaded for Qayrawān since I was afraid that time would be running out and we would miss the sailing altogether.

Specification of the shipments to Qayrawān:

Boat of Abu 'l-'Alā' ("The Excellent")[3] 19 bales

[1] Flax was the staple export of Egypt in those days. Therefore bales containing flax were not described as such.

[2] See no. 22, n. 35, above.

[3] Here sailing from Alexandria to Tunisia in the spring. In a letter to

Boat of Ibn al-Mawwāz ("Banana seller")[4]	22 bales
Boat of Othmān (The Seller of Lac)[5]	10 bales
Boat of Ḥasan of Barqa[6]	3 bales
Total	54 bales

One bale arrived[7] on this very day on which I am writing this letter; it will go to wherever God, the glorious and exalted, will grant.

Specification of the shipments to Palermo:

Boat of the shaykh Abū 'Abdallāh, al-Andalusī[8]	20 bales and 1 barqalū[9]
Barge[10] of Ḥusayn ("The Seller of Lac")	10 bales

The bale with the textiles was opened by me. I sent one part with Ibn Dhīsūr,[11] and the other bundle with al-Andalusī.[12] May God ordain safety for all of them.

You, may God preserve your honored position, had instructed me previously to send the four bales of pepper to Qayrawān. Accord-

---

Ibn 'Awkal (TS 12.223, margin, ed. S. D. Goitein, *Tarbiz* 36 [1967], p. 392), it returns to Egypt in the fall.

[4] "The *new* boat" of this shipowner had to undergo repairs in Alexandria during the winter according to another letter to Ibn 'Awkal (Mosseri L 52, l. 10, *Tarbiz* 37 [1968], 50).

[5] Presents to this shipowner by Abu 'l-Khayr Moses Tāhertī, the writer of no. 11, above, in University Library Cambridge Collection Or 1080 J 35, l. 35.

[6] The medieval name of eastern province of Libya (see no. 72, n. 15, below).

[7] In Alexandria, sent from Fustat.

[8] The Spaniard mentioned also in no. 70, below. In TS 8 J 20, f. 2, the Andalusian ship arrives in Alexandria, sailing from Denia, Spain. Here, on the way back, it makes a stop in Palermo.

[9] A smaller bale. See *Med. Soc.* 1, 335.

[10] Ar. *qarrāba* (see *Med. Soc.*, 1, 477, n. 13). This "Seller of Lac" may, or may not, have been a relative of the one whose boat sailed to Qayrawān, mentioned here before.

[11] Occurring about ten times. Possibly different ships of the same proprietor, one replacing the other, are meant. In TS 13 J 17, f. 11, l. 23, ed. *Tarbiz* 36 (1967), 387, where a boat of Dhīsūr sails from Palermo, it is expressly said that it had come there (as in our letter) from Alexandria.

[12] Finished textiles were particularly valuable. Therefore, as a measure of precaution, they were loaded by the writer on two different boats.

ingly, one camel load[13] was loaded on the boat of Ibn Abi 'l-Shi'shā' ("The Man with the tendril"),[14] and another with Ibn [al-] Iskandar.[15]

In your letter which arrived today you ordered to send the pepper to Palermo. This, however, was not possible, for I could not unload them and I had already paid the freight. I was about to direct most of the flax to Palermo, when news was received here that the amir Sharaf al-Dawla ("Glory of the Dynasty"),[16] may God preserve his power, had returned to Tripoli and defeated his enemies. I hope that this is true, if God wills. Consequently, I asked God, the glorified and exalted, for guidance and directed our things to Qayrawān. I hope it will be to the good.

You ordered me to return the textiles (from Alexandria to Fustat).[17] This is the right thing to do, for they are not like flax or pepper, which could be sold locally (namely, in Alexandria). They are being sent to you in their entirety, and also the bundle (men-

13 Two camel loads correspond here to four bales. It is proper that a camel load should comprise two bales, Ar. *'idl,* which means lit., a package being exactly of the same weight as the one fastened on the other side of the camel's body. The Ar. term for justice, *'adl,* is derived from this word.

14 A nickname. In the huge account TS Box J 1, f. 54, col. IV, l. 30 (see no. 63, end, above), this boat is on its way back from Tunisia to Egypt.

15 In the Greek name *Alexander* the Arabs took *al* as the Ar. article. For reasons unknown to me the writer here deleted the *al* after he had written it. The boats of this family of shipowners (which might have been Christian) are frequently mentioned, but, as far as I have noted, always with *al.* The usual form of the name today is *Iskandar.*

16 This is the princely title of Mu'izz b. Bādis, the contemporary ruler of Tunisia, 1016-1062. In early spring of 1023 he made indeed great preparations for an attack on Tripoli, but finally did not carry his plans through (see Idris, *Zirides,* p. 161). The "news" reported here early in May 1023 had been received from travelers who had seen Bādis marching through al-Mahdiyya, their port of embarkation, at the end of March. Their reports might have been true. Bādis might have had initial success, but did not pursue the war because of the general situation within his state (see Idris, loc.cit.). The historians had no reason to mention these early gains, because they were not followed up; the merchants were very much concerned with them because the success of the business season depended on the safety of al-Mahdiyya, the port of Qayrawān.

17 Certain textiles concerning which intelligence had been received that they did not sell overseas.

tioned in your letter) with Ibn al-Wazzān ("The Weighmaster"),[18] to whom I have also handed over a letter destined for you.

I gave your letter to the shaykh Abū ʿAbdallāh al-Andalusī.[19] I shall settle accounts with him on the freight and take promissory notes from him, if God will, provided he does not put me off.

This very day, the bale of lac and the camel load of myrobalan arrived. In accordance with your instructions, I shall ship the lac to Qayrawān and the myrobalan to Palermo. I have given to ʿAbd al-Salām[20] all the specifications concerning our shipments to these cities. May God grant safety to all of them.

I have transmitted your letters to Masarra ("Happiness") and he has already answered you. Let me know what should be done in this matter.

The ships are ready to set sail. They wait only until the heavy warship will be repaired.[21] This is what kept them until this time. May God grant them a safe passage.

God willing, you will receive additional letters from me with all the details and all the news coming in; may God let us hear good news.

I have written this in a hurry on the evening of Friday (Thursday evening);[22] please, my lord, excuse this lack of details. (Added in small letters:) As I have written, I shall inform ʿAbd al-Salām about my shipments and I have already informed him about all I have loaded.[23]

[18] A Jewish family name, common throughout the centuries.

[19] This shipowner from Spain (see n. 8, above), had done business with the addressee, but not paid him yet.

[20] A Muslim factotum of the recipient. Larger Jewish businesses, like that of Ibn ʿAwkal or the Tustarīs, always had among their employees a Muslim, not because they believed in desegregation, but because it was practical, for instance, if a boat carrying shipments for them arrived on a Sabbath. A slave could not be used for such and similar tasks, since a slave was bound to observe the Sabbath like his master. Salām, peace, is one of the names of God.

[21] The convoy of the merchantmen was accompanied by a flotilla of the navy consisting of an *usṭūl*, or heavy warship, Greek *stolos*, and light galleys. See no. 70, below.

[22] In the Middle East, the day begins in the evening (cf. Genesis 1:5, etc.: "There was evening and there was morning, one day"). The mail couriers seem to have left Alexandria for Fustat on Friday. See *Med. Soc.*, I, 287.

[23] The second item listed the expenses (transport to the boat, customs,

I extend kindest greetings to your noble self, to my lords, the elders (the addressee's two brothers), and to my lord, the illustrious elder Abu Sa'īd Sahlawayh b. Ḥayyīm.[24]

(Address, right side:)

(To) his excellency, my lord, the elder Abū Naṣr ("Victorious") al-Faḍl b. Sahl ("Bounty, son of Ease"), al-Dustarī.[25]

(Left side:)

From Ṣadaqa, son of 'Ayyāsh, (may his) s(oul) r(est in peace), who is grateful for his kindnesses.

70 NAVAL ESCORT AND OTHER PRECAUTIONS

Alexandria to Fustat
Ca. 1025

This letter, like the preceding one, reflects a war situation: the spring convoy of ships sailing from Alexandria, Egypt, to the West, again is accompanied by a heavy warship and galleys manned with soldiers. But this time, all goods go to Tunisia, none to Sicily. This would fit the crisis of 1025-1027, when the Byzantines invaded the island, which then was in Muslim hands.[1]

One single shipment of 180 bales (sec. C), worth perhaps half a million dollars, is the largest noted by me thus far in the Geniza papers. Its proprietor was the merchant prince Joseph Ibn 'Awkal, the recipient of our letter, about whom the introduction to no. 1,

---

freight, considerations for the officials, and sailors, etc.) for each bale and the names of the persons to whom they were entrusted. The first contained descriptions of their content, for goods arriving from Fustat often had to be repacked for the overseas transport.

24 This great Karaite banker, who is repeatedly mentioned in connection with the Tustarīs, must have been a close relative of Abū Naṣr, the addressee, probably his brother-in-law.

25 With *D* instead of *T*, because polite style derived this family name not from its real origin, Tustar, the Iranian city, but from the Persian word *dastūr*, high dignitary.

---

1 A. R. Lewis, *Naval Power and Trade in the Mediterranean, A.D. 500-1100*, Princeton, 1951, pp. 194-196.

above, may be consulted. His representative in Alexandria, the writer of the letter, was a nephew of Mūsā (Moses) Ibn al-Majjānī, whom we have met before and meet here again as Ibn 'Awkal's agent in Qayrawān, then the capital of Tunisia (see no. 1, sec. F). Four other letters to Ibn 'Awkal by this Alexandrian representative have been preserved.[2]

University Library, Cambridge, Taylor-Schechter
Collection, TS 13 J 17, f. 3.[3]

(Four lines of introduction, which contain also the date: 27th of Iyyar, approximately mid-May.)

A. Merchantmen and warships ready for sailing

You know, my lord, from my preceding letters that not a single bale of ours has remained on land and that all the bales in the ships are in the best places. I ask God to guarantee their safe arrival for us.

We have heard pleasing news from the West; for, by God, my lord, there had been many hideous rumors about Qayrawān, and every man added his own version, so that we had been very much upset. I ask God to let us hear good news from them, but we shall have no peace of mind, until their letters have been received, confirming that the city is safe.[4] I ask God that it will be so.

The ships, my lord, are in the last stage of preparations. Not a single soldier charged with their protection has remained on land. They have already loaded their water and provisions and are waiting now for the completion of the warship; they will set it afloat and sail, and the boats (of the merchants) will sail with them (the soldiers). The day after the writing of this letter the galleys[5] will be set afloat, for today they have completed their repair.

[2] In addition to the three noted in *Tarbiz* 36 (1967), 369: BM Or 5563 C 19; Shaked, *Bibliography*, p. 178.

[3] Ed. S. D. Goitein, *Tarbiz* 36 (1967), 372-376, trans. Stillman, *East-West Relations* (see no. 1, n. 5, above), pp. 296-302.

[4] Read *bi-salāmatihā* (in the printed text *t* is omitted). See n. 20, below.

[5] Ar. *al-qaṭā'i*. The galleys, which were propelled by both oars and sails, moved swiftly and therefore could leave some time after the convoy and the heavy warship, *uṣṭūl* (see no. 69, n. 21), or if necessary, before, in order to explore the situation.

B. Letters sent in different boats

I wrote to M. Abū Sa'īd Khalaf b. Ya'qūb ("The Fortunate, Substitute, son of Jacob")[6]—may God keep him—a letter in four copies, sending each copy with coreligionists on different boats: namely, one with Salāma Ibn Abī Khalīl on the boat of al-Ba'shūshī;[7] another, on the boat of al-Andalusī,[8] with Sahlān, may God keep him;[9] a third copy, on the boat of Ibn al-Qaddār ("Mr. Potter")[10]—may God keep him—I gave to the owner of the boat, for no Jewish person traveled on it; the fourth, I gave to Salār ("Chieftain, leader"),[11] the "boy" (employee) of Ibn al-Ṣāhila ("The woman who neighs like a horse"). I instructed all our coreligionists, may God keep them, to watch carefully the seventy bales and one barqalū until they will deliver them in safety into the hands of Khalaf b. Ya'qūb, the Andalusian.[12]

C. Instructions to Ibn 'Awkal's agent in Qayrawān

I also sent a letter in five copies to Qayrawān, to my mother's brother, may God support him. I copied the letters which I shall send to you, my lord.[13] The letters indicated by you, twelve in all, were given by me to Wad'a ("Cowrie shell"),[14] may God keep him. I shall wrap up the remaining letters and send them with our coreligionists on five different boats.

6 Representative of merchants in al-Mahdiyya, the port city of Qayrawān. About this prominent Spanish Jew see *Med. Soc.*, II, 60, 61.

7 In another letter to Ibn 'Awkal (Mosseri L 52, l. 9, *Tarbiz* 37 [1968], 50), this boat wintered in the port of Alexandria and was repaired there. The name is derived from *ba'shūsh*, probably a Maghrebi version of *ba'ṣūṣ*, tail, etc.

8 The Spaniard. See no. 69, n. 8, above.

9 Possibly Sahlān b. Abraham, leader of the Iraqian Jewish community of Fustat, after the death of his father in 1032. See Mann, *Jews in Egypt*, I, 82-83, and passim.

10 Frequently mentioned.

11 This Persian word should be spelled Sālār.

12 A list of persons to whom the various bales had been entrusted was included in one of the preceding letters of the writer, which are referred to at the beginning of paragraph A, above.

13 Letters which had arrived in Alexandria from abroad were copied before being forwarded to Fustat.

14 A business agent who was legally a slave.

Likewise, I wrote five letters to M. Abū Zikrī Yaḥyā,[15] may God keep him, and informed him about all I had sent to al-Mahdiyya this year, a total of 179 bales and two barqalūs,[16] specifying the boats, the advances on the freight collected for them, and similar matters. I ask God to mercifully grant them a safe passage.

I have asked my uncle, may God preserve his honored position, to send his son M. Abū Zikrī Yaḥyā to al-Mahdiyya as soon as our bales would arrive, to receive them all, to sell them in al-Mahdiyya during the height of the business season[17] and send all the proceeds to my uncle in Qayrawān. I have asked the latter to buy for my lord all the goods you have ordered, such as lead, wax, brocade, textiles, saffron, etc.

D. Financial arrangements. Conclusion

I have already informed my lord, may God preserve his honored position, that I owed 30 dinars on account of the advances on the freight and that I had taken a *suftaja* of this amount from Ibn ʿAbd al-Qudra ("Slave of [God's] Majesty").[18] I also took the 10 dinars which were with Salāma,[19] may God keep him, and made payments with them.

All the ships are ready to sail—may God grant them a safe passage. I intended to send Salāma, when I learned that the ruler of

[15] The son of the uncle of the writer, Mūsā al-Majjānī. The letter translated in no. 18, above, was written by Yaḥyā about fifteen years later.

[16] This shows that another convoy had left Alexandria for Tunisia a very short time before. Ships did not sail before the very end of April.

[17] Ar. *fī nafs al-mawsim*. Merchants often adopted an opposite course, keeping their goods until later in the year. Intelligence must have reached Alexandria that in the West there was a great demand for Egyptian flax. Perhaps by European traders? This also explains why, despite a threat of war, such huge quantities were shipped.

[18] For *suftaja* see no. 67, n. 1, above. Stillman's rendering "cashier's check" is more to the point than the usual "bill of exchange." The banker Ibn ʿAbd al-Qudra, who issued the suftaja, was a Muslim.

[19] One of the Ar. names corresponding to Heb. Solomon. The man was a factotum of Ibn ʿAwkal.

Qayrawān had been defeated.[20] There was great confusion[21] here in the city and I was afraid that [. . .] and there were many bad rumors. (A few more disconnected words follow; the remainder, probably not more than two or three lines, is torn away. Of the greetings in the margin only the name of Ibn 'Awkal's youngest son, Abū Sa'īd,[22] is preserved.)

(Address, right side:)

To his excellency, my lord, the illustrious elder, Abu 'l-Faraj Joseph, son of Ya'qūb Ibn 'Awkal, (may his) s(oul) r(est in peace). May God make permanent his honored position, eminence, happiness, and prosperity.

(Left side:)

From his servant,[23] Ephraim, son of Ismā'īl, (may his) s(oul) r(est in peace), al-Jawharī.[24] (To be delivered) in his office[25] in Fustat, God willing.

71 SHIPWRECK IN WAR TIME

From Palermo, Sicily, to Damsīs, Egypt

Ca. 1025

The writer of this letter had lost everything in shipwreck, and when he finally arrived in Palermo, Sicily, found that part or all of his property had been alienated. His state of utmost privation was aggravated by the Byzantine attack on Sicily, which threatened

20 The rumors referred to here and in sec. A, above, were well founded. The mighty Berber tribe of the Zenāta (or Zanāta) had launched formidable attacks against the ruler of Tunisia, but were finally defeated in the course of the Muslim year ending in March 1025 (see Idris, *Zirides*, p. 162). The travelers arriving in Alexandria with the first boats which had sailed from al-Mahdiyya, brought the good tidings.

21 The manuscript has *dahj* (see Dozy, *Supplément*, I, 465*b*), which is related to the more common *dahsh*.

22 His name occurs also in Bodl. Libr. MS Heb. d 80, f. 43*v* in the fragment of a legal document in Ar. characters.

23 Absolutely exceptional.

24 Dealer in gems, a family name.

25 See no. 1, introduction, above. Ar. *bi-majlisihi*, lit., the place where one sits and receives guests. Meaning probably: not to his home.

to sever the communications between his temporary domicile, Palermo, and his home in Egypt, where he had left his young wife and little boy. Despite this dire situation we do not read a single word of lament or despair; all the letter contains is a succinct factual report, followed by practical instructions, culminating in the writer's main concern, the education and upbringing of his little boy.

The approximate date of our letter is provided by the reference to an impending enemy attack on Palermo and the name of the recipient, Isma'īl b. Abraham (or Barhūn) Tāhertī, who lived at the end of the tenth through the first third of the eleventh century. Letter no. 12, and the account from the year 1024, no. 63, above, are addressed to him. Thus the dreaded enemy attack must refer to the Byzantine invasion of Sicily in 1025-1026.[1]

Isma'īl Tāhertī, a native of Qayrawān, spent many years in Egypt, where he acted as a kind of representative of his compatriots, taking care of their affairs in that country.

Damsīs, whereto this letter was sent, was a small town on the right arm of the Nile, which was frequented by Maghrebi merchants who supervised the cutting, combing, and packing of flax destined for export. It seems even that a letter from Damsīs, written by one of these merchants, a nephew of the great merchant prince Joseph Ibn 'Awkal, makes mention of the stay of Isma'īl Tāhertī in that locality. For he writes: "I sought the advice of Ibn Tāhertī."[2] To be sure, several Tāhertīs commuted between Tunisia and Egypt. But since our letter shows Isma'īl stationed for some time in Damsīs, it is likely that he is meant in the letter sent from there.

Joseph b. Samuel, the writer of our letter, as indicated by the handwriting, style, and content, was a young man from the Muslim West who had settled in Egypt and married there. In addition to part of a house acquired there he possessed one in Palermo, no doubt because he used to commute between Egypt and the West. After suffering shipwreck he decided to settle in Sicily and asked his wife to follow him there. As was sometimes done, he had given her a conditional bill of divorce, in order to enable her to marry again in case he perished on one of his travels, by acts of God or men, without leaving an eyewitness of his death. He was doubtful

[1] See no. 70, n. 1, above.

[2] Jewish Theological Seminary, New York, E. N. Adler Collection 2727, f. 41, l. 6, ed. S. D. Goitein, *Tarbiz* 37 (1968), 166.

whether his wife would agree to leave Egypt, for wives were normally reluctant to join their husbands in another town, let alone country, where they lacked the protection of their fathers or brothers.

It is remarkable that our writer decided to settle in Sicily despite the Byzantine menace. (Since he was prepared to travel to Egypt in order to bring his wife to Palermo, he was apparently not afraid of a new voyage by sea.) Obviously, the inhabitants of the Sicilian capital were confident that the Byzantine attack would be repulsed or would peter out. Events proved that these expectations were justified.

University Library, Cambridge, University Collection, Or 1080 J 22.

My elder and master, may God prolong your life and make your welfare and happiness permanent. May he augment his bounty and gifts granted to you.

I am writing you from Palermo[3] on the 6th of Tishri; may God make this a blessed year for me and for you and for all Israel.[4]

What you wish to know: I was shipwrecked in Zahlaq, between Surt (Syrta, Sirte) and Hawwāra (Lebda),[5] and came out of it without a dinar or even a dirhem and no garment to wear; I arrived naked in Tripoli. By God, had I not met there a Jew who owed me a qinṭār of wax (sent to him) from Zawīla[6] and with whom I agreed on a price of 5 dinars,[7] which I received from him and with which I bought clothing and provisions, I would have been destroyed and forced to have recourse to philanthropy.[8]

[3] Siqillīya must here be translated with Palermo (and not Sicily), since it is later referred to as "town."

[4] The Jewish New Year is celebrated on the first and second days of the month of Tishri and falls mostly in September.

[5] Hawwāra (or Huw[w]āra, see *EI*², s.v.) is the name of a widely scattered Berber people; according to Ibn Duqmāq, v, 14, many of them settled in Lebda, Libya (see no. 36, above), and perhaps this town was called after them. In TS 18 J 3, f. 19, l. 8 (dated 1089), Lebda seems to be referred by that name.

[6] A suburb of Al-Mahdīyya.

[7] Compare this remark from a letter from Qayrawān: "The market price of a qinṭār of wax is 6 3/8 dinars. But we got it for 5 dinars less 5 qīrāṭs, because there were no ships (for export)." Bodl. MS Heb. d 65 (Cat. 2877), f. 17, ll. 6-7.

[8] Text: *wa-nkashaft*.

Arriving in Palermo, I found that a man from Barqa had pulled down my small house[9] and built there another. I quarreled[10] with him, but, by God, I had no dinar or even a dirhem to spend (on a lawsuit). Then I did not find my brother here so that I could not get from him part of what he owes me.

I sent you ten pounds of silk with Ḥayyīm b. Saʿāda and sent you also 6 dinars gold, numbering 6 1/4.[11] With you I left 2 dinars and with them in the house 1 dinar and the olive oil I bought from you. As you know, 10 dinars are due the girl[12] as her second installment (of her marriage portion). I wrote her a *bill of divorce* fearing the vicissitudes of fate, nor do I know whether I shall be able to return to them in the course of two or even three years, for this town is menaced by enemy attack, and, at present, I do not have a thing.

I left with you promissory notes of: the "Son of the Swollen Woman," 6 1/2 dinars; Isaac Qābisī,[13] 1 1/2 dinars; Ḥayyīm Ibn Jāsūs,[14] three qinṭārs of tragacanth gum;[15] all this besides what is owed me by Muslims.[16] Collect these debts and keep the proceeds for the *alimony* of the boy. If she accepts the *divorce*, I shall send every year the *alimony* for the boy. But if she prefers not to accept the *divorce*, deal with this matter cautiously in a way deserving my thanks: ask her whether she is prepared to settle with me in Sicily. (In case she does), let her confirm this by oath and inform me accordingly. I shall then sell my apartment[17] and bring her here

[9] This might imply that a larger house in the neighborhood of the smaller one also belonged to the writer. But it could mean also that he possessed only that small house.

[10] Text: *mutashārir*. Dozy, *Supplément*, I, 739*a*, has form 7 in this meaning.

[11] He sent 25 (Sicilian) quarter dinars. The silk was worth about 20 dinars. See *Med. Soc.*, I, 222.

[12] His wife. The second installment was due at divorce or death of husband.

[13] Family name derived from the town of Gabes in southern Tunisia. This man, Isaac (b. Abraham) al-Qābiṣi, bought in about 1044 a house in Qayrawān from a lady divorced by an Ibn Jāsūs (see next note). Bodl. MS Heb. c 28 (Cat. 2876), f. 41, ed. S. Assaf, *Tarbiz* 9 (1938), 214.

[14] "The Spy"—a Maghrebi family name often found in the Geniza at this time.

[15] Ar. kathīrā (here, *ā* is missing). A medical plant much traded in the Geniza period. In TS 8 J 21, f. 29 (ca. 1050) the price of 4 1/4 dinars for a qinṭār was regarded as bad. Thus the quantity sent here was worth about 15 dinars.

[16] In Damsīs. For these he presumably wrote to a Muslim business friend.

[17] Text: *rbʿy*, which could mean also "my quarter," namely of a house.

together with my boy. By God, I did not write her the *bill of divorce* because I do not love her, but because I was afraid of the punishment of the Creator.[18]

And, o God, o God, my lord, the little boy! Concern yourself with him in accordance with your [religiosity], so well known to me. When he becomes stronger, let him pass his time with a teacher.[19] I shall write to you and i[nform you about my situation]. By God, at this moment I have nothing, [. . .] But as soon as [. . .].[20]

(Address on verso, which is blank otherwise.)

To my elder and master Abī[21] Ibrahīm Isma'īl b. Abraham, may God be his protector.

From Joseph b. Samuel, known as al-Dny.[22] *Many greetings!*

To Damsīs, if God will.[23]

72 REPORT ABOUT BOATS EXPECTED FROM THE WEST

Alexandria

Ca. 1050-1065

The letter was written on the third day of Av, which, in the period concerned, and practically always, fell in the month of July, when the seafaring season was at its height. A total of over 52 ships is reported here as being on their way from the Muslim West to Alexandria or as having already arrived (see n. 9). Most of the ships mentioned by name are known from other Geniza letters.

18 This is a religious alternate for the "vicissitudes of fate," mentioned in the same context before. A violent death was normally regarded as a punishment for a sin.

19 Instead of wasting time playing in the streets.

20 Only a few words seem to have been lost. Obviously, the writer wanted to emphasize that, at the moment, he was unable to pay for tuition.

21 This might be an attempt at correct Arabic grammar or a fixed usage (Abī for Abū) in some Maghrebi circles.

22 Probably for al-D'ny, that is, Dānī, a family name derived from the town of Denia, Spain.

23 Published first in *Archivio Storico per la Sicilia Orientale* 67 (1971), 20-23, but thoroughly revised and adapted.

The recipient of the letter was Nahray b. Nissīm in Fustat (about him see *Med. Soc.*, I, p. 153-154, and nos. 5, 29-35, 64, 66, 67, above), its writer Ibrāhīm b. Farāḥ (Ibn al-) Iskandarānī, who operated a mail agency in Alexandria (see *Med. Soc.*, I, p. 304, and no. 28, n. 24, above). Like the imperial postmasters, the commercial mail agents served also as transmitters of news.

University Library, Cambridge, Taylor-Schechter
Collection, TS 13 J 15, f. 9.[1]

I am writing to you, my lord and master, . . . from Alexandria, on the 3rd of Av, may God let this month be a most propitious time for you.[2] . . . I received your letter, . . . in which you announced to me the arrival of my letter to you. Meanwhile I have written two other letters to you—I hope they have arrived—in which I informed you about the arrival of the *Shāmī*,[3] one of the ships of Ibn Abī 'Aqīl.[4]

The day before yesterday, on Monday, several boats arrived, among them that of Muhammad al-Ghazzāl ("Spinner"),[5] the proprietor of the small Shāmī barge. They had set sail from Tobruk[6] twenty-five days ago. The passengers told me that there were fourteen ships in Tobruk, four Sicilian[7] boats in Shaqqat al-Wa'r ("The Rugged Crevice") and seven in Rās Tīnī ("Cape of the Figs"),[8]

[1] *Nahray* 61, ll. 1-19 and *verso*, ll. 4-8.

[2] Av is a month of mourning, and the proper blessing would have been "may God convert it into a month of joy," as in many other Geniza letters.

[3] Shām was the region comprising approximately the present day states of Syria, Lebanon, Israel, and Jordan. The meaning of the term Shāmī in relation to a ship meant that its home port was Tyre, Lebanon, or any other of the sixteen or so more prominent harbors on the east coast of the Mediterranean.

[4] Ibn Abī (so spelled here) 'Aqīl was an affluent Muslim judge of Tyre whose ships, frequenting Sicily, Tunisia, and Egypt, are often mentioned in the Geniza. See *Med. Soc.*, I, 296, 310-311.

[5] Mentioned, e.g., in TS Arabic Box 18(1), f. 101, ll. 5-6, as arriving in Alexandria from the West.

[6] Tobruk, of World War II fame, is a small port in eastern Libya. Strong winds blowing from the east (see n. 19, below) must have accounted for the extraordinarily long time spent on the comparatively short passage from Tobruk to Alexandria.

[7] The word is only partly visible.

[8] So also in TS 12.372*v*, l. 17, and other Geniza letters. On modern maps of Libya: Ra's at-tīn. The name originally was perhaps a Greek word.

among them[9] Ibn al-Shārī,[10] Ibn al-Baladī,[11] Mufaḍḍal,[12] Ibn al-Aṣfāṭī ("Chest maker"), the Nile barge, Ibn al-Barr ("The Godly"), and Ibn al-ʿŪdī ("Trader in odoriferous wood").[13] May God, the exalted, in his mercy grant them an easy passage.

A man arrived with them[14] who had sailed from Tripoli in a barge carrying oil to Barnīk,[15] which got stuck in Bandariyya.[16] He brought good tidings from your family and reported that prices in Ifrīqiya were very low: 25 thumna of wheat cost in Qayrawān 1 dinar, and oil from one-half dinar upwards.[17] He had left behind twenty ships loading cargo in al-Mahdiyya and five in Sfax. Reports from Sicily were now better than they had been before. The man had traveled ten days from Tripoli to Bandariyya and twenty days from there to Alexandria.

I have no doubt that God the exalted—if God will—will bring

[9] This must refer to the ships sighted, not those already arrived, for them the writer would not have to rely on the report of one single unnamed man. Jewish passengers frequently traveled on the ships named.

[10] "The Buyer," or rather, "The Quarrelsome" (TS 20.122, ll. 16, 20, and *verso*, ll. 16-17); arriving in Palermo and sailing from Mazara, Sicily, to Egypt.

[11] *Balad* means "place," "town." Several localities bear this name.

[12] Mufaḍḍal, a shipowner from Haifa, possessed both a *qārib*, or barge (see *Med. Soc.*, I, 305), and a ship, *markab*. They appear together in TS 16.163, l. 14, and *verso*, l. 9.

[13] Frequently mentioned as sailing on the route Palermo-al-Mahdiyya-Sfax-Alexandria.

[14] The ships that arrived on Monday, as reported before. The writer mentioned only one of those ships by name, because the others probably did not carry goods in which the recipient of the letter was interested.

[15] The ancient (Greek) Berenike, today Benghazi, the main city of eastern Libya. This district was called Cyrenaica in ancient times and Barqa in the Middle Ages.

[16] Presumably because of the adverse winds (see n. 6, above). A letter written about half a century later (ULC Or 1080 J 178*v*, l. 1), reports that all the ships on their way from al-Mahdiyya to Alexandria had to take refuge in Bandariyya and were waiting "for rescue by God," that is, propitious winds. A sign over the name of that place in ULC Or 1080 J 178 might mean that it was pronounced Bundariyya.

[17] Wheat was measured, not weighed. According to Hinz, *Masse*, p. 52, the *thumn(a)* contained 6,318 liter. Thus, 25 thumna would correspond to approximately 2 1/2 American bushels of wheat, for which 1 dinar would indeed be an extremely low price. Several different measures of oil are mentioned in the Geniza papers of this period. The writer either forgot to specify or assumed the recipient knew to which measurement he referred.

these ships here soon in safety. I shall keep you informed about any new happenings. May they be good.

(Several smaller business matters.)

Some people say that the barge of Yusr al-ʿAttāl ("Ease, the Porter") is coming back.[18] If it does, I shall take receipt of what you have in it, if God will. Of all the other ships no one has reported that they are coming back. May God, the exalted, make it easy for all in his mercy. The wind we had a short time ago was of no avail for the ships, for all those in which you have goods have not yet moved from their moorings.[19] May God ease in his mercy.

73 AN ATTACK BY THE ENEMY'S NAVY

Postscript to a letter in the hand of
Ibrāhīm b. Faraḥ al-Iskandarānī
Ca. 1060

Of the letter itself, only the end, providing no self-contained information, has been preserved. For the writer see no. 72, above.

University Library, Cambridge, Taylor-Schechter
Collection, TS 8 J 24, f. 21, ll. 20 - verso, end.

Then there happened something which I am not able to describe to you. It is not something which (often) occurs. The people felt safe as if they were in their own city. I have never seen nor even imagined what happened. I had rolled out my sleeping carpet and spread my bedding, as if I had been at home. My money bag was under my head and I felt safe and calm—until hell broke loose.

Ten galleys had penetrated the roadstead, each carrying 100 warriors, part of whom disembarked, while the others remained aboard. People said there were 200 galleys. This happened when the moon rose, but the sky was overcast. Land and sea became crammed. They

[18] The returning of boats to the port of embarking was a calamity very frequently mentioned in the Geniza. See *Med. Soc.*, 1, 322-323.

[19] In a previous letter, the writer had reported that a favorable east wind was blowing in Alexandria. But before the ships carrying most of Nahray's goods started moving, the wind had already ceased.

threw firebrands into all the ships to burn them, but the fire did not catch.

(Added in larger letters:)

Praise be to God that the end was good! Thanks to God, the exalted! *And Peace.* Accept special greetings for your noble self. And greetings to my lord, the Rāv.

(Continued in writer's regular script:)

They cut loose the ship of the Damascene and towed it behind them. But the wind was against them, so they turned it back, took out all they wished and left it on the rough ground. The two rudders of the ship of the employee of Ibn Shiblūn were on its stern and without sailyards and sails. The rudders of the ships of the 'Aṭṭār ("Perfumer") and of the Khammār ("Wine-seller") were on land. All this was the cause that they could not take them. The firebrands thrown into them were not effective, for the wind there was not strong. Finally the people quenched the fire, working in shifts. But I am unable to describe what happened. *And Peace!* I threw the firebrands into the sea with my own hand!

74 THE HORRORS AND AMENITIES OF TRAVEL

Sicily to Egypt
Ca. 1140

Despite the horrors experienced by the writer and his family on the short voyage from the town of Tunis to Sicily, he invites his brother in Egypt to make the long journey to Palermo "for both pleasure and business," *nazāhan wa-tijāratan*. Life in the Norman capital appeared to him attractive, economically and otherwise, after it had become so miserable in the once-flourishing country of Ifrīqiya ("Africa," designating present-day Tunisia and some adjacent districts).

The fragment of an earlier letter by the same writer (TS 8 J 23, f. 13), establishes his full name and provides more of his personal history. That letter, like the one translated here, was addressed to his elder brother Abu 'l-Barakāt ("Blessings"). He himself was called Abū Sa'īd ("Blissful") b. Abu 'l-Ḥasan al-Abzārī ("Dealer in Seeds," the family name), and, as his beautiful hand and good style indicate, was a well-educated man. The earlier letter (TS 8 J 23, f. 13) tells us that Abū Sa'īd had traveled from Egypt on a Christian ship, which met the warship (or fleet, *uṣṭūl*) that had conquered Jerba. This, no doubt, refers to the conquest of that Tunisian island by the admiral of the Norman king Roger II in 1135, an event echoed in several Geniza papers.[1] Abū Sa'īd and his non-Christian fellow travelers were horrified, but no harm befell them. He arrived safely in Bijāya (Bougie), Algeria, where he did profitable business. He intended to return to Egypt that same year, but "the Rūm rammed and toppled the ship of the Laqantī [that is, one belonging to a man from Alicante in Muslim Spain], "and a war was on," *wa-waqa 'at as-sayf*. Whether, as a result of that obstacle Abū Sa'īd remained in the West, married there and had two children, as evident from our letter, or whether he had commuted between Egypt and the West some years between the two letters discussed here, cannot be said.

Our letter, sent from Palermo to Fustat, reflects the situation around 1140, when the Normans cut Ifrīqiya from its life line, the trade route to Egypt. For a merchant like Abū Sa'īd, who specialized in the export of Oriental spices to the West, this meant that he had nothing further to do in the countries of North Africa. The distance between the town of Tunis and the shores of Sicily is very small, but bad storms could have a devastating effect: instead of one day or so our traveler needed thirty-five to reach his goal, and most of those who had set sail simultaneously with him perished.

University Library, Cambridge, Taylor-Schechter
Collection, TS 13 J 26, f. 10.

"And say to him: All your life—peace upon you, peace upon your house, etc."[2]

"The Lord will guard you from all evil, he will guard your soul.

[1] "Today [October 14, 1136] there arrived the prisoners of Jerba," namely in Egypt, to be ransomed (TS K 6, f. 47). "The captive cantor, of the Jerba captives" (TS 10 J 15, f. 26).

[2] I Samuel 25:6. This translation is in accordance with the commentaries contemporaneous with the writer of the letter.

"The Lord will guard your going out and coming in, from this time forth and forever."[3]

To the presence of my brother, the delight of my eyes, my lord and leader, most esteemed by me, the crown of my head, and the one on whom I rely. May God prolong his life in happiness, guard and keep him and never deprive him of his good guidance.

Dear brother, may God protect and never forsake you, may he be *your help and sustainer, your support and trust from this time forth and forever.*

I entered Sicily with my family coming from Tunis because of the privations suffered there and the horrors witnessed in Ifrīqiya and also because of my longing for you. I intended to travel to Egypt via Sicily, for it is no longer possible to travel to Egypt directly from Ifrīqiya. I planned to arrive in Egypt this very year, but God had willed otherwise. The obstacle to my travel and coming to you was illness in the family, which lasted four months. By Israel's religion, my misfortune[4] forced me to spend 50 Murābiṭī dinars,[5] for the wife fell ill and also the two little ones, and God willed that one of them died, the baby, he was one and a half years old—may your life be prolonged!

Then on the voyage to Sicily I was overcome by a disaster (see n. 4, above), the like of which I have never witnessed. A great storm seized us on the sea and we were forced to land on an island called Ghumūr.[6] We stayed there for twenty days with no food other than nettles.[7] When we set out from there we did not have the look of human beings any more. The seas tormented[8] us for thirty-five days and we were regarded as lost.[9] For we set sail in four barges (*qārib*), but only ours survived. After arrival in Sicily we were so exhausted from our sufferings at sea that we were unable

[3] Psalm 121:7-8. These verses may allude to the writer's own successfully concluded adventures.

[4] The word *ḥaraka*, lit., movement, is used here and below in the sense of *événement grave*, as in the *Arabian Nights*. See Dozy, *Supplément*, I, 276*a*.

[5] The "dollars" of that period. See *Med. Soc.*, I, index, s.v.

[6] Presumably one of the little islands between Tunisia and Sicily.

[7] Nettles: *ḥurrayq*. The tender stalks of the nettles are edible during springtime. As the date of our letter shows, this voyage was undertaken approximately in April in order to catch the boats going from Sicily to Egypt in May.

[8] Lit., "the seas wanted to get at us," *tamannatna 'l-biḥār*.

[9] These words are repeated in the text, albeit in different order.

to eat bread or to understand what was said to us for a full month.

This is the reason which prevented me from coming to Egypt this year. After all we have endured this year we are not prone to travel. You must see us with your own eyes; no description can do justice to our state.[10]

Furthermore, it is now three years since I have seen a letter or an answer from you. I am very much upset, and this, too, makes me reluctant to come. Dear brother, by God, do not withhold your letters from me, for I am waiting for them. I am staying here in Sicily, by God, do not withhold your letters from me[11] . . . for I am yearning after you and my mind is very much perturbed since the time your letters ceased to come. Write also about the poll tax.[12]

If you intend to move, the best thing is to come to Sicily (or, Palermo), for the spices of the Orient sell here well. Thus, it will be for both pleasure and business. We shall help one another in enhancing the prestige of the family[13] and shall be happy with one another.

(Greetings to four persons and to "my paternal aunts," which suggests that the family had been settled in Egypt for at least two generations.)

This letter was written on the New Moon day of the month of Sivan.[14] By God, I need not entreat you again to answer quickly, if God wills. Peace upon you and God's mercy and his blessings. *And may your welfare increase forever and never decrease. Amen.*

My son Abu 'l-Ḥasan[15] sends greetings to you all, and so does the dweller of my house[16]—to everyone, young and old.[17]

[10] Text: *lays al-ḳhabar ḳal-ʿiyān,* a proverbial expression.

[11] Such repetitions are frequently found in similar contexts. One word is illegible here.

[12] Although the writer had been away from Egypt for at least four years, he was afraid that he was still registered as resident, and, at arrival there, would have to pay the poll tax for the years of his absence, although he had certainly paid the tax at his domicile in the Muslim West.

[13] Text: *wa-nataʿāwanū fī rufūʿ al-ahl.* I am not entirely sure about the correctness of the translation; *rafaʿ* means "move someone up in the row of seats of honor."

[14] Falling in the month of May.

[15] So called after his grandfather.

[16] His wife.

[17] Published first in *Archivio Storico per la Sicilia Orientale* 67 (1971), 24-27. Revised here.

(The address on the reverse side is largely effaced, but the main elements are recognizable:)

To my brother . . . Abu 'l-Barakāt, son of . . . al-Abzārī . . . Fustat. From his brother Abū Sa'īd.

75 SKIPPING ALONG THE COAST

From Messina, Sicily, to Mazara, Sicily

Ca. 1153

The warm invitation extended by the India trader Abraham Yijū to his family in September 1149 (no. 41, above) did not find immediate response. Letters were exchanged, but no action was taken. Finally, after a lapse of about four years, we find here Yijū's nephew, Peraḥyā[1] b. Joseph, on the first leg of his trip to Egypt, where, again after considerable time, he finally married his cousin, the only remaining child of the India trader.

Peraḥyā's family had left Tunisia, probably in 1148, when it was partly occupied by the Normans, and settled in Mazara, a port on the southwestern coast of Sicily. During the eleventh century, Mazara was a lively entrepôt, serving as a bridgehead to Tunisia and a terminal for ships going to the Levant. After the Norman conquest of Sicily, however, and the subsequent severing of close relations between Tunisia and the island, Mazara lost its importance as a seaport. Peraḥyā had to look for another way to get to Egypt. He turned first north overland to Palermo and from there went by boat to Messina on the east coast of Sicily. This voyage is described in our letter.

With a craving for adventure—attested in the Geniza for other young men, too—Peraḥyā's younger brother Moses insisted on accompanying him to the foreign country.[2] After some mishaps—Moses was captured by pirates—the two finally arrived and were later

[1] No such Heb. name exists in the Bible. This is one of the pseudo-biblical names invented during the Geniza period and I suspect that the verb contained in it was understood as Ar. *faraḥ* ("Joy in God") rather than Heb. *peraḥ*, "flower," which makes no sense.

[2] See, for instance, no. 57, above.

followed by the rest of the family. Many letters concerning this family have been preserved in the Geniza, which is to be explained by the fact that the youngest brother, referred to in this letter, became a judge of the rabbinical court in Old Cairo.

The writing is effaced in several places, but can mostly be restored by reasonable surmise.

Jewish Theological Seminary, New York, E. N. Adler Collection 151 (2557).

This is to inform you—may God . . . keep you—that we arrived in Messina in safety and good health—for which we must thank God, and not ascribe it to our own merit or good deeds—after we had passed eight days on our journey. For a rainstorm kept us back in Baqṭas (Patti).[3] We paid the Christian skipper of the boat a fare of 2 rubāʿīs[4] less one-quarter and stipulated that he should let us disembark at the lighthouse near Messina[5]—the town is, indeed, visible from it.

We embarked on Friday night, in the company of a Jew, a Kohen, from Salerno, and were at sea until . . . day, when we arrived at Baqṭas (Patti). There, however, a rainstorm befell us, and we stayed until Friday. We boarded the boat again in the morning and arrived at a place called Mīlāṣ (Milazzo).[6] There, the above-mentioned Jew, along with Isaac, the son-in-law of Giovanna's son, disembarked and continued their travel by land. The Christian skipper told us that we would not reach the lighthouse—the place where we had agreed that he would let us off—before Sabbath[7] and added that we could disembark there whenever we arrived, but that he could not take a shortcut. As I was afraid of desecrating the Sabbath, and of other things (as well), I took another boat for two-thirds of a rubāʿī, and we arrived in Messina on Saturday.

On the following Sunday, I inquired about my uncle Mevassēr[8] and found him there. He did not fall short (of his family duties),

[3] A town and a gulf of the same name on the northern shore of Sicily.

[4] A quarter of a gold dinar, the standard coin of Sicily at that time.

[5] Spelled here, as in other Geniza papers, *msyny*, which indicates that the name was pronounced Messīnī or Messēnī by the writer.

[6] A town on the eastern end of the gulf of Patti, the ancient Mylae.

[7] The Sabbath begins on Friday evening with nightfall.

[8] This is Abraham Yijū's brother, to whom no. 41, above, is addressed.

and we stayed with him. Then I inquired about Ben Siṭlūn and Ben Baruch[9] and found them. Ben Siṭlūn said: "I shall take care of your fare, and you will go up (i.e., to Egypt) with me, if God wills." Then I consulted my uncle and Ben Siṭlū(n) about Moses' travel, and they said: "There is nothing to be gained by it. He had better go back to his father." But he insisted on setting out with me, so that he would not come back empty-handed. Thus I am uncertain with regard to him, and I have not received a letter from you giving instructions, or about your well-being, as might be expected. Now, please do not neglect to send a detailed letter with information about your well-being and that of my mother and my brother, and do not worry about us, for we are well.

Ben Siṭlūn let me copy the commentary on 'Eruvin by Rabbēnū Nissīm for him,[10] and most of the people in the town have asked me to serve as a schoolmaster in his house, for the town lacks everything. Were not the town unfit for you to live in (you could find a good job here). However, the town is mediocre; one cannot live here. (. . . Here, it requires an) effort to study and to pray. Since we arrived, there has been no public prayer in the afternoon and the evening, while the morning prayer is said before dawn; at daybreak, they are already through with it. If we lived here . . . , we would miss the prayer; and it is impossible to walk in the streets here because of the (dir)t.[11]

(After dealing with some sundry items, the writer asks his parents not to worry too much about their absent sons and, in particular, not to fast too much for them—it was customary to fast as a means of enhancing the efficacy of prayer for relatives on travel. He then

[9] Business friends of his uncle, the India trader. The usual spelling of the first name was *Ṣiṭrūn* (citron), a family name still common among so-called Sefaradi, or Spanish, Jews.

[10] The frequently quoted book of the great Tunisian Jewish scholar is lost, except for three pages found in the Geniza, which are indeed in the handwriting of our Peraḥyā! Obviously, they were his first attempt before he made the copy mentioned here and he carried them with him to Egypt. MS ENA 2936, ed. B. M. Lewin in *Jacob Freimann Jubilee Volume*, Berlin, 1937, pp. 72-80.

[11] Both Muslim and Jewish writers used to decry the low standard of their coreligionists in Sicily in Norman times. Mazara, the town to which this letter was directed, was of a different type, owing to its close connections with Tunisia (see above).

reiterates a medical prescription for his mother, which he had previously sent from Palermo, and concludes with a series of greetings, which shows that the community in Mazara must have included quite a number of scholars.)

(Address:)

To our dear father, may God keep him with his never ceasing watch, Joseph, the teacher, b. Peraḥyā Yijū, God is his protector! From his sons Peraḥyā and Moses, who are longing for him.

May salvation be near![12]

76 DIVERTED TO TARSUS

From Alexandria to Cairo
Ca. 1212

Reading this fragmentary thirteenth century letter one regrets that not more material of a similar type has been preserved. A Jewish shipowner from Alexandria, Egypt, was on his way to Cyprus. At that time the island was under Christian domination, and he, coming from a Muslim country, certainly possessed a letter of safe-conduct, permitting him to land at Cyprus and to do business there. But a storm diverted him to Tarsus, the birthplace of the apostle Paul, in southeastern Asia Minor—Turkey today, but at that time the capital of Lesser, or New, Armenia, a Christian kingdom ruled by Leon II, "The Great" (1187-1219).[1] In these unforeseen circumstances the shipowner was without protection and afraid that the king would force him to take up his residence in Tarsus instead of Alexandria. For Leon II was eager to attract the maritime trade to his city, as is known from Venetian and Genoese sources.[2]

[12] Published first in *Archivio Storico per la Sicilia Orientale* 67 (1971), and revised here.

---

[1] He received a crown from the Pope of Rome, but was recognized as king also by Byzantine and Muslim rulers. See, for instance, Jacques de Morgan, *The History of the Armenian People*, trans. E. F. Barry, Boston, 1965 (reprint), pp. 222-225.

[2] Heyd, *Commerce du Levant*, I, 369-372. At that time the river on which Tarsus is situated was still navigable and accessible to seafaring vessels. See

But a Christian business friend, most probably himself a native of Egypt,[3] helpfully secured a strong letter of safe-conduct: the writer had a good time in Tarsus and would have remained longer, had not illness forced him to hurry back to Alexandria.

The second part of the letter reports the successful treatment of the writer (most Geniza letters report the opposite) and mentions the names of four physicians, but is otherwise fragmentary.

In the third section we find ourselves again in a larger historical context. The writer recommends an "illustrious" person, "a scion of the noblest families" of Sicily, who, for reasons not indicated, had lost everything and was forced to leave his home. The community in Alexandria was unable to take care of him, for at the same time a large company had arrived from France, and the cost of their stay in the town and the expenses for their travel (to the Holy Land) put a heavy strain on public charity. It has been recognized long ago that the exodus of "300 rabbis" from France to Palestine did not happen in the one year 1211, for which it was reported, but was a more protracted process.[4] This is confirmed by several Geniza papers. Here, too, the arrival of a large group of needy travelers from France is reported as nothing very extraordinary. It was common practice to send persons whom the community of Alexandria was unable to take care of to the far more populous and richer capital. Letters to this effect have been preserved from the eleventh to the thirteenth century.

The beginning of the letter, and with it the address, which was written on the reverse side, is torn away, but not much can have been lost, since the first two lines contain the end of the introductory blessings.

University Museum, University of Pennsylvania E 16 522.

May He ḳeep your boys, the esteemed notables, the brilliant[5]

Heyd, p. 367, and G. Le Strange, *The Lands of the Eastern Caliphate* (Cambridge, 1905), p. 133.

[3] He is introduced in a way which shows that he was well known to the Cairene recipient of the letter.

[4] S. Krauss, "L'Émigration de 300 rabbins en Palestine en l'an 1211," *Revue des Études Juives* 82 (1926), 333-352; E. N. Adler, ibid. 85 (1928), 70-71.

[5] Heb. *h-mḥyrym* is a slip for *h-mhyrym*. The letter was written by a clerk.

youth, and may you be granted to see their joy and wedding. Amen, may it be ordained thus.

When I parted from your excellency, I intended to sail to the island of Cyprus, but a strong storm diverted the boat to Tarsus.[6] I was very much afraid that the king would take hold of me and detain me. Therefore the boys[7] who traveled with me went up to Fahd b. Karīm ("Cheetah panther, son of Noble-minded"), and informed him of my arrival. Fahd came on board and said to me: "Disembark, do not be afraid, the king has granted you safety." He carried with him letters of safe-conduct from the king assuring me that I was permitted to return to my place, and I found with him safeguards the like of which no one has received before. The ministers[8] were very happy with me and thought that I would remain. They made me all kinds of offers ensured by guarantees. I said to them: "Until the first of the next month." I offered[9] a sum of money to the Christians in the town; Fahdān[10] is an in-law of theirs. But the illness of which you know remained with me and I could not stay any longer [for I needed] treatment. [Four lines torn away.]

I found my paternal uncle present in Alexandria and he brought me to the physician who let me take medicine three times. I found[11] healing through it, God lit up my eyes in his bounty and goodness. I am very much indebted to the illustrious elder, the physician Abu 'l-Karam Ibn al-Wāsiṭī,[12] the son of your paternal uncle, may God let many people be like the two of you.[13] [Most of three marginal and four main lines lost.] . . . and the elder Abu 'l-Manṣūr ("Victorious"), . . . and the physician 'Abd al-Kāfī ("Servant of the All-

[6] Spelled *Tarṣūṣ* for the usual *Ṭarsūs*, i.e., with interchange of the emphatics.

[7] The writer's sons.

[8] Ar. *al-dīwān*.

[9] Ar. *a'raḍt* (fourth for first form, as often). The offer was probably for the purchase of goods.

[10] Meaning Fahd. This is an attempt at classical Arabic for *Fahdun*.

[11] Ar. *'ṣbh*, with two dots on the *h*, again a wrong attempt "to go classical."

[12] From the town of Wāsiṭ in southern Iraq. A common family name among the Jews in Egypt through three centuries. Physicians bearing the names Abu 'l-Karam and Ibn al-Wāsiṭī are mentioned in Ibn Abī Uṣaybi'a, *Biographies of the Physicians* (Cairo, 1882), I, 255-256, II, 141-142, but cannot have been identical with this one, who was Jewish.

[13] From here one gets the impression that the recipient, too, was a physician.

sufficient"), . . . the physician 'Abd al-Raḥmān ("Servant of the All-merciful"),[14] *may our God remember them by bestowing on them blessings, life, bounty, and peace, and may thus be his will.*

The bearer of this letter,[15] the illustrious elder R. Isaac, the son of R. Abraham, is one of the illustrious men of Sicily (or Palermo); many here in Alexandria know him as a prominent and fine person and a scion of great families. His arrival in Alexandria coincided with the presence of a large company from France. Our community has made a large collection for them and has also taken care of their maintenance and expenses during their stay here, so that there is no possibility to provide for this or any other man at present. Your bounty is now besought that you may act for this man in accordance with your [noble] habits and your munificence, so that he will part from [you] full of thanks, as all people who pass your house.

To all of you[16] kindest regards, greetings, and respects. *And peace.*

I need not impress on you the urgency of action for that man, so that he should be treated well and kindly, for he is suffering utmost deprivation. Any good done for him—he is worth. *And peace.*[17]

77 A BILL OF LADING

This bill was given to the traveler who accompanied the shipment and took care of it. Another copy would be sent to the recipient in another boat.

University Library, Cambridge, Taylor-Schechter Collection, TS NS J 300.

[14] These Muslim physicians obviously had been invited to a consultation by their Jewish colleague who treated the writer. Cf. *Med. Soc.*, II, 254.

[15] Lit., "service," *khidma.*

[16] Such an informal conclusion was possible only between relatives or very close friends.

[17] It was customary to recapitulate the main purpose of a letter in a P.S. and to conclude it with a second "*and peace.*"

O God, in your mercy grant safety for Joseph, son of Khalfa,[1] (*whose*) *s*(*oul may*) *r*(*est in peace*), to a bundle containing:

32 Tripolitanian cloaks

2 red cloaks

2 hides serving as covers

40 Sicilian cloths wrapped in a washed mantle

4 boxes of saffron

5 Sicilian cloths, a turban made of cotton. All are wrapped in underpants.[2] May God decree safety for it. Amen. O Lord of the Worlds! *And Peace.*[3]

78 PROVISIONS FOR A JOURNEY

A stranger writes to a travel companion, who was accompanied by his wife or a servant. Script of early thirteenth century.

Mosseri Collection (Private) L 101.1.

In (*Your*) *n*(*ame*), *o Mer*(*ciful*).

It so happens that your servant must go on travel today. I am sending to you some chickens and quails as provisions on my way, for I have no one who could prepare them. Please excuse this impertinence and treat me in this matter in accordance with your kind character and noble disposition, for [as the proverb has it] "strangers are kinsmen to one another."

May the welfare of your excellency increase steadily and forever. Selah.[1]

[1] Known from other Geniza papers with the family name *al-Qarawī*, from Qayrawān, Tunisia. He lived in the second half of the eleventh century. See ch. IV, introduction, n. 1.

[2] Men did not wear trousers but their underpants were very wide. When no longer in use, they served as wrapping material.

[3] This greeting is addressed to both the bearer and the recipient of the bill.

---

[1] This enigmatic word, which concludes many Psalms (e.g., Psalms 3, 9, 24) appears often at the end of letters or their introductions.

79 THE ABANDONED CONCUBINE

In the Sudanese port 'Aydhāb
Probably December 19, 1144

Muslim law entitled a master to use his slave as a concubine. The Church and the Synagogue emphatically denied this license. They permitted sexual relations solely in marriage, and marriage was possible only between free persons. Therefore, a master who fell in love with a pretty slave, had first to free her. But this was not an easy matter, since Christians by statute and Jews by custom were monogamous. Still a considerable number of such cases is attested to by the Geniza papers.

It is natural that social concepts and practices of a majority should influence minorities living within it. Cases of a bachelor living with a slave girl or of a husband absconding with one are reported in the Geniza, although such cases were far rarer in the East than in thirteenth century Spain. See *Med. Soc.*, I, 134-135.

As to travel, I have found only one case of a man suspected of visiting prostitutes (in Aden, South Arabia) and one, the document translated here, of a traveler accused of having kept a slave as a concubine. An attentive reading of the text shows that the core of the accusation was not the fact of the concubinage, but the mean way in which the girl had been treated. After having borne a son to her master, she was abandoned by him in Berbera, Somaliland, at that time a wild part of Africa. The girl most probably was Indian and a complete stranger in those parts. The matter was aggravated by its religious aspect. The proper thing would have been for her master to free and then marry her. Later, since he was certainly married, he should have divorced her, before or at coming home, and given her means enough for being a good match for a Jewish man of a lower social class. The Geniza contains several marriage contracts of freedwomen marrying men other than their former masters, and bringing in a substantial dowry. See *Med. Soc.*, I, 145.

By one of those ridiculous coincidences in which the Geniza is so rich, a marriage contract between a freedwoman and a freedman has been found in which it is stipulated that the bride receive as domicile a house connected with the house of Abū Sa'īd Ibn Jamāhir, the man accused of concubinage in our document. Without wishing to reflect upon the mores of a man dead so long, it is perhaps not farfetched to surmise that another affair of Ibn Jamāhir was brought to a close in a more humane manner by that marriage.[1]

Abū Sa'īd Ibn Jamāhir ("Multitude")[2] was an important merchant of good standing, whom we find repeatedly in India[3] and also in Aden, where he was involved in ecumenical Jewish affairs in the year 1134.[4] Our document is from the Sudanese port 'Aydhāb at a time when Ibn Jamāhir was on his way home.

Ibn Jamāhir's accuser Ṣāfī was the business agent, and legally slave, of the head of the yeshiva, or Jewish high council, which then had its seat in the capital of Egypt. As such, Ṣāfī, probably a native of India, was a respected member of the merchants' community, and, as repeatedly found in such circumstances, more Jewish than the Jews.

In order to cleanse himself from Ṣāfī's accusations Ibn Jamāhir charged him before the governor of the town with calumniation. The governor seemingly accepted the word of the influential merchant without making any inquiries and had Ṣāfī flogged publicly and thrown into prison, from which he was freed only after the payment of a substantial sum. The Jewish merchants present in 'Aydhāb clearly disapproved of Ibn Jamāhir's action. A record of the affair was drawn up, destined, of course, to be submitted to a Jewish court in the Egyptian capital. This document, however, is not signed, which means that it was never produced in court. Ibn Jamāhir must have had second thoughts about the wisdom of his action and probably compensated the slave for his humiliation and his losses.

Ibn Jamāhir, as is proved by the letters in which he is mentioned, was active in the India trade during the fourth and fifth decades of the twelfth century. Abū Sa'īd, the head of the yeshiva, or Jewish high council, can be none else than Abū Sa'īd Joshua b. Dōsā, who is mentioned in a document from the year 1143-1144 as the highest Jewish religious authority in Egypt. In this year Tevet 21 fell on

[1] University Library, Cambridge, TS 15, f. 65, sec. I.

[2] See no. 63, n. 12, above.

[3] *India Book* 28, 298.

[4] *India Book* 86, 87, ed. S. D. Goitein, *Sinai* 33 (1953), 225-237, and *India Book* 254, which is the continuation of no. 86, but was found after 1953.

Tuesday, December 19, 1144, and this date is the most likely for our document, for Abū Sa'īd Joshua was in authority for a very short period only.[5]

University Library, Cambridge, Taylor-Schechter Collection, TS 12.582.[6]

This deposition was made before us, we, the witnesses signing below. This is what happened:[7]

We were present in 'Aydhāb on Tuesday, the 21st of the month of Tevet of the year [ ],[8] when Abū Sa'īd b. Maḥfūẓ ("Propitious, son of Protected [by God]"), known as Ibn Jamāhir, appeared before the chief of police,[9] launched a complaint against Ṣāfī,[10] the "boy" of the elder Abū Sa'īd b. [. . .], and appealed for help against him. The chief summoned the slave Ṣāfī, and the aforementioned Abū Sa'īd procured as witnesses Muslims, some of those with whom he used to associate. They testified in favor of Abū Sa'īd that this Ṣāfī made false accusations against him, and that Ṣāfī had said words which cannot be repeated to the aforementioned Abū Sa'īd, that he called him bad names, saying: "You had a slave girl, made her pregnant, and when she bore you a boy, you abandoned her together with her b[oy] in Berbera." Abū Sa'īd appealed to the chief for help and demanded satisfaction from his adversary Ṣāfī.

Upon this the chief of police sent a herald to assemble the Jews who happened to be in the town and to bring them before him. Some hid themselves, others were brought into his presence by police. When the chief saw that Abū Sa'īd persisted in his demand

5 Mann, *The Jews in Egypt*, II, 270. The calculation made in *Med. Soc.*, I, 432, n. 10, is wrong.

6 *India Book* 170, ed. S. D. Goitein, *Tarbiz* 21 (1950), 185-191. Small, but regular script, such as used in court records.

7 The beginning and end of a record used to be written in Aramaic, the language that had been used by the Jewish courts for over a thousand years. The main text is in Arabic.

8 The year was filled in when the witnesses signed. Since this document remained unsigned (see below), the space for the year remained blank.

9 Ar. *wālī*. In a town of moderate size, such as 'Aydhāb, he held also the office of governor.

10 "Pure, sincere," a common name given to a slave serving as business agent.

for satisfaction, he ordered Ṣāfī to be flogged. But Ṣāfī protested, and shouted: "I am the 'boy' of the *Rayyis*,[11] the head of the yeshiva," while Abū Sa'īd declared: "I shall not renounce my claim." After the flogging, Ṣāfī was put in jail in the presence of his adversary, who had appealed to the chief for help, and in the presence of all the Jews who had come to the audience hall.

Before the flogging of the slave Ṣāfī one of the Maghrebi merchants had gone to the chief's house in order to save the slave. But when Abū Sa'īd Ibn Jamāhir learned that he wanted to save the slave, he began to incite some Muslims against the stranger; they gave him trouble and [threatened] him with fines and other matters, after having made false accusations against him.[12] Ṣāfī was set free from jail only after incurring loss of money.[13]

This is what happened. We wrote it down during the last ten days *of the month of Tevet*[14] *of the year of the Creation*[15] *in the city* of 'Aydhāb, *which is situated on the shores of the Great Sea. Written between the lines*: the Jews.[16]

Correct, valid, and confirmed.

(Room was left for at least twenty signatures, which may indicate that the Jewish travelers passing through 'Aydhāb contemplated concerted action against the high-handed Ibn Jamāhir. No signature is attached. For a possible explanation see the introduction.)

[11] The Ar. term for the head of the Jewish community.

[12] Ar. *ba'd al-ikhrāq bih* (fourth for first form, as common). In the edited text *b* is printed for *k*.

[13] He made a deal with the chief of the police. The document purposely remained vague on this point.

[14] At first sight it seems strange that the document, being dated on Tevet 21st, is again dated in a more general way at the end. This was done in order to enable witnesses to add their signatures to the original two signatures required by the law. A similar custom is found in Muslim and in pre-Islamic Coptic documents.

[15] See n. 8, above. The writer of this document was from the Maghreb or from Alexandria, where it was customary to count from the Creation. In the capital of Egypt Jewish documents were dated according to the so-called Seleucid era, which began in the autumn of 312 B.C.

[16] When words were added between the lines in a legal document, the addition had to be indicated as such at its end. The reference is to the last sentence of the second paragraph, where the text originally had: "all those that had come, etc."

80 IDENTIFICATION PAPERS FOR A FEMALE TRAVEL COMPANION

A man from Ceuta, Morocco, was imprisoned in Bijāya (Bougie), Algeria, and his goods confiscated, because he had been unable to produce identification papers for a woman accompanying him.

The note is written on a minute piece of thin, dark gray paper, and probably was inserted into a letter as a postscript. The handwriting is that of the thirteenth century.

University Library, Cambridge, Taylor-Schechter Collection, New Series NS J 286.

Furthermore, I inform you that I long and yearn for you. I also inform you that someone arrived here and told us that your son Nissīm traveled from Ceuta to Bijāya, where the governor of the town[1] found that a woman was in his company. He asked him: How is this woman related to you? He answered: She is my wife. However, when he was asked for her (marriage) certificate,[2] he replied that she had none. Upon this the governor took all his goods and put him into prison. Nothing remained in his possession. By God, do not tarry.[3]

Take note of this. Greetings. *And Peace.*

[1] Ar. *ṣāḥib bijāya,* which could also mean: the *ruler* of the town. Most likely the reference is to a governor of the Ḥafṣids. The Ḥafṣids took the town in 1230 (see *EI*², III, 66), and, in the early period of their rule, still adhered to the stern regime of the Almohads.

[2] Ar. *aina ḳitābuhā.*

[3] Ar. *tataḥarrā,* spelled *ttḥr'y,* which spelling has not yet been found by me in other Geniza papers.

LIST OF GENIZA TEXTS TRANSLATED

	Number in this Book
British Museum, London	
BM Or 5542, f. 9	31
5566, D, f. 6	40
Bodleian Library, Oxford	
(In parentheses is the number of the manuscript in the printed Catalogue, as far as listed in the latter, see Abbreviations)	
Bodl. MS Heb.	
a2 (2805), f. 17	18
20	28
a3 (2873), f. 13	23
19	37
26	17
b11 (2874, no. 21), f. 22	9
c28 (2876), f. 34	26
55	58
d66 (2878), f. 15	69
43	55
52	6
66v	36
d74, f. 41	59
e98, fs. 65*a*, 64*a-b*, 65*b*	64
David Kaufmann Collection, Budapest	
DK 3	52
13	1
E. N. Adler Collection, Jewish Theological Seminary of America, New York	
ENA 151 (2557)	75
2739, f. 16	45
4020 I, f. 55	47
Institut Narodov Azii, Leningrad	
INA D-55, f. 13	33
Jewish Theological Seminary, New York	
(see also ENA)	
JTS Geniza Misc. 15	19
Mosseri Collection	
Mosseri L 5	29
12	43
39*b*	20
101	78
Taylor-Schechter Collection, University Library, Cambridge, England	
Glasses (mss. kept under glass)	
TS 8.12	13
TS 12.133	11
.144	3
.224	12
.291	14
.320	39
.389	24
.435	7
.582	79
.657	35
TS 16.163	25
TS 20.76	22
.180	30
TS 24.64	38
TS 28.11	44
Bound volumes	
TS 8 J 19, f. 27	5
24, f. 21	73
TS 8 Ja 1, f. 5	4
TS 10 J 9, f. 3	27
10, f. 15	41
13, f. 4	51
16, f. 19	57
TS 13 J 13, f. 18	61
15, f. 5	15

INDEX

Rīf, Egyptian countryside, 120, 127, 234, 268
risāla, "shipment," 279
robes, 68-69, 77, 99, 108, 152, 184, 200, 242, 248, 288; of the bazaar type, 108; of the homemade type, 108; wedding, 265
Roger II, Norman king, 324
Roman, 23, 175
Rome, 23
ropes, 199, 235
rose marmalade, 89, 91, 94-95, 98-100, 119, 185, 268, 287
rose-water, 295
Rosetta, Egypt, 209
rubāʿī, quarter dinar, 274
Rūm, 324
Ruqqa, Tunisia, 240
al-Ruqqī, 240

Sabbath, 222, 240, 328
sabīb, currency, 195
Saʿdān b. Thābit Baghdādī, 255
Ṣadaqa b. ʿAyyāsh, 307, 311
Ṣadaqa b. Yaḥyā, 255
Ṣadr al-Dīn, 270
Ṣāfī, agent, 336-338
saffron, 58-59, 99, 112, 116, 118, 122-123, 125-126, 314, 334
al-ṣaghīra (young wife), 211
al-Ṣāḥib, vizier, 37
Ṣāḥibī robe, 37
Sahl Tustarī, 35, 74
Sahlān b. Abraham, 313
sailors, 40-41, 86, 88, 277; Jewish, 125
sal ammoniac, 98, 100, 113, 116, 131, 133
Saladin, 212, 217
Salāma, 280, 314
Salāma, agent, 243
Salāma b. Jaysh, 90, 92-93
Salāma b. Mūsā b. Isaac (of Sfax), 138-139, 158, 162
Salāma Ibn Abī Khalīl, 313
Salāma of al-Mahdiyya (al-Mahdawī), 30, 86-87
Salāma, son-in-law of Furayj, 31
Salār, 313
Salerno, 42, 328
Ṣāliḥ b. Barhūn Tāhertī, 32, 115
Ṣāliḥ b. Ephraim, 39
Sālim, 183
Sālim, son of "the (female) broker," 210
Salmān, 241
Samḥūn b. Dāʾūd Ibn al-Siqillī, 34
Samuel b. Abraham Tāhertī, 80
sappan wood, *see* brazil wood
sarcocol, 45, 100
sari, 199
Sayf al-Dīn Sunqur, 217
Sayf al-Islam, 217
scales, 266
scammony (a strong purgative), 52, 55, 179
scarfs (*radda*), 248
Schechter, Solomon, 6, 209
scholarship conferring social prestige, 9
scribes, 251-252, 271
secret police, 18
security, 92, 109, 312, 322
Senna, 118
sex, 306
Sfax, Tunisia, 124, 129, 132, 138-139, 202, 206, 321
shāh-bender, 15
Shalwadh, Spain, 215
Shām(ī) (Syria-Lebanon), 47, 242, 246, 251, 282, 320
Shaqqat al-waʿr, roadstead, 320
Sharaf al-Dawla, 309
Shavuot, 197, 217-218
shawls, 68-70, 280
Shaykhiyya dinars, 140
al-shayyāl, 242
sheep breeding, 19
Shemarya b. David, Nagid, 216
Shemaryah Ibn al-Maḥāra, 104
ships, 65, 81, 98-100, 103, 114, 129, 131, 139, 181, 188-189, 191, 193, 197, 200, 210, 236-237, 245-246, 250, 262-263, 306, 310, 312, 319-322, 324; *see also* boats, barges
ships, new Spanish, 106
shipowners, 62, 64, 177, 187-188, 191, 193, 330

Library of Congress Cataloging in Publication Data

Goitein, Solomon Dob Fritz, 1900-
Letters of medieval Jewish traders.

1. Jews in the Levant—History—Sources.
2. Jewish letters. 3. Merchants, Jewish.
4. Commerce—History—Sources. 5. Cairo Geniza.
I. Title.
DS135.L4G6 915.6'06'924 72-14025
ISBN 0-691-0512-3